ALIENS, GHOSTS, AND CULTS

ALIENS, GHOSTS, AND CULTS

Legends We Live

Bill Ellis

University Press of Mississippi / Jackson

www.upress.state.ms.us

09 08 07 06 05 04 03 02 01   4 3 2 1
∞

Library of Congress Cataloging-in-Publication Data

Ellis, Bill, 1950–
   Aliens, ghosts, and cults : legends we live / Bill Ellis.
      p.   cm.
   Includes bibliographical references and index.
   ISBN 1-57806-325-6 (cloth : alk. paper)
   1. Legends—United States.   2. Tales—United States.   I. Title.

GR105.E43   2000
398.2'0973—dc21   00-048104

British Library Cataloging-in-Publication Data available

When we consider the matter carefully, we can determine that the constant motion and lasting security of folk legends represent the most reassuring and most refreshing of God's gifts to man.

—*Jacob and Wilhelm Grimm (1816)*

Contents

Acknowledgments

This book represents work that I planned and carried out over more than twenty years, and there are many people who deserve recognition for supporting me through this journey. I value the help given by all these friends, many of whom have been silenced, some by death, some by the economic trends that have decimated the field of folklore over the last decades. In this space, I can only thank a few by name.

The first level of ideas in this book represents the heady days of the 1970s, when folkloristics broke its ties with older research and began to address important issues of social communication. When I encountered the exciting narrative tradition of Hiram House Camp, Moreland Hills, Ohio, I saw that it could provide material for theoretical essays. At this time I was encouraged by my mentors, Daniel R. Barnes, Patrick Mullen, Jean MacLaughlin, and the late Dudley Hackell. Fieldwork was made facilitated by the directors of Hiram House Camp, notably Kenneth Bonsell and Ron Vederman. Jeff Jeske, Bill Henry, and Ross Johnson, former counselors and taletellers, provided important early leads and contacts. To carry out this fieldwork, the late Stanley Kahrl loaned me an automobile and the former Carol Ann McClish (soon to be my wife) offered the use of her VW Bug, accompanying me to many of the interviews.

A second level spun off of this project, recognizing that the folklore of adolescents could provide new insights into the problems of youth culture. Pat Mullen again helped by giving me free access to the rich archival materials in the Ohio State Folklore Archive, and Phyllis Gorfain helped make my Gore Orphanage field research possible by providing a nearby base from which to work. Linda Dégh, recognizing the potential of this work, kindly made it possible for me to teach a summer course at the Folklore Institute of Indiana University, at which time I became acquainted with many fundamental works on legend.

In the early 1980s, I recognized that much of what was being defined as "satanism" was based on a profound misunderstanding of adolescent folklore. I also saw that ostension, a concept then recently defined by Linda Dégh and Andrew Vázsonyi, was central to understanding this emerging social problem. Sylvia Grider was an early inspiration in this research, and she, the late Carol

ix

Edwards, and Dan Barnes all helped prepare the first version of "Death by Folklore" for the 1984 AFS meeting. Subsequently, Jeffrey S. Victor, Robert Hicks, and Phillips Stevens, Jr., assured me that there was merit in my approach and encouraged me to return to this theme. They, along with Philip Jenkins of the Penn State Religious Studies Program likewise provided needed support at a difficult time. In addition to material included in this volume, this research led to the book *Raising the Devil* published by the University of Kentucky Press in Fall 2000.

During the 1980s I was invited to participate in an exciting group of annual seminars held at the University of Sheffield on "Perspectives in Contemporary Legend." Much of the theoretical work in this book was first presented at these seminars, where international mentors like Mark Glazer, Sigrid Schmidt, W. F. H. Nicolaisen, and Véronique Campion-Vincent helped refine my raw ideas through the exhilarating give-and-take debate for which these early seminars were famous. I owe a special debt to Paul Smith and Gillian Bennett, these seminars' organizers, for their commitment to seeing that the excitement of these initial seminars was not lost but incorporated into the International Society for Contemporary Legend Research.

I had the honor of editing this new group's newsletter for several years. Being on the firing line of emerging legends gave me a detailed perspective of how legends interact with social structures, as shown in several of these essays. Alan E. Mays, my News Editor, was tireless in locating press clippings and Internet references to these legends, and much of the detail in these chapters I owe to his industry.

Penn State University provided support for travel to conferences so I could present early versions of many of these essays. Theodore Kiffer, former Associate Dean of the College of Liberal Arts for the CES, was especially supportive of my research during the 1980s, in spite of its unorthodox orientation. A number of Research Development Grants during the same time also made transcription of fieldwork possible. A travel grant from the American Council of Learned Societies allowed me to present a very early version of one of these chapters at the Ninth Congress of the International Society for Folk-Narrative Research, Budapest, Hungary, in June 1989. Thanks also to the *Fortean Times,* who invited me to the "UnConvention 95," London, England, in April 1995 to present an updated and much-revised version of this same chapter. The Committee for the Scientific Investigation of Claims of the Paranormal (CSICOP) likewise invited me to present a material at their 1991 Annual meeting in Oakland, California.

Finally, Monica Gregory, Director of Academic Affairs at the Hazleton

Campus, kindly allocated funds necessary to underwrite the publication of this book.

Some of the material that appears in this book appeared in tentative form in the following articles and is reprinted with permission: "The Camp Mock-Ordeal: Theater as Life." *Journal of American Folklore* 94 (1981): 486–505; "Ralph and Rudy: The Audience's Role in Recreating a Camp Legend." *Western Folklore* 41 (1982): 169–81; "Legend-Tripping in Ohio: A Behavioral Survey." *Papers in Comparative Studies* 2 (1983): 52–69; "*De Legendis Urbis*: Modern Legends in Ancient Rome." *Journal of American Folklore* 96 (1983): 200–08; "What Really Happened at Gore Orphanage? Legend as Submerged Urban History." *Urban Resources* (Cincinnati, OH), 4:3 (Spring 1987): 19–24; "The Varieties of Alien Experience." *The Skeptical Inquirer,* 12:3 (Spring 1988): 263–69; "The Fast-Food Ghost: A Study in the Supernatural's Capacity to Survive Secularization." In *Monsters with Iron Teeth: Perspectives on Contemporary Legend III.* Ed. Gillian Bennett and Paul Smith, 37–77. Sheffield: Sheffield Academic Press, 1988; "When Is A Legend? An Essay in Legend Taxonomy." In *The Questing Beast: Perspectives on Contemporary Legend IV.* Ed. Gillian Bennett and Paul Smith, 31–53. Sheffield: Sheffield Academic Press, 1989; "Death by Folklore: Ostension, Contemporary Legend, and Murder." *Western Folklore* 48 (1989): 201–20; "Introduction" [to special issue: *Contemporary Legends in Emergence*]. *Western Folklore* 49 (1990): 1–7; "The Devil-Worshippers at the Prom: Rumor Panic as Therapeutic Magic." *Western Folklore* 49 (1990): 27–49; "Satanic Ritual Abuse and Legend Ostension." *Journal of Psychology and Theology* 20:3 (Fall 1992): 274–77; and "Review of Leea Virtanan, *It Must Have Been ESP!*" *Southern Folklore* 51:1 (1994): 95–101.

Because these essays were prepared in so many formats and over so long a period, the job of getting them into one manuscript with one standard format was daunting. I appreciate the patience and long-suffering faith of Craig Gill, who helped me find faith that there would be a book at the end of so many trials. The loan of a laptop computer from Penn State University helped get those produced recently on an IBM computer translated into a consistent language, while my student assistant, Timothy Poodiack, was able to scan many others that were produced on a typewriter or in an irrecoverably obsolete computer language. I am especially grateful to Tammy Oberhausen Rastoder, whose detailed copyediting has saved me from many inconsistencies and errors. I remain responsible for the rest.

Finally, over all these years I acknowledge the sacrifice made by my wife, Carol Ann, whom I met during the opening phases of this research and who has stayed by my side during the lonely path that it led me down. Following the "path less taken" has meant that we both had to give up many of the professional contacts and opportunities that would have been possible in conventional academic departments. For myself, I accept this fate as a consequence of having let my heart choose my research topic. But I regret that my choice has also meant financial and social hardships for my family.

Recognizing how much writing these essays has cost her, I dedicate this volume to my wife.

Introduction: Legends in Emergence

In the last decades, the study of legends has undergone dramatic change. Before, traditional folklorists looked mainly at stories "believed to be true" that focused on older supernatural beliefs assumed *not* to be true by academics and indeed not shared by "hard-headed, rational" Americans in general. These ideas were challenged in the late 1960s and early 1970s and scholars began to document the vast numbers of legends circulating in European and North American countries.[1] Simultaneously, a number of scholars from Europe and North America have begun to collaborate to try out new approaches to this fluid, seemingly formless tradition. Sometimes called "urban legends" or "modern legends," they are in fact not confined to cities, nor is their form or content especially new. Since they allege to deal with events that have "just happened," or with threats that have recently emerged, it is more accurate to call these stories "contemporary legends." We must keep in mind, however, that the genre is by no means contemporary with us. Such narratives have circulated at least since ancient times, always dealing with issues that were contemporary for their tellers.

Beginning in 1983, many of the truisms of older legend scholarship were reconsidered in the light of this new material. Scholars ultimately agreed to disagree about many of the issues: What constitutes a legend? What rhetorical form, if any, distinguished it? How can it be classified? How should it be transcribed? What is its relationship with other related forms such as belief, rumor, anecdote, memorate, practical joke, and ethnic humor? Overall, folklorists have come to see the contemporary legend as an *emergent* form best understood as a folk process, not a static form.[2]

Legends grow out of social contexts, which they intend to alter, so contemporary legends are "emergent" on three levels. First, they emerge as *news* freshly arisen from the teller's social setting. Their motifs and structure may be quite old, but the events or beliefs described are directly relevant to the audience's past, present, and future.

Second, they are emergent in that their primary meanings *emerge out of specific social conditions and roles.*[3] Those who tell a legend have a goal in doing so; likewise, audiences have implicit expectations they want fulfilled. Legend telling embodies a complex event, in which the performer not only narrates a story but also gains (or fails to gain) social control over a social situation. The best tellers—and the most popular legends—have the potential to transform social structures for better or worse. Hence legend telling is often a fundamentally *political* act.

Although folklorists have been slow to acknowledge the political role of contemporary legends, historical documents show that they were already used in ancient times to justify controversial acts like the Greek desecration of the Jewish temple at Jerusalem and the peremptory execution of Catiline's cohorts by Cicero and his supporters.[4] On the other hand, food contamination legends recounted by Upton Sinclair in *The Jungle* were instrumental in winning long-needed reforms in Chicago meatpacking plants. With the balance of power shifting dramatically in many parts of the world, contemporary legends continue to play an important role in expressing the goals of common people or in manipulating their perceptions of their governments and the governments' rivals.

Third, contemporary legends often embody an *emergency*—a social problem that urgently needs attention. Legends embody social stresses and attempt to define ambiguous feelings of threat in vivid, dramatic form.[5] However, this sense of "urgency" oftentimes makes academic analysis difficult. The tendency of old-fashioned folklorists to assume that legends are "not true" frequently oversimplifies complex social situations in a way that impugns the credibility (and intelligence) of those who pass them on.[6]

One role of legend is to redefine reality in a way that restores the narrators' control over situations. This is what I call "the Rumpelstiltskin Principle." That is, an ambiguous situation produces stress until witnesses find a "name" or a statement of it in acceptable cultural language. Once this is done, the experience can be translated into a narrative and shared with others, and the act of narrating gives observers power over the event. When the princess guessed Rumpelstiltskin's name, she reduced his uncanny nature to words and saved her child by giving her magical power over the threat. The difference between "supernatural" and "urban" legends may be far less than traditional folklorists have thought. If we expand the conventional definition of what constitutes a "legend," we may find that there is "magic" of some kind always at its core.

Folklore literature—up until the last few years—has contained surprising gaps: the Vietnam conflict, puzzling phenomena like cattle mutilations or crop circles, incidents such as near-death experiences and alien abductions, UFO lore generally. Legends now spread more rapidly using new forms of media such as popular literature, fax, and, ever increasingly, the Internet and world-wide web. Most dramatically, folklorists allowed misinformation about "satanic cults" to reach alarming proportions before even recognizing that it was even potentially a topic for research. Far from being marginal, mere phantasms in the fog, topics like these constitute major portions of the world-views of millions.

The essays in this collection try out ways of analyzing legends that credit their emergent nature and force. Some of them discuss the ambiguous role that folklorists must play in dealing with polarized groups of believers and skeptics; others suggest more fruitful models for looking at the legend as a process, not as a collection of texts. All of them acknowledge the important role that legends play in revealing social tensions and in motivating actions that will relieve these anxieties.

ALIENS,
GHOSTS,
AND
CULTS

PART ONE   THE LIFE OF LEGENDS

The strength of folklorists is sometimes our weakness. The thing we study, the everyday culture of common people, lies all around us. And as we have seen in the last quarter of a century, the inroads made by media and technology have by no means destroyed folk culture but empowered it in often exciting ways. We find ourselves at the start of a new millennium with no dearth of topics and data to discuss: if anything, our problem often is where to begin, what to choose.

Yet the discipline of folklore remains a weak one, whose voice often does not carry far into other disciplines' work on similar topics. And folklorists often do not listen carefully to other disciplines' work even when it is directly relevant to ours. Our link with sociology is stronger than most, but the natural sciences too provide useful ideas and metaphors for folklore research.[1] Many folklorists have turned from analyzing isolated texts "to the dynamics of telling and transmitting stories from person to person and from people to people, through means of direct contact, interaction, and resulting processes responsible for the formation and continual recreation of narratives."[2] These "legend biologists" rejected earlier folklorists' emphasis on texts alone and stressed that one should be concerned with the processes through which traditions were transmitted.[3] Such an approach looks at narratives not as inanimate art objects to be appreciated by themselves but rather as one part of a complex process of communication. Thus seen, stories can best be understood as "living" in a kind of ecological setting. The hallmark of the narrative biologist, Linda Dégh says, is the willingness to "view individual versions as unique and independent creations."[4]

Particularly she denounces some scholars' tendency to edit and retouch texts in terms of some academic idea of cultural absolutes. With some irony, she quotes Edwin Sydney Hartland's nineteenth-century call for verbatim texts: "Every turn of phrase, awkward or coarse though it may seem to cultured ears, must be unrelentingly reported; and every grotesquerie, each

3

strange word, or incomprehensible or silly incident, must be given without flinching. Any attempt to soften down inconsistencies, vulgarities or stupidities, detracts from the value of the text, and may hide or destroy something from which the student may be able to make a discovery of importance to science."[5]

Such calls for literalism, she notes, often meant only care to represent the typical *content* of narratives, not the literal transcription of specific tellings. By contrast, the narrative biologist ought to be committed to recording "the primary data appropriate for scientific research . . . the faithful recording and the observation of creative processes of storytelling."[6] Neither Dégh nor the scholars she surveys take this approach to its logical extreme, which would consider stories as entities with lives of their own independent of narrators. But neither would a trained biologist see any species as entirely independent. For the narrative biologist, however, stories are like living organisms existing in relationship with many ecological factors: other story lines with which they compete and share material, the tellers whose brains they inhabit, the communities through which they disseminate. Dan Ben-Amos has argued: "any definition of folklore on the basis of . . . abstracted things is bound to mistake the part for the whole. To define folklore, it is necessary to examine the phenomena as they exist. In its cultural context, folklore is not an aggregate of things, but a process—a communicative process, to be exact. . . . And in this framework, which is the real *habitat* of all folklore forms, there is no dichotomy between processes and products. The telling is the tale; therefore the narrator, his story, and his audience are all related to each other as components of a single continuum."[7]

What are the goals of the legend scholar? As folklorists' scholarship grows, the need also grows for defining our goals and methods to suit the peculiarly elusive nature of the living beast we are chasing, or at least trying to observe from the underbrush. The essays in this section look at the communicative process of legend telling from a variety of perspectives. First we deal with basic issues: what a legend is, and what we mean by a *traditional* legend. Then we deal with issues that have led to widespread confusion among folklorists and other academics: what we mean by *contemporary* legend and why we often call two texts equally "legendary" when in form they seem nothing at all alike. Finally, we will return to the natural sciences and see what concepts developed recently in the field of biology itself have to offer our quest.

Chapter 1

WHAT IS A LEGEND?

Few concepts have provoked so many varied definitions and characterizations as the legend. While the earliest students of folk narrative recognized a basic distinction between fantasies ("tales") and allegedly factual stories ("legends"), the exact traits that distinguish the ones from the others have been the subject of controversy. Some have evaded the issue by studying legends under the general heading of tales, even though "this form of tale purports to be an account of an extraordinary happening believed to have actually occurred."[1] To reconcile this contradiction, folklorists have assumed that such happenings "cannot have happened, rather they have been formed by the fabulating gift of the people."[2] Thus the legend came to mean any story believed by an informant and *disbelieved* by a folklorist.

In defining legends, folklorists have unsuccessfully tried to apply three criteria: (1) their departure from objective truth, (2) the degree to which their narrators believe them, and (3) their stylistic characteristics as a peculiar form of narrative. The first of these, however, assumes that the collector is more in touch with "reality" than the folk. True, some widespread legends can be objectively disproved, but many more are accurate oral history, and still more cannot be "proved" as either true or untrue.

A second, more currently found criterion is the belief factor: the legend is supposed to be *believed*, by narrators, by their audiences, or, ideally, by both. "The strong element of belief in the legend as told, or in the individual folk beliefs inherent in the legends, constitutes the hallmark which sets the legend apart from the folk tales," argues Wayland Hand.[3] While such a definition avoids the ethnocentrism of the first criterion, it too is difficult to apply in practice. Many folklorists have identified some narratives as "ficts," that is, stories told as the truth but actually intended to scare children and other trespassers away from places where they are unwanted. In style and performance these may be indistinguishable from other legends, even though narrators and many of their listeners may recognize them at once as politic lies. Similarly, scholars have shown that legends reinforcing folk beliefs strongly held in a community will coexist in tradition and in performance with "fabulates" or entertainment legends. These have little or no connection with local beliefs and persist mainly because they are interesting stories.[4] In fact, some European folklorists have taken a position exactly the opposite of Hand's, claiming that the only narratives that deserve to be called legends are those that lack documentation by the teller and hence are probably *disbelieved* by the community.[5]

If objective truth is hard to determine, so too are the internal thoughts of narrators. They may be telling what they sincerely believe, or may be telling a story because they think that is what the collector wants, or they may even be trying to mislead the audience or collector. Attempting to define belief or disbelief among members of a storytelling audience likewise often proves futile. Not only may they misrepresent their beliefs for the same reasons noted above, but even in natural context their responses may vary considerably, from active corroboration to open scoffing. Thus belief alone cannot be used to define the genre, or we would have to redefine narratives after the fact based on new information of which the collector was originally ignorant.

Still, there is a grain of validity in this criterion, in that belief is nearly always a factor in legend performances. Even after discrediting truth as a defining criterion, Dégh and Vázsonyi still maintain that "the legend tells explicitly or implicitly almost without exception that its message is or was believed *sometime*, by *someone, somewhere*. . . . general reference to belief is an inherent and the most outstanding feature of the folk legend."[6] Thus even the most hardened skeptic who relates an alleged encounter with a ghost, only to refute and ridicule it, nevertheless concedes by so doing that this is a narrative that requires disproof. He also enables listeners of the opposite party to pick it up and repeat it as evidence for their own belief. In sum, folklorists agree that while tales are certain fiction, needing no refutation, the legend is regarded as no less than *potential* fact.

Is There Such a Thing as Narrative?   A legend might be defined as a narrative treated by a storytelling circle as "possible" and requiring documentation or disproof. But even this definition presents difficulties. This should not be taken as a sign that folklorists are uncertain about what they are studying but only as a recognition that previously defined boundaries of the genre are less distinct than once thought. Is a legend a narrative?

If by that we mean that all legends are characterized by conventional opening and closing formulas and follow coherent, conventionalized plots, then the answer is no. While some stories may present experiences in full detail, the same teller may drastically abbreviate them on other occasions, reducing them to mere allusions that the audience does not need to hear in full again. Similarly, extended discussions of beliefs make it difficult to draw sharp boundary lines between a circumstantial narrative about how a storyteller saw a ghost by the bed last Sunday and related forms of conversation. Such a story might merge imperceptibly with discussions of what ghosts are, statements of belief in ghosts, and allusions to experiences not actually narrated: "Well, what about last Sunday?" Since all these statements communicate the message "Ghosts may exist," it is often a moot question which ones we would identify as legends, even implied legends.

Henrik Lassen has recently placed the dilemma of defining the concept of "legend" in the context of modern narrative theory. Surveying a broad range of recent theoretical studies, he argues that the concept of "narrative" has become more and more problematic for scholars. He notes that the study of stories has to distinguish between two objects of study, which in European-based research have been termed *sjuzhet* and *fabula*. The first of these refers to the actual linguistic strategies involved in communicating any specific rendering of a story. Thus, in folkloristic terms, the *sjuzhet* would be the actual collected text of a legend, in as much or little verbatim detail as could be recorded. By contrast, the *fabula* would be the "deep" structure underlying the individual performance that would allow one to link it to many other collected texts. The folkloristic equivalent would be a tale type, motif number, or footnote leading to a scholarly discussion of the legend in all its forms. The two, theorists note, have to depend on each other: the audience has to use the evidence of the various *sjuzhets* to construct a concept of a *fabula,* while the teller has to rely on the audience's sense of the *fabula* in order to produce an individualized performance or *sjuzhet.*

But scholars working in the theoretical field of narratology have become increasingly skeptical about the validity of *fabula* as a concept. Barbara Herrnstein Smith, in particular, has critiqued the actual practice of constructing "basic stories" or "deep plots" out of corpuses of texts. When these are examined closely, she says, they turn out to be "quite manifest, material, and particular retellings—and thus versions—of those narratives constructed, as *all* versions are, by someone in particular, on some occasion, for some purpose, and in accord with some relevant set of principles."[7] In other words, the alleged "core plot" of a given tale or legend is the analyst's individual performance of it, no more, no less. Herrnstein Smith observes that the "Cinderella" tale exists in many variants across the world, such that any attempt to identify "the" story of Cinderella is "an artifact of folkloristic assumptions and methodology." In other words, the tale type or standardized title of a given narrative reflects merely the set of versions that the scholar decided were related to each other, "in accordance with some particular but *arbitrary* set of relational criteria."[8] In point of fact, though, there are no underlying basic stories but an unlimited set of possible narratives that the scholar, storyteller, or audience could see as related to it. More important, there is also an unlimited set of possible narratives that each of these parties could construct in the future *in response to* these existing narratives.[9] That is to say, whatever else we could propose "a legend" to be, it is *not* an underlying plot but *rather a social impetus to create new narratives in the shape of the old.*

Lassen finds no convincing evidence that there is any universally shared sense of "narrative" in a deep mental or epistemological sense. The apparent "similarity" of narratives in a given "family" is, he proposes, a mental construct only so far as it allows one to observe *unique* features in a given text. He concludes:

> We shall have to accept, in other words, that the quest for an understanding of narrative as a one-dimensional, entirely mappable phenomenon remains an impossible one, and content ourselves with the fact that the pragmatic working-hypothesis of narrative structure may function as an especially useful perceptual instrument, a general-purpose construct conducive to the enterprise of analyzing the variable functions of narrative . . .
>
> If we choose to operate with the axiom of the existence of *narrative* (and from a pragmatic perspective at least, this is certainly not inappropriate) and employ the abstract construction of narrative structure as a convenient means for focusing, in concrete terms, on what is different between individual performances, versions, variants, and types rather than speculation on the subject of what is ostensibly *shared* by them, the idea of narrative structure may, then, in fact function as an enabling concept, a worthwhile and effective tool.[10]

Text-based research too often gives more attention to a perceived a priori tradition that the researcher sees as central to folklore. Lassen correctly sees this sense of tradition as something heuristic, a means to an end rather than a form of knowledge in itself. In other words, the sense of "sameness" is useful only to the point to which we can give full value to the features that make each collected version more or less individual creations. Lassen's approach suggests ways of moving the *process* of narration into the center of critical attention, thereby giving the same credit to performers' innovative skills that "the folk" do in the context of narration.

This discussion, interestingly, is not new to folkloristics. In its most extreme form this position has been advocated by Robert A. Georges, who sees "stories" not as linguistic entities, or texts but "nothing more than a written representation of one aspect of the message of complex communicative events."[11] Similarly, he asserts that every storytelling event is absolutely unique and that it is "misleading" to suggest that two or more such events might be variants of each other or carry the same message.[12] If we grant this point of view, "legends" are scholars' creations, artificially abstracted from continuously changing legend-telling events. Certainly traditional approaches deny rather than affirm what is unique about each unique, not-repeatable telling.

Legends more than any form of oral discourse are subject to communal composition and performance, and the specific interests of one group, which determine to a large extent the text being narrated, may have little in common with the interests of other groups. Thus, fragmentary, incoherent plots are the norm rather than the exception among legends. Since the essentials of a given experience can many times be assumed, storytellers will often omit them, presenting only the outline of a plot, which can be implicitly realized by the listeners individually. For this reason folklorists have often proposed that "the legend has only content and no fixed form at all and depends on the nature of the message it communicates."[13] If legends consist of content alone, then there is no craft of telling, and many scholars have said so. Dégh comments that the legend-teller "is no artist, he has no artistic inspirations, he claims only to tell the truth."[14] From this argument it is only a short step to say that there is no formal distinction to be made between legends, belief, customs, and rituals, and that there is nothing in the style of any given legend that could be said to define a distinct genre of oral narrative.

Nevertheless, it is a mistake to assume that the legend has no form, only content. To begin with, early field-workers consistently confused the narrative with that being narrated, thus reducing many legends to statements of belief alone. In other cases, narrators' own styles of storytelling were not considered artistic enough to record, so the collectors simply retold the stories in their own words, making whatever changes they thought were necessary or desirable. Both field techniques falsified legends. Collectors often did not distinguish legends that supported beliefs active in the community from those told for the sake of entertainment alone, reducing both to "folk beliefs" attributed to the community, superstitions or customs not actually active in tradition. Likewise, one reason the stylistic conventions peculiar to legends have been so difficult to isolate is that such elements have usually been eliminated or misrepresented in printed texts.[15]

But what is the quality in legends that must be transcribed literally? Given traditional content-focused approaches to legend, the real text is not what is verbalized but what lies behind the skull of the informant—the cultural attitudes that motivate his speaking. If this is so, then surely all that is necessary for scholarly analysis is a clear, grammatical summary of the performed text. But if belief is the crucial factor, why not study beliefs? If content is primary, why consider a story about the content a self-sufficient genre? Why study "urban" legends and not attitudes about cities? The problem with this conception of legend is that it ultimately destroys the thing it defines. If all is content and there is no art of legend telling, then the thing as verbalized is nothing in particular. The study of legends is often a flight from the utterance itself toward something else whose presence can only be inferred from the linguistic details that the researcher finds significant enough to notice.

Yet the discipline of folkloristics is founded on the notion that some traditions have continuity over time and space. Given texts that vary widely in wording and even dramatically in the presence and order of motifs, though, we must try to say as closely as possible *what* it is that continues. Even Dégh has noted: "The acceptance of the validity of the legend is expressed by its convincing *style*. Claim for belief lies in the style of the legend, in the way it is structured, in its painstaking precision to present witnesses and evidence. If there is artistry in the way a legend is told, it is in the skillful formulation of convincing statements."[16]

Tales contain more consciously formulaic patterns and phrases that survive even in heavily doctored texts. But all events, whether they happened to narrators or to someone else, must be interpreted, organized, and dramatized to make them tellable. Even the humblest form of legend telling is consciously artistic, but such art is difficult to abstract from texts that have been "corrected" according to the collector's notion of literary artistry. Legends normally form part of an ongoing discussion and are continually subject to contributions, corrections, comments, and objections from the other participants. Unlike tales, which usually are separated from normal conversation and attended without interruption, legends must be seen as part of a communal event, in which the audience's role is as important as the narrators'. It therefore has been argued that what we should be trying to define is not the style of legend *texts* but rather the style of legend *performance*. In other words, legends are not folk literature but folk *behavior*.

Legends may appear in more than one legend-telling event, but the particular form they take in any one telling reflects the dynamics of that particular event. The same narrator may tell what he considers the same story in radically different ways at different times or may alter the style of narrating because of the social dynamics of the telling. It follows that the *message* communicated by such different tellings may also vary, even if the narrator is the same. And while folklorists can suggest *general* social functions for legends that remain approximately the same over many different retellings, they must also deal with other narrations that are unique to only one event. These too must be seen as part of a behavioral, not textual, tradition and deserve study as much as the more widespread legends.

What then is a proper definition of the legend-telling event, regardless of whether the text being told is well traveled or unique? In the same essay in which Dégh claimed that the legend-teller had "no artistic inspirations," she nevertheless identified a recognizable narrative frame. Although she admits that the sequence of elements in this frame may vary from text to text, still, she says, "I certainly can tell what belongs to it." Characteristic of this frame are (1) a reason for telling the narrative (for example, a moral or warning), (2) detailed identification of the persons involved, and (3) accurate fixing of the time and place.[17] And the events recounted are not everyday, trivial happenings but unusual, anxiety-provoking incidents, ones that place the group's norms in question.[18] Hence we can say that two features define the typical legend. It begins by placing the events that follow as precisely as possible in the group's conception of the real world, and the events it narrates or alludes to challenge in some way the boundaries of what the world is or should be. Bearing in mind that the legend is not self-contained but is part of an ongoing conversation, we see why the text cannot be separated from the legend-telling event, since the performance arises from the group's concerns and in turn provokes further discussion and performance.

Suppose we approach the genre from another angle, asking not what formulas legends contain but what these formulas embody. What are people *doing* when they tell legends? From experience, we can see that people gather to share information about happenings that they accept both as significant and as actually, allegedly, or potentially part of the real-life world they inhabit. Sometimes these events are merely alluded to; at other times, however, events are narrated; that is, they are "replayed" in such a way that both teller and audience can vicariously re-experience what took place.[19] When many such events are replayed (doubtless accompanied by many more in abbreviated form) and when these narrations are embedded in a larger conversational context, then we are looking at the behavior that we call "legend": participants using the extremes of experience, their own and others', to explore, test, and redefine their perspectives on the "real" world.

In brief, *legend telling is the communal exploration of social boundaries.* By offering examples of the extremes of experience—unusual, bizarre, inexplicable, unexpected, or threatening incidents—members of the legend-telling circle attempt to reach some consensus on the proper response to what is arguably "real."[20] Not only is a narrative criticized by an audience as "pointless" when it describes events not relevant to the issue being explored, but even when a point is made, it may be subject to extensive "negotiation," in which narrators and the audience refocus and restate the narrative. Legend telling in its natural context is a means of expressing anxieties about a group's cultural worldview, as well as a way of redefining it in the light of individual experiences. It also provides a safe way of questioning what important institutions define as "real" and "proper."[21] Found among nearly every cultural group, from peasant societies to intellectual college groups, legend telling deserves folklorists' attention in all its forms. Theoretically, there are an infinite number of "points" that could be made in a legend-telling event, and it is possible that a given narrative's message might be unique, not shared by any other in tradition. But in reality, each narrative ought to conform to points already shared by other members of the group, so legends will tend to embody a limited number of messages, which will recur from event to event.

Accordingly, by observing and comparing the way legends are performed in groups, and especially by observing the ways in which points are verbalized or negotiated, the folklorist can identify concepts central to the group's definition of cultural reality. From this point of view, Dégh's assertion that the legend is not motivated by "art" makes a certain sense. For the important part of the legend-telling event is not so much the plot portrayed by the storyteller but the discussion through which all the participants relive the event in their own ways. It further follows that it makes little sense to consider the legend a text apart from its performance. The interaction that precedes, follows, and often interrupts the telling is as central to the event's meaning as the plot alone.[22]

The majority of printed legend texts, therefore represent not legend telling but rather legend summarizing. Collected in interview situations in which the normal interaction of performer and audience was absent, they represent only the subject of what the narrator would flesh out in performance. Given this, it truly makes little difference if such a summary is literally transcribed or rewritten, since the printed text is already twice removed from the event itself.[23] It is surprising that, only recently, scholars of Anglo-American narrative have acknowledged the need to provide fuller reports of the texts they collect. Elizabeth C. Fine's use of such precedents in transcribing and analyzing English-language texts has demonstrated beyond doubt that fine linguistic details are not, after all, trivial. Rather, she indicates, existing methods of transcription record such details in trivial ways. *Every* transcription is, in her terms, an "intersemiotic translation," insofar as it attempts to represent through the visual channel of print all the linguistic and paralinguistic messages communicated through the spoken voice, further modified and amplified by the speaker's gestures, expressions, and postures.

Fine too insists that the keynote of performance is its aesthetic qualities, and that the ideal text would enable the reader to reconstitute these qualities in the original performance. This can be done partially through commentary on the normative characteristics of the genre but can only be completed through recording "the aesthetic transaction (manifested through observable behaviors) between the performer and audience."[24] Collecting and transcribing legends in performance thus is necessary to determine exactly how specific performers control specific situations and to what specific techniques their audiences respond. If our analysis requires verbatim texts, it is inconsistent to transcribe all the linguistic evidence available as if it were spoken in an inartistic monotone. We risk falsifying the aesthetic nature of legend telling if we do not in some way indicate in print the ways in which the performer and his audience relive the events narrated.

Finally, the verbatim text needs to present the legend in its natural domain—a free, spontaneous conversation. If collectors can simulate the usual setting of legend telling, perhaps with the help of a tradition-bearer, they can take on the role of sympathetic outsiders whom the group needs to "initiate." In fact, collectors' relative ignorance to the legends already known by the group can encourage performers to produce unusually full texts, filling in details normally taken for granted. While the dynamics of such an event will inevitably be somewhat artificial, the performance nevertheless will preserve more of the features of a natural event than a content-based interview. With some effort, legends may even be taped in one-to-one situations, depending on how capable a collector is of adopting an active role as audience and how easily narrators adapt to performing to a tape recorder.

The danger is that, if the situation is too artificial, storytellers may relate mere summaries of legends they would freely elaborate in front of an active audience. Yet even such a text will show narrators compensating for the lack of an audience by breaking up the legend with comments, explanations, and other seeming digressions. These features may be one's only evidence of how the legend would be negotiated or realized in actual performance. Although such a text may appear inartistic or incoherent, it is still more valuable than one that has been misrepresented or doctored to produce a literary text.

"He's Not Mine"   To illustrate how texts can be misleading, let us compare two texts submitted to the Ohio State Folklore Archive by Rob Wakely, a lifelong resident of Marion, Ohio, and an expert on allegedly haunted places in the area. His first text was written out in literary fashion from his memories of legend-telling events held among himself and his high school buddies. It is similar, unfortunately, to many "edited" texts in printed anthologies.

The story itself begins around the turn of the century. It takes place in a two-story brick house on Irvin-Shoots Road.

There was a young man in his twenties who had married a woman in her thirties. They never had any children. She was known to fool around quite a bit and although everyone knew about her affairs he seemed to ignore their gossip. One day he reported her missing and everyone just thought she ran off with some man, but some believed he had killed her.

About twenty-five to thirty years later the man did remarry. She was young and in spite of his age she loved him. They seemed to be happy. A child was born and that's when it all began. Because of his first wife he began to think his second wife was just like her. He started to accuse her of seeing other men. One day while she was preparing dinner waiting for him to come home, she went upstairs to get the baby which was usually crying for his dinner by then. As she went upstairs she had a feeling something was wrong. As she opened the door she began screaming because of what she saw. The child was dead. Someone had taken a hatchet and killed it, there was blood all over, and written on the wall in blood was the words "HE'S NOT MINE."

As she was running from the room she saw him standing at the end of the hall with a hatchet in his hand smiling at her. She ran down the stairs and headed for the door but she stopped and closed it again and decided to hide in the closet. She heard him open and go out the door. After what seemed hours she decided to come out of the closet. She opened the closet door slowly and stuck her head out and all of a sudden the door flew open and there he was waiting on her. He brought the hatchet down and killed her. From this day on if you go there at dusk you can still see a hatchet floating around and hear screams.

From this text alone it would be difficult to analyze this narrative as a legend. True, it begins by locating the events in a specific place (Irvin-Shoots Road, north of Marion) and in at least a general time in the historical past ("around the turn of the century"). But no effort is made to make the events realistic. No source for the legend is given, nor is any reason given for relating it. The events described are indeed threatening but, as they stand, not very credible. One wonders, for instance, how narrators learned about what the young wife was feeling, since she was murdered without telling anyone. This inconsistency, the obvious borrowing of the "closet scene" from John Carpenter's popular horror film *Halloween,* and the unexpressive, flat language used might lead us to conclude that narrators did not believe the story and thus it would be better considered a tale. Although the ending implies present-day consequences of the murder, again no source is given, nor does the narrator say whether or not he ever witnessed the screams or floating hatchets. From the text alone, in short, we can only conclude that the narrative *might* be told as a legend. But it is not so told in this text, nor does it allow us much evidence about the context in which it might be told.

By contrast, Wakely's second text was collected in a near-natural context. Knowing that his sister Penny and another acquaintance of hers, Melody Christian (who lives near the house in question), had both made trips to the place and had told stories about it, Rob invited them to share a pizza and their recollections. The tape recorder's presence was acknowledged but was soon forgotten during the storytelling. As a result, this version became six times as long as the edited text, with several significant passages of negotiation and evaluation. This text in its entirety follows, with portions corresponding to the edited text in boldface for reference.

Melody: First time I ever heard about this was in high school. My brother told me about it. It's supposed to be haunted and a lot of kids used to go over there. There's this stone road that runs across and it's used as a party road. Kids when they get real drunk they go over there and dare each other to go inside the house by themselves. They had to go upstairs and shine a flashlight out the window—I wouldn't be able to do it! (*Laughter*) Especially at night (*laughs*).

Penny: I was afraid to in daylight. (*Laughter*)

Melody: It didn't help much when we walked up to the door and you see a rope hanging there and the words "You're doomed" (*laughs*). Hang on in there (*laughs*). That's the way I felt about it. (*Long pause and laughter*) OK! This is the story behind the house—

Penny: Well, what is it? (*laughs*)

Melody: **Well—there was this guy and he was a farmer, like most people in that area—um—he had this big house and he got married when he was young to an older woman and she fooled around, but he ignored it because he was in love with her and stuff—and—um—he could always hear people talking behind his back, but he acted like he didn't hear them—**

[*Recording interrupted.*]

Penny: Go on with the rest of the story (*laughs*).

Melody: OK, this is part one, take two (*jokingly*).

Penny: Are you sure you didn't take it back to the beginning?

Melody: Yes, this is act two, part one then.

Penny: OK.

Melody: **Well, no one knows what really happened to—It was just one night—uh—she just disappeared!**

Penny: Did she run away or did he kill her?

Melody: **He told the police that his wife was gone and he couldn't find her. Since she fooled around, everyone thought she ran off with a man. They didn't really know, but—uh—I think, you know, he killed her** (*laughs*). **Well, he didn't remarry until he was an old man.**

Penny: How old was he?

Melody: Maybe twenty-six (*laughs*).

Penny: Sure—you think twenty is old (*laughs*).

Melody: Well, then he was in his fifties. **His new wife was young and really loved him. But—he couldn't get it through his head—he thought all women were deceitful, that they fooled around and stuff. Well—she had a baby and he didn't think it was his**—you've got to help me out here—

Penny: He didn't think it was his (*laughs*).

Melody: Come on, Penny, you can think of something (*laughs*)—you're supposed to be helping me out on this.

Penny: Well, you had a real good story going on here. I was listening (*laughs*). What am I supposed to say? This is where you're supposed to tell about his going up and killing the baby, isn't it?

Melody: **Well, you see he starts asking questions around and stuff and she didn't have any lovers or anything.**

Penny: Well, why would he kill them?

Melody: Well, he couldn't get it through his head that it was his kid and stuff.

Penny: He was nutty (*laughs*).

Melody: Yeah, he was crazy! He should have been locked up.

Penny: He sounds a little weird.

Melody: He was a little weird. I wouldn't marry someone like that. No way—

Penny: When is this supposed to be taking place?

Melody: About thirty years ago.

Penny: I thought it was longer than that—the way I heard it you know.

Melody: Well, you saw the shape of the house.

Penny: I know, that's why I thought it was longer ago than that.

Melody: OK, it took place two hundred years ago.

Penny: (*Laughs*) Not that long ago?

Melody: A little newer, huh? (*laughs*)

Penny: Yeah!

Melody OK—one hundred years ago.

Penny: There you go.

Melody: The turn of the century.

Penny: Which century?

Melody: The next one, of course (*laughs*).

Penny: That's good (*laughs*). They didn't have any kids, right?

Melody: Right.

Penny: I guess not, how old was she [*the first wife*] supposed to be? Maybe she was too old to have kids.

Melody: She was older than he was—

Penny: Yeah.

Melody: Like the guys in my class said, you know, I think it was a football wedding—one of those where you marry her and wait for the kick off (*laughs*).

Penny: Maybe we ought to get on with the story.

Melody: **OK—well, he asks around and it finally drives him crazy**—you know, over the hill.

Penny: He was already crazy (*laughs*).

Melody: Well, he was walking that thin line—and then he hung himself after he had killed them.

Penny: Oh yeah, that noose hanging on the door, I don't think he could have used it, though, unless he was a midget (*laughs*).

Melody: You know—I just thought why we couldn't see the blood on the floor.

Penny: There was too much junk there (*laughs*).

Melody: No—

Penny: Why?

Melody: Because you've go to go there at dusk—when he killed her—we saw the blood on the floor. Barry said that it looked like someone drug a dead animal in there.

Penny: Well, you still can't see it for all that stuff on the floor.

Melody: **Well—he was driving her crazy, she just couldn't get it through his crazy mind.**

Penny: She stayed too long (*laughs*).

Melody: Yeah, she waited too long, I tell you I wouldn't hang around, I'd say, "Forget you, man, I'm going home to my Mom." (*Laughter*) "I'm not going to stay here and convince you it's your brat" (*laughs*). **It was getting late and it was getting to be the baby's feeding time and—she couldn't figure why the baby wasn't crying, she went about fixing dinner, well, he was supposed to be out working in the fields, he wasn't even supposed to be home. Well, she was cooking dinner and she finally went upstairs to check on the baby—she could tell something was wrong,** you know, women's intuition.

Penny: Yeah.

Melody: I get that sometimes.

Penny: Uh-huh.

Melody: **But she went up—she opened the door and started to scream at the top of her lungs—just screaming. Here was the baby all cut up in the criddle—in the criddle? (*Laughter*) (She clucks her tongue) In the cradle. And on the wall it said,**

"HE'S NOT MINE." Well, she turned around and he was standing at the end of the hall with a hatchet in his hand smiling at her. Wouldn't that freak you out? A guy standing there with a hatchet and smiling at you?

Penny: Yeah!

Melody: Oh, God, time to go, play is over, exit stage down the stairs, you know, bye— (*laughter*)—I would take off.

Penny: Yeah, I wouldn't hide in the closet either—I just keep running.

Melody: Yeah—it was right there by the front door.

Penny: Why didn't she just keep on going out?

Melody: It—**and what happened was she went down the stairs and started to go out the door—she opened the door and closed it again and she thought, "Maybe if I hide in the closet he'll think I went out and take off—she hid in the closet for what seemed like hours and hours and hours—so finally she heard the front door—**

Penny: Maybe he did the same thing that she did?

Melody: **Well, she heard him go out.**

Penny: Oh.

Melody: **She stayed in the closet so long that she decided to look out to see if he was really gone—suddenly the closet door flew open and the hatchet comes down and chops her up. And to this day if you go there at dusk you can see a hatchet float down the hall and down the stairs and—**

Penny: Aren't you supposed to hear her scream?

Melody: Yeah—

Penny Well, you didn't say that.

Both: **You can hear her scream** (*laughs*).

Melody: **You can see the hatchet stop at the closet doors and then disappear through the front door.** Well, what's weird is if you go up there during the day, well, Rob can tell you this, there are those birds that come in the windows at you.

Penny: Yeah, I remember—

Melody: Did you see the way I ran out the door?

Penny: Yeah, you said to watch out for the birds coming in the windows at you (*laughs*).

This transcription makes it clear that the narrative did in fact circulate as a legend. While Melody carries the main thread of the story, both she and Penny interrupt its progress constantly to evaluate its significance and to compare its content with their perception of the real world. The importance of audience comments during tale telling has been noted, but such comments are still more important to understanding legends. Beyond the simple telling of a narrative, in this performance we can identify three major kinds of interaction: remarks about the performance itself, definition of the story's time, place, and characters, and evaluation of the story's point.

Comments about the performance of storytelling itself make it clear that the participants consider the narrative as an entity exclusive of performance. Most obvious of these are floor-taking formulas, in which Melody takes on the role of narrator and Penny acknowledges that she now is the audience.

Melody: OK! This is the story behind the house—
Penny: Well, what is it? (*laughs*)
Melody: Well . . .

Melody: Yes, this is act two, part one then.
Penny: OK.
Melody: Well . . .

Another set of comments addresses what the audience sees as error, digressions, or discontinuities in the performance.

Penny: Maybe we ought to get on with the story.
Melody: OK—well . . .

Penny: Aren't you supposed to hear her scream?
Melody: Yeah—
Penny: Well, you didn't say that.
Both: You can hear her scream (*laughs*).

Such comments clarify a distinction sometimes blurred by scholars. While some discussions may be central to the circle's sense of the legend and thus are not digressive, though some outsiders may see them as such, yet other discussions *are* recognized by the participants as nonessential. This by no means indicates that such a digression is irrelevant to understanding the social context of the legend; it only means that the participants recognize that it is not necessary to the performance of the legend. Narrators do digress, then, and audience members often correct them or object when significant details are omitted. Conversely, narrators may request help from the others when trying to recall details:

Melody: Well—she had a baby and he didn't think it was his—you've got to help me out
    here—
Penny: He didn't think it was his (*laughs*).

Melody: Come on, Penny, you can think of something (*laughs*)—you're supposed to be
   helping me out on this.
Penny: . . . This is where you're supposed to tell about his going up and killing the baby,
   isn't it?
Melody: Well . . .

A final significant type of remark involves audience members' aesthetic
responses to the telling:

Penny: Well, you had a real good story going on here. I was listening (*laughs*).

Penny: Which century?
Melody: The next one, of course (*laughs*).
Penny: That's good (*laughs*).

Such comments, of course, need not be complimentary, or even expressed
in words, since audiences often respond to "gross" moments with wry facial
expressions or statements like "Blaaach!!" These comments need to be preserved in transcription, as their presence isolates moments when implicit aesthetic expectations were conspicuously fulfilled or violated.

A second, more significant kind of interaction involves "orientation"—the
definition of the narrative's time, place, and characters.[25] In legend telling, it
is necessary only to observe that when specifics are lacking in any of these
three areas—time, place, and characters—active negotiation may take place
at any point of the narrative, often at the beginning, but often also at the end.
That this is more than a mere linguistic "clue" is apparent from its presence
in tall tales, which narrators know are untrue, as well as in legend. Even
though the two are dubious about whether the murder did in fact occur, still
they actively discuss when it *might* have occurred.

Penny: When is this supposed to be taking place?
Melody: About thirty years ago.
Penny: I thought it was longer than that—the way I heard it you know.
Melody: Well, you saw the shape of the house.
Penny: I know, that's why I thought it was longer ago than that.
Melody: OK, it took place two hundred years ago.
Penny: (*Laughs*) Not that long ago!
Melody: A little newer, huh? (*laughs*)
Penny: Yeah!

Melody: OK—one hundred years ago.
Penny: There you go.

The tone of this exchange is jocular, implying that neither feels any particular need to verify the event's date. Still, the care with which they agree on a "credible" date—Marion was not yet settled in 1782, and the house is plainly older than 1952—indicates that both choose to orient the story's events in actual local history, not in a fantasy "long, long ago." Since both participants had recently visited the house, there was no need to negotiate the events' location as extensively, though they do remind each other of specific details of the house important to the narrative.

Melody: . . . and then he hung himself after he had killed them.
Penny: Oh, yeah, that noose hanging on the door . . .

Penny: Yeah, I wouldn't hide in the closet either—I just keep running.
Melody: Yeah—it was right there by the front door.

The precise age and mental status of the male antagonist, however, needed to be characterized before the tragic story's catastrophe could be narrated credibly.

Melody: . . . Well, he didn't remarry until he was an old man
Penny: How old was he?
Melody: Maybe twenty-six (*laughs*).
Penny: Sure—you think twenty is old (*laughs*).
Melody: Well, then he was in his fifties.

Penny: Well, why would he kill them?
Melody: Well, he couldn't get it through his head that it was his kid and stuff.
Penny: He was nutty (*laughs*).
Melody: Yeah, he was crazy! He should have been locked up.
Penny: He sounds a little weird.
Melody: He was a little weird. I wouldn't marry someone like that. No way—

The last exchange is especially revealing, as the participants negotiate not only a credible age for the husband but also a credible motive for his actions. Rather than being an inexplicable villain in a fairy tale, the antagonist is merely a "weird" fellow such as one might meet and potentially marry in real life. The effect of such orientation is to place the issues and events of the narrative against a backdrop of local history, so that the two girls can share both a story and their opinions about what future husbands are "really" like.

The interactions in which this sharing take place, where the participants *evaluate* the narrative, deserve most attention. These are the comments that most directly address the legend's "point" and allow us to identify the cultural attitudes behind this point. In some cases narrators or their audiences "make the point clear" by providing an explicit moral at the story's ending. In the following case, the narrator, an ex-Marine conversing with other ex-Marines, leaves his story's moral implicit, but a listener caps it with a proverb. Again, the narrative proper is in boldface.

A: Did you ever hear, here's a story that I have always heard. It got to be Marine Corps folklore, and I can't remember the guy's name, because—I—like I don't even know if it's a real name, but they always say **this guy, Private so-and-so, in boot camp—was the range champion, had the highest qualifying marks, and then he was on float, and he was in the first wave going ashore and he was shot to death as soon as he stepped off—never fired a shot—as soon as he stepped off the landing craft, shot right between the eyes**—(*laughs*)—Did you ever hear that one? The most deadliest Marine there was—greatest shot in the Marine Corps, never heard that story?

B: There's always one with your name on it.[26]

In most legends, however, the point is not so gift-wrapped, so we need to pay attention to several common types of evaluation: (1) comparison of the legend's events with one's own experiences (including both narrators' comments on their stories' events and the audience's comments on narrators' experiences), (2) reference to other persons' experiences confirming or denying the legend's validity, (3) direct criticism or approval of the characters' actions, and (4) appeal to other members of the circle for agreement. In the case of the Irvin-Shoots haunted house, the evaluation is rather complex, since there are actually two points at issue: whether the house is really haunted and whether the second wife could have escaped had she been more sensible. As for the first issue, both quickly agree that the place provokes fear:

Melody: . . . Kids when they get real drunk they go over there and dare each other to go inside the house by themselves. They had to go upstairs and shine a flashlight out the window—I wouldn't be able to do it! (*Laughter*) Especially at night (*laughs*).

Penny: I was afraid to in the daylight. (*Laughter*)

By referring first to other participants who have to "get real drunk" in order to enter the house on a dare, Melody immediately characterizes the place as one avoided under normal sober conditions. When she imagines herself in such a situation, she admits fear and elicits a like response from Penny. Later on, though, Penny is not so supportive, and they part company on the issue of whether uncanny things do happen there.

Melody: You know—I just thought why we couldn't see the blood on the floor.
Penny: There was too much junk there (*laughs*).
Melody: No—
Penny: Why?
Melody: Because you've got to go there at dusk—when he killed her—we saw the blood on the floor. Barry said that it looked like someone drug a dead animal in there.
Penny: Well, you still can't see it for all that stuff on the floor.

Here two personal experiences are being opposed. Melody, the one more likely to agree that the house is haunted, alludes to a visit in which she saw the indelible bloodstain, and she corroborates her sighting with "Barry's." Yet on a subsequent visit "we" (the two girls) saw no bloodstain. Melody suggests that the phenomenon occurs only at a specific time—"when he killed her"—but Penny withholds support, offering only the mundane excuse of "all that stuff on the floor." Similarly, at the end of the narration, Melody describes another uncanny experience.

Melody: Well, what's weird is if you go up there during the day, well, Rob can tell you this, there are these birds that come in the windows at you.
Penny: Yeah, I remember—
Melody: Did you see the way I ran out the door?
Penny: Yeah, you said to watch out for the birds coming in the windows at you.

Again Melody offers herself as an eyewitness to strange events, supporting her account with "Rob's" experiences, but again Penny stops short of agreeing that the event was in fact "weird." She only acknowledges that Melody "said" that the birds came at her. The transcription breaks off here, and we cannot tell if this difference of opinion led to further negotiation. Perhaps Penny's admission that she was afraid to enter the house by daylight was enough agreement that the house was spooky, regardless of what specific uncanny manifestations happened. But in general, the two agree to disagree about the nature of the house's haunting.

Where they agree, however, is the point of the tragic love affair that causes the haunting. This is the part of the narrative that is most actively discussed and, in the two girls' eyes, is the most relevant to their lives. In particular, the young wife's actions are commented on at every turn, and the two quickly agree that she was foolish.

Melody: He was a little weird. I wouldn't marry someone like that. No way—

Melody: Well—he was driving her crazy, she just couldn't get it through his crazy mind.
Penny: She stayed too long (*laughs*).
Melody: Yeah, she waited too long . . .

Penny: Yeah, I wouldn't hide in the closet either—I just keep running.
Melody: Yeah—it was right there by the front door.
Penny: Why didn't she just keep on going out?

The wife's actions appear even more dim-witted since the narrator indicates that she has a normal woman's intuition that ought to have warned her of danger. ("I get that sometimes.") By contrast, the two participants agree that they would have acted long before to keep from getting into any similar situation.

Melody: Wouldn't that freak you out? A guy standing there with a hatchet and smiling at you?
Penny: Yeah!
Melody: Oh, God, time to go, play is over, exit stage down the stairs, you know, bye— (*laughter*)—I would take off.

The sarcasm here betrays a serious suspicion of male attitudes and behavior. The wife in the legend is a "good" woman from a husband's point of view. She is completely faithful, bears a child and stays at home to care for it, does the chores and fixes dinner. Nevertheless, she is still "not good enough" and dies for it. Thus the legend is primarily a cautionary narrative, at least in the eyes of these two tellers. It warns young women not even to try to live up to this sterile ideal; a person shouldn't have to put up with suspicions from a "weird" husband and his unfair accusations of infidelity. Rather than accept marriage on these terms, both girls agree to break off the relationship: "I wouldn't hang around," "I would take off," "I just keep running." Within this male-dominated institution, according to the terms of the narrative, the only alternatives are insanity—"he was driving her crazy"—or death. Significantly, earlier on in the discussion Melody jokes about a similar male perspective on wedlock.

Melody: Like the guys in my class said, you know, I think it was a football wedding—one
of those where you marry her and wait for her to kick off (*laughs*).
Penny: Maybe we ought to get on with the story.

Perhaps this point more than any other illustrates what normally gets left out of edited legend texts. Where the abstract given first would appear to be a narrative explaining why a house is haunted, in fact the legend-telling event transcribed is primarily a discussion of "men" and how to deal with their unreasonable demands. Whether or not the house is haunted is not important enough for the two to resolve; what is threatening is the possibility of being trapped in a male-dominated marriage. Of course the same legend may appear in other conversations to illustrate entirely different points. Further collections and analyses, however, would be necessary to demonstrate this.

This analysis shows that the narrative has been used in female female circles to discuss tensions surrounding the gender roles that become important during adolescence. Close examination of the evaluation of this legend reveals not incidental digressions, but interchanges central to our understanding of the event. Contemporary legend scholarship should be cautious of losing our disciplinary identity in rushing to adopt concepts and methods devised by other disciplines. But the theoretical issues have in fact been addressed by scholars, and in forms apropos to this material. If we have no sounder rationale for interpreting texts than our subjective sense that we can gain something by doing so, then our conclusions do not logically follow. All we are doing is retelling the stories we collect, replacing our informants' language with scholarly language appropriate for this time and place. But rather than contributing to our knowledge of the texts we study, we are simply adding one more performance—our own—to the corpus.

Chapter 2

WHEN IS A LEGEND
TRADITIONAL?

"Scary stories"—those horror-filled legends related by camp counselors to their adolescent charges—compose an important body of folk narrative active in the Midwest. Recounting the mayhem wrought by spooks, maniacs, mutants, or uncanny animals, these stories may run as short as five to ten minutes for a simple anti-legend like "The Walking Coffin" or as long as an hour for some camps' epics.[1] But while such stories make up the major extended narrative genre in the area, folklorists have been slow to study them. Several reasons for this neglect can be suggested. To begin with, adequate texts are hard to collect, since many tradition-bearers are reluctant to tell horror legends out of context, and as many folklorists are unwilling to tote their tape recorders up and down ravines to reach proper context. Thus nearly all published and archival texts are no more than outlines of the versions actually performed as part of a campfire event.

More important, though, such narratives are performed in situations controlled by adult counselors and are rarely performed by the campers or passed from one to another. Indeed, many horror stories are so associated with specific counselors that they do not circulate even among adults but remain the "property" of one respected storyteller. Thus it could be maintained that these legends are really "fakelore," manufactured to have the look of traditional stories but actually imposed on audiences by counselors' whims. There would seem to be little to study, then, since these narratives cannot be shown to be traditional in history or transmission.[2] Finally, even those who have studied camp legends have discussed them as hoaxes, perpetrated by their narrators to intimidate audiences, just as white racists once invented night horrors to subjugate blacks.[3] Such narratives could not even be called legends, since the degree of belief central to the genre is absent in the teller and present in the audience only insofar as they have been tricked into believing a lie. It is not surprising, then, to find folklorists not only disinterested in the camp horror

26

legend but actually prejudiced against it as a fabrication, both as legend and as tradition.

But such prejudice fails to recognize that there may be narratives that mimic the "true" legend, yet are not intended to inspire literal belief. Conventional definitions of "legend" have often assumed no middle ground between the legend proper, "regarded as true by the narrator and his audience," and the tale, "regarded as fiction . . . not to be taken seriously."[4] Such definitions in fact discourage folklorists from studying narratives strongly endorsed by traditional audiences. Looking at the camp horror legend from this dualistic perspective can only result in a distorted image of the audience's participation in the performance. If we are to believe that the legend "deals with experiences an ordinary man has to face passively . . . who remains helpless before the events he encounters," so too the audience must respond to the performance with the same passivity.[5] By fabricating "true" details about horrifying forces, the storyteller would seem to ensure his total control over an intimidated audience.

John M. Vlach, for example, has argued that many narratives told to children are built around realistic "legend cores" that produce fear and tension in the listeners. He examines a version of "The Encounter with the Horrible Monster," a common "shaggy-dog story" about a furry monster or green gorilla that pursues a character implacably. When he corners his victim, he simply touches him and says, "Tag, you're it!" Vlach concedes that few children would find the premise of the story credible. Still, he counters that "if a more realistic character were substituted as the bad guy (e.g., an escaped lunatic or prisoner) and if the punch line were discarded, then the story would be similar to one which appears not infrequently in newspaper headlines."[6] So far as Vlach goes, his point is valid, in that motifs frequently show up in more than one kind of narrative. But by reducing the narrative to content alone, he ignores the behavioral fact that not all stories about realistic subjects are treated by audiences as "real." A version collected by Richard M. Dorson does present the incident as fact. It begins: "Oh yes, I went up to that darn place up there called the insane asylum. I was in Bangor and I thought I'd call up and see an old fella, a neighbor of ours that they'd sent up there. I don't know much about it anyhow, but there was a couple of guards had some fellas out along there with pruning shears and sickles and different things that they had in their hands, cutting the grass around the bushes. So this big fella, black whiskers, he had a sickle." The narrative ends in the same way as the "shaggy dog" story, with the supposed lunatic pursuing the narrator only to say "Tag" at the climax. Dorson, although more an outsider than a traditional member of the informant's audience, clearly took the story as potentially true. Even though he notes variant texts, he still comments, "Conceivably this laughable incident could have happened to Curt [the storyteller]. I had a peculiar experience myself once when I entered that same asylum to meet a mentally sick folklore collector."[7]

By contrast, Vlach's version begins: "There this guy. He had this big gorilla, thirty-two foot tall and forty foot wide. And he thought he'd go and see if he was still there in a cave. So he got in his car and he drove and drove and drove and drove. And then he came to this curve and he stopped. And then he got out and he walked and walked and walked. Then he climbed and climbed and climbed and climbed. And then he came to this cave and says, 'Open Sesame,' and the cave door opened." In contrast to Dorson's text, no specific character is identified as the protagonist, just "this guy." Likewise, the story takes place in no specific place, while Dorson's text relies on common knowledge of the Bangor asylum and the peculiar things that both storyteller and audience know happen there. Vlach, significantly, observes that "it was apparent from the outset of this version that the intent of the teller was to evoke humor. The overly repetitive use of verbs pointed immediately to that purpose and at varying intervals the audience was amused by the silly behavior described in the narrative."[8]

Vlach chides previous folklorists for having classified only the punch lines of such narratives. In fact, though, the more crucial differences occur at the beginning, where the storyteller communicates to the audience whether the narrative is located in the real world they both share or in a fantasy world outside of time and topography. That both narratives end with the same punch line is not a compelling argument for considering them both tales, nor is the alleged credibility of the "legend core" in itself sufficient reason for calling them both legends. By recognizing the genre of the narrative, the audience in fact gains considerable control over the storytelling event, something that all experienced campfire performers understood and anticipated.

Robert A. Georges, referring to such narratives told by Scouts, asks, "Do they *believe* that these accounts are true?" and responds neither yes nor no, "for the answers are somewhere in between."[9] This essay is partly an effort to follow up Georges's appeal for sounder concepts of legendry, precisely by exploring the narratives that fall "in between" more conventional legends and tales. More important, this study looks at the traditional audience of such narratives and the powerful influence it can have over the storyteller. For, as we shall see, campers are neither passive nor hoaxed in the face of the camp horror legend.

Admittedly, some performers may use legends to intimidate and manipulate, especially in the case of younger children. In such cases, tales are indeed a more wholesome diet. But early adolescents often want to leave "strictly fictional" narratives behind in the nursery and insist on a "real" scary story. Camp counselors have observed that campers aged twelve to fourteen will demand stories that are open-ended and apparently factual. One commented that "if you tell 'em it's not true that ruins the whole thing. You have to leave that fact that it might actually be true in there."[10] By enforcing this aesthetic choice, such an audience may determine the narrative's direction, either actively, by interacting with the narrator while the story is being told, or passively, by approving or disapproving parts of the story. Such involvement suggests that early adolescents *choose* to hear such stories because they see them as entertaining, not because adults want to threaten them. This in turn indicates that their response is not anxiety, however often they may say "That's scary," but a reaction similar to what Goffman has termed "being engrossed."

Crucial to such a response, he argues, "is not an individual's sense of what is real, but rather what it is he can get caught up in, engrossed in, carried away by; and this can be something he can claim is really going on and yet claim is not real."[11] Such a response, based not on belief but on *suspended disbelief*, is a liminal one, exactly appropriate to the camp's overall position between civilization and wilderness and analogous to the campers' ambiguous status in the woods. If we confuse content with performance style, we risk confusing engrossment—aesthetic involvement with fiction—with fear. Storytellers rarely confuse the two. The camp horror legend therefore is an intermediate form of folk narrative, presented *in terms of* reality, but implicitly recognized by both performer and audience as fantasy. When adolescents thus become collaborators with the storyteller in sustaining the illusion of "truth," at the same time they assume significant control over both the legend's success in performance and its future development in tradition.

A test case for such audience control is a camp horror legend titled "Ralph and Rudy." This is, at first appearance, a complex but unique narrative about a "wild man" who menaces campers and counselors. It is, however, an example of one of the most widespread camp horror legends, which we might term "The Dismembered Hermit." In legends of this sort, a tragic accident or cruel prank horribly disfigures a person. This person becomes a recluse and, to avenge his deformity, periodically attacks campers. "The One-Armed Brakeman," from Camp Clifton, near Clifton, Ohio, illustrates this plot:

The story was more or less that the one arm brakeman was way back when 4-H camp started. Had both arms then, was working on the railroad and some 4-H'ers from the camp went down to the railroad tracks and played around and threw the wrong switch or something and the next train that came by, it caused it to wreck and everyone was killed except the brakeman and he had one of his arms chopped off. So he kinda went crazy as a result of that and finally got a hook put on the end of his arm instead of having the rest of his arm and hand, and became a hermit and lived in the gorge.[12]

Another variation on the theme involves an innocent person who is accidentally or maliciously decapitated, and who returns as a ghost or revenant to the camp, hoping to find a camper whose head he can rip off and use for his own.[13] Both these story types draw material from the many "Hook" and "Baby-sitter" legends widespread in suburban communities and passed on mainly by the adolescents who attend camp.

"Ralph and Rudy" was put together by a group of college-age counselors, at Longview Riding Camp near Georgetown, Kentucky, in the summer of 1972. Bill Henry, then twenty-one, was the counselor most noted for telling the legend that year and the following summer of 1973.[14] After this, Henry moved to northeastern Ohio to attend graduate school and, in the summer of 1975, came to work at Hiram House Camp, just east of Cleveland. He worked there each summer through 1978, telling the legend often and with success. Even though the story gained quite a reputation at the camp, few other counselors attempted to tell it at their own campfires, and when I began fieldwork at Hiram House in 1979, I found only one who could even summarize the plot.[15] Likewise, although campers continued to show familiarity with the legend, asking for it at campfires through the summer of 1981, I found no evidence that they performed it to each other. This legend, then, would seem to fit the stereotype of scary story as fakelore: it did not circulate in tradition, even among adults, and remained exclusively the property of one storyteller, who presented it according to his own sense of how it should be told. But if this stereotype were accurate, we would expect its audience to have been passive and the content and style of the story to have changed little over the years. But "Ralph and Rudy" was never frozen in tradition: it changed radically when it was transplanted from Kentucky to Ohio and continued to evolve during Henry's tenure at Hiram House. The direction of these revisions, moreover, indicates that the storyteller was conforming not to his whims but to specific audience expectations.

We can discuss this story as traditional on three levels. First, although the legend itself is unique, its incidents and overall structure are based on earlier horror legends and urban belief tales. Second, the story itself developed over a number of years, incorporating motifs demanded by the audience's traditional expectations. Finally, the style of performance, particularly its "proto-dramatic" nature, conforms to campfire conventions reinforced by campers' responses. In short, the "traditionality" of "Ralph and Rudy" needs to be defined not exclusively by history or content but also by the type of active control the audience exerts on the performer.

Traditional Roots   "Ralph and Rudy" went through two stages of development, according to Henry. It began as an extended contemporary legend at Longview, then became a longer, more complex narrative at Hiram House. Like "The Dismembered Hermit" and the more widespread contemporary legends on which it was based, "Ralph and Rudy" initially consisted of three sections: (1) an explanation of the "maniac's" origin, (2) a close brush with the maniac, proving his dangerous nature, and (3) a warning not to put oneself in his power.

The "origin" section was presented in this way:

They [Ralph and Rudy] were brothers and they worked as hired hands on the farm. And they both were really hard workers and really good people to have around, but they were like day and night. Ralph was an alcoholic, he drank a lot, went on benders and came home, and every time they'd come home they'd have a big fight.[16] Besides, when Ralph wasn't on one of his drunks, they worked real hard and they would bring vegetables and stuff up from the yard. . . .

One time Ralph was out on one of his drunks and he came home all drunked up and Rudy was waiting for him. And—which usually happened—they'd get in a big fight, every time he comes home they get in a big fight. So they got in a *real* big fight. And they really tore up the house, rolled out into the yard, and in the yard they—they were farmers and you know if you're a farmer or any kind of a skilled craftsman or anything you keep your tools in excellent condition. It's something that—you know you just don't—like our houses [at the camp], you don't have anything in it that isn't as sharp as it should be or anything. But these guys really kept their tools—they sharpened their shovels and took really good care of things.

So they roll out in the yard and in the yard was a chopping block . . . and in it was a double-edged axe. OK, and they rolled around and they were fighting and Ralph picked up the axe and tried to swing it at Rudy but it slipped out of his hands and flew out into the yard. So they're really, *really* fighting, it's a good fight, they're really hitting each other and there's a lot of cuts and bruises and they're rolling around. But the story takes a turn for the worse now because they roll near the double-edged axe. And Ralph picks up the axe and swings it and cuts Rudy's head off at the neck with just one big swipe 'cause it's so sharp.

Now you know what happens, like the two veins going up your neck that carries all the blood about every minute or two to your head and back to your body? So when that is severed all of a sudden like that, the heart keeps pumping, it keeps pumping it out like a fire hose. Well, this stuff pumped out and hit Ralph right in the face, through Rudy's head, just really splattered his face.

(So then you just stop. I stop the story and I'd say, "Well, the next day)[17]

This explains how Ralph became a "wild man," and the story then turned to accounts of close encounters with people at or near the camp. Unlike "The Dismembered Hermit" Ralph, the wild man, is not himself mutilated or decapitated. Still, the way that the two brothers are portrayed, as "night and day," suggests that they are, in fact, inseparable because they are two sides of a single personality. The wild Ralph corresponds to impulses dominated by the id, while the moralistic Rudy represents a super-ego figure that attempts to impose restrictions on Ralph's search for pleasure. The climax of the opening, Ralph's murder of his brother, is his ultimate rebellion against the super-ego, but by eliminating this side of his personality, Ralph does not liberate himself but instead becomes a prisoner of his unbridled animal nature. The "close encounter" sections of the story make his bestial characteristics explicit.

The first of these again makes explicit links with the adolescent contemporary legends that served as models for the legend.

About three weeks later Pauline [the camp owner's wife] who is sitting in the—it's a mansion actually is what it is, it's a huge house—but she's sitting there and her husband's gone to bed and the girls are in bed and she likes to—after the news is over—just sit and look through the paper, re-read it. It's a hot summer's evening and there's a breeze and she's sitting in a chair, nice, big, with a high back, and right behind her to the right there's a screened window that is open.

And she's sitting there and she's just leafing through the paper and all of a sudden she hears this breathing, really heavy breathing. And didn't hear it for a minute because she's reading it, and then she looks and pretty soon she hears scratching at the screen; she looks behind and what she saw was really very, very scary, 'cause behind her was *Ralph!*

His hair—his eyes were real wide like he was really a wild man. It was just like—real wide and he had grown a beard in the last three weeks, it was streaked with white because—I don't know, he was a young man, in his mid-twenties, but it was streaked with white.

And one thing I failed to mention was that Ralph and Rudy were big men—they weren't my size, they were—I think Ralph, mention six-five and he weighed in excess of 250 pounds so he was a *huge* man. And he's there and his eyes were real wide and he's kinda frothing at the mouth.

But that *scared* her, but what *really* made her flip out was in his right hand was Rudy's head. And after three weeks of running around the forest the skin was falling off and the hair was in big mats and there were worms and bugs and flies all over it.

(So you sing the old song, "The worms crawl in, the worms crawl out, through your nose and out your mouth"—that's all I know of it but I usually put that in there and everybody just goes, "Yuck!")[18]

And the *smell!* Like that smell hit her too, but it didn't hit her until she finally saw the head and a big puff of breeze came in and blew the smell, and it's really—you know—rotting flesh—you know, it's just—(gags)—just an incredible smell.

The woman screams, which drives Ralph away for a time, but this encounter is followed by a string of others, equally graphic. Bill Henry here injects himself as a character in the legend, initially functioning as a skeptic who, when first told the story, responds "I don't really believe that, I'm not a dummy—I mean, that's a neat story, but that doesn't sound real true." He is convinced, however, when he investigates a disturbance among the stock one night and surprises Ralph slurping raw organs from a horse he has disemboweled.

This series of confrontations is the typical structure of the extended camp horror legend, normally moving to more and more gruesome murders or attacks.[19] "Ralph and Rudy" is perhaps unusual in that Ralph does not follow up his initial murder with others but instead seems content to slaughter animals for food and to startle people. Many elements, however, connect him with the traditional psychopaths in adolescent legendry. The "really heavy breathing" in the first scene, along with the isolated position of the female victim, derives from legends like "The Entrapped Baby-sitter," in which the maniac invariably announces his arrival with heavy breathing. Similarly, the scratching at the screen not only recalls "The Roommate's Death" and "The Boyfriend's Death," in which the dead or dying victim terrifies an isolated woman by scratching a partition, it is also found in its own right in other camp stories.

Camp Clifton's "One-Armed Brakeman," for example, was said to claw at the screens of cabins, trying to get in and abduct campers. Even the dismembered animals are paralleled in adolescent legends. Near Zanesville teenagers tell stories about "Short Arm," a one-armed hermit (possibly a ghoul) who slaughters and eats sheep for food. And near Athens and Montgomery students have recorded legends of finding disemboweled animal bodies, apparently related to "witch" rituals that legend-trippers try to observe.[20] Finally, the most distinctive element in Ralph's behavior, his carrying around Rudy's decomposing head, has also been reported elsewhere in camp legends. At Camp Robert Meecher, in the northern tip of Kentucky, "Headless Haddy" rides around after dark on a horse, wearing "a flowing gown with a chain of heads around her waist." She carries a scythe and attacks only men: "at least once a year somebody in town, at night, gets a little carried away and loses their head."[21] Even though Ralph is a unique creation, therefore, he is recognizable as a wild man in the best tradition of traditional narrative.

With these graphic confrontations set during "last summer," the Longview version of "Ralph and Rudy" concluded with this episode:

> There was a full moon, clear sky, and one night John [a fellow counselor] comes out and he says, "Get, get out of bed, get your boodie [backside] upstairs and see what's happening." Go out and the counselors were all standing around and we look up and on the hill is what looks like the outline of a man, a large man, and under his arm was a white object, which we thought was probably the skull of Rudy because by this time everything, all the meat had fall off and just a white skull.
>
> And he's standing up there going, "RUUUUUUUDY!" Kinda baying at the moon, you know? "RUUUUUUUDY!" You know just—really—just every time he said it, sent chills up and down everyone's spine. It was just really scary. That's the last time we saw him that summer.[22]

The narrative thus comes to a natural end, with animals beginning to disappear "this year" and with a warning to campers to stay put after dark or else. The tale's stern moralism again suggests the contemporary legend: "Ralph and Rudy" serves as an admonition to those who rebel against adult authority and suburban mores. Ralph, like the traditional legend maniac, is a mindless, motiveless fiend-animal who rids himself of his conscience-like superego nature but who does not gain freedom from his own antisocial impulses. Indeed, instead of deforming his brother, the story makes him the deformed one, doomed to carry around the disgusting remains of his brother's head in the same way that other camp hermits have to live with their own twisted limbs or bodies. The closing tableau shows Ralph as a "really scary" boogieman, but at the same time makes him pathetic, implying that he is crying out his brother's name out of loneliness.[23]

Thus the legend's primary function at Longview was to reinforce traditional authority roles. "I used it to keep kids in their tents," Henry admitted. "It was basically because we'd have—half the tent would be up walking around, and I used it for that reason, to actually frighten the kids." One of the pranks played after a performance of "Ralph and Rudy" illustrates this use of the story.

> We were coming back [from a trip to a nearby country club] and we had two high-school kids that worked at the country club come down and get in the house. And then we waited, came off the bus, said, "Listen, listen!"

And they were all down banging around going, "Ruuuuuuudy!" We ran down over the hill and they had flashlights and flashing around going, "Ruuuuuuudy!" and banging around, and it's not that far, and it just was real effective and all the kids went back over there were crying, and I can remember Janet [one of the female counselors] coming out and going, "You—come in here and tell them"—she was just screaming—"and tell them it's not true, they're crying!"

And oh, she was so mad at me for doing that.

Intimidation was not the sole function of the legend at Longview: Henry noted that "we had fun with it too," and recalled that campers made the story the subject of a musical-comedy skit. Nevertheless, the core of this version of "Ralph and Rudy" was terror—the gruesome details of the murder, the rotting skull, the uncanny, bestial Ralph. And the terror stems from Ralph's daring to strike out against Rudy's moderating "good" influence, in the same way that the unwise camper who disregards the "good" counselor's warnings puts himself in Ralph's power. The story thus validates conventional power structures and mores in a way wholly appropriate to its context: an elite riding camp for politically conservative upper-class and upper-middle-class suburban whites.

The Hiram House Version   Suburban white values, however, did not play well at Hiram House, a service camp for disadvantaged inner-city Cleveland youth, nearly all black. While most other camps could rely on counselors' authority being accepted as a matter of course, Hiram House had to deal with streetwise adolescents, many of them gang members, who were not eager to submit to "the man's" leadership. Moreover, the philosophy of Hiram House, since its founding at the turn of the century, was not to oppose the gang spirit but to co-opt it, encouraging its campers to express ethnic identity and rebellion in a harmless, constructive manner.[24] Thus the kind of moralism central to the Longview "Ralph and Rudy" would have clashed with this audience's traditional expectations. Indeed, when Henry arrived in 1975, the most popular narratives among the campers followed a different pattern, which held conventional authority up to question and presented counselors, not campers, as the most common victims.

"The Bloody Hammer," a variant of "The Fatal Fraternity Initiation," showed the counselor/narrator as the one violating cultural taboos and as a result putting himself in the power of uncanny forces. Another horror legend, certainly the most popular campfire narrative at Hiram House, celebrated the social struggle of Majaska, a modified urban badman, against the repressive bigotry of the ogre Hermit Dan. Majaska's victory at the end of this narrative clearly invited campers to identify with this monster as a wish-fulfillment hero. The narrative tradition into which Henry entered, then, was predicated on horror not as a means of producing conformity but rather as a way of reversing the conventional hierarchy, in which accepted authorities (like counselors) were brought low and ethnic outsiders (like campers) elevated in status. To succeed in front of such an audience, "Ralph and Rudy" had to be radically altered.

In one respect the most important change Henry made was the most conservative: rather than relocating the events of the story in Ohio, he left the core story far away in Kentucky. But then, to explain these events' relevance to the present context, he added a long coda to the legend. "Next summer," in this version of "Ralph and Rudy," actually comes, and Ralph returns to molest the camp, terrifying both the kids and the counselors. Then, one night, they make plans to defend themselves.

I had put a baseball bat under my bed. You know, just in case anything ever happened. So I lay down, and when I go to sleep I like to lay and just relax for fifteen minutes before I finally fall asleep.

And so I'm laying there and . . . if I look behind my bed were the stairs, to my right just this wall. Or to my left there's just the wall and on my right, to the front of me there, I'm looking at four windows. So I'm laying there and just kinda looking at the end— there's a door, a window, window, window.

And as I look at the door I see something pass the door. "I wonder what that is?" So I looked at the next window and something passed that window.

And it *dawned* on me that the person was high because the windows are fairly high off the ground and I could see this person from his *chest up*. You know, it's filling quite a bit of window. And as he passed the window right here next to me I saw it was Ralph. And I reached under the bed for the ball bat.

And all of a sudden there was a blood-curdling scream and the door, kitchen door flew off its hinges into the kitchen. And immediately right to the kitchen was my room. He comes *screaming* in, he's just yelling, "Ruuuuudy!" and he's just screaming and he comes charging at me and I give him—grab the base bat, jump up, and I swing and hit him right in the ribs. You know, right in the stomach in the rib cage.

And—the—you know—and his eyes—you know—just—nothing had really—up to the point nothing had really hurt Ralph, you know? I mean, he would, he's been, you know, kinda—he got *cut* but I mean as far as anybody really hurting him he's never been hurt by a human being or anything else, since he's so big and just such a wild man and—and this *stunned* him, you know? And we surmised we broke a couple—I broke a couple of his ribs when I hit him.

And he just—it just—a *surprised look* and a hurt—a pain—a look of pain and surprise crossed his face and he just turned around out the door, you know? And just *split*.

And everybody's just going, "Wow!" You know, everybody's up by this time, they heard, they came running out and they saw Ralph exit. And they're going—I'm standing there and I'm really shaking, you know, I'm just really upset. And everybody's going, "Wow, great job!" and I said, "Boy, I don't know, you know, it—it—you know, what really happened."

So everybody thought, "Well, we're not going to see him again, he's *afraid* now." And I didn't really *believe* that.

(So what I go into now is . . . I say what happened when I hit him.)

He had never been hurt before and it kinda knocked some sense back into his head. . . . I was the first person to ever really hurt him. And it kinda jarred back some of his human qualities—I mean, he was still a wild man, very insane.

But what made this worse was, actually it made him a worse, a more dangerous type of person to be around and to be involved with, because not only was he as wild and as insane as before, but [before] he was just going around killing and just *living,* you know, he wasn't really doing anything, but *now* he's starting to think and ponder different ideas. And *one* of the ideas that he pondered was getting me.

And so what had happened was he kept sneaking around camp unbeknownst to us. And the big mistake—and this is why (now this is what I'd say if I was telling a bunch of kids) this is why it concerns *you* guys. The big mistake that was made at that time was even mentioning my name.

From eavesdropping on Henry's colleagues, Ralph learns his name and present address, and immediately begins to trail the counselor. State police come to Hiram House to warn Henry that disemboweled animals have been located all across Ohio, forming a beeline from Longview to the Cleveland-area camp, the last being found in the immediate vicinity. As before, the story ends with a warning to campers to stay in their tents, but now it is the counselor, not the campers, who is in deadly peril.

"You better be careful," I said, "if you hear anybody out here, if you hear a lot of screams, stay in your tent. He's just after me. But he *has* attacked humans before, I mean, he hasn't *eaten* anyone, but he's attacked humans before and you know you're pretty *vulnerable* in these tents. . . . And I said, "If you hear anything, don't come out and try to rescue me. . . ."

(At Hiram House I just say, "He's after me," and tell them "in the area," and that's basically it. That's where the story—there's no ending, the story's an ongoing type of story which never ends.)

The motifs included in this coda are, again, not unique to this story, although Henry's combination of them is unusual. The scene in which the counselor confronts the maniac and defeats him is paralleled by versions of "The Cropsey Maniac," collected from around New York State by Lee Haring and Mark Breslerman. Here a respected adult male goes berserk and commits a series of gruesome murders until a counselor corners him and wounds him in the leg with a hatchet; after this he is traced down and (apparently) killed.[25] Similarly, the variant of "Headless Haddy" from Camp Meecher cited earlier concludes with the reassurance that campers are safe when they are with counselors, because "she at one time tried to behead one of the camp counselors and the counselor grabbed her scythe. One of the heads on the chain [around her waist] told the counselor if he gave the scythe back, Haddy would promise not to bother the counselors."

On the other hand, the open-ended conclusion, in which the narrator claims to be in imminent danger, is surely derived from "The Fatal Fraternity Initiation," already in tradition at Hiram House when Henry arrived. In this local variant, members of a fraternity trespass in a haunted house; four are killed at once, their brains bashed out and their hands spasmodically pounding the ground (thump, thump, thump) with a bloody hammer. Each year another member of the fraternity dies in the same way, at the exact date and hour of the trespass, and the narrator concludes by admitting that he is the only survivor and that tonight is the anniversary.

And this is *my* turn.
So in the morning or sometime in the night, you hear somebody . . . [*pounding on table*: thump, thump, thump, thump] . . . beating, don't be alarmed, just sleep until the day. Don't worry about anything, it's probably me over there.
  (Maybe I'm not going to be here this evening, maybe I'll just leave or something.)
  (You'll read it in the paper, or somebody will tell you about it.)
  ((Want all you to remember—one thing—))
  I'M NOT CRAZY![26]

But while individually these motifs are conventional within the tradition of camp horror legends, Henry's combination of the two seems unique. Counselors' encounters with Cropsey and Headless Haddy end with victory and at least partial relief from horror, although in both cases the boogieperson escapes final capture. "The Bloody Hammer," by contrast, shows the counselor's encounter with the supernatural ending with defeat, leading to horror intensified. That is, until the shouted "catch" ending provides a closing frame to the narrative and lets the audience know that they have been hoaxed. Like

"The Golden Arm," the effect of the catch forces the audience to jump, but in so doing it dissipates the anxiety generated. True, one Hiram House counselor admitted that some staffers would occasionally sneak out after the story and pound on a tree to mimic the hammer's arrival, but even he commented that the campers who stayed awake "wanted to stay up anyway so they had a good time."

By contrast, "Ralph and Rudy" presents a victory over the maniac, but its nature is ambiguous and Pyrrhic. Instead of relieving the danger, ironically, Henry's actions actually put him into greater danger by transforming Ralph into a worse maniac than before, and the conclusion of his legend provides no catch or closing frame to mitigate the story's anxiety. This, combined with his first-person perspective and his constant stumbling to get specific details of the scenes exactly right, makes Henry's narrative unusually convincing, and it is not surprising that even some of his fellow Hiram House counselors initially took the story as autobiography:

> Like Jackie [one of the female counselors], I had her convinced for a number of weeks at Hiram House, that it was a totally true story and that I was the bravest person around. And she was real disappointed—she's unit leader for Indian Girls now—and she was *really* disappointed she found out it wasn't true.
>
> Somebody told *her—she* was telling someone, she said, "I think Bill is so brave—did you hear about that story and what happened to him?" And somebody—it was an old staff member—she says, "He hit this guy Ralph right in the stomach and this guy's after him now, you know, to come out at night, and this person's just sitting there!"
>
> He says, "*You* believe that?"
>
> She says, "Yes!"
>
> "That's just a story he tells."[27]

Yet I found little evidence that the campers were so totally hoaxed by the narrative; however unconventional, the ending seemed to have been wholeheartedly accepted by its audience.

The new ending, though, was only the most dramatic revision; its effect was reinforced by more subtle internal changes that took place during performance. These revisions were determined by several types of audience response. First was simple refusal to react to parts of the story that had been accepted by the Longview audience. In particular, the earlier version used the decomposing head of Rudy as a dramatic focus throughout Ralph's attacks. "In Kentucky the head was the whole story," Henry recalled, "whereas as it came up north, then I had to—I spent more time doing other stuff and leaving the head kinda out of it." Partly this shift was caused by Hiram House campers' apathy to descriptions of the head after its first appearance. But in addition the audience had more direct ways of suppressing unwanted parts of the story. Henry remembered direct challenges to details: "See, the problem was, when you're at Hiram House, the kids there, you had to come up with the head . . . If I said I had the head, they would say, 'Where is it?' "

In the absence of a real-life prop, then, the Ohio campers lost interest in the head of Rudy, and it gradually disappeared from the legend. Conversely, when he saw that campers were apathetic, "not really believing" a given episode, Henry chose to start "playing with the story"—improvising—"to see what I can get away with." This tendency to keep adding to the narrative, combined with the Hiram House campers' habit of reminding the storyteller of "important" details he had forgotten or altered, in essence "edited" the legend through successive retellings. While Henry provided raw material, his audience took the initiative in selecting what they wanted kept or dropped.

But the campers did not merely edit what Henry produced. The Hiram House version of "Ralph and Rudy" was also altered to allow breaks in the storytelling, where campers could comment directly on the narrative. One such pause came at the very start of the performance, when Henry and his unit would start a "discussion about the story's overall theme." As Henry recalled, they would talk about "how much pressure you can put on our minds," and about "people in mental institutions, and why are they really there? Is it because they can't handle the pressure, or really what's the real problem, what really makes a mind snap?" This version, then, took as its starting point a discussion of maniacs not as bestial menaces but as unfortunate people, responding to pressures not much different from those felt by the group. Thus the story turned from evoking an incomprehensible threat to comprehending "the real problem"—what made Ralph a maniac?

Similarly, after the scene where Ralph burst on the scene as "wild man," bearing Rudy's rotting head, instead of dwelling on the horror of this image, Henry again broke off the narrative for a discussion of "what really *happened* to Ralph."

First, he really *did* love his brother, but he was drunk and he—and he *killed* him.

Second of all, he's hit in the face with blood, which is real warm, it was just really—you know really—I mean, to be hit in the face like that with blood is just really gross. It's just—it just—that was too much for his mind, killing his brother and being in that gore just, his mind could not handle all that and he kind of, he just—his mind *snapped*.

He was part animal and he still has human capabilities and he carried a big knife, but he was part animal. And he just, he was living off the land by killing domesticated animals or anything else he could. And it was just too much for his mind.

(Now sometimes we got, we've gotten group discussions of what really happened to him. I mean, it takes a long time sometimes, this story, because you open up for group discussion of what really happened to Ralph. . . .)

(I kinda feed it but everybody, they'll start throwing in like, "Well maybe he had some other problems," or just something else that I didn't think of. There's been a whole myriad of things that's been thrown at me that really surprised me that the kids would come up with . . .)

(Like I didn't—carrying a big knife didn't *dawn* on me until some kid brought it up. Now—and living off the land, like for a while I had him living off the land but then we put a cave in because somebody thought he just can't live off the land, what's he do in the winter time?—so we put a cave in.)

(So some of the kids have fed in, especially right here of the character of Ralph and who he is and what his hair looked like—I didn't have anything on hair, but they said, "Man, it must have been standing on end," so all of a sudden you had Ralph with his hair all mussed up, it was kinda sticking out.)

(And the white streaks in the beard were later brought in by the kids. Said, "Aw, yeah, like it probably have white streaks," and that's kinda how his character's been built up. He's not the original character.)

Such discussions gradually transformed Ralph's role in the legend. Rather than a boogieman, used to warn campers not to disobey authority, he became an unlucky human who went insane almost by accident. Not only do the added details add realism and logic to the narrative (how else could Ralph disembowel horses; he *had* to have a big knife), they also make it clear that his insanity is more the result of Ralph's horror and remorse at what he'd done than his rebellion against his conscience. These changes humanize the maniac, making the coda, where Ralph returns partially to his human nature, both credible and satisfying. Henry gives the Hiram House campers credit for this transformation, conceding, "I think if there's anyone responsible for the character as it now stands of Ralph, it's the kids . . . it's been their reactions that's made Ralph what he is, and some of the things have come directly from them. That's why I like—that's why I'm happy with that story."

Horror and Ostension   Just as Hiram House campers responded actively to the legend in performance, sharing in its creation, so too they involved themselves in its *ostension*, or dramatic extension into real life.[28] Since both versions of "Ralph and Rudy" were open-ended, the audience was left responsible for providing some sort of closure, through a form of protodrama. Thomas A. Green declines to call any sort of patterned nonserious activity "folk drama," but he still observes that there are borderline events that use dramatic techniques, even though they are not fully scripted plays.[29] A performance of "Ralph and Rudy" can be dramatic in this sense: the antagonist (in this case, Ralph) does not actually appear, but both narrator and audience make believe that he is nearby and thus act out roles appropriate to people preparing for his arrival. The large numbers of hoaxes and genuine dramas that grew out of this legend and others like it show that participants recognize the core material as dramatic in nature. In fact Henry told me that he had always wanted to get someone to act the part of Ralph and break in at story's end, but had never gotten the chance to make these plans.

Longview campers may have responded with fear, but it is not clear how genuine this anxiety was. Certainly the roles adopted by Hiram House campers showed they were not intimidated by the legend. They responded aggressively, mimicking either Henry's role as protector of the camp or Ralph's part as challenger of authority. Both responses show that the audience accepted the legend not as truth but as an entertaining fantasy. To be sure, the proper effect of the narrative depended on its being "realistic" enough to encompass their real-life concerns about the pressures of conforming to a violent, often maddening society. Yet at the same time it had to be "fantastic" enough to assure them that they were in no real danger in their tents. Here the text alone is not enough to determine "Ralph and Rudy's" precise place in the gray area between legend and folktale. We must pay close attention to the way campers injected themselves into the narrative, playing at being in danger—or being the endangerer.

Part of the function of the coda, in fact, was to deflect personal anxiety away from the audience by assuring them that Ralph only sought to attack the counselor. The campers thus were encouraged not to worry about their personal safety but rather take some kind of stance concerning the counselor's well-being. Some adolescents, Henry remembered, responded ironically: "They go back to their tent and say,—'You stay *outside,* don't come near me!'" But a more typical response was sympathy: "I had some kids that would want to stay up with me and say, 'We'll protect you,' you know, 'We'll stay with you.'" Such sympathy, in fact, was exceptional if we remember that the normal audience was made up of black street youths more used to defying authority than seeking to protect it. But the activities that followed gave campers the opportunity to show themselves not as passive victims, like the typical character in a white urban belief tale, but as active counterattackers. Again Henry gave them the lead, underscoring that Ralph is no supernatural boogieman but a human who feels pain and thus can be defeated. "One of the things that they would ask," Henry recalled, was "What would happen if he comes in our tent?' I say, 'Well, hey! Eight strong guys like you, you know, just jump all over him! . . . You guys are strong—jump all over him! Beat him!'"

Similarly, once the campers had distanced themselves from the legend's performance, they took on the persona of the wild man as a joke, again extending the narrative into the camp week and turning the tables on the authority figure. Many counselors recalled how campers initiated into the legend would go around camp the rest of the week, calling out "RUUUUUUUUDY!" in the most threatening of tones. "I'd be in the barn," Henry told me, "and I'd hear kids walking by, going 'RUUUUUUUUDY! I want your *head*!' . . . Or, 'I've *got* your head!' I think it is." Likewise, he remembered having some of his campers lie in wait for him on the trails and jump out of the bushes, shouting "Rudy!" to startle him.

In this context it is significant that the campers used the cry "RUUUUUU-UDY!" as if it were a threat, not a pathetic "baying at the moon" out of loneliness. Their actions, it seems, interpret the cry as signifying, "*You* are Rudy, and I'm coming to get your head (or I've already got it); your life is in my hands!" In either case, then, we see campers playacting roles that imply that *they* are the ones responsible for the counselor's welfare, either by offering to "save" him from the wild man's attack or by pretending to "kill" him. In a setting where lower-class black adolescents have to adopt ambiguous attitudes toward educated white counselors, such activity again indicates that they take the story as fantasy and use its elements to play at taking authority away from traditional authority figures.

This creative response is far from the mere political function that earlier folklorists found in horror stories. Indeed, while Henry admitted that one of the story's good points was that it kept campers in their tents, even at Hiram House, still his best memories were not those of intimidation. "I think the *best* experience was having the kids wanting to stay with me, and 'We'll protect you.' You know, that made me feel real good."

Still, the ability to participate in such a "real" fantasy, to the extent that one can behave as if maniacs actually were part of real life, is a sophisticated aesthetic response that seems not to be mastered before adolescence, and even then it can be a fragile thing. When asked how far he would humor campers who would "attack" him in the persona of Ralph, Henry replied, "A couple of times I'd just, you know, act really scared. See, what *that* did was—I don't know if it's really bad, but—one group jumped out one time and scared me and I got, I acted real scared and fainted, you know, and—well—it reinforced the story in their minds and they got scared that night because of my reactions. So I reacted after that but not nearly as dramatic."

He also recounted other "bad experiences" with the story, when he unintentionally terrified groups of campers too young to separate the pretended reality of the legend from literal history. Significantly, Henry found the best way to calm such audiences was to make this distinction openly and explicitly.

They'd be in there crying, and what I did was say—I would sit them together—"That is *not* a real story. It is totally made up, there is no such man. I am in no danger." I would completely deny the whole story and just say, "I'm sorry that I told that," and then they'd be mad at me for telling them. "Why did you tell us to scare us?" you know, and I'd say, "Well, I'm real sorry, you know, I didn't really think it'd affect you that way. . . ." I said "It's really kind of a way to keep you guys in your tents." And they kinda went to sleep after that.

After such experiences, Henry chose his audiences more carefully, refusing to perform to campers under the age of eleven and testing the group beforehand to see if they seemed mature enough for a horror legend. It is clear that in order to enjoy "Ralph and Rudy," the campers must have mastered the skill of suspending disbelief, yet not be credulous enough to take the legend aspects of the narrative seriously. The effect of the story, in the best performances, was to engross the campers to the extent that they colluded with the storyteller to maintain the illusion of "real life" that it projected. And when the story worked, "all week long you'd hear kids going around going 'RUUUU-UUDY!' you know, and having a lot of fun with it."

"Fun" would seem to contradict what folklorists have seen as the essence of the camp horror legend, indeed, of legends in general. Max Luthi, for instance, has described the local legend as an interpretation of "a weird frightful event," which, far from alleviating anxiety in the telling, "lets the threatening and horrifying aspects of the experience reappear more strongly than before in a new way."[30] At first glance, "Ralph and Rudy" would certainly fit this description, but fright, threats, and horror make strange bedfellows with fun. Yet in the liminal context of the summer camp, neither civilization nor wilderness, full of real anxieties about leaving home and having to obey strangers and rely on them for safety and comfort, nothing is quite what it seems.

In cases like these, we must take Bascom's seemingly rigid dichotomy and bend it: yes, ostensibly the narrator and his audience regard the story as true, and, yes, their actions show that they do not take it seriously. Such narratives are neither "real" legends nor tales but narratives deliberately designed to fit the gray area between. They arouse anxiety, but it is the entertaining kind of fear one feels watching John Carpenter's *Halloween*;[31] it tempts the audience to give in to the feeling of being alone in anguish but stops short of convincing it that the boogieman is waiting outside the theater. Such a legend—a mock one, recognized by its audience as talelike in execution and function—can be useful too, and in its light we need to broaden our conception of legends. Legends actually believed and told as literally true may be stylistically similar to legends meant as fiction and told to an audience that demands the illusion of strict realism. In such cases the actual nature of the narrative is determined, not by its style, nor by its content, nor even by the teller's degree of belief, but *by the audience's perception of the narrative in context.*

Given this, one can see easily how the same story, told in the same way, may provoke different aesthetic responses, especially among listeners of varying age. The pre-adolescent may "read" "Ralph and Rudy" as a true legend and react with frightened passivity, while the twelve-to-fourteen-year-old normally will interpret it as a talelike fantasy and proceed to playact within its terms. Most counselors interviewed agreed, though, that the second response is the one they aim for—not to oppress audiences but to enlist them as collaborators in the fictive world of the legend. In the case of Henry's narrative, campers did collaborate, not only responding creatively to the performance but also actively shaping its form and content. They thus were able to take charge of the narrative's progress, as younger children influence tales, as a means of expressing violent, antisocial desires and even of acting out rebellion against traditional authority. Even if we admit that Bill Henry was the only performer of this narrative, it still follows that he was a traditional interpreter of his audiences. To the extent that "Ralph and Rudy" was created and altered to fit different campers' aesthetic expectations and social needs, it indeed passed into "tradition."

In short, a legend becomes traditional not only when it passes from performer to performer but also when it is accepted, influenced, and re-created by a traditional audience.

Chapter 3

WHEN IS A LEGEND CONTEMPORARY?

Scholars began discussing the genre of narratives variously titled "urban legends," "contemporary legends," or "modern legends" mainly as recent responses to current social changes. Jan Harold Brunvand traces only "The Vanishing Hitchhiker" into records before 1900 and states that such legends demonstrate that "whatever is new and puzzling or scary, but which eventually becomes familiar, may turn up in our modern folklore."[1] Other researchers have stressed the stories' "immediacy" and "ephemeralness" or "the flavor of modern existence" they contain.[2] Recently the term "urban" has been criticized, because not all examples circulate in cities, while "the generic term 'modern' could be applied to all because they are in contemporary oral circulation."[3] But this term too is a misnomer, because not all legends in contemporary tradition are newly born, nor is the genre limited to "modern" times.

For this reason, folklorists suggested "contemporary" legend as a more accurate term. This suggests that such legends may in fact be quite old but that in context they are perceived as immediate or modern. But this term too has been challenged as an inexact way of referring to legends that happen to have been collected during the later twentieth century. Such terms as "contemporary" and "modern," Alan Dundes argued, "unnecessarily date the material and unwittingly relegate the writings to instant obsolescence."[4] Others have challenged the concept on the grounds that there is no reason to believe that the legends of the past were different from those being collected and analyzed today.[5] But there is a broader way in which we can interpret "contemporary," meaning not "contemporary with the folklorist" but "seen as contemporary at the time it circulates." Legends may have been "current" (or actively circulating at some previous time in history) or "modern" (relating to events seen as contemporary by people who circulate them).[6] The contemporary legends now being studied are clearly "current" and "modern," and so they are "contemporary" in every sense of the word. But in "ancient" and "medieval" periods there were also contemporary legends that were "modern" then just as they are modern now. Many legends current now have elements in them that can be found in historical records. Adrienne Mayer has studied legends dealing with gifts of disease-tainted blankets used to decimate minority cultures. She found that its central motif is identical to the "Nessus Shirt" familiar in the mythology of Hercules. This in turn seems to have been based on ancient outbreaks of diseases such as smallpox, which inspired atrocity legends blaming the disease on rival cultures such as the Spartans.[7] Similarly, she found that Roman stories about omens involving dogs that vomit severed fingers are at least cognate with the recent "Choking Doberman" legend.[8] Recent stories about economical carburetors and everlasting light bulbs closely parallel ancient stories dealing with suppressed inventions such as unbreakable glass.[9]

But continuity of content is not enough, for "contemporary" legends occupy a different niche in culture. Many legends about historical or supernatural events may circulate quietly and steadily over many years because of their narrative value, but contemporary legends emerge briefly yet explosively as truth claims requiring immediate response. An event felt to be emergent requires a different mode of narration and a different audience response from one that is current but said to have happened long ago and far away. It is therefore important that we look not just at the content of "ancient contemporary legends" but at the context that shows that they behaved like the legends studied in our time.

"The Gang Initiation" in Modern Times   One modern example, "The Gang Initiation," may well be the oldest contemporary legend for which we have records. The first version of this legend type to gain folklorists' attention was called "The Castrated Boy." Widespread in the United States during the 1960s and 1970s, it told about a child who goes alone into a shopping mall's restroom. When he does not return, his mother investigates and finds him in a pool of blood, his penis cut off. In one collected text we learn: "Subsequently they found three little black boys walking through the store with a bloody penis in their pocket. As it turned out, they had cut the little white boy's penis off as a orientation, a method of getting into a gang that they wanted to belong to. And to get into the gang they had to cut the penis off a white boy, which they did do."[10]

Other versions held that the culprits were white, Mexican American, Native American, or "hippie." In fact, the story had circulated actively some decades before. Janet Langlois, for example, noticed that a similar contemporary legend about a gang who abducted and murdered a baby had helped spark the 1943 racial riots in Detroit, Michigan.[11] Paradoxically, black audiences heard that a white mob had murdered a black baby; white audiences heard the opposite story. In either case, the symbolic image of the innocent child murdered as a token of the "other" race's gang loyalty and hostility to "us" stirred up and justified racial hatred in response to the alleged atrocity.

And additional versions of the "initiation" continued to develop in American culture in the following decades. As early as 1978, gangs were said to be operating in the parking lots outside shopping malls, where they would hide underneath cars and assault the ankles of young girls, then pull them under the car to rape them.[12] The story became widespread in the late 1980s and early 1990s, and was often accompanied by bizarre details. In one version, the gang member was supposed to slash the girl's ankle with a sharp knife, then, when she reached down to see what was happening, cut off her fingers.[13] This dismemberment element also showed up in a cycle of stories current in the Boston area, in which gang members would follow women to department store dressing rooms, then overpower them and cut off one of their fingers for the sake of their valuable rings.[14] And in another version that emerged close to Christmas in Wichita, Kansas, gangs of blacks were said to initiate new members by requiring them to grab white babies out of strollers and toss them over the balcony of a two-level mall lobby.[15] In all cases, police and mall owners were said to be conspiring to keep the matter private by keeping details out of local papers.

The element of the horrific initiation became a standard feature in the Satanism Scare. In 1988, Gary Sworin, a Pennsylvania law enforcement specialist in cults, conducted a series of public meetings in the Wilkes-Barre area, warning parents that cults were seeking teenagers to "brainwash." Once involved, teens might begin "just listening to some heavy metal rock music [or] starting to read Satanic bibles." But they would soon be induced to participate in a "Black Mass" in which they would be "initiated" into the cult. At this point, Sworin cautioned parents, "Statistics show that people who were involved—and I'm talking hard-core cultists saying this, people who've been involved with sacrifices, people who have been involved in mutilating even themselves—their rate of deprogramming to get that out of their system, to get them back into the mainstream is zero. *Zero*."[16]

This had been a standard motif among anticult propagandists at least since the 1970s. *Jay's Journal*, purportedly the journal of a teenage suicide, described the fate of a naive sixteen-year-old who fell under the control of a local coven. "It's like I'm a puppet," Jay writes toward the end. "Like I'm controlled and I don't want to be controlled! . . . Actually the occult movement is kind of a

Pied Piper sort of thing: we want to go but we don't want to go . . . in the end we have no choice . . . we've just got to see what's in that mountain."[17] At the book's climax, the coven leaders involve Jay and two friends in a ceremony involving ritual mutilation of a cow, from which gallon jugs of blood are drained. Their initiation involves a baptism in the blood, laced with hallucinatory drugs, after Jay enters a "zombie" state: "I couldn't stop myself from saying and doing things I didn't want to say and do." The initiates invoke Satan and thereafter are slaves to the cult, eventually committing suicide.

The themes of mutilation and ritual sacrifice appeared regularly in rumor panics inspired by this complex of beliefs. Before Friday, March 13, 1992, rumors circulated in Lehighton, Pennsylvania, that a blonde, blue-eyed virgin would be abducted from a local school and murdered by cult members. "There are 151 people in it, 65 from our high school," a teen told a local reporter, adding that she had heard that the sacrifice was needed to "worship Lucifer. . . . They'll cut out her heart and drink the blood." Although no evidence of a criminal cult ever emerged, the local district attorney agreed to come in to investigate, and the chief of police distributed a statement to churches for public reading: "Contrary to popular belief, Satan is alive and well and living here in Carbon County. . . . within the past few weeks local authorities have been receiving information at an alarming rate as to the cult's activities. The entire law enforcement community here in the County are working together to combat this activity. . . . There allegedly are activities planned by the cults for Friday the thirteenth. We will be ready for them."[18]

An even more extensive panic was set in motion by a story emerging in September 1993 about a gang who drove around at night with car lights on high beam or turned off. When another motorist flashed his lights as a courtesy, the gang members would follow this car and murder the occupants. On September 1, the Chicago FBI office sent a version of this warning out on a teletype, and soon after faxed and photocopied warnings appeared in a variety of public places. One said:

BEWARE!! *There is a new GANG INITIATION!!*

This new initiation of <u>murder</u> is brought about by Gang Members driving around at night with their car lights off. When you flash your car lights to signal them that their lights are out, the Gang Members take it literally as "LIGHTS OUT," so they follow you to your destination and kill you! That's their initiation.

Two families have already fallen victim to this initiation ritual. Be aware and inform your families and friends.[19]

None of these cases ever led to successful prosecution, but all of them provoked intense public discussion and certainly contributed to hostility against the various ethnic and religious groups targeted by these stories. And we find commingled in the various versions the themes of initiation into a sinister conspiracy connected with a crime against an innocent person, usually a child or young woman, and often involving mutilation of a body part. It may well have been the most popular contemporary legend during this time period, and so it is instructive to see that it was equally popular nearly two millennia previously.

"The Gang Initiation" in Ancient Times   Variants of this legend can be found as far back as 63 B.C., and it is probably at least a century older than that. It circulated actively in Rome and other major centers of the Roman Empire for more than three centuries. Moreover, contextual information given in the ancient records shows that in form and in function it was identical to the contemporary variants. Then as now, these legends exhibited four basic traits: (1) they spread rapidly as accounts of actual, recent happenings; (2) official investigations found no firsthand witnesses and no factual substantiation for any of the stories; (3) the culprits were ethnic, religious, or political groups rising in prominence; and (4) the stories expressed the existing anxieties and taboos of the established majority rather than knowledge of the scapegoated group. We are fortunate to have two full accounts of one early form of this legend—the anti-Christian version—not only recorded but analyzed in its social context. Both witnesses, Tertullian (ca. 150–220 A.D.) and Minucius Felix (fl. second or third century A.D.), were lawyers trained in the courts of Rome, though the former returned to his home city of Carthage and the latter probably came from that area as well. Both had opportunity to witness official proceedings against Christians and to participate in the investigations occasioned by anti-Christian stories. Both credit outrage at the irregular treatment that Christian defendants received before magistrates as one reason for their conversion to the faith. Since nothing is known about Minucius except what we can deduce from his sole surviving work, the *Octavius*, we cannot ascertain if he and Tertullian were contemporaries, but the latter's best-known work, the *Apology*, is textually related to the *Octavius*. Which came first is a matter of controversy among classicists, but today it seems more widely accepted that Minucius borrowed from Tertullian.[20] Still, their accounts of the anti-Christian legend vary widely, probably because Tertullian took his variant from oral tradition while Minucius relied on a literary source, a now-lost oration by Marcus Cornelius Fronto attacking the new sect. As Minucius's text is the fuller of the two, let us examine it first. It is to be found in the context of a debate between Caecilius, a pagan advocate, and Octavius, a

Christian apologist. After repeating a number of slurs against Christianity, Caecilius comes to the story:

> Details of the initiation of neophytes are as revolting as they are notorious. An infant, cased in dough to deceive the unsuspecting, is placed beside the person to be initiated. The novice is thereupon induced to inflict what seem to be harmless blows upon the dough, and unintentionally the infant is killed by his unsuspecting blows; the blood—oh, horrible—they lap up greedily; the limbs they tear to pieces eagerly; and over the victim they make league and covenant, and by complicity in guilt pledge themselves to mutual silence. Such sacred rites are more foul than any sacrilege.
>
> Their form of feasting is notorious; it is in everyone's mouth, as testified by the speech of our friend of Cirta [Fronto]. On the day appointed they gather at a banquet with all their children, sisters, and mothers, people of either sex and every age. There, after full feasting, when the blood is heated and drink has inflamed the passions of incestuous lust, a dog which has been tied to a lamp is tempted by a morsel thrown beyond the range of his tether to bound forward with a rush. The tale-telling light is upset and extinguished, and in the shameless dark lustful embraces are indiscriminately exchanged; and all alike, if not in act, yet by complicity, are involved in incest, as anything that occurs by the act of individuals results from the common intention. (9.5–7)[21]

Tertullian's account, part of a quasi-legal defense of Christianity directed at provincial magistrates, includes the same motifs, but (doubtless following oral tradition) presents the infant killing and orgy as part of the same bizarre ceremony. First he summarizes the story: "We are said to be the most criminal of men, on the score of our sacramental baby-killing and the baby-eating that goes with it and the incest that follows the banquet, where the dogs are our pimps in the dark, forsooth, and make a sort of decency for guilty lusts by overturning the lamps. That, at all events, is what you always say about us." (7.1)[22]

Then, as part of a *reductio ad absurdum*, he presents a fuller account as a burlesque set of instructions supposed to be given to the neophyte before the ceremony:

> Come! plunge the knife into the baby, nobody's enemy, guilty of nothing, everybody's child; or, if that is the other man's job, do you just stand by (that is all), by this human creature dying before it had lived; watch for the young soul as it escapes; catch the infant blood; steep your bread with it; eat and enjoy it.
>
> Meanwhile, as you recline on your couch, reckon the places where your mother, your sister, may be; make a careful note so that, when the darkness of the dogs' contriving

shall fall, you can make no mistake. You will be guilty of a sin, unless you have committed incest. So initiated, so sealed, you live for ever. (8.2–3)

Later, Tertullian gives yet a third anti-legend parody version in which he ironically details the catering instructions that would have to be given: "*item* a loaf, to catch [the baby's] juicy blood; add lamp stands and lamps, a dog or two" (8.7). He also ponders the social embarrassment that would occur if the neophyte's mother and sister did *not* show up at the initiation (8.8). Minucius's and Tertullian's variants differ on some points, such as whether the baby is killed unintentionally or not, or whether its flesh is eaten or merely its blood. They do agree on the central motif, however: that the new Christian's initiation consists of the ritual murder of an infant, procured for the purpose. The guilt of having participated, actively or passively, in such a crime is the factor that binds the neophyte to the group, since he would fear punishment if he broke faith with the cult and revealed the story (Tertullian 8.9).

The authors agree on the story's extraordinary popularity in Rome. "It is in everyone's mouth," says Minucius's pagan spokesman (9.6), and his Christian opponent admits that "the demons were for ever setting fables afloat without either investigation or proof" (28.2). As we have seen, Tertullian presents his story as "what you always say about us; and yet you take no pains to bring into the daylight what you have been saying about us all this long time" (7.2). Both point out that investigations revealed no evidence that such ceremonies had occurred, and Minucius records that the orator Fronto, although he repeated the legend, "did not produce evidence as on affidavit, but spattered abuse like an agitator" (31.2). In short, the narrative appears to have taken the course of an urban legend, becoming widely known and producing severe persecutions, but remaining anonymous and unsubstantiated, even though torture was used in an attempt to make suspects confess to the ritual murder (Tertullian 2.5).

These two writers deal with the legend as it circulated in Rome and possibly in North Africa during the latter half of the second century. But the same legend had already led to investigations in Asia Minor in 112 A.D. Pliny the Younger, sent as governor to Bithynia and Pontus that year, wrote back to the emperor Trajan asking advice on the matter of Christians. Shortly after his arrival, Pliny records, "An anonymous document was brought before me containing many names." After interrogation and torture of past and present members of the sect, he concluded that the Christians had been in the habit of gathering "to take food, but perfectly ordinary and harmless."[23] This last reference suggests that Pliny knew some form of the baby-eating rumor, although he does not repeat it, perhaps because the emperor was already familiar with it from Rome. Thus the legend of the ritual murder had apparently circulated between 112 and 200 A.D., both in Rome and in the provinces, occasioning local persecutions but never receiving concrete validation by authorities. "Who yet," demanded Tertullian, "came upon a baby wailing, as they say" (7.5).

In passing, Tertullian gives us an additional hint about the legend's history. After mentioning the customary shedding of blood to seal a treaty, he comments, "Something of the kind was tasted in Catiline's plot" (9.9). The reference was too familiar in his day to need development, but we are fortunate to have the whole narrative preserved by Sallust in *The War with Catiline*. At a crucial point in his conspiracy against Cicero and the Roman government in 63 B.C., according to this source, Catiline gathered together the whole body of his supporters. He promised them "abolition of debts, the proscription of the rich, offices, priest-hoods, plunder, and all the other spoils that war and the license of victors can offer." This incident, allegedly, followed:

It was said at the time that when Catiline, after finishing his address, compelled the participants in his crime to take an oath, he passed around bowls of human blood mixed with wine; that when after an imprecation upon traitors all had tasted it, as is usual in solemn rites, he disclosed his project; and his end in so doing was, they say, that they might be more faithful to one another because they shared the guilty knowledge of so dreadful a deed. Others thought that these and many other details were invented by men who believed that the hostility which afterwards arose against Cicero would be moderated by exaggerating the guilt of the conspirators whom he had put to death. For my own part I have too little evidence for pronouncing upon a matter of such weight.[24]

We find no infant sacrifice, at least in this version, but we do find the motivation central to the later narratives: guilt at "so dreadful a deed" being a motivation for greater unity and ruthlessness. Moreover, Sallust tells us that the narrative circulated "at that time," when "men were uneasy and apprehensive, put little confidence in any place of security or in any human being, were neither at war nor at peace, and measured the peril each by his own fears." The story thus expressed not only prejudice against Catiline's conspirators but fear of his supporters in general, the commons, whose desire for change alienated the more conservative classes in Rome. Sallust expresses this rather modern-sounding stereotype: "in every community those who have no means envy the good, exalt the base, hate what is old and established, long for something new, and from disgust with their own lot desire a general upheaval."

Significantly, Sallust could not substantiate the narrative, though he had access to official records of the investigation, and his doubtful ending suggests the characteristic "well, it *could* be true" attitude of contemporary American urban legends. Certainly Tertullian took it as true, and thirty-five years after him, Cassius Dio had no scruples about attributing the whole infant sacrifice motif to Catiline in his *Roman History*. Having gathered "the lowest characters," Dio tells us, "upon the foremost and most powerful of them, including Antonius the consul, he imposed the obligation of taking a monstrous oath. For he sacrificed a boy, and after administering the oath over his vitals, ate these in company with the others."[25] It is not important that the added motif of human sacrifice may have derived from some form of the anti-Christian legend; clearly the two motifs were functionally identical in inspiring horror and prejudice.

And the Romans also suspected other groups than the Catalinians and the Christians of similar initiations. The adherents of the Bacchanalia, a female-focused religious movement focused on Bacchus, the god of wine, were said to attract new members by inviting them to feasts. After participants had indulged in wine and normal sex, the Roman historian Livy says, "all varieties of corruption first began to be practised. . . . If any of them were disinclined to endure abuse or reluctant to commit crime, they were sacrificed as victims." A contemporary consul assumed that those involved had higher goals than self-indulgence: "It is already too great to be purely a private matter: its objective is the control of the state." As a result, the Roman senate took harsh measures to suppress it, and large numbers of people denounced as cult members were executed.[26]

After its ultimate victory over persecution, the emerging institution of the Christian church immediately appropriated the myth to attack its rivals and enemies. As early as 330–340 A.D., the Alexandrian bishop Epiphanius claimed to have defected from a sect called the Phibionites, who worshipped a snake, identified each other by secret signs, and practiced ritual intercourse during their services. Whenever a child was conceived during these orgies, they aborted the fetus, mixed it with other foodstuffs, and devoured it as "the perfect mass." Many other early Church fathers blamed a variety of other gnostic and dissident factions for orgies and cannibalism. The story was revived in Western Europe and applied to a variety of heretical sects. In 1019, a group of clerics at the collegiate church of Orleans formed a religious movement that challenged many of the tenets of orthodox Christian doctrine. They were convicted at a special Synod and burnt at the stake, the first heretics in Europe to be executed in this way. Afterwards, rumors circulated about the real nature of their rituals: they assembled at night by the light of lanterns to call out a litany of demons' names. Suddenly, a demon in the shape of an animal appeared, and the lights were at once put out. At this point, "everyone, as quickly as he could, seized whatever woman came to hand and abused her, without thinking of the sin, or whether he was possessing their mother, or sister, or a nun; and they considered that intercourse to be something sacred and religious."

As with the Phibionites, if a child was conceived in this way, it was ritually burned eight days after its birth, and the ashes preserved as a kind of holy sacrament. "There was such power of diabolical trickery in those ashes," a contemporary source claimed, "that anyone taking even a little of those ashes could scarcely ever afterwards forsake that heresy and walk in the ways of truth."[27] Theologian Guibert de Nogent made a virtually identical claim in the early twelfth century, except now *bread* was made from the burned baby: "Part of it is distributed for the [heretics'] Eucharist; once they have eaten it they almost never turn away from that heresy."[28] For a century to come, persons claiming to have managed to overcome the power of the initiation came to inform on so-called "synagogues of Satan." And from the thirteenth century on, Jews were widely accused of abducting and murdering a Christian child to use its blood in sacramental bread for Passover. At this point, the so-called "blood libel" appeared in so many forms that it was eventually given its own motif number in folklorists' references.[29]

Contemporary Functions for Ancient Cultures   Where then did the narrative come from? Historically we can point to the repeated uses of infanticide and ritual sacrifice for horror in Greek epics, especially those associated with the House of Atreus. And in fact the earliest related version of this legend is recorded from Greek tradition by Josephus, who wrote ca. 100 A.D. but associated the story with the upheaval resulting from the plundering of the temple at Jerusalem by Antiochus IV Epiphanes in 167 B.C. and the ensuing Jewish wars of liberation. Here it is allegedly a Greek who is kidnapped, fattened for a year in the temple, then ritually killed and eaten while the Jews swear "an oath of hostility to the Greeks."[30] Minucius and Tertullian, however, were interested not in tracing the story to a historical source but rather in why it was so perennially repeated. Minucius took the easy route, calling it "the handiwork of demons" (28.2, 8; also 31.1).

Tertullian gave a more psychologically astute explanation. The period when the "Christian Gang Initiation" contemporary legend was circulating, as all agree, was one in which the sect was growing considerably, both in the cities and in rural areas and villages.[31] Local pagan rites were sometimes neglected, and butchers who sold the flesh of animals killed as sacrificial offerings sometimes had trouble doing business because such meat was proscribed by Christians. Later in the century Tertullian wrote, "Men proclaim aloud that the state is beset with us; in countryside, in villages, in islands, Christians; every sex, age, condition, yes! and rank going over to this name" (1.7). Minucius's pagan agrees: "Already—for ill weeds grow apace—decay of morals grows from day to day, and throughout the wide world the abominations of this impious confederacy multiply" (9.1). The inroads made by this foreign religion, with its radical departures from Roman and Jewish cosmologies, confused many, and the immediate response to novelty was fear.

In addition, the Rome of the second century was an overcrowded city, with perhaps more than one million inhabitants packed mostly in apartments of up to six stories. It was among this lowest economic class—peasants, workers, slaves—that Christianity took its firmest roots. After the relative calm of the first century, internal dissent was becoming more troublesome and the central and regional governments less capable of keeping the Pax Romanorum. In such a crisis situation, it was not surprising for the established conservative classes to seek scapegoats, to pin on newly insurgent minorities rumors that "protect and justify emotions which, if faced directly, might be unacceptable."[32] Or, as Tertullian put it: "If you would realize that these sins are found among yourselves, you would see that they are not to be found among the Christians. The same eyes would assure you of both facts. But two sorts of blindness easily meet, so that those, who do not see what is really there, seem to see what is not" (9.20).

In his analysis of the legend, Tertullian provides eleven paragraphs of comparative detail, showing the fascination of Romans with human sacrifice, infanticide, and blood-drinking. He observes that the motif of human sacrifice of children was ubiquitous in myth, ranging from Saturn devouring his children to the Iphigenia in Aulis plot. He accuses the Gauls and North Africans of ritually killing humans until just recently; indeed, he suggests that in Africa the cult "to this day . . . persists in secret" (9.3). Some of the Roman spectacles included the killing of a prisoner sacred to Jupiter of Latium, he continued, so the Romans were guilty too, even if such a prisoner would have been executed anyway (9.5).

As regards infanticide Tertullian points to the common practices of exposing unwanted children and ending pregnancies by abortion. Both were baby-killing in his view, "since there is no difference . . . whether you do it as a sacred rite or just because you choose to do it" (9.6–8). Finally, he surveys the role of blood-drinking in current rituals. First he cites Herodotus on "how some tribes have used blood drawn from the arms of both parties and taste it to seal a treaty" (motif P312). Then he comments on the contemporary

Roman belief that blood caught flowing from the wounds of a dying gladiator was a cure for epilepsy (9.9–10). Thus he proves that the very motifs mentioned in the anti-Christian legend were in fact characteristic of pagan Roman culture rather than the Semitic background of Christians, which prohibited human sacrifice, exposure or abortion of infants, or even the trace of blood consumption. What was feared in the legend, in short, was what pagans most feared in the roots of their own culture.

After citing Vergil's famous attack on "Fama" (Rumour) as "swiftest of all curses" (*Aeneid* 4.174), Tertullian concluded:

The wise man does not believe uncertainty. It lies with everybody to reflect that, however widely Rumour has been put about, with whatever assurance it has been contrived, it must necessarily have originated at some moment with some single person who started it. After that it creeps through ramifications of tongues and ears; and something wrong in the little seed, whence it sprang, so obscures all else in the rumor, that no one reflects whether that first mouth sowed the lie, as often happens, from an envious nature, from wanton suspicion, or from that mere pleasure in lying which with some people is no new thing but inborn in them. [7.11–12]

"Nothing new" should be the motto for studies of contemporary legends. What we see today as our modern folklore may in fact be only universal human hates and anxieties in a contemporary cloak. Today the same impact is produced by the same symbol of castration to "take away the power of the majority,"[33] and the same fear that "they" have already formed a secret society to attack us where we are most vulnerable. Thus, what Catiline and his thugs "were said" to have done, today gangs of black/white/Chicano/Indian/hippie thugs "are said" to do. What is constant is the tendency to suspect new ideas, desire to hold on to "what is old and established," and project our own insecurities onto newly ascendant minorities. What is modern is only the identity of the culprit; otherwise, the genre is "nothing new" but the externalization of urges "inborn," the evidences of which we could doubtless trace farther back than 167 B.C.

We should not speak of modern legends, only modern texts of *contemporary* legends.

Chapter 4

WHEN IS A LEGEND?

Robert A. Georges has proposed that "a legend is a story or narrative that may not be a story or narrative at all; it is set in a recent or historical past that may be conceived to be remote or antihistorical or not really past at all; it is believed to be true by some, false by others, and both or neither by most."[1] In the previous chapters we have seen that legends may not follow a straightforward narrative sequence but might proceed in a seemingly random way, continuously interrupted by lengthy descriptions or discussions that have apparently little to do with the actual events represented.[2] And legends may allude to an immediate past but in fact retain content and dynamics that are millennia-old.

Should we then follow some folklorists and define the legend as no more than a belief surrounded by a variable cloud of "contextual elements"?[3] But as we have seen, "belief" is too vague a term for us, as it tempts us to look beyond the legend we directly observe and define it in terms of functions and motives that we can only infer. We risk discarding what we can observe and studying what we would *like* to observe.

It is equally dangerous to stress the narrative qualities of some legend texts, considering them as good stories, deserving close explication in the same way as literary short stories.[4] While this attitude encourages us to look at every legend with respect, it also tells our sources that we consider their stories first and foremost, and above all, "noble lies."

Folklorists seem to be embarked on a quest like Don Quixote's—an attempt to find order in a disorderly world. In seeking to define the exact quality of legend, scholars embark on a quest for something that we rarely glimpse and almost never capture—a legend that will stand still long enough to let us appreciate it in both its aesthetic and experiential sense. The Grimm Brothers, at the dawn of modern collecting, were aware of this dilemma. When challenged for rewriting the texts they collected in a folksy style, Jacob responded enigmatically that "in order to get to the yolk of an egg, you have to break the shell, but if you do it with care, the yolk will remain intact."[5] This principle has led some folklorists to reject the texts they collect as imperfect. Instead, they collate collected and uncollected versions in an attempt to reconstruct ideal texts.[6] Such practices reflect not so much sloppy methodology as misguided zeal. They discard the incoherent texture of texts that reflect only the artificial dynamics of "collecting" in a desperate attempt to re-create the uncollectable legend's spirit in scholarly language.

I suggest an alternative way of talking about legends, whether collected and transcribed, uncollected and untranscribed, or, more frustratingly, uncollectable and perhaps untranscribable. Rather than attempt to impose rigor and consistency on the phenomenon, I will instead ask the question, "When is a legend?"

This is not a riddle: I am not asking "When is a legend a legend?" The question hinges on the genre's chameleon nature, fixable but not fixed.

What Is "Narrative"?   Structural theorist Tzvetan Todorov describes the minimum narrative as "a movement between two equilibriums which are similar but not identical." That is, each story begins with (or infers) a stable situation and likewise ends with (or infers) another such situation. In between, something occurs that upsets this equilibrium, and the characters then have to react to this complication. "Every narrative," Todorov says, "includes this fundamental schema, though it is often difficult to recognize: *its beginning or its end [for example] may have been suppressed*."[7] Thus the text as performed may not seem to be complete and may leave characters still in flux. But narrators and audiences may silently supply appropriate beginnings and endings for the story.

Legends are narratives that share two features. First, they assume that the narrator, the audience, and the central character of the narrative initially share the same stable equilibrium. Second, the legend does *not* return to a positive equilibrium; that is, it suppresses its end. Hence, it moves quickly from positive to negative equilibrium and stays there. To paraphrase Linda Dégh and Andrew Vázsonyi, we tend to assume that the world is a rational, predictable place, but, of course, the legend insists that it isn't.[8] Supernatural elements—or at best grotesque, unparalleled, or psychologically threatening elements—enter this calm, stable world. Characters in the narrative find themselves forced to redefine their expectations of the way things are—as we do as listeners.

Few of us have experiences exactly like those told in contemporary legends.

But the narrative allows us to consider what would happen if we did. That is, we can temporarily set aside normal definitions of reality without being considered deviant. Nevertheless, as Dégh and Vázsonyi point out, "freedom of criticism in this case also means the compulsion to criticize. The teller of the legend, and often the listener, the active or passive participant of the legend-telling event, has to speak his mind. . . . this is the time of dispute."[9] The legend does not presuppose or compel belief, but it does demand that the teller and the listener take a stand on the legend: "Yes, this sort of thing could happen"; "No, it couldn't"; "Well, maybe it could"; "No, I don't believe in such things, but this I did see with my own eyes." Each individual participant in the legend-process is therefore responsible for the narrative's return to the "similar but not identical" equilibrium predicted by Todorov. So *a legend is a narrative that challenges accepted definitions of the real world and leaves itself suspended, relying for closure on each individual's response.*[10]

This definition says nothing about the *content* of legends; nor about whether they occur in the distant or recent past, the present, or the future; nor about whether they are told first-person or at secondhand; nor about the "beliefs" they reveal. Such issues are important, and the categories they project are often paralleled by categories recognized by the narrators themselves— ghost stories, belief legends, oral history, memorates, and the like—but these matters do not define the genre, nor are they central to its development.

What distinguishes the various kinds of legends is *when* they are: each narrator of each legend faces this puzzling question. Elizabeth Fine argues that a transcribed text is an intersemiotic translation from one medium of communication to another. The resulting text seemingly allows folklorists, or their readers, to replicate the original performance. The more detailed the transcription, we might think, the more exactly the original can be reconstructed. Fine's methodology, however, presupposes that every speech act can be repeated verbatim without altering its meaning. And this is not always true.

In fact, legends cannot be reperformed without radically altering their nature as a speech act. Each successive performance is a kind of intersemiotic translation, but the end product is a different kind of narrative. Todorov, again, has noted this about fantastic literature. This popular literary genre comes close to legend because it links realistic and supernatural events in an unstable way that forces the reader to "hesitate" between two worldviews.[11] Habitually, it presents events through the limited perspective of a narrator's eyes—a technique that forces the reader to identify with the main character. So the fantastic story, more than other kinds of fiction, can only be read in one direction. If, by caprice, we skip ahead in a conventional novel, we anticipate events that the novelist knows but that we readers, in the normal course of reading, ought not to know; still, Todorov argues,

> the loss suffered is not so great as if we were reading a fantastic narrative. If we know the end of a fantastic narrative before we begin it, its whole functioning is distorted, for the reader can no longer follow the process of identification step by step. . . .
>
> Hence the first and the second reading of a fantastic story produce very different impressions (much more than for other types of narrative). Indeed, for the second reading, identification is no longer possible, and the reading inevitably becomes a metareading, in the course of which we note the methods of the fantastic instead of falling under its spell.[12]

This feature is common to many forms of folklore, including, as Daniel R. Barnes noted, both the contemporary legend and the practical joke. They are structurally identical in habitually withholding important information, thus keeping their audience—their victims—in the dark. Ironically, once the performance is complete and each participant has reacted in his/her appropriate way, the story or prank immediately changes character without any necessary change in form.[13] Hence, when a narrator tells the same legend a second time to the same audience, the narrative now becomes in reperformance an aesthetic event, during which we appreciate the methods of narration instead of falling under its spell. Further performances yield further transformations.

The Half-Lives of the Legend   It is as if each legend, in the narrative repertory of each individual performer, were composed of radioactive material, created in some complex but explosive interaction of personality and environment. Initially full of energy, it has but a brief half-life, gradually but invariably decaying into simpler but still unstable forms, until finally it grows inert. Tentatively, we can recognize five such forms in the typical life of a legend. In its first and most transient state, it provides an individual with convenient language to identify an uncanny event or a social stress; it *names* a marginal experience. Second, it shares this experience, in the form of words, with others, who evaluate and comment on it; it *translates* marginality into language. Third, with the help of this evaluation and existing tradition, the performer reduces idiosyncratic elements in the narrative to good form. The resulting performance can be repeated at will to convince or entertain; it becomes *a finished narrative.* Fourth, the story no longer requires performance but instead remains a familiar part of the group's knowledge; it becomes a *metonym,* a kernel narrative, an inside password. Fifth, as it decays farther from its original energy, it becomes dormant. Known but no longer relevant, it circulates only in parodic or summary form; it is no longer a legend but a *legend report*. Obviously these five categories are neither rigid nor irreversible. But unlike the folk song or the folktale, which might be learned in its finished form and maintained through a lifetime with only trivial changes, the very survival of the legend depends on its capacity to change.

1. *Name.* For every legend told, obviously, there must be a legend born. But the reverse is not the case, for not every person who hears a legend is compelled to perform it. Tradition is no bully that forces narrators to pass on traditional material merely for the sake of perpetuating the tradition. Each legend performance, then, requires that these should be palpable, but previously undescribed, stresses on the individual and narrative elements in tradition that allow the individual to express these stresses. Such stresses may be empirical experiences or they may be unresolved psychological or cultural stresses.[14] In any case, the individual feels both internal and external pressure to control these stresses by *naming* them. This is the "Rumpelstiltskin Principle" discussed earlier. As Hufford notes, "When one has an experience and is aware that others have had a similar experience, that knowledge is generally accompanied by the availability of words and phrases understood to describe the experience or some of its aspects. . . . Not only does general knowledge allow for convenient language, but the presence of convenient language indicates the presence of a consensus, which in most cases provides assurance that one's experience is not somehow monstrous."[15]

That is to say, so long as an experience remains outside the realm of tradition, it is recognized as marginal but is not yet "named." It is Rumpelstiltskin without the happy ending. But language quantifies the experience, and the process of translating it into words exorcises the monster.

A major function of legends, then, is to serve, individually and collectively, as convenient language for the experiences that lie, actually or potentially, at the very boundaries of existence. This stage of the legend is, practically speaking, uncollectable, unobservable, and untranscribable. The fitting or crafting of convenient language to experience is silent, perhaps preconscious. Through careful interviewing and extensive background research, we can sometimes reconstruct this initial stage after the fact.[16] We must be careful, though: not every legend derives from an actual experience, however transformed in transmission. Most "friend-of-a-friend" contemporary legends clearly do not. As with proverbs, one can never freely identify the content of the legend with the content of the experience it names; nor is it possible to derive any universal social "meaning" from a legend by merely analyzing its component parts.

Folklorists need to deal more with the conditions that encourage such legends to spark into life.[17]

2. *Translation.* Nevertheless, each legend must be narrated for a first time, and such tellings can be observed, collected, and transcribed. Still, it is difficult to do so unless one can predict when such a narration is about to take place. Yet this stage is in many ways the most intriguing, since it involves the actual translation of individual experience into words. Such performances are often unresolved and inconsistent, with frequent use of verbal stalls and formulas. In the usual context, they are heavily interrupted and continued by comments from the listeners, who demand, in often unexpected ways, additional information, elaboration of points, and even retractions.[18]

This stage of the legend comes closest to the absolute form of "words as experiences." That is, the narrator uses words to describe not the words of tradition but the actual events as the narrator knows or imagines them to be. I would, however, hesitate to follow Gillian Bennett in calling this stage told "for true"—though the stylistic features she has identified obviously apply to narrations in this stage.[19] The term "true" introduces the notion that all legends narrated at this stage are implicitly believed. This is not always the case, and exceptionally versatile narrators may learn and repeat stories not so much for their "truth" as for the social power they gain by introducing so many of a given kind of legend.[20] Rather, such legend performances present the events "for real." The tellers identify the narrative situations with their own and those of their audiences, even to the extent of impeding or losing the thread of the story.

Good texts of translation legends are difficult to come by, for the obvious methodological reasons. Hufford has perhaps done better than most by letting it be known (in public lectures, for instance) that he is interested in the actual events underlying Old Hag stories. He also is willing to take his informants at their word. The resulting texts, often described as first tellings, are extremely incoherent and filled with false starts and expressions of tension. Hufford notes that this difficulty in composing sentences, combined with self-consciousness "often prevents people from speaking of their experiences" and observes that, only when he indicated support and willingness to accept such experiences as legitimate would most informants "begin to verbalize their experiences freely."[21] Most professional folklorists, however, are not as willing to provide support; indeed, our quickness to shift the topic of discussion from real life to traditionality often makes us the worst possible audience for this kind of legend.

A tape recorder often bears the implicit message that words spoken will be collected as aesthetic events, not as signs for real-life experiences. It is not surprising, then, that many of the published texts that illustrate this stage of the legend's life were collected with *concealed* tape recorders. Undercover recording preserves the event of translation in enough detail to allow us to describe it fully. But if we take our informants' rights to privacy as seriously as our own, we perhaps *should* not collect them. Or else, like Hufford, we should come to terms with the sensitive nature of these performances and agree, at least temporarily, to hear and record them as "real." Alternatively, we are reduced to post hoc reconstructions, which inevitably fail to record important linguistic information but at least do not disrupt the context. Folklorists need to discuss further how far their right to study their material extends over their informants' right to set social rules of conversation.

3. *Finished narrative.* When legends are told again, they change again, both for narrators and for hearers. Keeping in mind the first reactions of their audiences, narrators will replicate not the original translation but the previous telling; now they present "words as words." That is, the more narrators tell their stories, the more they will focus on the narrative elements that most efficiently re-present the most successful translation of the events described. One of the most telling is the deliberate use of suspense to compel audience interest. Narrators know from past performance the moment of peak tension, the fulcrum point at which the positive equilibrium of the start shifts to the negative equilibrium at the end. Instead of presenting it directly, surrounded with the halo of orientation and evaluation that would make it convincing as fact, they play with listeners, drawing them in little by little, before turning the world around.

Both the translated and the finished legend, therefore, choose an indirect, tangled thread of narrative, but for different reasons. The translation subordinates plot to experience; the finished legend re-creates the legend experience through dramatic techniques. Such techniques transform each listener into a surrogate of the original (perhaps hypothetical) experiencer. Simultaneously, each narrator "acts" as the marginal stress that the legend names. Put briefly, the legend as name allows narrators to identify with the otherwise monstrous experience; the legend translation allows them to confine the monster inside words; the finished legend allows them to embody the monster. Dégh's comment—"The tale gives relief from anxiety; the legend arouses it and leaves man alone with his anguish"—is the reverse of the truth.[22] Narrators use the legend to impose form on marginal experience; thus they can comprehend, control, and share anxiety. When anxiety is shared, one is no longer alone.

4. *Metonym.* Eventually narrators, however successful, exhaust the available audiences: and however intrigued by the events described, they no longer need to reexperience them through performance. At this point the legend

becomes a name in form as well as function. If the group has experienced the legend, they may reduce it to a simple allusion to one of its distinctive elements[23]—a protagonist's body part (the Hook); a piece of dialogue ("Have you checked the children?"); even a sound effect ("scratch, scratch, scratch"). Such an element is a "metonym," a part that stands for the whole.[24] In such cases, the allusion recalls the whole story simultaneously present in the minds of the group's members, without interrupting the topic of conversation to replay it.

Legend metonyms show up everywhere but are often opaque to outsiders. To that extent, they define the boundaries both of the group's world and of its membership. Typically, the only time they will revert to finished form is when a new member enters the group, or needs to be initiated with the legend's aid. Again this stage of legend poses methodological problems: our broad knowledge of legend motifs allows us to recognize metonyms, but we are in the awkward position of being unable to collect them in finished form unless the group agrees to accept us as at least potential members.[25]

Sometimes, though, legends simply resist the reverse entropy needed to restore them to narrative form. "The Razor Blades in the Apple," as Sylvia Grider has found, is a metonym, since even the allusion to the allusion universally represents a narrative that is almost never performed.[26] In such cases we can reconstruct the "implied" text only by surveying the cultural uses of the metonym, just as the compiler of a dictionary produces the implied definition of a new word by comparing its various uses.

5. *Report.* For folklorists, the alternative is simply to collect legend texts, whatever and however. Unfortunately, however, this shortens the legend's half-lives and rushes it to a state where it serves only the function of recalling a tradition. When collectors are interested only in the legend as legend, that is, as interesting stories, then their sources will want to oblige. However, in so doing they will strip away the details that should interest the collector the most, and reduce narratives to the bare bones of the plot. The difference between the lively translation or finished legend on the one hand and the dormant legend report on the other can be quite pronounced.

The Organist and the Maniac   As illustration, here is a version of a local maniac legend that circulates among female undergraduates at Miami University in Oxford, Ohio. The story is attached to a chapel near a cluster of buildings—Fisher Hall and Pines Hall—that, according to tradition, had once been used to house "lunatics."

Theresa: Did you ever hear any about Kumler Chapel?

Amy: When you mentioned that story about the hair turning white. Yeah, I remember hearing that one.

Theresa: Had you heard that?

Amy: Not very often.

Theresa: I had heard that um, OK, the girl had gone over to practice.

Amy: And the crazy man broke out of—

Theresa: Yeah, another maniac!

Amy: Pines or Fisher Hall.

Theresa: She turned around and there's a guy with bandages all wrapped around him, standing there in back of her. Amy: And whenever she stopped playing he would come closer.

Theresa: Yeah. So, she just kept on playing madly and madly and madly through the night so that he wouldn't start moving towards her, and then in the morning—they found her and she had just gone berserk. And her hair had turned white and they had to put her in Pines.

Amy: [*bursting out in laughter*] That's a nice one!

[*Informant's comment*: "This legend has the traditional motifs of a maniac who is loose, and a girl whose hair turns white from fear. Realizing the legend contains these two motifs makes me believe that the legend is not true. Some Freshmen students may still believe in it though, since it is told as a true story."][27]

As this is no more than a summary of a legend, the means used to transcribe it is adequate, for here is little to analyze beyond content. The version that follows, by contrast, is a finished narrative, performed in full dramatic detail, and it deserves a far more finished job of transcription. The unrecognized problem is that words, including tags and stalls, do not carry meaning in or by themselves. Rather, speakers consciously and unconsciously use paralinguistic devices, which subtly affect the ways in which their words are interpreted by their auditors. "Uh-huh" means nothing in particular; add pitch, and it can mean "I approve. Go Ahead"; or "That's that. Move on"; or "Wait a moment. I think I missed something"; or "Yes, I see and appreciate what's coming next," or any number of socially defined messages. All of us successfully decode these utterances every day, but a transcription that includes them may be literally verbatim yet just as misleading as a rewritten text.

So what should a text of a finished narrative include? Theoretically, as Elizabeth C. Fine argues, it should "provide the most information for the greatest number of people," using a variety of techniques to represent in print the variety of communications available in speech and kinesics. To this end, she uses not only standard orthography but also iconic devices to represent pitch levels, stress levels, use of rasp and falsetto, pauses, and pelvic tilts. Marginal and interlinear "stage directions" represent additional semiotic devices: gestures, postures, changes of location, and fine distinctions of characterization in voice and expression.[28] Her use of videotape to capture all these fine details, however, may often be beyond the capabilities of the legend-collector. And the Heisenberg principle of folklore holds that the act of recording inevitably influences the event itself.[29] The use of a small sound tape recorder, in the hands of a nonprofessional who may not be capable of recording the fine nonverbal acts of communication, irretrievably limits the details preserved to those audible on tape. Simultaneously, the performance recorded in so limited a form may be far more spontaneous and natural than that captured by a videotape recorder in the hands of a team of practiced professionals.

Assuming that the primary document is a sound tape, then, a full text would account for as many of the speaker's inflections as possible. The following is an attempt to do this without overloading the intended audience with puzzling orthography.[30]

Mary: [*Preceding narration concerned ghostly events said to have occurred in Fisher Hall*]
OH.
This is not really a ghost story but it, it's something that
scary that happened to
someone there [*near Fisher Hall*]
Um—
over on Western College—
which used to be the Western College for women
but now it's just the Western College, Miami University, Miami bought it.
◇
Um—there's the Alumni—
◇
Alumni Chapel.
◇
no, *Kumler* Chapel.
(I'm sorry.)
Carol: Umm?
Mary: The Alumni Building of the Kumler Chapel.
Carol: Oh.
Mary: [*inaudible*]
Over on Western campus and there's a—a big pipe organ in there, it's one of the nicer ones on campus, well one of the two that are on campus.

    And—
    ◇
    one of the music majors was over there practicing one night—
    and she always practiced over there
    and uh—
    ◇
    late at night and
    um—people all over campus could hear her practicing, it was such a
    a beautiful organ and it
    had such a nice sound to it
    and she would always just turn on the light right above the *organ*
    you know, she wouldn't bother to turn on the rest of the lights 'cause she didn't think
        it was necessary.
Carol: Uh-huh.
Mary: Well—
    ◇
    ◇
    ◇
    ◇
    that particular day
    someone, some group from Cincinnati or Dayton or someplace had brought a group
        of special education—people, you know, RETARDED people
    to CAMPUS and they had been taking them on a *tour*.
    And they had happened to come *in*
    while she was *PLAYING*, it was in the—early evening
    and they were just getting ready to leave and they thought they'd come by and see
        who was playing the ORGAN.
    And uh—
    ◇
    she knew they were THERE and she kept on playing and then they LEFT—
    And uh—
    ◇
    it got to be later on in the evening, she was **a real dedicated music student**
Carol: [*an ironic laugh*] *Huh*!
Mary: she practiced for hours every day.
    And uh—
    ◇
    she was sitting there and she *finished practicing*.
    ◇

And she heard someone walking down the aisle of the church and she couldn't *see* who it *was*.

◇

And it **scared** her so—

she called out to—see who it *was*

◇

and uh, no one answered her

and they just kept walking down the aisle and so she started *PLAYING* again and they—whoever it was would stop *WALKING*.

◇

You know, they'd—go BACK (or whatever.)

And uh—

◇

◇

she—finished that song and she stopped—

◇

and whoever it was would start walking down the aisle aGAIN.

And so she started PLAYING again. You know to keep—make them quit—stop—quit *walking* towards her. And uh—

◇

◇

this went on all *night* well, *finally she got—so—SCARED*, that she just kept

playing and playing and—

[*quickly*] people didn't-think-too-much-about-it-I-mean-they-could-hear-her-playing-all-night-but-they-didn't-really-think-too-much-about-it

And uh—

◇

so the next *morning* she was still *PLAYING*.

[*quickly*] When-everyone-woke-up-the-next-morning-she-was-still-playing so

FINALLY

a bunch of people went in there

to SEE, you know, *WHY* she was still *PLAYING*.

And she was UP there just—she had gone crazy.

And her hair had turned completely white, 'cause she was so scared.

She—it scared-her-to death.

And—

she was up there playing, just [*mimes playing keyboard rapidly*]—going nuts and they had to put her in **an insane asylum—probably over in Pines Hall.** [*laughter*]— or Fisher. [*laughter*] but uh—

◇

what had HAPPENED was

one of these special ed. people

had COME

and had *enjoyed her playing* so much and they—they—somehow they broke away

from the group

and had *come BACK.*

And whenever she'd quit *PLAYING*

they would start walking down the ai—aisle.

You know, they didn't know any better and just start walking down the aisle towards

    her—

    ◇

you know, they were—trying to get her to play some

more whenever she'd go ahead and *play* some more—

then they'd—*be satisfied* and they'd go back to the back of the church, you know,

    and they'd, you know

listen to her—*play*—some more.

And—

actually the person had only been there for about

fifteen or twenty minutes when—when he finally left, they finally

came and got him or something and—

but she didn't know it.

And she thought they were still out there, so she just kept (playing all night and

    just—she just went crazy.)

Carol: ((Huh.))

Mary: (So that was sort of a scary thing.)

Carol: Yeah, I saw that in the folder. *[i.e., the sample texts I had given the class; the text*

    was the one given above]

Mary: (Yeah [*laughs*].)

Carol: That was—

    I think

    my—

    professor told it.

    My folklore professor.

    Told a version of it—it was somebody—

Mary: Oh I'm sure there are several—versions of—

    You know it's probably not true

    it's just a—

Carol: No—

Mary: Um, then there's the . . .

    [a *version of "The Hatchet Man" follows.*][31]

The most obvious difference between these two texts is in length, but this does not in itself *define* the difference. We must see *how* the second one is longer. First the initial version contains no characterization beyond stereotype. "The girl" is a victim who happens to be there at the wrong moment; the "crazy man" appears, menaces, and leaves without a trace. Why he is charmed by the music into coming no closer is left a mystery. By contrast, much of the length of the second version comes from explanations of why the girl was there to begin with: she was, to begin with, "a music major," attracted to "a beautiful organ" with "such a nice sound." Later, Mary makes it clear that she is a "real dedicated music student . . . she practiced for hours every day," which in turn explains why people on campus "could-hear-her-playing-all-night-but-they didn't-really-think-too-much-about-it." The "maniac" turns out to be a harmless "RETARDED" person who "*enjoyed her playing*" and was merely "trying to get her to play some *more*." The second legend, then, elaborates the actions and the motivations of the characters, linking them to real-life situations. In the first, the incongruous "bandages" instead link the story to familiar movie plots involving creatures like the Frankenstein monster and the Mummy.

A second major difference lies in pacing. In both cases the performer and the listener know the story's conclusion from the start. In fact, the first begins with the climax, "the hair turning white," a metonym. Theresa and Amy plunge headlong into the plot, putting the crazy man on the scene in the first exchange, then wrapping up the consequences as quickly as possible. Mary, on the other hand, lingers over the same scenes, continually halting them with seemingly irrelevant details—the girl's habit of turning on the light above the organ, for instance, or the description of the special education class. Mary knows these bits are necessary to the plot but, in accordance with the art of the finished legend, she makes no effort at the time to explain. As we go along, we recognize that the organist cannot see who the intruder is because she has left the hall dark. Since we assume that the strange man is a "RETARDED" person, we, like the organist, irrationally fear that his actions will be unpredictable and possibly dangerous. The narrator knows that the man is harmless, but she deliberately withholds this vital detail until after the story's climax. Then she forces the audience to reinterpret the narrative by reenacting it from the perspective of the "special ed." person. By contrast, the first version withholds nothing and therefore leaves us with an incoherent narrative.

More important, the intonations preserved in the second version suggest interpretations in a way that the bare bones of the first cannot. Close listening and transcribing reveals, for instance, that Mary habitually stresses certain words in the story. The music major keeps *playing* and PLAYING the ORGAN, while the RETARDED person, who has COME, keeps *WALKING* towards her whenever she stops. Americans frequently load the terms "playing," "coming," and "organ" with sexual connotations. The legend is thus connected to other contemporary legends about isolated young girls who are sexually menaced by real or apparent "lunatics": the assailant in the back seat, the man in the barber's chair cleaning his glasses, and so on. All of them contain the telling double perspective that withholds important information until near the end, and then forces the audience to reexperience the story from a second perspective. The unique quality of this legend is that, ironically, the girl keeps playing and "playing" with the "organ," while the man, whom we would expect to keep "coming" and "coming" all the while, instead has a seat to watch the exhibition and soon disappears altogether! The poor music major, however, trapped by her fantasy of male domination, "plays" by herself (with herself?) all night and goes insane, which is again a fitting end, as many Americans have heard the Puritanical claim that excessive masturbation is both a cause and a consequence of "lunacy."

This interpretation may be valid, but there is no guarantee that it is not the product of the analyst's mind. For another listener, the legend may name quite a different anxiety. My wife, for instance, saw in this transcription a literal event uncannily close to one she had actually had when she was an undergraduate. While she was practicing on her college's chapel organ, a strange man had indeed walked in and sat down to listen to her practice. In this case, the legend helped her verbalize her fear of being with strange men: "You never know who you're going to meet in a college town," she concluded. If we could hear how Mary discussed her version of the legend, we might be able to judge which interpretation is more valid, the psychological or the literal. In this transcription, however, we get no discussion, for as soon as the collector suggests that Mary has uttered folklore, Mary hides behind a disclaimer. Thus the legend, seemingly in front of us, suddenly and frustratingly vanishes in spite of all my orthographic subtlety.

So we end where we began. Granted, the narrator has neither had this experience nor knows who did have it; still, she has visibly lavished verbal art on it. This indicates that it named something marginal, previously unexpressed, that it survived her translation of it into her own experiential terms, and, in finished form and metonym, it still serves to name something. But what? The legend text allows us to ask the question, but it is shy to give the answer.

Verbatim Texts: The Impossible Quest   Don Quixote, in Cervantes's view, was a madman and a fool who attempted to do what no sensible person would think to try—to find sanity in an irrational world. So, too, legend scholars seem trapped in a futile quest for something that cannot entirely be grasped. The quest for a whole legend, a totally verbatim text, is quixotic in every sense of the word. Two of the crucial stages of legend development, its use as name and its birth as translation, are virtually impossible to collect. Two more—the metonym and the report—can easily be collected but reveal little of their meaning, which can only be reconstructed through detailed background work. This leaves us with the finished legend, which fascinates and leaves us with tantalizing, but limited, conclusions. As repeated and repeatable narrative, it necessarily emphasizes aesthetics, not experience, and the act of identifying it as folklore, transcribing it, and discussing its artfulness necessarily heightens this aesthetic slant. Worse yet, our technology enables us to preserve more and more aspects of performance, but it necessarily skews the context of performing away from person-to-person communication toward conscious artifice. So we unconsciously but inevitably misrepresent every performance that we capture. Our sources do not tell us the legend; they play themselves telling the legend. To this extent, folklorists are quixotic in Jorge Luis Borges's sense. In his short story, "Pierre Menard, Author of the Quixote," Borges depicts the archetypal legend scholar.[32] Menard devotes his entire life to writing—not translating, not copying, not rewriting—but *writing* as if for the first time some pages from Cervantes's masterpiece. He made it his quest to say what Don Quixote said, as if the words were being written for the first time. After a lifetime of research, experience, rough drafts, revisions, he apparently succeeds. But Borges ironically notes that the words written in the twentieth century by Menard now have a completely different meaning and significance from those written in the sixteenth century by Cervantes.

In the same way, contemporary jazz musicians despair over the problems created by recordings of improvised music by great artists like Jelly Roll Morton and Louis Armstrong. Again, technology proves a mixed blessing: it preserves moments of brilliance, but in a frozen, lifeless form, since the musicians' intuitive choices result only in a disk or tape that plays back the same notes over and over. "How do young musicians re-create music originally played in a combustible, semi-intuitive manner?" critic Whitney Balliett asks. Note-for-note transcription of solos misrepresents the original nature of the music; attempting to turn oneself into the original artist leads inevitably to pale imitation. "Poets, not copyists, are needed for such work," he concludes.[33]

We folklorists are in the same situation. To refer again to the Grimms' dilemma, we may try to remain true to the literal words, the shell, or to the allegedly ideal content, the yolk. Either way, we end up with a document different from that we try to capture. A broken egg, however aesthetically fried or scrambled, is a poor substitute for the living entity that produces and is produced from it. We need to stop making omelets and start chasing chickens. The legend is a polyform genre whose stages equally reflect humans' need to define, name, and share every part of their world and every margin of their experience. All these stages are equally legend, even when they differ in function and form.

So if we are to understand any legend, we must know *when* it is. The verbal art of the finished legend does not define the desperate incoherence of the translation; nor is this the same incoherence of the report. The legend as name is not quite the same as the legend as metonym. Every single legend, to survive, will invariably appear in different forms at different times. No single stage can define the whole genre; yet the genre is not formless.

The Broadway reinterpretation of Cervantes's work turns the fool into a hero of our time. Quixote's impossible dreams make his "sensible" antagonists look pedantic and nihilistic. So too the quest for verbatim legend texts is quixotic: impossible, but not for that reason foolish. What we need to do, though, is to stop trying to make our chameleon texts stay one color long enough for us to put them in their pigeonholes.

Chapter 5

WHY IS A LEGEND?

Folklorists are often called on to explain why a given legend has emerged. This is often hard to do, because legends circulate for reasons independent of the narrators' personality. French sociologist Jean Noel Kapferer demonstrated this by taking a series of surveys on a widespread contemporary legend: the "Blue Star Acid" story.[1] According to this story, which has circulated in the United States since the 1970s, drug dealers give free LSD to small children in the form of "lick-and-stick" tattoos laced with drugs that can be absorbed through the skin. When this legend went through France in 1988, Kapferer distributed a questionnaire to his students. He found that two-thirds found the legend credible and 60 percent passed on the story to others, either orally or by copying a flyer with a version of the legend. But the 60 percent who circulated the rumor were *not* all drawn from the 67 percent who believed it. Of the believers, 27 percent said they did nothing, a factor made up by the 26 percent of nonbelievers who nevertheless passed on the warning to others. Interestingly, the percentage of those who physically duplicated the leaflet was actually higher among nonbelievers and those inclined to disbelieve than among firm believers and those inclined to believe.

In old-fashioned folkloristics, the goal of studying folk narrative was to determine the personality of the narrator and the function or significance of the story for the teller and community. But legends circulate for many reasons and so may not have a set significance, even for one narrator. Can we answer the question that many in the general public often assume we can answer: what do legends mean? I propose that, in and of themselves, legends *have* no meanings. This does not mean that meanings aren't constructed *from* legends. This is the one thing that we can be sure about: that legends *compel* their hearers to construct meanings. But it would be lost labor to study their content, history, and morphology as a key to some "hidden message" intrinsic to all variants of a given narrative.

This suggests that legends do not match their tellers' beliefs or interpretations in a simple one-to-one way. Rather, these narratives may, in some cases, behave more like organisms in an ecosystem, which develop through natural selection to exploit the conditions in which they are passed on. Richard Dawkins, a zoologist at the University of Oxford, has recently suggested such an original approach. He proposes that some ideas are "mind viruses," packets of information with the apparently autonomous ability to pass from brain to brain. They resemble on the one hand the DNA strips that have developed biological strategies of forcing hosts to replicate and disseminate them. And on the other, they mimic computer viruses that silently encourage terminals to duplicate and pass them on without notice of the user. Dawkins speculates that human consciousness itself, being both biological tissue and biocomputer terminal, can be a host to a third kind of virus that can be expressed directly through words. We may differ from many of his preconceptions, particularly his assumption that mind viruses are always parasitic and so detrimental to their hosts. But as he approaches our data with a novel scientific mindset, we can hardly ignore his conclusions.

In a field of study that has come to be termed memetics, he formulates theories of behavior founded on empirical biological research motivated by Darwin's theories of natural selection. In his popular book *The Selfish Gene* (1989), Dawkins boldly argues that organisms' behaviors are motivated by the essentially "selfish" aim to perpetuate the information encoded in their DNA. Such an aim, he says, is intrinsic to the DNA molecule itself, and organisms themselves, including human beings, ultimately are "survival machines— robot vehicles blindly programmed to preserve the selfish molecules known as genes." Dawkins first applies what biologists have learned about how DNA molecules develop strategies for replicating and preserving themselves. This occurs in its purest state in viruses, which often are no more than strands of information encoded in DNA sequences. These are enclosed in a simple structure that protects the molecule and allows it to penetrate another organism's cells. Once there, the virus's gene takes over the cell to replicate and spread itself. Dawkins, drawing on the work of behavioral scientists, suggests that even more complex organisms are motivated fundamentally by the desire to perpetuate their genes in competition with those of other species and even with those of their peers. Such strategies, he argues, are explained by Darwin's theory of evolution.

In particular, he holds that every aspect of life is ruled by essentially biological drives of selfishness and altruism. The popular conception of natural selection is that traits that contribute to the good of the overall species govern evolution. Dawkins notes that this belief in fact distorts Darwin's actual argument: natural selection is driven by the desire of individuals to perpetuate their genes at the expense of others. He summarizes his thesis: "I shall argue that a predominant quality to be expected in a successful gene is ruthless selfishness. This gene selfishness will usually give rise to selfishness in individual behavior. However, as we shall see, there are special circumstances in which a gene can achieve its own selfish goals best by fostering a limited form of altruism at the level of individual animals. . . . universal love and the welfare of the species as a whole are concepts that simply do not make evolutionary sense."[2]

Dawkins describes a number of cases in which apparent altruism equates with genetic selfishness. When an animal shares food or defends another of its species from attack, its decision may be determined by the degree to which it is genetically related to the other. Helping out a close relative, say a sibling or child, might outweigh the loss to the individual, because it does after all ensure the perpetuation of genes that are shared by both individuals. Dawkins stresses, however, that he does not mean to suggest "that the individual animal works out what is best for his [sic] genes. What really happens is that the gene pool becomes filled with genes that influence bodies in such a way that they behave as if they had made such calculations."[3]

In moving to the human condition, Dawkins proposed the most controversial of his concepts, that of the "meme." If DNA is essentially a form of encoded information that acts to perpetuate itself, he reasoned, then other forms of information might act in equally selfish ways. The "meme" is an information packet that acts like an organism in that it manipulates hosts to reproduce and distribute it. Only in this case, it is expressed in symbolic language rather than DNA, and it relies on human consciousness for its life. A meme, that is, is a unit of culture that is transmitted from one organism to another in a competitive environment that encourages it to develop strategies to ensure its own replication. He argues: "Examples of memes are tunes, ideas, catch-phrases, clothes fashions, ways of making pots or of building arches. Just as genes propagate themselves in the gene pool by leaping from body to body via sperms or eggs, so memes propagate themselves in the meme pool by leaping from brain to brain via a process which, in the broad sense, can be called imitation."[4]

There is a biological link between the evolutionary forces that create a human brain and those that control the development of the meme pool that inhabits it, Dawkins continues. But it is no longer a direct parallel; that is, conditions have arisen in which the memes themselves have become a new type of replicating information packet, and have begun a form of evolution of their own. The direction of this evolution is focused on their own survival as memes, not the survival of the brains that transmit them. That is, a meme may circulate widely not because it gives any biological advantage to its host but simply because it has become well adapted to its mental environment.

Indeed, in his boldest argument, brains are not necessarily *controlled* by memes; through foresight and critical analysis, our consciousness may in fact rebel against memes that are recognized as pathological. Repeatedly he uses the Roman Catholic "co-adapted stable set of mutually-assisting memes," such as belief in a god, life after death, faith, and fear of hell, as examples of virulent memes that circulate widely simply because they have evolved selfish means of perpetuating themselves. It is possible, he says, that Catholic priests might have planned hell as an indoctrination device. "However," he continues, "I doubt if the priests were that clever. Much more probably, unconscious memes have ensured their own survival by virtue of those same qualities of pseudo-ruthlessness that successful genes display. The idea of hell fire is, quite simply, *self-replicating*, because of its own deep psychological impact."[5] He stresses that when we study memes as entities governed by natural selection, we must avoid the fallacy of thinking that every meme confers biological advantages to its host: "a cultural trait may have evolved in the way that it has, simply because it is *advantageous to itself.*"

Chain Letters as Mind Viruses   In *The Selfish Gene*, Dawkins often compares highly successful memes to viruses with high infective power. He claims only the power of analogy for such statements, but he also quotes a colleague, N. K. Humphrey, who makes more sweeping claims: "memes should be regarded as living structures, not just metaphorically but technically. When you plant a fertile meme in my mind you literally parasitize my brain, turning it into a vehicle for the meme's propagation in just the way that a virus may parasitize the genetic mechanism of a host cell."[6]

In a later essay, "Viruses of the Mind" (1993), Dawkins publicly adopted Humphrey's position, arguing that the human brain, being essentially a computer, was a "virus-friendly environment." Using the observed behavior of computer viruses as a model, he hypothesized that minds were hosts "to parasitic, self-replicating ideas or information, and that minds are typically massively infected." Such a parasitized mind might not recognize the presence of a virus, he suggested, and may in fact strongly reject the idea. Still, he said, the mind affected by a mind virus "typically finds himself [sic] impelled by some deep, inner conviction that something is true, or right, or virtuous: a conviction that doesn't seem to owe anything to evidence or reason, but which, nevertheless, he feels as totally compelling and convincing."[7]

Dawkins's evidence for mind viruses is general and anecdotal. For instance, he comments that "yo-yos, hula hoops and pogo sticks, with their associated behavioral fixed actions, sweep through schools, and more sporadically leap from school to school, in patterns that differ from a measles epidemic in no serious particular."[8]

But most of his essay incorporates extended attacks on the dogmas of organized religion, which he sees as clusters of mind viruses that "gang up" and mutually support each other, just as groups of genes do in complex organisms. He describes "mind viruses" such as the Catholic doctrine of transubstantiation and Orthodox Jewish dietary codes as objectionable because they rely on "blind faith" rather than scientific method. Science, by contrast, is *not* a virus:

Scientific ideas, like all memes, are subject to a kind of natural selection, and this might look superficially virus-like. But the selective forces that scrutinize scientific ideas are not arbitrary or capricious. They are exacting, well-honed rules, and they do not favor pointless self-serving behavior. They favor all the virtues laid out in textbooks of standard methodology: testability, evidential support, precision, quantifiability, consistency, intersubjectivity, repeatability, universality, progressiveness, independence of cultural milieu, and so on. Faith spreads despite a total lack of every single one of these virtues.[9]

Beyond such critiques of religion, Dawkins did not at this time present any precise, testable, quantifiable, or nonsubjective evidence for the existence of mind viruses.

But his faith was justified: in 1994, a common chain letter was received by the wife of Oliver R. Goodenough, professor of law at Vermont Law School, who was studying legal doctrines in terms of memes. Folklorists will recognize the format: it begins with a homiletic statement and instructs the recipient to copy it and pass it on. It continues with a long string of case stories of people who passed it on and received money or who broke the chain and suffered from bad luck.

Goodenough sent the letter to Dawkins, and the two coauthored an article in the flagship British science journal *Nature* announcing the discovery of the first documentable mind virus. Calling the letter "The 'St Jude' mind virus" because it contains the cryptic line "St. Jude," they argue that it is a virus since it contains "duplicate me" instructions. Along with appeals to "guilt, fear, greed and piety," it essentially compels a certain number of recipients to replicate it, thus ensuring its survival. Goodenough and Dawkins themselves claimed immunity, though both admitted to "waves of mild, irrational anxiety on deciding not to comply, and we could be said to seek a modicum of good luck by sharing it, on a purely scientific basis."[10] Indeed, the text of their article includes a full transcript of the chain letter, with the article functioning, in the authors' words, "a form of meme therapy, for we have attached our own information package to a mind virus of proven virulence."

Goodenough and Dawkins conclude by expressing hope that identification of this mind virus might lead discussion of the topic from theory to concrete data. In turn, such study might in time lead to "a more general theory of more complicated mental parasites and symbionts." In a popularization, *American Scientist* quoted Goodenough as saying, "We can now move from the question of 'Do such things exist?' to 'What do these things do?' "[11]

The same article notes that scientists interested in Dawkins's meme concept have launched a new field of study called "evolutionary culture theory," which takes a quantitative approach to how ideas circulate across populations in time and space. This field has more recently been termed "memetics," perhaps because any term similar to "cultural evolution" is bound to remind scholars of the numerous ways in which Darwinian thought was distorted to fit political aims in previous years.

Difficulties with the "Mind Virus" Concept   Dawkins deserves credit for looking at traditional materials from a novel perspective. But the discovery of memes and particularly of the St. Jude mind virus was new only to biologists. In fact, even before the *Nature* article was published, sociologist William E. Fox (1993) was referring to the St. Jude chain letter as an "obvious example" of Dawkins's meme concept. While "meme" is a broader term than our "folklore," the two clearly cover the same field of reference and focus on the same issues: dynamic variation within a coherent, documentable tradition.[12] And "mind virus" clearly fits the observed social dynamics of contemporary legend, even though Dawkins, to the detriment of his argument, uses mainly examples of beliefs domesticated and imposed by the mass media or by institutions. The logic of natural selection should have directed him to the wilder, more competitive habitat of oral and unmoderated media-enhanced conduits such as e-mail networks, where ideas that do not develop survival strategies simply disappear without a trace.

Goodenough and Dawkins cite none of the scholarly literature on chain letters or their ancestors and reference only anecdotal "personal communications" and a variety of press releases from such sources as the *Washington Post* and *Daily Telegraph*. Had the authors examined the history of the letter they received, materials exist to trace it into the eighteenth century. The *Himmels-*

brief, or Letter from Heaven, contained a similar instruction to copy and distribute its contents, with a similar mixture of supernatural promises and threats.[13] Such a review might have saved Goodenough and Dawkins from some premature judgments. They comment that the St. Jude chain letter's demand for 20 copies "is perhaps counterproductive . . . Twofold duplication might, paradoxically, show more effective penetration."[14] Indeed it did: the 1935 Springfield, Missouri, chain letter craze, which asked recipients to send a dollar and pass on the chain, did require only two copies. Participation was so great that it produced mob scenes outside stenographers' offices and brought much of the town's business to a halt for a few days. A similar scheme, which affected Denver earlier that year, involved sending a dime and making five copies; postal officials processed as much as 95,000 extra letters per day at the height of the craze and ended up with more than 100,000 undeliverable letters.[15] The fallacy in Goodenough and Dawkins's comment can be diagnosed by using Dawkins's own logic. The more virulent a computer virus, the more quickly it will draw attention to itself and be terminated; similarly, a biological virus that kills too many of its hosts too quickly will die of its own success. The 1935 chain letters were more successful in manipulating their recipients, but at a suicidal rate. In much the same way and for the same reasons, sociologists have noted that intense collective delusions are by their nature self-limiting; they burn themselves out or draw negative attention to themselves.

They might also have applied J. Maynard Smith's concept of the evolutionary stable strategy (ESS) to the letter's insisting on twenty copies, no more, no less. Such features in nature, Maynard Smith argues, are the result of a process of natural selection in which individuals using other strategies die off. In this case, we could say, the number of copies demanded is the ESS, the minimum needed to keep the chain letter circulating somewhere. Chain letters asking for fewer copies, presumably, burn themselves out; those asking for more do not find enough takers to keep them going. Goodenough and Dawkins simply do not carry their logic far enough.

Goodenough and Dawkins refer briefly to the Craig Shergold appeal for cards as a "particularly virulent" mind virus but cite only journalistic sources that ignore important elements of the phenomenon. In truth, the version that spreads the most widely is often altered in significant ways from the original story. The real Craig was from Carshalton, was thirteen at the beginning of the appeal, and asked for get-well cards. But as the appeal developed, he was more widely described as American, eight years old, and in need of business cards.[16] But the appeal was more than simply "virulent." It certainly did misguide and hence waste some people's energy, but it also resulted in bringing the child much-needed medical attention, which in fact healed his otherwise lethal brain tumor. The phenomenon also attracted attention to the needs of London children's hospitals and to organizations like the Make-a-Wish Foundation that provided aid to other sick children. The cards, it turns out, were recycled as scrap paper for money used to benefit handicapped and sick children, and the Royal Marston Hospital, where Craig was initially treated, raised more than £20,000 for leukemia research by selling the postage stamps on cards sent him.[17] Dawkins's characterization of "mind viruses" as being measures of "gullibility" is imprecise and insufficiently supported by evidence.

This in itself seems a common meme, as Gary Alan Fine has noted that the popular press often characterized other such "redemption rumors" as "cruel hoaxes."[18] In fact such appeals often do result in benefits to medical patients, though perhaps not in the way or to the extent that the chain implied. The Shergold affair demonstrates that there are often real-world dimensions behind legend chains that folklorists need to recognize and value. The Shergold family was participating in a tradition of appeals on behalf of sick or distressed children dating at least to the 1850s. Many of these are apocryphal, such as the widespread appeals for aluminum drink can tabs or UPC codes. Yet even these have produced realities of their own, when sympathetic organizations have found ways to cash in huge collections of these items for medical equipment.

Such problems suggest a more fundamental problem with Dawkins's approach to the concept of mind viruses. He expresses faith that scientific ideas spread rapidly because they are, after all, good and useful, "satisfying the demanding standards of scientific method." In the 1989 endnotes to *The Selfish Gene* he notes the surprising popularity of the term and comments, "The word meme seems to be turning out to be a good meme."[19] In another endnote, though, he denies that scientific ideas behave in the same ways as memes. In the realm of science, after all, some ideas "are actually right, others wrong!" A wrong idea can be popular "at least for a while." But "their rightness and wrongness can be tested; their logic can be dissected. They are really not like pop-tunes, religions, or punk hairdos."[20]

Unfortunately, Dawkins's associate philosopher Daniel Dennett does not share this optimism, even though he admires it: "not all good scientific ideas spread," he counters, "and not all bad ones are extinguished."[21] Biologist Stephen Jay Gould likewise has argued for humility rather than aggressive faith in scientific method, at least the way it is often practiced in a nonreflexive way. In a survey of contemporary textbooks he was surprised to find that nearly all authors treat evolution in a way that "is virtually cloned." Textbook authors, he found, copied each other so frequently that they too often gave students "an ill-considered and virtually Xeroxed version with a rationale lost in the mists of time."[22] His many other historical studies of evolutionary theory honestly admit that racist, sexist, and class-privileged ideas have frequently influenced evolutionary research even in the presence of contradictory data, and have only grudgingly given way.[23]

In short, Dawkins's concept of memes and mind viruses must be accepted with caution. First, it is based on theoretical and subjective preconceptions and does not take into consideration the large body of solid, verifiable, and quantifiable data readily available in academic publications. Second, it comes close to privileging any research that claims the name of the hard sciences. He ignores evidence that much of what passes as science is in fact based on faith or on uncritical copying of other sources. His approach to what he calls mind viruses needs to be tempered with the reflexive and self-critical approach championed by David Hufford in dealing with alternative belief systems.[24]

The core of the scientific method is reflexivity and response to rebuttal. Many of the notions behind the concept of "mind viruses" seem inadequately examined and deserve challenge. Such rebuttal must itself be reflexive and ready to concede value to the other side. But at minimum we should expect scientists to obey their own tenets when discussing cultural material. And if "memes" and "mind viruses" are to be discussed as organisms, even in analogy, we members of a 150-year-old discipline should insist on the scientifically recognized principle of priority in nomenclature. For this reason, I will from this point on call "memes" by their proper name, which is folklore, and "mind viruses" by the more objective and academically established name, which is "contemporary legend."

The Dialectics of Legend and the Immune Reaction   Like the Native Americans present when Columbus arrived in America, folklorists may be underwhelmed by Dawkins's discovery. We knew folklore was there all along. But if narrative or legend biology is to survive in the next century, then we need to show how and why present theories and methodologies can contribute to those that might be proposed by memetics. Therefore I propose some modifications of Dawkins's concept that would bring his image of mind viruses in line with what folklorists have seen as typical characteristics of contemporary legend. With equal justice to his biological background and our folkloristic research, we could see legends not simply as pathogenic but as part of a complex process in which information systems respond cautiously to foreign ideas. That is, we could see legends either as the invader or as an individual's or community's response to invasion.

1. *Legends as Immune Reactions.* Considering legends as mind viruses at first seems to make a great deal of sense. We easily apply the concepts and methods of epidemiology to the contemporary legend. Much of our language, after all, already implies such a fit: we already stress oral or face-to-face transmission and define legend conduits through which we can document legends spreading. Recent folkloristic research has begun to focus on many of the epidemiological issues.[25] But the main weakness in memetics is its tendency to understate the important differences among its three ecosystems. Biological viruses are created through random mutations of DNA, and they circulate among symbiontic organisms, who replicate and pass them on unwillingly and unconsciously. Computer viruses, like biological viruses, circulate silently among terminals, who replicate them unwillingly, but they are created consciously by human minds and do not mutate, at least not so far. Mind viruses, as they circulate from brain to brain, seem to be different from the other two, in that the act of replication involves not only a conscious choice but also an opportunity for creative variation. In describing "immunity" to the St. Jude chain letter, Goodenough and Dawkins imply that that choice is itself determined by one's background; either one resists the virus or one is "gullible" and thus compelled to pass it on.

Dawkins emphatically denies that his theory is deterministic and repeatedly says that humans have a special capacity to rebel against the biological imperatives both of their genes and their memes. This, however, is challenged by Dennett, who describes the human mind as "itself an artifact created when memes restructure a human brain in order to make it a better habitat for memes."[26] Implying that one has a free will to choose to reject memes, for him, implies a privileged point of view. "When should we say that a particular 'virus of the mind' *exploits* the other memes that it encounters," he asks, "and when should we say that *we*, masters of our ideas, *evaluate* and *choose* the doctrines we will live by?"[27]

One possible resolution is suggested if we combine the insight that legend-telling is a communal exploration of boundaries with insights biologists have found into how organisms' immune systems work. Intense debate, both within groups and within an individual, is the classic sign of the legend process. Similarly, both sociologists and folklorists have noted that especially popular legends show an initial outbreak leading to a sharp peak in transmission and observed effects followed by an equally sharp disappearance of the legend from public. Such a reaction matches more closely the ways in which an organism challenged with a protein that it recognizes as foreign to itself develops strategies for disarming it and either assimilates or expels its information package. Biologists now know that part of this natural process involves special cells with constantly mutating genes, which randomly develop small numbers of antibodies that react to foreign proteins. On detecting such an intruder, the cells produce large numbers of these antibodies, which target the invading virus for destruction. After this is done, though, some of these cells remain in the body as "*memory* cells that . . . boost the immune system's readiness to eliminate the same antigen if it presents itself in the future."[28]

Even before the details of immunology were publicized by the AIDS pandemic, Dégh and her students already saw that when legends entered a community's tradition, they inspired "anti-legends" that attempted "to attack and destroy the legend as a whole."[29] Thus the epidemiological model suggests a general theory for why legend telling is characterized by debate and by what Dégh has termed "anti-legends." Such a reaction represents the informational analog to an *immune reaction* to something that hosts recognize as a foreign and potentially infective information package. Hence we could expect the viroid nature of contemporary legends to be marked by a vigorous defense and the emergence of informational antibodies, or anti-legends. I should add that the defense itself is a mental reflex: its presence owes nothing to innate skepticism or gullibility and certainly nothing to the objective veracity of the legend itself. It simply reflects the brain's natural defense against potentially infectious ideas.

We can see these elements in an especially clear way in the "Good Times Cathy" computer virus flap that tied up much of the Internet during the first days of December 1994. Itself an obvious mutation of the well-known "AIDS Mary" contemporary legend, it claimed that a hacker named Cathy had devised a virus that could be sent by e-mail under the subject heading "Good Times." If anyone attempted to read the message, the virus would destroy his hard drive. As experienced Internetters soon saw, this warning *was* the "Good Times" virus, since as it circulated, it generated "transmission headers" as long or longer than the forwarded messages. Further energy and computer space were taken up by rebuttals, which likewise were actively circulated with lengthy headers and did little to clear the virus from the Internet.

In fact the end of the debate was signaled by the emergence of anti-warnings that garbled the original message by alluding in a comic way to other common legends. One in fact borrowed material from the St. Jude chain letter, beginning "The instructions in this message must be followed exactly or an ill fate will destroy you! First, you must read this message in its entirety. Then you must erase the contents of your hard drive! Then you must send this message to ten others, adding your name to the list below. Expect to dispense ('win') one million dollars U.S. ($1,000,000!) within a month!" And ending:

> This is not a virus.
> This is NOT a virus.
> Erase your hard drive NOW.

Another referred to the "Lights Out" gang initiation warning, which also had circulated widely on the Internet: "If you receive a message from AOL entitled VIRUS ALERT! DO NOT FLASH YOUR LIGHTS AT IT! Your computer will crash! This is part of a secret initiation ritual that all AOL members have to go through. I know this is true because I read it on the Internet."[30]

The strategies of these anti-legends is close to what biologists would expect: they garble the original by attaching information to it from other plot lines recognized as harmless. Hence the original information is recognized as absurd and the host responds with mirth rather than concern. Interestingly, psychologist William Sargent found two effective strategies against brainwashing. One was previous acceptance of an extreme religious doctrine such as that of the Jehovah's Witnesses, but the other was "controlled and continued amusement on the part of the subject at the efforts being made to . . . win him over."[31] This suggests that legends are best resisted either by prior inoculation by similar ideas, or else by a strategy of inverting and ridiculing the infectious legend shell, hence the tendency of popular legends to survive in parody form as jokes.

2. *Patterns of Behavior.* The life history and pattern of variation seen in contemporary legends, as in folklore in general, could be viewed in terms of memetics. If we accept that contemporary legends are selfish ideas that spread much like viruses, then we may be able to comprehend why they behave in such an intense but short-lived fashion. We note, for instance, in the research above that legends emerge in a much more explosive way the first time they enter a culture, afterwards circulating in a much more limited and less intense form. This suggests that successful legends tend either to die of their own success, as Gustav Henningsen notes of sociopathic witch crazes, or else gravitate toward a steady-state relationship with hosts that resemble what biologists call an evolutionarily stable strategy.[32]

Such an ESS, we might suggest, demands less energy or risk from its hosts to survive, much as legends such as "The Stolen Kidney" first circulated as alleged incident, then quickly jumped to frankly fictitious habitats such as the comic strip "Dick Tracy" and the TV series "Law and Order." In another example, it is revealing that the Craig Shergold appeal began by asking recipients to go out and buy get-well cards for the dying child, a small but complex behavior change. But the version that proved most successful in tradition asked for *business* cards, a request that demanded far less energy, in line with other evolutionarily successful appeals for drink can tabs and UPC labels.

Yet we occasionally find legendary materials penetrating some communities in an obviously sociopathic way, but without the usual debate or anti-legend occurring. Or when it occurs, skepticism is paradoxically defined as a social problem and sanctioned. The clearest instances are demonologies of the kind that have motivated witch crazes, including the present satanism scare. In multiple instances, including Sweden in the 1670s, Salem in 1692, the McMartin Preschool affair in Los Angeles in 1983, and the Orkney Islands ritual abuse case, children's testimony was obtained under unusually liberal legal standards describing human sacrifice, cannibalism, and bizarre sexual acts. These were admitted as court testimony against defendants, often in the absence of any physical evidence and in the face of common-law standards of reasonable proof.

Often the argument has been made that the charges are so horrifying that, paradoxically, even the possibility that some of them may be true is grounds for convicting defendants against whom there is no other proof. One professional, lecturing on satanic cults' involvement in multiple personality syndrome, told a scientific meeting, "if even 10% of this stuff is true, then we're in big trouble."[33] Such a tendency suggests that demonologies assault one's social and biological taboos to such a degree that, once one agrees that *some* bizarre charges *may* be true, the observer no longer can say with certainty that *any* of them are *false*.

Such events are preceded, often decades earlier, by the introduction of quasi-scientific ideas giving warrant for a demonic or ritual-satanic origin for poorly understood psychological problems. It seems likely from a biological point of view that such ideas constitute an AIDS-like information packet that compromises precisely the normal debate that novel and unconfirmable ideas normally produce. Henningsen has observed that demonological traditions are generally not harmful, at least in a community-wide fashion, so long as they remain in the religious and folk belief contexts in which they are most often found.[34] But when such beliefs are syncretized with existing legal and scientific communities, he observes, the result can be lethal on a megascale. In biological terms, this makes perfect sense when we recognize that AIDS normally uses another organism, a monkey, as its host and develops its frightening effects only after a latency period in which the human host can spread the subversive DNA to many others. Thus the morbidity of the infection, like that of the legends that motivate witch panics, may not be recognized until it is widespread among communities.

Happily, the obviously sociopathic impact of such legend complexes makes them by nature self-limiting, though elements from them remain latent in some communities and particularly in printed sources produced during such panics. Religious communities, for all Dawkins's hostility, have in fact been more able to control such outbreaks, perhaps because their previous exposure to similar ideas confers immunity to their most sociopathic features. A representative of the Spanish Inquisition, for instance, was responsible for suppressing the Basque witch scare, and the Salem witch scare was stopped largely at the insistence of Puritan church leaders. In our time Christian fundamentalists have critiqued the Satanism scare far more incisively than representatives from within secular institutions such as law enforcement, social work, and clinical psychology.[35]

(3) *Morphology.* Much research has confused what Alan Dundes has characterized as text and texture: in particular, the modern diffusionist research that analyzes or attempts to construct an "ideal" version by comparing the elements common to most versions circulating.[36] Biologists' understanding of how real viruses work might help folklorists in distinguishing two aspects of legends' formal characteristics that are often confused. Legends, like viruses, consist of encoded information and a "survival machine" whose sole purpose is to see that hosts pass it on consistently enough to ensure its survival. This latter constitutes what Alan Dundes would call the *texture* of the legend that in some way tells the person who hears it, "This is a good story: tell it to someone else," or "This is an emergency: spread the warning." Such an approach has the effect of focusing on the parts of a legend that have been most successful in replicating themselves; this by no means proves that these are the parts of the legend that were most meaningful to the persons who passed them on. They are simply the parts that, by chance, proved to be the most successful in replicating themselves. We have simply described an especially successful mind virus shell; we still have not established what message, hidden or otherwise, was encoded within.

Our methodology needs to be more exacting in isolating what legend features derive not from the artistic or political aims of narrators but are implicit in the laws of natural selection as applied to information packets. Many contemporary legends are "mini-mysteries," in which a significant narrative detail is withheld until the end, at which time the listener must reinterpret the entire narrative. The truck driver apparently chasing a lone woman is actually saving her from the murderer in the back; or the helpless little old lady is really a murderer with hairy hands; or the maniac threatening the organist is a harmless music lover. Such features may have developed precisely because they are striking, and encode implicit messages to the host personality that assure the story's repeated telling.

Folklorist Daniel R. Barnes says that the "memorable irony" of the legend may "set into play a kind of retrospective interpreting on the part of newly-informed listeners. They set into play, that is, the interpretive act itself." The telling of contemporary legends often provoke lengthy discussions, in which tellers and their audiences share impressions and similar stories. Barnes notes:

> This is . . . what is really significant about all those explanatory codas that so often show up at the conclusions of urban legend-tellings and legend-texts.
>
> . . . For what makes urban legends so compelling finally is not the story they tell but the one they don't tell, and the demands they accordingly make upon us as tellers and listeners, *forcing* us as it were to assume the role of interpreters.[37]

The memetic biologist might see these responses as our best evidence of what messages the legend encodes, and not the formal characteristics of the most common or fullest variant of the legend. In other words, the content of the legend lies precisely in these metanarratives, which most collected versions arbitrarily strip away as unimportant.

4. *Function.* Finally, much of the research Dawkins cites on self-protective strategies of organisms is relevant to contemporary legend. We may take with a grain of salt his assumptions that "mind viruses" are always self-serving and produce only signs of gullibility and irrational behavior in their hosts. This is, after all, the universal response to contemporary legends among the general public, and itself may be an innate reaction to ideas that we interpret as novel and potentially parasitic. We can hardly blame him for accepting it uncritically.

But folklorists have demonstrated that not all legends are obviously delusive, even when they provoke the immune or anti-legend response we have noted above. We must consider whether at least some contemporary legends are themselves part of the community's immune reaction to some media-driven information seen as potentially harmful. Initially, this seems to contradict Dawkins's essential thesis, which is that genes seek only the individual's survival, not that of the community or the species as a whole. But memes are not genes, in that they are passed on or mutated by choice.

We should ask whether some legends originate and function in the context of other cultural material that in itself provokes an immune reaction from individuals, who in turn pass it on selectively to others in their groups. An individual does not pass on antibodies to others except under rare instances, such as a mother to a developing fetus. But anti-legends can be circulated as freely as positive legends. Thus mind viruses, if we accept the concept, are unlike either biological or computer viruses in that the responses they provoke circulate as widely as they do. Hence an anti-legend response created by an individual may in fact be transmitted in an altruistic way to the rest of his community.

This transmission, however, would follow the biological risk analysis described by Dawkins: that is, to run the risk of transmitting a legend or anti-legend implies that the teller will gain some benefit in return. Hence, we could predict, legends would not be circulated in a broadcast fashion but would follow set patterns that identify strong social obligations.[38] Fine's work on corporate legends also implies that extraordinarily successful advertising campaigns seem to draw contamination legends to such products or their companies in a self-regulating process that appears to be evolutionary in nature. Similarly, Patricia Turner notes that when a product is intensively promoted within a black community, contemporary legends arise as soon as the risk of using it outweighs its utility. These legends could be characterized in terms of a community's immune response to media propaganda, which is quite explicitly deliberately designed to infect and influence listeners' minds. Turner's research suggests that many contemporary legends among African Americans may function as "early warning calls" intended to identify a potential danger to their community and encourage collective action against it.[39]

What Next?   In conclusion, the concepts of "meme" and "mind virus," like "the biology of storytelling," challenge our tendency to see legends as isolated texts with hidden meanings. Dawkins's approach has much in common with Linda Dégh's call to pay attention "to the dynamics of telling and transmitting stories from person to person and from people to people, though means of direct contact, interaction, and resulting processes responsible for the formation and continual recreation of narratives." Both approaches are similar in that they encourage us to see legends not as stable texts but as constantly mutating entities that survive because of the complex ways in which their strategies for survival parallel and perhaps prey on human brains' strategies for survival. Analysis of legends as virus-like may help us focus on elements that facilitate their spread in the emergent, epidemic-like waves that distinguish contemporary legends from other forms of folklore.

We can determine the "where" and "how" of legend telling. And vital statistics such as tellers' age and sex are important data about the legend's epidemiological strategies. But can we continue to claim that we are thus able in any all-encompassing way to say *why* a given legend circulates? Dawkins does not suggest or imply a means for extracting logocentric meaning from mind viruses seen as scientific data, nor do folklorists possess such a magic mirror. Whatever general theory we adopt for legends, we need to own up to the fact that literary scholars faced a generation ago: storytellers' personalities are not open books to us. We may never be able to say with any precision what legends mean to them, even after intensive fieldwork during which we elicit the legend from them repeatedly.

Seen this way, the meanings we extract from legends may simply reflect the effects the legend has on us scholars as individuals, and these may not have any priority over any other construction of the legend by any one of our sources. Individually or collectively, legends may have no determinable meanings, hidden or otherwise. In a parallel sense, the biological information contained in the AIDS virus has no "meaning," hidden or otherwise: it is what it is. Therefore, any general theory we produce ought to focus on facts we can ascertain and limit itself to the questions that these facts can document.

As biologists learn more about our field, more sophisticated attempts to exploit it will follow. What follows may be a benign and whole altruistic sharing of data and ideas, a hybridization that will strengthen the warrant for future folklore studies and firm up our understanding of how legends confirm or modify evolutionary theories. But if history does repeat, and if Dawkins is right in claiming that ideas and groups of ideas have essentially selfish reasons for establishing dominance, then I expect that we are in for a turf war of no little vehemence in the next decades. The study of folklore is a marginal and embattled discipline; biology is a respected and well-funded cornerstone of the modern academy.

We temporarily have one advantage over the new biologists interested in mind viruses: we have the data they need to draw valid scientific conclusions, and we know where it is. But, after all, the Indians held their land and knew it well, and still lost it.

Folklorists' reliance on old-fashioned pseudo-Darwinian cultural evolution has done political damage to the field's credibility within the academy. Moves toward rigorous interpretive analyses have been artificially inhibited by uncritical reliance on scholars who have not felt it necessary to document the social fears that legends ostensibly express. In such a "fossilized" critical environment, Gillian Bennett concludes, it is "easy for the untidy performed text to be dispensed with in favour of the sort of neat résumés and paraphrases which lend themselves best to abstract analysis." Our failure to develop a real *discipline* of legend scholarship has left us working in a field of "endless possibility of discourse," in which "one person's interpretation of the data is no better or worse than any other."[40]

A genuine discipline of legend scholarship would require interpretations to be falsifiable, and if challenged, they should be revised or retracted, just as scientific ideas develop in the face of rebuttal. The alternative is playing a perpetual Trivial Pursuit game.

Biology, like it or not, is a discipline; the study of contemporary legend at present is not. I nevertheless have faith, perhaps myopic but not wholly blind, that our ideas and methods will endure, if not prevail. Still, I would appreciate it if each of you would tell at least two other scholars the gist of what I have written in this chapter.

PART TWO LIFE AS LEGEND

A journalist in the Allentown, Pennsylvania, area, who had a reputation as a "ghost hunter," was once contacted by an informant with a story that concerned his visions of his dead Uncle Frank:

> For several months, perhaps once or twice a week, I received mysterious telephone calls from a man who said he lived in Wyomissing but offered little else in the way of identification. He claimed that he was "too well known" in the community to allow his name to be attached to something as misunderstood as ghostdom. This man was scared. His conversation turned hushed or ended abruptly when his teenage son entered the room in which he was speaking. His voice, authoritative and rational, quivered as his stories intensified, lending credence to my belief that he was really experiencing what he told me, and his "haunting" was no imaginary tale.
>
> "One time, my wife and son and I were walking through the Berkshire Mall," the caller whispered over the phone. "I was glancing over at the people walking up the other side, toward us, and to my shock, there was Uncle Frank!" A chuckle of amazement leaped from my lips and struck like a bullet of incredulity on the other end of the line. The man shot back. "Yeah, I know you don't believe me," he snorted. But for some quick psychological jousting on my part, my chuckle may have cost me this story. I assured him that the giggle was not born of disbelief, but of amazement. Even as I tried to soothe the man, I added that I had never heard of a ghost being sighted in an enclosed shopping mall.[1]

The dynamics of performance on both sides are significant. The informant alternates between an "authoritative and rational" tone of voice and a more intense "quivering" intonation as he demands credibility from his audience. Yet he is almost painfully reticent, stopping even when he fears he is overheard by his own family. The journalist's reaction is also revealing. Versed in all the popular ghost-story motifs of the area and generally sympathetic, he

93

still cannot resist a "giggle" when someone tries to tell him about a ghost in, of all things, a *shopping mall*.

We seem to be stumbling over the boundaries of what the Hungarian folklorist Mihaly Hoppal has termed "a belief-language." Each culture has a "belief-vocabulary," he argues, with which it can "compose meaningful communications."[2] But this culturally derived vocabulary limits which supernatural experiences can be shared with license. Thus, while it is not intrinsically foolish to say, "I feel God's presence," or "Last night I saw a ghost," one must be careful not to make such statements in what we might call an experientially ungrammatical way.

We instinctively smile at the notion of meeting ghosts in fast-food restaurants or in shopping malls, *because* such statements are patently ungrammatical in terms of the belief-language. Such places are dangerous, contemporary legends tell us. We might unwittingly purchase a poisonous snake or spider in a department store, or encounter ruthless criminals in the parking lot, or risk losing one's child to gang initiations. But in tradition we do not meet *ghosts* there. Contemporary legends confront us with forces that we recognize all too well from the media and our own experience: they may be extreme in their horror, but they are not uncanny. To put it another way, the contemporary world may be marginal and culturally dangerous, but it is not numinous; it is not holy ground.

Yet ghosts do appear in public places, but only those that are self-conscious links with earlier days and modes of thinking. In this context, far from being a threat, ghosts often provide good advertising. Many "country inns" in the United States combine atmosphere, family-style cooking, and the thrill of the supernatural. The Maple Grove Hotel, in Berks County, Pennsylvania, uses as its logo "a 'gentlemanly' ghost wisping forth from a doorway," and the menu combines local history and legend in a self-consciously quaint way:

The Inn, built ca. 1783, had a long and vicarious history. . . . an Indian was supposed to have been hanged in the 'common room' and another 'guest' was supposed to have been murdered in a second floor closet.

In any case, the ghosts of these unfortunates still are reputed to be haunting the Inn where the present owner, Colin Heffley, is serving the most delightful drinks and dinners in a country Inn full of charm and history . . . and a ghostly atmosphere.[3]

Such legends are often far more than creative writing: owners and employees of such establishments are quite willing to give circumstantial accounts of their supernatural experiences. In a setting where legends of the romantic past are expected, personal contact with the supernormal is sanctioned, even encouraged. Going to such a restaurant, in this sense, is like going to an adolescent legend-trip site,[4] in that it gives the diner and the employee license to experiment with unconventional modes of perceiving "reality." A sympathetic journalist ended his account of the Maple Grove Hotel, saying: "You can believe what you've just read, or dismiss the various incidents as natural, not supernatural, occurrences. But if you're enjoying a quiet meal or a few drinks at the Maple Grove Hotel one evening and the chandelier starts to sway, the iron fireplace crane starts to shimmy, or you feel a ghostly presence sitting next to you, you'll believe . . . you'll believe!"[5]

At the same time, such cultural license allows adults to leave the spirits behind in the past. They can pretend they are in an antiquated world and so can tell stories that in another setting would be ridiculed as superstitious. The actual events described by reticent sources are not, after all, so different from those described by those who experience the supernormal in teenage haunts and quaint old restaurants. Why then the discrepancy?

One answer might be that such cultural license is denied to those in an environment associated with the contemporary world. Take this statement: "Last night, when at the haunted house on Erwin-Shoots Road, I saw the ghost of the wife that was murdered there." This statement may provoke any of the conventional responses within the tradition of contemporary legends—ranging from admiration to crass skepticism—but it is a grammatical experience, in that such things are, according to the tradition, seen there. A person who says he saw a ghost at that spot may be sincere, mistaken, or even lying in order to get a girlfriend to accompany him there that night. But he is acting within the terms of the belief-language.[6]

But if a witness's empirical experience cannot be fitted into cultural belief-language, then its shock hits the listener without insulation. Many supernatural experiences are never translated into legends and are told, if at all, under extremely restricted circumstances. David Hufford, as we have noted, has identified the crucial role that legends play in "naming" experiences. When convenient language exists for a given event, those who undergo it are reassured that others have had similar experiences. But when such language does not exist, he says, "the experience remains largely unshared and unknown," even when this leads to considerable psychic stress.[7] For example, perhaps more than 15 percent of Americans have experienced a supernatural paralysis-attack experience. Persons relaxed but apparently awake suddenly find themselves paralyzed and in the presence of some nonhuman entity. Often the sensation is accompanied by terrifying hallucinations—of shuffling sounds, of humanoid figures with prominent eyes, even of strange, musty smells. Often the figure even sits on the victim's chest, causing a choking sensation.

The experience, apparently, is based on a unusual and poorly understood disturbance of the sleep pattern, akin to narcolepsy. During this event, the brain functions as if asleep, and so the body does not respond to impulses to move. The result is an illusion of paralysis; further, when the impulse to gasp and breathe harder results in no action by the lungs, one may feel choked or suffocated. Despite the relative frequency of this event, Hufford found, published descriptions were difficult to find in cultures that lacked a folk tradition "naming" this experience. Yet even in the absence of such a tradition, many of the specific details of the Old Hag experience recurred in victims' accounts, leaving them profoundly confused and reluctant to talk for fear of ridicule. Hence the Old Hag remained largely unstudied by psychologists and practically unknown to the general public. Ironically, then, one function of contemporary legends is to insulate our hard heads against the shock of totally unprecedented and hence "irrational" experiences. Perhaps this is why the Grimm Brothers insisted that "the constant motion and lasting security of folk legends represent the most reassuring and most refreshing of God's gifts to man."[8]

In the following section I will explore three dimensions of the ways in which legends provide convenient language for extraordinary events. First, I will take an unusual series of phone calls received by a Pennsylvania State Police trooper and examine the ways in which the area's contemporary legends could explain it. This will traverse a lightly explored area—the study of "anomalies," or unexplained phenomena. A vast network of loosely connected networks has emerged, many of whom call themselves "Fortean" after Charles Fort, who gleaned dozens of such unexplained events from media sources and published them as a challenge to conventional science. Following in his traces, many researchers in the United States and Europe have gathered information on puzzling events in the hopes of finding unconventional theories that would explain them. True, the scientist will justifiably require extraordinary evidence for extraordinary claims. But it does not follow that all the experiences investigated by Forteans are obviously misinterpretations of mundane events. More important, the willingness to entertain the reality of the paranormal does not mean total willingness to accept every alleged paranormal event as valid. In fact, we will see that Fortean networks frequently include active debates, and the cultural language provided to explain anomalies is not one-sided but pluralistic.

Second, we will look at a single awkward translation of a paranormal experience, one that is ultimately unsatisfying for the narrator, who retreats into silence. Such "failed translations," however, show how intense the battle may be between cultural language that supports "consensus reality" and the demands of experienced details. Through the media, cultural custodians continually show us what to observe and how to interpret it, harmonizing the teller's experience with authoritative language. Those who support a "common sense" definition of reality often marginalize those who have had experiences outside the norm. Some are subjected to *nihilation*, in which a "rational" explanation for what they have undergone restores faith in consensus reality. Failing this, experts may simply reject the experience the tellers present in their stories, and refer them to psychological therapy, in which their perceptions are defined as an "illness" to be cured. Still others may be told, bluntly, that their experience never occurred.[9] When an abnormal experience happens to someone who previously had faith in consensus reality, an extraordinarily intense internal debate results.

The Wyomissing informant, in short, is "scared"—not so much of Uncle Frank, whose manifestations are, we find, characterized by a wry sort of humor and friendliness, but of the social sanctions that would be invoked if he tried to communicate his experiences. And these penalties are hardly limited to ridicule. Stewardesses who claimed to have seen the ghost of a dead pilot aboard an airborne jetliner were hesitant to speak to an equally sympathetic journalist, for fear that they would be labeled as neurotic and forced by management to see the company psychiatrist. One said to him, "referral to the company shrink is no joke . . . It's the first step in getting laid off. Also, we could be just plain held up to ridicule. That's hard to take, too. We're taking a big chance right now in trusting you not to identify us."[10]

Finally, we will turn to the subject of alien abductions, where those who have undergone such experiences find themselves in the middle of a debate among cultural custodians. Again we recognize the strategies of nihilation and therapy among the rationalists, but those who support the reality of such deviant experiences, as we will see, have agendas of their own. The assistance they give in making such experiences tellable, ironically, distorts the actual experience in the same way as those who try to explain such experiences away.

Chapter 6

THE FRACKVILLE ANGEL

The 1993–94 winter was one of the worst in the history of eastern Pennsylvania. At the end of the previous winter, on March 13, 1993, residents had been stung by a blizzard that dropped as much as three feet of snow in the area. Then, starting on December 22, a stubborn weather pattern brought snow after snow, punctuated by spells of subzero weather. The fifth major storm in less than a month hit on January 17, 1994, with two feet of snow (bringing the season's total to six feet). Two days before, the nearby Reading area suffered a significant earthquake on January 15, the first to occur in Pennsylvania in years and the strongest ever recorded there. We were wondering how and when it would all end.

Monday, January 31 brought another blast of icy cold, with temperatures dropping to all-time records of −20°F. That morning, between 6 and 7 A.M., Sergeant Barry Reed, station commander of the Pennsylvania State Police Station at Frackville, a small town in the mountainous Anthracite region of northwest Pennsylvania, got a phone call. A motorist wanted to report something strange that had just happened to him. He was on the way to work along State Route 61, just south of town, and stopped to pick up a hitchhiker, whom he described as "a tall, thin man with long dark hair and wearing a long dark coat." After getting into the back seat, the man told the motorist, "I am here to tell you the end is near." When the driver looked into the back seat, the hitchhiker was gone. Reed was further mystified when this call was followed by three similar reports, two placing the hitchhiker on Route 61, and one on Interstate 81, the major freeway that bisects Route 61 at Frackville. While he did not record the identities of the persons who called, he described them as reputable local citizens. "All of them were scared and appeared to be telling the truth," Reed later told a reporter. "They were from different towns. I have no reason to believe they could have gotten together to make something up."

The exciting world of Forteana consists of a growing network of researchers and enthusiasts. Amateur investigators into ghosts, mystery animals, and other forms of the paranormal have been collecting and organizing their material for nearly 150 years.[1] This network is one that deserves to communicate with the academic discipline of folklorists. Since the early nineteenth century, after all, folklorists have also been collecting huge numbers of narratives describing anomalous and bizarre events. This body of information is housed in archives located in many parts of Europe and North America. Active and productive data sharing between the two groups would seem to be natural, indeed inevitable.

But it is rarely so. The narratives collected and archived by folklorists seemingly provide us with a world of ideas to discuss. But academics often see this world through the screen of their own *words*. To improvise on a theme by T. S. Eliot, the difference is that Forteans stress "words as the world," while folklorists often consider "words as words," a narrative told as a story. And the academic words that folklorists use can blur rather than reveal the information that these narratives reveal. Take the most common term for a narrative that describes an anomalous event, "legend." This implies a final product, something artfully finished and (to render the Latin literally) "ready to be read." This suggests a "proper" approach to these narratives in which we appreciate them as words, not as the world. That is, we look closely at the language our informants use, use intellectual methodologies to trace what they are *really* trying to say, and so reconstruct what academics believe are hidden messages about our contemporary world.

There is an element of readily observable truth in this approach. Even the most committed believer in the paranormal recognizes that not all evidence is equal in quality. An anonymous thirdhand story is far less likely to preserve information about the world than a narrative told by a good firsthand witness of the phenomenon. But to understand such complexes of legend and life, we need to look at legends in a simple, clear-eyed way rather than replacing the words of our informants with a more "rational" but perhaps facile academic language of our own. For the legend does not, after all, live through contemporary systems of folk belief as understood by academics. It lives through experience, past, present, and future.

To illustrate how folklorists and Forteans could profit by a broader range of inquiry, I would like to begin by focusing on the verifiable event that took place early this bitterly cold morning outside of Frackville. First I'll analyze it as a conventional folklorist would, as an example of a traveling contemporary legend. Then I'll look more closely at its context and suggest a more Fortean context for this legend type. Finally, I'll use the this expanded context as a basis for suggesting how the two groups could cooperate profitably.

Enter a Hitchhiker: Folkloristic Approaches   The area around Frackville is ethnically diverse and rich in oral history and legend. Originally it was settled by a mixture of English and German settlers in the early nineteenth century.[2] During the 1860s the developing coal industry created hundreds of "patch towns"—company-owned settlements—and populated them with more recent immigrants. The Irish dominated the workforce at first, bringing with them a strongly Catholic worldview. Starting in the 1880s and continuing to the present, new waves of immigration came to the coal region—Slovak, Polish, Montenegrin, Italian, Tyrolean, and still others. They brought with them their distinctive religions and sets of belief. Today the area remains ethnically diverse and economically depressed.[3] Overlook, or evil eye, is still widely feared and remedied by magical rituals. Satan is alive and well, and the local newspaper regularly prints petitions to various saints and divine beings. These hold that if you say the prayer given for a certain number of days, they will grant any request, "no matter how difficult it may be." Thus the idea of a mysterious apparition that appears to deliver a message is by no means deviant in the community's belief-language.

Sergeant Reed, however, was no credulous sort as he immediately remembered having heard essentially the same story ten years ago when he was stationed in the Lancaster County area, some hundred miles south in the ethnically distinct Pennsylvania Dutch region. Folklorists too had been alert when the story circulated a few years before in the Harrisburg/Carlisle/Shippensburg area, just to the west of Lancaster County. Folklorist Yvonne Milspaw also was told of a young couple who found an old man walking in the rain along the Pennsylvania Turnpike. At one point in their conversation, the man suddenly said, "The Lord is coming soon!" then vanished, leaving behind only a damp spot on the backseat. One lady told Shippensburg folklorist Mac Barrick that the incident had happened along I-81: the hitchhiker was a woman who, when asked where she was going, said only "Jesus is coming" and disappeared. A state policeman stopped to investigate and commented, "You're the 7th car that's happened to."[4] These folklorists at once recognized their old friend, "The Vanishing Hitchhiker."[5] Both Sergeant Reed and most folklorists would have been content to disregard this call as an obvious prank.

But Reed was particularly impressed by one woman who called in to explain that she had never before stopped to pick up a hitchhiker, but given the bitterness of the weather and the appearance of the tall thin man, she felt "compelled" to stop for him. Reed told press, "I regarded [this] person as the most reliable." Reed and his fellow officers were thus surprised and bewildered about how to react. In the end, they did treat the event as a real happening, sending a cruiser out to the last reported location of the stranger (to no avail). The officers also checked with the neighboring state police stations at Hazleton and Schuylkill Haven, but neither of them had received reports. Further investigation turned up nothing, and the incident was filed away by state police as officially unsolved. Initially, Reed's official conclusion was ambivalent: "I believe it is a hoax. But the people are reliable." Later, speaking more personally to another reporter, Reed was even less definitive: "I don't know what to make of it. . . . My personal belief? There's a lot more on heaven and earth than science can explain."[6]

Can folklore help explain what mystifies science and the police? The most immediately obvious explanation is that the incident was, despite Sergeant Reed's ambivalence, a well-orchestrated hoax perpetrated by four people already familiar with the plot of the legend. There are indications that the story had been active in the area before the Monday morning phone calls. When a local paper reported the incident on Friday, February 4, the story noted that "unofficial" versions had already been phoned in. These said that the hitchhiker had also made comments "about the weather, the turbulence of society or the Angel Gabriel 'tooting his horn for the second time.' " Other versions phoned in to the newspaper said the hitchhiker warned "Jesus is coming! Jesus is coming!" before vanishing. All of these either were or became widely distributed motifs in what folklorists recognized as the vanishing hitchhiker complex.

Two days after the local publication of the Frackville incident, for instance, this item was posted on an Internet newsgroup: "A friend tells the following story: His girlfriend's mother was driving in Los Angeles the day after the earthquake [a damaging 6.6 tremor that hit the area on the morning of January 17, 1994]. She usually does not stop for hitchhikers, but saw an old man with a flowing gray beard, impeccably dressed in a dignified suit. He looked so dignified that she let him in." He allegedly told the Internetter's friend's girlfriend's mother, "I am the angel Gabriel . . . come to toot my horn!" and promptly disappeared.[7]

And the story resurfaced a few weeks later in the Lancaster area. The hitchhiker now was described as a middle-aged, neat-looking man. According to various sources, he and the motorist began talking about the weather. "You think you've seen a big storm, wait until you see the next one coming," one version went. Another has him saying, "It's going to be a very bad snowstorm, up to the second-floor windows of homes." Often the hitchhiker gave March

13, the anniversary of the blizzard of 1993, as the specific date for this killer storm. Then the guest vanished; the motorist "pulled alongside the road because he was really freaked out." The traditional coda follows: a police car appears; the motorist tells his story; the officer says, "You're the third person that's said this to me."[8] Given concerns about the harsh winter, it's likely that similar stories were circulating earlier in the Frackville area.

In fact, we have evidence that stories sharing the major motifs of the story had been circulating among evangelical Christians for more than a decade. A variant of it was printed in a booklet of daily meditations sold by televangelists Jim and Tammy Bakker in 1980. This secondhand story involves a Christian couple who "don't usually pick up hitchhikers," but who did give a lift to a young man, who repeatedly told them "Jesus is coming soon." He then vanished, and a local sheriff told them, "You're the seventh or eighth couple in the last few days to tell us the same story." "Wasn't that strange?" the Bakkers comment. "Could it have been an angel?" Similar stories likewise traveled internationally among evangelistic conduits. It was reported in New Zealand in 1990 ("Jesus is coming back soon"; officer says "you're the 10th [or some other number] person to tell me that story"). Then it cropped up in Holland in 1991 (he announces the End of the World and says he is an angel; the officer says "You are by no means the first to tell me this story").[9] Oral Roberts used the story as a homily during the last week of April 1994, emphasizing how the mysterious hitchhiker told the motorist, "His lips are near the trumpet" before vanishing. The thunderstruck police officer let him off without a ticket; he had been the sixth one that night to have the same experience. Roberts, obviously moved, told his viewers that the wonder of this story had nearly brought tears to his eyes.[10]

So folklorists could say they can finger the source of the story—a migratory legend distributed nationally and in fact internationally. The elements of it are all part of oral tradition: the motorist who does not normally pick up hitchhikers but feels mysteriously compelled to do so; the mysterious man who utters a prophecy and then vanishes; the police officer who arrives to validate the experience by saying it has happened repeatedly in the same area. Therefore, a traditionally based folklorist would infer, an event that tradition claims happened in many different places to many different people could not have happened and could never happen.

Hoax?   But, one might reply, it did happen. The phone calls to the Frackville State Police station are a matter of record, and they were made by people claiming to have had the experience themselves, not friends-of-friends. A traditional folklorist would say that the details are still "too good to be true." What "really" happened is this: a group of people who had heard the legend as it circulated before January 31 decided to perform it. But rather than telling it orally in the usual way, they chose to enact it in life through the perform- ance medium known as ostension.[11] The Frackville incident might have been a practical joke perpetrated by a group of people familiar with the traditional vanishing hitchhiker legend. Working out their story in advance, they called state police headquarters, one after another, giving stories that jibed with each other and placed the hitchhiker at various places nearby each other. Sergeant Reed thus may have been an innocent participant in this ostensive perform- ance. It is not clear whether the motorists ever identified themselves by name; certainly Sergeant Reed confirmed that no names were recorded in the state police's computerized report on the affair. In any case, by making sure that the officer on duty would hear four versions of the same incident, they in fact transformed Sergeant Reed into a character in the legend, the policeman who says, in all truth and sincerity, "You're not the first person who told me this story."

One motive might simply have been to pull the legs of the officers on duty and cause a sensation, an incentive that lies behind much of the pseudosatanic activities of teenagers. One Ohio adolescent admitted that he had told a ver- sion of the "classic" hitchhiker legend to a friend, then drove him to a nearby graveyard where he had planted a sweater on top of a tombstone. The victim promptly fainted from shock, to the delight of five accomplices who were hidden in the underbrush to watch the hoax. The perpetrator had a more complex reaction: "I can't really explain the emotion I had at that moment. It was a kind of fear that I had caused Joe to have a heart attack or something, mixed with the feeling of a strange sort of power that I had in my possession through the telling and manipulation of this story."[12]

Alternatively, the perpetrators might have felt that the story was valuable as religious propaganda. By involving Sergeant Reed in the legend, they might have felt they were creating an atmosphere in which end-time evangelists could use the "true" story to gain converts. If it was a hoax, at least it was a holy one that expressed a deeper truth in the eyes of fundamentalists—namely that the apocalypse is indeed near. Certainly the persistent use of the story by evangelists indicates that they see it as useful, even if not verifiably true.

And, of course, Sergeant Reed himself either might be part of the hoax or might have made up the calls, for either of the above reasons. I admit, though, that this seems unlikely since he received the calls in the presence of other officers at the station and took responsibility for an official report on the case.

If the Frackville incident were a hoax, however, it was a remarkably ambiguous one. In all the thirdhand versions surveyed, the prophecy was clear and unambiguous: Jesus is coming; Gabriel is about to blow his horn; the next snowstorm will be a monster. Sergeant Reed, however, insisted that "I am here to tell you the end is near" were the words the callers attributed to the mysterious hitchhiker. The end of what? The end of the world? The end of the millennium? The end of this cold spell? The end of Democratic control of the United States Congress? If the event were a planned hoax, one would expect the perpetrators to build their story around a prophecy that is at least as specific as the tradition on which it is based, if not more so. It is difficult to reconcile a motive for the hoax with the vagueness of the reported prophecy.

And, while we can prove that this version of the legend had been around for some time, we can't absolutely prove that this incident sprang directly from the emergence of it as an actively told story in the Frackville area. The event on January 31 is the first documented version of the vanishing hitchhiker in the present flap; even the one attributed to the January 17 California earth-quake wasn't actually put into documentable form until February 6, two days after the local paper published it. And since the paper notes that the discussion of the story had been going on all week, there is ample time for it to jump through numerous means of communication to California. This jump might have in fact been facilitated by the nearly simultaneous earthquakes that affected both areas. Though it is unlikely, we cannot rule out the possibility that actual events taking place in Pennsylvania on January 31, shared informally soon after and then in the media by the end of the week, were the catalyst for all the remaining American versions that spring. We also cannot rule out that it is possible, even probable, that the incident was indeed a hoax. But leaving it at that takes an intriguing situation and reduces it to the level of consensus reality. This approach risks being frankly boring, and in any case does not help us understand the cultural language that helped make the account tellable and even credible within the region where it circulated.

Expanding our Horizons: Fortean Perspectives In any case, the major limitation of the folklorist's perspective is that it presumes that if a story is found in variant form attached to many places and times, then that is proof presumptive that it never happened at any place or time. This is naive, as Gary Alan Fine discovered when he analyzed legends concerning dead mice in bottles of Coca-Cola.[13] He consulted some readily accessible legal references and found dozens of authenticated cases in which mice and other vermin were found in bottles of various sodas. Granted, the vanishing hitchhiker circulates widely and usually in anonymous or friend-of-a-friend form. But does that in itself impugn every firsthand account?

One advantage of being a folklorist means that one can entertain options that one does not have to prove, at least not in a scientific way. One need only show that the same options have been entertained by other people to explain similar phenomena. There is no easy way to investigate such phenomena objectively, notes Hufford. The least we can do, he argues, is to examine what witnesses say sympathetically. Prematurely replacing their evidence with our own cultural or psychological explanations may produce a superficially more rational picture of "what really happened." But Hufford notes that these explanations are often themselves untestable and say more about the analyst's own preconceptions than the witness's experience.

Let's consider, then, for a moment some of the meanings that a Fortean might find in the Frackville events. (1) As some of the variants that circulated soon after suggest, the hitchhiker might be an angel or divine being. (2) As some of the older versions of the vanishing hitchhiker suggest, he might be a ghost returning from the dead to pass on an important message. (3) As some lesser-known versions suggest, he might be a diabolical figure appearing to frighten and confuse humans. (4) Finally, we might speculate, he might himself be a kind of cosmic trickster, who enjoys thwarting our assumptions about "what really happens."

I don't intend to do this to find "the truth" behind the Frackville incident. There may well be several lessons derived from a given complex of narratives, perhaps mutually exclusive but equally valid. Active legend complexes will generate intense debate in which competing explanations will emerge, even within a single performance. In a culturally rich area, there may well be a surfeit of convenient language that would help construct such an experience. Each of these constructions is equally part of the legend process, whether it be religious, supernatural, or skeptical. Only by valuing these other levels of the event can we hope to come to a holistic understanding of the Frackville incident as a legend, as a communal exploration of the boundaries of reality.

Hitchhiker as Divinity   The initial press coverage did not give any interpretation of who or what the vanishing hitchhiker might have been, calling him only "the mystical man" and alluding in a playful way to the current American television series *Unsolved Mysteries*. But the "angel" theory quickly emerged and became the dominant one. Sister Adrian, principal of Holy Spirit School in Mount Carmel, an adjoining town, found children commenting avidly on the story the day after. She got a copy of the newspaper clipping and passed it on to Tom Kutza, host of a radio talk show on station WISL in Shamokin, another Anthracite-area patch town. He told of the event on one of his shows and received calls from listeners who christened the mysterious man "The Angel of Frackville." Sister Adrian, interestingly, was rather skeptical about the incident: asked if she felt the figure was really an angel, she laughed and commented, "I'm a doubting Thomas. Unless I picked him up and he disappeared before me, I would tend to discount it."[14] Nevertheless, as we noted with skeptics of the "Blue Star Acid" legend, she served as a conduit for passing the story on to many people who took it much more seriously.

As noted, there are many traditional versions in which the vanishing hitchhiker is later revealed to be a divinity. Among these is this version, known as "The Black Lady," a common contemporary legend type found in Poland. Here a motorist picks up a woman dressed in black, who asks him to take her to a shrine to one of the many Black Madonnas in Catholicism. "During the trip, she predicts a frightening future for the whole world, except for the Polish people who remain under the protection of the Black Madonna. She asks him to promise that he will spread this message to all the people and adds, to cancel any doubt that she can tell him the future, that within an hour he will have a corpse in his car. After these words, she suddenly disappears from the speeding car. After two kilometers, the police stop him and ask him to take a critically injured person to the nearest hospital. On the way, the injured person dies."[15]

Here the mysterious lady in black is obviously connected with the Virgin Mary herself; in fact, she may be the Mother of God. If so, then the following text from a broadside dated April 5, 1890, may be the ultimate ancestor of this vanishing hitchhiker tradition:

In the last days of June, 1889, there appeared at the railroad station of Ancona a woman in mourning. She said she was to go to Rome but lacked the money to pay for her ticket. The train left the station but after a while it stopped. Though 5 more engines were added, it would not budge.

A gentleman on the train, named Chev Morelli, thought of the black dressed lady who could not board the train at the station for the lack of the money to pay her fare to Rome. He went immediately to find her, and he offered to pay for it. He paid, in fact, 47 lires for a first class ticket to Rome. This the lady accepted under the condition that she travel alone. No sooner had the lady boarded the train, than it started up speedily, to the astonishment of all.

Chev Morelli, upon reaching Rome, wished to pay his respects to the lady. He went to the car where she had been seated. However, no one was there, and on the seat he found

2,000 lire in money and a note in golden letters, which read, "I am the Mater Dolorosa Virgin; and I wish to tell the sinners of the world that they must redeem themselves, believe in God and serve Him. Otherwise, a great calamity will soon befall Christianity."[16]

Most of these legends are anonymous or at best thirdhand, but not all. One intriguing variation, collected by Linda Dégh, happened to a Gary, Indiana, woman, about 1980. It was related by the woman's son, who himself participated in some of the events. It seems that on the way to do shopping, the woman saw an infirm old lady standing on the corner. "My mother said that normally she wouldn't just pick up some old lady," the narrator said, "but something told her to pick this lady up." She helped her do her grocery shopping, then accompanied her to the bank. When she came out, the account goes, "She opened her purse and she had all this money—a whole lot of cash—like she just withdrew a bunch of cash. So my mother asked her what she was doing with all that cash and with as much trouble as she has getting around somebody could have swiped her money. The old lady said that she didn't worry—she had lots of money and was an old person."

In the end, the woman took the old lady home, carried in her groceries, and asked if there was anything else she could do. The lady then asked if she could bring some gallon jugs of water over later, as she did not have running water at her house. She agreed and stopped by later with her son (the narrator). Oddly, no one came to the door, and when the son looked through the window, he found the house vacant. Fearing the old lady had had an accident, they roused a neighbor, who informed them that no one had lived in that house for ten years.

> My mom just looked at me . . . you know how you turn all white and your hair gets all up on your head . . . she got all scared . . . she got in the car and she was really scared. She said, "Mike, I know I dropped her off, that lady at that house." And my sister [who had gone with his mother to the old lady's house] said the same. . . . My mom called my grandma and my grandma's really religious and she said maybe it was somebody . . . like acting like God to see if you would help somebody out . . . That's why she had all that money to see if you'd take that right away from her because she was helpless.[17]

While certainly not the conventional vanishing hitchhiker story, it does include many elements familiar to folklorists, particularly the motif of feeling "compelled" to pick up a person in obvious distress. And it, together with the other traditional variants, allows us to appreciate the detail in the Frackville case: an old man, walking along a road in the midst of a bitter weather pattern that was especially hard on senior citizens. It was realistic that a motorist unaccustomed to picking up hitchhikers would feel "compelled" to stop. It would take only a modest leap of faith to see such a figure as a divine being, testing whether passers would in fact be Good Samaritans and reward their faith with a supernatural message.

Hitchhiker as Ghost   The Frackville incident itself did not immediately suggest the more widely known ghost-girl version of the legend. But soon after, a local reader sent a letter to the local paper to explain that the Angel was not the only phantom hitchhiker known. "Do any of you old timers remember the old lady who walked the back road into Frackville?" she began. "The woman wore felt boots and sympathetic drivers picked her up because it was cold and uninhabited. When they got to their destination the woman had simply disappeared, leaving behind a felt boot. It was a scary stretch of road in the night and you could not have paid my daughter enough money to drive that road after dark."

She also recalled that in her lifetime a car of high school students returning from a prom had slipped into a lake, drowning one of the girls. "Anyhow, every year on the date of that prom night, at midnight, when the accident occurred, a lovely girl in an evening gown, dripping wet, is picked up by sympathetic drivers, many of whom are truckers, only to find themselves left with nothing more than a wet seat in their vehicle." As further evidence for her point of view, the author narrated a more conventional vanishing hitchhiker story, alleged to have happened to Canadian journalist Edwin Hill. "Mr. Hill was not the type of man to swallow such a story—but it happened to him." She concluded, "The area of Bucks I lived in is over 300 years old and many of the mansions and a lot of other very old homes are haunted."[18]

We find similar complexes of narrative in many parts of the world, where the phantom is explained as the ghost of a human who has been trapped between worlds or who returns to do a good deed. In Austria as recently as December 1981 stories circulated about an "enigmatic 'black lady'" who stopped motorists and traveled with them for a few hundred meters before saying, "If you hadn't stopped and taken me along, you would have had an accident." Residents connected the narrative to the recent death of a waitress in an auto accident, and it gained so much credence in the Salzburg area that the local archdiocese issued an official denial of the story as "overexcited imagination or hallucinations."[19] And another Polish contemporary legend tells about a veiled lady, dressed in black, who stops a motorist and asks to be driven to a cemetery. This time she gets out and goes to a grave before vanishing. The driver, following, hears the sound of a child crying and notifies authorities, who open the grave. They find that the child's cruel stepmother had managed to bury him alive, and the motorist later positively identified a photograph as the lady he had picked up: she was the child's natural mother, dead for two years.[20]

Forteans recall the Uniondale, South Africa, case, well documented by Cynthia Hind. In May of 1976, Anton La Grange was driving down the Uniondale road during a heavy rainstorm and stopped to pick up a girl wearing dark slacks and a navy blue jacket. She gave him an address, and when he turned to ask for more details, he found she had vanished. Puzzled, he notified authorities and later learned that the place where he had picked up the mysterious rider had in fact been the site of a 1968 fatal accident in which a girl, going to tell her parents of her newly announced engagement, had been killed. At the time of the accident, she was wearing dark green slacks and a navy blue duffel coat, and when given a photograph of the girl, the motorist said, "I cannot swear for sure, but I think that is the girl."[21]

No evidence directly corroborating this reading has come from the Frackville area, but the intersection in which the events occurred is a heavily traveled area, and the nearby interstate highway is almost continually the site of fatal accidents, especially during bad winter spells. Truckers and tourists from the southern part of the state often find that the weather and driving conditions deteriorate markedly as they climb from the Lancaster Valley into the rugged Appalachian ridges of Schuylkill County. We could reconstruct the story as one in which the victim of a previous snowstorm appeared to warn motorists that if they did not drive carefully, the end of their lives might be near. Alternatively, the ghost might be reassuring them that, no matter how bitter the present weather conditions, the end of the winter would in time come.

Hitchhiker as Demon   But there is no reason to assume that the apparition appeared for benevolent reasons. The area's most notorious haunted site is an abandoned cemetery near Weatherly, a small town between Hazleton and Frackville. Here, a woman in black is said to appear beside the road, and if you see her, a friend of yours will die the next day. This superstition is obviously related to the many similar local traditions connected with defying death during the adolescent bravery test that folklorists call the legend-trip: if you sit on a certain stone couch three times, you will die; if you see red eyes looking at you out of an abandoned church, you will die, and so on. But this legend connects up with a more serious narrative complex in the Hazleton area concerning a mysterious woman in a nun's habit (which of course would be black also) who stands along the Stockton Mountain Road. Any motorist bold enough to pick her up will find that she "has no face." This motif parallels the Mexican-American contemporary legend-complex concerning "La Muerte," a seemingly beautiful girl whom young men pick up by the road but then find that "she had no face, it was just skull."[22]

Starting about the turn of the century, these patch towns were swept by a series of panics focusing on a mysterious woman in black who haunted the fringes of town after dark, accosting travelers. A contemporary news account, which appeared in a Hazleton paper on March 14, 1907, gives a characteristic version:

Strange as it may seem, the woman in black, who has figured so extensively throughout the coal region towns, has now made her appearance in the Third Ward [i.e., in downtown Hazleton], and has already stricken terror to the young men who reside in that ward. She was first encountered by Allen Weir, brother-in-law to Letter Carrier Edward Hughes, on Monday morning about 12:30 o'clock, but the story did not leak out until yesterday.

Weir was on his way home after spending the evening with friends. He was jogging leisurely along Hazle Street and when he reached the corner of Mine Street, he was startled to be confronted by the woman in black.

She commanded him to halt, and the next moment she pointed a revolver at him. By this time beads of sweat were coursing over Weir's body, he believing that his last hour had come.

The woman looked Weir over carefully and after she was through she told him that he might move on, as he was not the one she was looking for. Weir promptly obeyed the command, in fact he was in such a hurry that he took to his heels and was soon out of sight.[23]

Accounts come to mind of strange old ladies who ask unsuspecting women for rides home from shopping malls.[24] As many of these stories develop, the old lady has strangely hairy hands and is later exposed as a murderous man with a hatchet or meat cleaver. The Hazleton lady in black, though, really is a woman, and a Wilkes-Barre informant remembered one popular explanation: the lady in black was the widow of a miner killed by the terrorist labor group the Molly Maguires. Perpetually in mourning, she devoted her life to looking for her husband's murderers. The man encountered "was not the one she was looking for"; presumably when she found what looked like the right man, she would revenge her dead husband.

But the problem is complicated by other residents' discussion of this complex. For example, Helen and John Scarcella of Hazleton actually encountered the woman in black, and their experience gives us another set of clues on how to classify this legend complex. They were driving through Hazleton one day and suddenly spotted a "lady all in black" standing by an old lilac bush.

You know what?
We got her by surprise because *they* say
they wander
you know, but,
but they have—you have to see them first, then they can't move.
And—when—*both of us looked*
and she—
(you should have seen them eyes on her.)
(O—h, God.)
Them eyes were as BIG as saucers.
And she just kept *GLARING* at us and *she must have been in—about EIGHTY years old.*
Now *what would an eighty-year-old woman—?*
if that wasn't—[**Ironic**] *that was out of the ordinary.*
What would an eighty-year-old woman be doing under a lilac bush there—?? because
    she was *caught.* . . .
WELL!
HE [her husband] stepped—*on—the—gas*
and *boy—did—we—get* out of there.[25]

This memorate clearly describes the woman in black as a supernatural entity, not simply as a bizarre criminal or lunatic. Her inconspicuous "because *they* say" announces a complex series of "namings," in which she suggests several ways in which the events relate to traditions of the anomalous. Her casual-sounding "*They* wander" implies that the woman is not human but an omnipresent entity seen by accident, just as German peasants see dwarfs only when they chance to knock their fog-caps off.[26] The notion that if one sees such a woman first, "then they can't move" connects the experience with fairy-lore, who likewise cannot escape if held in a human's glance.[27] And the eyes, described after a dramatic hush, are "as BIG as saucers," like those of mysterious black dogs, whose eyes often grow alarmingly.[28] The "chills" her glance throws relate to the concept of overlook, since those who cast the evil eye also can make the victim feel supernatural dread. Whatever the lady in black is, for the Scarcella she was not only something "out of the ordinary" but positively demonic.

This is also implied by some hitchhiker stories, like the Austrian one mentioned, that say that if one does not pick up the hitchhiker, the motorist will have an accident at the next intersection. Alternatively, the figure will appear in the car anyway. Such an element appears in the Hawaiian tradition, in which the figure is the volcano goddess Pele: in one secondhand account, she was picked up by two Mormon converts. Just before vanishing, they saw her in the rearview mirror, "dragging on a cigarette and sipping a cup of coffee." These two acts are strictly forbidden for Mormons, which makes the hitchhiker's demonic nature clear.[29]

So one might construct the event assuming that the hitchhiker was diabolical in nature. He might appear to cause panic on the part of the motorists and confuse true Christians by implying that the apocalypse is in fact predictable. In fact, as the New Testament makes clear, the schedule of the end time is not known even to the angels, so a divine being who claims to know that the end is near must be a lying demon. By making a false prophecy, such a demon might be encouraging people to join tribulationist cults like David Koresh's or Marshall Applewhite's and discouraging believing Christians when the end turns out not to be as near as the message states.

Hitchhiker as Cosmic Trickster   This final alternative is one that might appeal to both folklorists and Forteans. We might see the Frackville "angel" (if angel he was) as an example of the way in which anomalous events explicitly challenge our ability to sort things out. William C. Clements has argued that legends are essentially based on "interstitiality," providing convenient cultural language to describe the things and the events that appear at the margins of experience or that show up anomalously in the middle of otherwise ordered life. Mass culture, as he notes, provides most of us with a standard "classification system" that allows us to make sense out of most of our world. But Fortean experiences challenge this system: the Frackville hitchhiker falls between two worlds and does not give us enough information to place him definitely as angel, devil, or former human being. This ambiguity is not a fault in the tradition, however. Clements argues that such elements "stretch the imagination to allow inclusion of materials that do not conform to the conventional, the established, the ordered. The legend-teller and audience may participate in basic creativity by demonstrating their ability to go beyond the system as innovative narrators and interested hearers and to explore unfamiliar—and maybe socially unapproved—concepts."[30]

And in fact some hitchhiker or co-traveler stories seem to be dramatic expressions of just such a challenge: the phenomenon that is just verifiable enough that it can't be discounted but not verifiable enough to constitute scientific proof. A contemporary legend collected in the remote area of Mongolia comes to mind: "One driver was telling me he had met a girl stripped naked. He was driving slowly across the steppe and suddenly noticed that a naked girl was running parallel to his car. She ran like that for some time, and then grabbed the door handle. The driver thought she wanted to get into the car and stopped. So he got out to ask her where she wanted to go. But the girl was gone."[31]

"Drivers report many such events," the informant concluded. "It was not just a single case." And indeed it isn't: Anglo-Americans in Northern Arizona often relate "skinwalker" legends, in which mysterious entities, sometimes balls of fire but more often human in appearance, appear alongside speeding cars and flank them for miles. "A guy, a friend of my friend," one version went, "was driving down the road on the Res[ervation], going about forty, looks over and sees a guy running along beside him. And he's going forty! And the guy's running along and looking over at the guy and smiling. This is true it happened to him."[32] Similar experiences, with nudity but without the supernatural element, seem widespread among American professional truck drivers: the most common legend they tell concerns "a woman driver in a state of undress": "Sometimes she will be naked. Sometimes she will be wearing only a blouse, or only a skirt. Sometimes she will be completely clothed but her skirt will be hiked well above her knees. Often she passes by in a hurry, allowing the driver, high up in his cab, only a glimpse, but occasionally she adjusts the speed of her car . . . so that she runs beside the truck for mile upon mile."[33]

This experience, whatever its explanation, seems itself a graphic way of visualizing the way in which evidence for the anomalous oftentimes eludes us in a tantalizing way. Janet and Colin Bord have noted the odd way in which cameras malfunction or photographs disappear in several different realms of the paranormal.[34] Skeptics may say that this is simply a reflection of hoaxers' ability to come up with multiple excuses for their lack of conclusive evidence. But we may look at it in another way as a Fortean analog to the Heisenberg Principle that makes subatomic particles behave in an almost intelligent way when they "know" they are about to be observed in a certain way. Such cosmic tricksters, like the naked co-traveler in the automobile flanking the trucker, allow themselves to be seen but not contacted. The end is near, yet so far away.

And when folklorists have analogous encounters with cosmic tricksters, these behave in an even more interstitial way. Instructed by a folklore professor to read a book on UFOs, a graduate student at the University of Pennsylvania looked up to find a gaunt, pale man dressed in a black suit, shoes, and a string tie inquiring about his reading. When the student commented that he did not find the book very interesting, the man in black screamed, "Flying saucers are the most important fact of the century, and you're not interested!?" Concerned about causing a scene in a public place, the student calmed down the stranger, who placed his hand on the student's shoulder and said something like, "Go well on your purpose." "It sounded religious," the student later recalled, "and I remember thinking that he was going to leave some proselytizing religious tracts with me. . . . I didn't look up to see him go." Within seconds, though, he was flooded with anxiety, sensing that the strange man was "otherworldly." He jumped up to follow the man, or at least to find a witness to this conversation, but he found that not only had his visitor disappeared but the normally crowded library seemed to be completely deserted as well.[35]

Folklorist Peter J. Rojcewicz published this narrative in 1987, crediting an anonymous source to whom he gave the pseudonym "Michael Elliot." Three years later, at a meeting in Minneapolis, he admitted that the experience in fact was his own, and the encounter had motivated his subsequent work on the phenomenology of UFO and man in black (MIB) encounters. Now, he believes, he was in an "altered state" somewhere "in the crack" between real life and another realm.[36] Whatever the nature of Rojcewicz's encounter, it seems clear that the gaunt, pale man dressed in a black suit that he encountered is experientially similar to the distinguished "tall thin man with long dark hair . . . wearing a long dark coat" who appears in the Frackville stories, and that the two inhabit much the same interstitial world that influences the world of consensus reality without quite residing there.

Conclusions?   We should see legends not as "texts" or as "beliefs" but as processes, as ways of naming otherwise "uncanny" or threatening elements of social experience. These symbolic expressions may themselves be horrifying, but because they explain events and give people personal ways of controlling them, they are less dangerous than unnamed and untold phenomena. As Clements noted, "That the legend-telling community can talk about interstitiality, speculate about its successful intrusion between the essential gaps in their culture order, and contemplate the effects of this intrusion indicates a sense of the system's resiliency, its ability to sustain even direct challenges to it."[37] Forteans thus help provide academics with a more complete picture of how the legend process actually works. Folkloristic motif indices that classify obviously false legends expressing similar beliefs often present a false image of the community's worldview. Studying belief systems that are tested empirically in the face of the anomalous might give us models more flexible than those proposed theoretically by psychologists and sociologists, who in the past have tended to give a priori emphasis to single factors like sex and social standing.

Scholars have in the past relied on such reductionist approaches, precisely because they are superficially safe and scholarly. Academic departments are still not very tolerant of "ghost-busters." But Forteana can help correct this imbalance by showing that such apocryphal stories often draw on a solid experiential basis. Some of the most intriguing research done in the last decade has valued the ways in which individuals and communities make sense of such experiences. Folklorist Ellen Badone found that a Breton woman describing supernatural events surrounding the unexpected death of a relative constantly juxtaposed details of the event with an encyclopedic recitation of local beliefs. The resulting narrative was "a reconstruction or ordering of past events which generates meaning and pattern where they are not otherwise apparent."[38]

Likewise, Hufford's study of the Old Hag has provided us with a picture of how individuals use several different cultural "explanations" to describe what appears to be a single common experience.[39] Ironically, "rational" readings produced by psychologists frequently prove more contradictory and ill-documented than those generated by the "folk." Fortean experiences are often quirky, with details not found in the most widespread versions of the legend and lacking the apparent polish of the folktale. But such events are valuable in helping sort out what details are probably cultural inventions and which are independently attested and hence evidence for phenomena still imperfectly understood.

This need not give "paranormal" explanations some kind of authority over "rationalist" readings when they arise together. The committed debunker is no less central to the legend's existence than the true believer. But if we see that alleged experience itself is the locus of debate, we can also see how a community responds in a polyphonic way to an anomalous event. We need to give full weight to all explanations, the "folk," the "oddball," and the "rational." The Frackville Angel might inhabit the domain of the University of Pennsylvania Library MIB only in the sense that both were well planned and successful hoaxes by persons enjoying "playing God." But even this reading acknowledges that the language found convenient by both hoaxer and victim plays a vital role in creating and sustaining one's definition of reality.

The folklorist and the Fortean thus share a common vision of the interstitial nature of such phenomena. Ultimately, this numinous or indeterminate quality keeps the putative event of the legend from being filed in any given niche of a society's natural or cultural order. Although all traditional beliefs and narrative structures do attempt to "name," contain, and explain such numens, no one can adequately comprehend such an experience. But then, not many scholars go to the Motif Index in search of insight.

Chapter 7

THE FAST FOOD GHOST

Supernatural elements have dropped out of many Anglo-American ballads, "presumably because [Americans] are hard-headed and practical," a prominent folklorist observed. Yet a few pages later the same scholar summarized surveys indicating that the level of "superstition" among American college students had remained at a steady, high rate since the beginning of the century.[1] Statistical surveys have shown that almost one-fifth of the American population has frequently experienced paranormal events, including extrasensory perception, clairvoyance, and communication with the dead.[2] Priding themselves in their capacity to leave the past behind and move ahead into the world of Star Wars, Americans seem unable to rid themselves of their fascination—and contact—with the supernatural.

There is, however, need to contain this potentially threatening contact. Churches are kept full, but only on Sunday, and contact with the divine is carefully mediated through ritual and a professional class of holy men. The outlying areas are kept full of haunts and ogres whom adolescents can contact, but only within carefully restricted limits and invoked by carefully prescribed rituals. The uncanny side of life is given its half-acre near most American communities, so that it can be invoked, witnessed, then left behind as the teenagers drive their technologically up-to-date autos back to the artificial light of their comfortable, safe suburban homes. American hardheadedness, therefore, does not eliminate the supernatural but rather seeks to concentrate it into culturally safe locations and channels of expression.

The result is illustrated graphically by the stories inspired by a puzzling apparition said to have been witnessed by employees of a Pizza Hut in a small town in central Ohio, which I shall call "Arbordale." Identical to thousands of others nationwide in its reinforced-concrete architecture and anonymous, interchangeable interior furnishings, the Arbordale Pizza Hut reflects the franchise's menu, unchanging from coast to coast, indeed, using a limited

117

number of sauces and flavorings for everything on the limited menu. Unlike fast-food restaurants specializing in quickly prepared, easily stockpiled foods, the Pizza Hut at least has a waitress to bring the pizza to the patron's very table. But this is because pizza cannot economically be prepared in advance and held indefinitely. For the employee, contact with other people is limited, personal choice is carefully restricted ("Extra cheese?" "Onions on your sub?"), and the entire operation of the restaurant is geared to convenience: getting customers in, served, out, and cleaned up after. The environmental surfaces, from the tables to the rest rooms, are sanitized, and service is brisk and impersonal. While waiting, though, diners can exercise a modicum of personal choice at the salad bar, where Osterized vegetables and vats of dressing (protected from germs by a hanging glass "sneeze guard") can be combined into an appetizer. For the customer, personality is quietly effaced in the interest of bland but predictable food, served quickly so that he or she can go somewhere else and do something more important. The intrusion of the paranormal into such a setting, therefore, is a jarring dissonance.

Traditionalizing the Supernatural   The first text was collected during a group conversation focusing on adolescent legends and scary stories told at summer camps and slumber parties. Tracy McCullough, an Ohio State University student had invited Louise, a former employee of the Pizza Hut, and two other girls from the Arbordale area over to make a tape for her folklore class.[3] The result was about an hour's worth of reminiscences, all more or less artificially focused on the topic of supernatural legends or "ghost stories." The participants first told the stories that most intrigued them; then, as they exhausted their active repertoires, they began to give more and more fragmentary or detached accounts of other supernatural legends. At one point, as Louise was giving a detailed account of a house owned by a friend that was the site of poltergeist activity, she commented, "I can tell about the Pizza Hut ghost too." But she continued with the story at hand, and this reference was not immediately pursued by the others. A few minutes later, though, after the girls had been unable to remember any other scary stories and the conversation had ground to a temporary halt, Louise reintroduced the subject.

Louise: [**Ironic**] Well then there's the <u>Pizza Hut</u> ghost.
Mary: [*Inhale*] There's one at high school too.
Tracy: That's not a ghost story.
     [*Laughing*] What was the Pizza Hut ghost.
     [*Indistinct; several people speaking simultaneously.*]

Alice: I know if you don't know.

Louise: Oh.

>   [*Laughs*] OK.

>   [**Ironic**] *OK—*

Alice: [*Laughing*] We all got white knuckles when we talked about that.

Louise: [**Ironic**] **The Pizza Hut ghost**

>   [**Narrative**] I ever tell you about the Pizza Hut ghost?

Tracy: Not that I know of.

Louise: [**Ironic**] Oh <u>yes</u>.

>   [**Narrative**] Um people would not close <u>alone</u> at the Pizza Hut in Arbordale
>   'cause of him.

>   'Cause there's supposedly a man was killed on the site where the Pizza Hut was built—
>   and

>   one—this is,

>   [**Conversational**] oh I don't know if it's all true or not, everybody, some people say
>   it is, some people say it isn't, but—

>   [**Narrative**] OK, Bruce was closing once and we had like this like little room in the
>   back for his office—and he said

>   he turned around once and he saw this—

>   somebody—was—standing—there.

◇

>   you know, and—and he
>   kind of shook his head and it was gone.

>   Then Jim Landers said HE was there once by himself at night and—

>   he—

>   was back in the back doing the books, and he came OUT and there was the guy
>   standing right *in the fridge—, right in front of the refrigerator—*

◇

>   and he said he—he saw him STANDING there and—

◇

>   the guy then kind of drifted out into the—

>   into the—

>   dining room and, Jim went up, by the 'frigerator and stood there, and it was, just ice
>   cold

>   even though the "frigerator wasn't open it was just *REAL COLD where he was standing*.

>   And he said there was *NO WAY* he was going to WALK OUT INTO THAT DINING room.

>   ***NO WAY!***

>   So he

>   Went back into the back and just [*laughing*] kind of sat there and—

>   [*two mock-"shivering" sounds*]

and I think then he left real quick [*brief nervous laugh*].

And then Molly Jones was going into the bathroom once—

◇

and she was coming OUT of the bathroom—

and—

she couldn't get out of the bathroom.

Alice: Oh.

Louise: Something was holding onto her and she couldn't get out.

She's going

["**Feminine**"] ***BRUCE!***

BRUCE! [*short laugh*]

[**Ironic**] and she **RAN**—

or he ran in there and said,

["**Feminine**"] *"What's the matter?"*

[**Ironic**] Then she yanked and she *got her purse out.*

But she couldn't get out.

[**Narrative**] And Lois Brown once was in there, cleaning the bathroom underneath the toilet—

[*Phone rings*]

Louise: and she felt, somebody tap her on the shoulder and she,
went up real quick and she knocked herself out.

◇

'Cause she was so scared.

[*Simultaneously, Mary answers the phone in the background; indistinct conversation: "Hello? Which one? Yeah this is her"*]

Tracy: [**Conversational**] Yeah but—

[*nervous laugh*]

um—

Well wha——

was there any story behind that though?

I mean like—

Louise: [**Ironic**] **YEAH**

[**Narrative**] there was a man that was supposed to be—

HUNG on that site.

[*Background phone conversation: "I THINK so—*]

Louise: he was—it was uh, supposed to he a farmer
cause

Jim said he had bibs on.

Or he had like—

a flannel, old flannel shirt on and—

JEANS.

Tracy: Uh-huh.

Louise: [**Ironic**] And a **HAT!**

Tracy: And he was buried on that site.

Louise: Uh-huh.

Tracy: [**Conversational**] Well isn't there supposed to be something about the high school
   was—buried, or over a graveyard or something?

Louise: I don't know, I never heard that.

◇

◇

The conversation continued for another half-hour, covering a variety of other adolescent legends including "Mary Ruth," a variant of the cursed witch's grave prevalent in the Midwest, as well as a lengthy account of a farm said to be inhabited by a coven of witches. The Pizza Hut ghost came up once more in conversation, and Louise recalled a few more poltergeist-type occurrences said to have happened there: pizza pans flying around and lights coming off their fixtures, for example.

Immediately we notice one puzzling feature: despite the incongruity of the setting, the story provokes surprisingly little interest. Although one of the listeners comments, "We all got white knuckles when we talked about that," the performer does not display any anxiety and the listeners remain impassive. Indeed, the key moments of the incidents related are performed with a calculated staginess: just before the ghost appears Louise breaks off a statement in mid-phrase, and after it appears, she pauses dramatically. The effect, once perceived, is almost parodic.

and we had like this like little room in the back for his office—

and he said

he turned around once and he saw this—

somebody—was—standing—there.

◇

Then Jim Landers said HE was there once by himself at night and—

he—

was back in the back doing the books,

and he came OUT and there was the guy standing right in the fridge—, *right in front of*
   the refrigerator—

◇

and he said he—
he saw him STANDING there and—
◇

    Yet none of the three accounts consists of any detail intended to make the apparitions seem concrete or verifiable. Rather, in most cases, Louise places much more stress on dramatizing the witnesses' reactions than on presenting the ghost itself.

And he said there was *NO WAY* he was going to WALK OUT INTO THAT DINING room.
   NO WAY!
So he
Went back into the back and just [*laughing*] kind of sat there and—
[*two mock-"shivering" sounds*]
and I think then he left real quick [*brief nervous laugh*].

She's going
[**"Feminine"**] *"BRUCE!*
BRUCE!" [*short laugh*]
[**Ironic**] and she <u>RAN</u>—
or he ran in there and said,
[**"Feminine"**] *"What's the matter?"*

    Significant here is the way in which Louise uses extreme contrast in dynamics to indicate fear, but only when she dramatizes the words or the feelings of other people. The supernatural details are told more flatly, and the resolution of each incident invariably comes as an anticlimax. Bruce has only to "kind of" shake his head, and the ghost is gone; Jim Landers feels an inexplicable chill in the air, which may or may not be related to his standing by a refrigerator; Molly Jones hysterically yanks her purse loose and then is free, suggesting that it was her purse that somehow was holding her in. The final, interrupted incident seems no different: Lois Brown knocks herself out "Cause she was so scared," but no effort is made to describe the tap on her shoulder as anything other than a momentary delusion. Nothing in Louise's narration, of course, makes it necessary that we see each incident as explainable in rationalistic terms, but neither is this specifically excluded; the debate between the rational and the supernatural simply never takes place.
    Louise thus adopts a self-consciously playful persona, from the beginning of her performance on. Twice she lets the others know this by using self-consciously ironic intonation in her opening phrases:

Louise: [**Ironic**] _The Pizza Hut ghost_
    ever tell you about the Pizza Hut ghost?
Tracy: Not that I know of.
Louise: Oh <u>yes</u>.
    Um
    people would not close <u>alone</u> at the Pizza Hut in Arbordale
    cause of him.

This point is further underlined by her admission that "this is—oh I don't know if it's all true or not, everybody, some people say it is, some people say it isn't but—" This statement does not prove that Louise disbelieves in the stories—she says only that she can't say that it is *all* true. But the persona she adopts here allows her to relate the stories at arm's length, playing with them as stories, not evidence for the reality of the supernatural.

Many of these consciously dramatic techniques appear a short time later in her performance of "Mary Ruth." Here again we see the same distancing of self from the story, combined with self-evidently dramatic gestures and overblown dynamics:

Louise: Oh she was the one that
    they accused of witchcraft
    and they burned her on the—
    burnt her on the <u>Square</u>.
    And that's the one that they say:
    [**Narrative**] If you spit on her grave
◇
    you get killed?
    And Diane Dugan knew these two boys?
    These two guys you know, they were in high school?
    Or junior high, and they were driving around—
    [**Conversational**] (no must have been high school 'cause they could drive.)
    Well that doesn't make any difference, they **COULD** have been driving—
    [**Narrative**] but one—
    they went out to the graveyard when the graves were still up?
    Mary Ruth's grave was still up?
Alice: [**Conversational**] Was this out at Greenfields?
    Or out by—
Louise: No, this is out on Dare Road.
Alice: Oh.
Louise: And um—

[**Narrative**] the one
one guy spit on the grave, and the one didn't.
And they were coming home
you know, they were just cruising around and they came back
from it [*inhale*]
and the one [*yawn*]
and they were in a wreck
and the guy who spit on the grave died
and the one who didn't
didn't die!
And the, doctor said there was
*no reason **why that** one shouldn't have died.*
But it was because HE spit on *Mary–Ruth's–**GRAVE!***
Tracy: Ok—
Right.

Again, the story is told in such a way as to preclude any debate. Although an authority known to the group is given ("Diane Dugan knew these two boys"), in this context it functions as no more than a conventional opening formula: "Diane Dugan told me this story about two boys." No doubt the graveyard is real, and it is important to one of the listeners to locate it more exactly. But the shift into high-pitched, parodic "feminine" intonation at the climax of the story makes it clear that Louise is acting as if she were a slumber-party "girl" (the same age as the alleged "boys") who could still be impressed by the legend's mechanical interdiction/violation/death format. That the "validation" is not to be taken seriously is signaled in advance by her conspicuous yawn. At the end the collector acknowledges the receipt of a story but does not respond with any further requests for evaluation or metacommentary; nor do the others.

Perhaps this lack of comment is a result of the artificial mode of collection: my student was aiming for a complete list of local supernatural legends, not just the ones that intrigued the group. Hence, the conversation had already been extended beyond normal length and, since these stories were already known to most of the group, further commentary may have been unnecessary. But other narratives in the conversation provoked many more details and discussions about the reality of the events narrated. It is more likely that both the Pizza Hut ghost and "Mary Ruth" are, for this group, so neatly harmonized with existing traditional motifs that no further dispute is called for. Louise begins both stories with schematic statements clearly tied to folk beliefs widespread in adolescent legends. The first:

people would not close *alone* at the Pizza Hut in Arbordale
'cause of him.
'Cause there's supposedly a man was killed on the site where the Pizza Hut was built—

connects the stories that follow the most widespread motif in Ohio adolescent legend-trips.[4] And, when Louise concludes her accounts, Tracy's somewhat flustered request for more information draws an ironic, slightly variant version of this schematic: "**YEAH** there was a man that was supposed to be—/ HUNG on that site." And the collector, trying to harmonize the story further with one she knows about her high school suggests another common motif.[5] Louise is willing to concur—perhaps the result of poor collecting methodology, but more likely a sign that she is more interested in accommodating her story to her audience than sticking to the "facts."

In general, then, we can characterize Louise's performance, adapting Dégh and Vázsonyi's terminology, as a "dormant legend." Typically, they observe, the keynote of active legends is "the compulsion to criticize. The teller of the legend . . . has to speak her mind."[6] Louise, however, cagily does not, and the listeners' criticism is defused by her detachment from the incidents; at least for the moment, "no one is interested if anyone believes them to be true."[7] This is not to say that the material community-wide is treated in a detached, humorous way; Louise's introductory remark acknowledges that "some people" say it is "true." Nor should we conclude that Louise adopts only one persona in this conversation. Elsewhere she is graphic and involved in presenting poltergeist activity, but in this particular context the incongruity of the event and the dispute of the legend have been rationalized within the terms of the tradition. On the one hand, the content is rigidly harmonized with a widely distributed legend-trip motif, which allows the teller to treat it half as a game. On the other, the reported experiences of witnesses are so described as to allow the listener to reject them as delusions or mistaken interpretations of natural happenings. At best, Louise is telling the group that it may be a verifiable case but she knows of others where the activity was more substantial and the informants more convincing. At worst, it is, like her dramatization, a case of overblown emotions.

Supernaturalizing Rationality Louise's version of the legend, however dormant, intrigued Tracy McCullough and she took the initiative of contacting one of the persons mentioned as an alleged witness of the ghost. "Bruce" was a former manager of the Pizza Hut and had been a high school classmate of Tracy's, though they had known each other only slightly. When contacted, however, he agreed to relate his firsthand experiences in the restaurant, and, on the night of February 22, 1979, he came over to Tracy's dormitory room, bringing a pizza. The second version of the Pizza Hut ghost legend exposes the powerful tensions beneath the defused, official version. The following is a transcription of the entire taped interview.

Tracy: [**conversational**] OK—
>   NOW.
>   *Just—*
>   (you know)
◊
>   *start* telling me.
Bruce: OK.
>   ["**Rational**"] The Arbordale Pizza Hut Ghost.
>   Uh—
>   *I* saw the Pizza Hut Ghost—
>   (now this was back in uh—)
◊
>   either late seventy-four or early seventy-five is the first time *I* saw him. (I don't
>   remember the exact date.)
>   (I was working late one night.)
>   I was in the back of the Pizza Hut. I was washing dishes at the time in these
>   large, industrial-size sinks.
>   Now there's a *wall*—
>   leading to a—yeah a *doorway* [*Clarifies positions with his hands*]
>   another portion of the wall (and then another doorway).
>   (And a—refrigerator there.)
>   ["**Amazed**"] I was *standing there and I had the damnedest feeling that somebody was
>   WATCHING* me.
>   (OK?)
>   Now I *KNEW I was the only one in the* store and that I had *locked the store.*
>   And I—*HAD this* feeling and I—*THOUGHT* originally that it was just uh (I'm getting
>   nervous and antsy about being in there—) late.
Tracy: Mm-hmm.
Bruce: It *kept up and I **finally looked up** and looked **over**.*
>   and I ***THOUGHT I SAW*** someone.
>   (OK, a, a) man.
>   Standing in that second doorway by the freezer area.
>   And I thought—*didn't think anything of it* and went *back to washing dishes* and it
>   *clicked—*

that

*there's **somebody STANDING** there.*

and I *LOOKED* again.

And I *looked at the* guy.

[**"Rational"**] and I *noticed that he was wearing* what look—appeared to be a *flat-brimmed* hat—

(a, a), FELT type hat.

Tracy: Mm-hmm.

Bruce: (OK, broad and [inaudible].)

[*Phone rings*]

And a—

and a, a *buckskin type jacket—*

BROWN.

buckskin jacket—

[*Phone rings.*]

couldn't make out his face.

[**Conversational**] (OK I'll let you stop there and get the phone.)

[*Recording interrupted.*]

Bruce: [**"Rational"**] OK I *think* where we were at would be—

uh—I had seen the guy, he was in the flat-brimmed hat and buckskin jacket.

[**"Amazed"**] I—*STOPPED what I was doing* and *STARED at* him *and*

when I *STARED at him he APPEARED to move SIDEWAYS.*

[**"Rational"**] OK, into the, another hallway (like where) the dishwashing area is (in the Pizza Hut).

Tracy: Mm-hmm.

Bruce: And move *SIDEWAYS* (just like) take a step to

his—

HIS right, my left.

[**"Amazed"**] Uh—I reacted and *RAN over* to see *who in the hell was* in the *store—*

OK?

NOBODY WAS THERE.

◇

NOT A SOUL.

And I **SAW him move** across—

out of the *picture—*

out of my *view—*

and nobody was THERE.

I *IMMEDIATELY checked all the* doors—

checked the restroom—

◇

RAN around the store—

PANICKING almost, thinking
There's GOT TO be somebody here—
It CAN'T be happening.
Uh—

◇

I didn't know what to do.
I was scareder as the devil, OK?
["**Rational**":] I *finally got myself back to the point* where
I was (you know, I was just imagining this, it couldn't be anything).
And went back, finished up the dishes and left and (didn't sleep worth a *damn* that night).
(OK, it) scared me—now—
later on there were other reports of it a *girl working there* named Mary Taylor—
Also saw him.
This is before Louise or any of the other people you may have talked to worked there.
Tracy: (Mmm.)
Bruce: SHE saw him.
Strange things would happen, noises, voices—
You'd be *SURE somebody was talking* to you—
calling *your name*—
and, and you wouldn't—
nobody would be there or—
the people were there would say you're NUTso.

◇

["**Rational**"] OK, it went on—
Jim Landers SAYS he had an experience with that—
in the Pizza Hut there's an area underneath where you MAKE the pizzas, where you store the COOKING pans.
OK, there's three sizes of cooking pans on two SHELVES.
OK, they're VERY HEAVY—
they're, they're oven type, heavy gauge *steel*.
He was closing one night, aGAIN washing dishes in the back where he's out of the way of the—
uh—

◇

view there.
S—UDDENLY he hears this
MASSIVE crash.
OK, and *all of these* pans—are—strewn from the *back* door
to the *cash* register.

Which in the *Pizza Hut's—about—*
oh—(twenty-four feet).

Tracy: (Mmm.)

Bruce: And—

["**Amazed**"] *there's* **NO WAY,** *the* **SHELVES** did not collapse—
(OK—)
And they *just didn't FALL OFF—not ALL of them would* have *fallen*.

◇

They were *ALL*—over.
Something appeared to have (knocked them out).
(just like) SHOVED them.
Out of the—
(the area they were at).
["**Rational**"] Now I *once again* saw the ghost
in—nineteen—seventy—SEVEN—
(that would have been).
Late SUMMER of seventy-seven.
(Late summer—is that right?—yeah 'cause the ground was clean).
Uh—
I was walking to the BANK (which is) right next door to the building.
And it was MY store so I always checked it out to check to see if any lights were
    missing outside and how it looked, looking through the windows.
["**Amazed**"] And I *saw someone* moving. And I thought—
IMPOSSIBLE.
CAN'T be.
CAN'T be, it's got to be *my reflection*.
["**Rational**"] Well I moved my arm [*waves his arm*] to see if it was my reflection
    and—it—didn't.
OK,
I thought, well somebody's walking out in front of the building, looked—
THROUGH the windows to see if anybody was moving and it WASN'T.
The *figure was moving*

◇

in a direction
OUT toward the FRONT of the store—
OK?
NINETY-degree angle to me.
[*Clarifies position with his hands*]

Tracy: Mm-hmm.

Bruce: Moving out toward the front of the store—

just on the other side of the salad bar (which is in the center of the dining area.)

["**Amazed**"] I **STOPPED—**

and WATCHED, thinking it's got to be *HEADLIGHTS* it's got to be something—***nothing moved except this*** figure.

AGAIN the guy in the flat-brimmed hat.

((OK))

He *started—*

◇

through the salad bar*—**not THROUGH the salad—beyond the salad*** bar, got to the ***end of the salad bar*—**and—just—vanished.

◇

Flat-out—

VANISHED.

◇
.
◇

["**Rational**"] Now I had *left everything in the* store.

I *wasn't quite* done, *that night* I just walked in, turned off the lights and (went out and left.)

Uh—*didn't complete* what I was supposed to do, caught all sorts of hell for it in the morning—

from my employees.

["**Amazed**"] (I have told them that they could do whatever they want [*nervous laugh*] I wasn't going to do it that night).

["**Rational**"] There were various sightings, Lois Brown felt someone touching her once while she was in the restroom

uh—

◇

voices as I've said.

It was kind of spooky at times.

People, some people flat-out REFUSED to close the store by them*selves* because they'd been *frightened.*

Guy named Dave Lucas, Dave's—

not an exceptionally BRAVE man but he's a BIG man, he's six-foot-six and three hundred pounds.

Scared to DEATH of it.

Told me he—I could FIRE him before he'd ever close that store by himself again.

Tracy: ((Mmm.))

Bruce: He was FRIGHTENED by it.

Uh—he SAYS he heard it (one night).

◇

["**Amazed**"] *It's kind of strange, I checked into it in* local history, now there's—

◇

WHERE the store is located is near where the original settlement of Arbordale was.
(OK)
Smith's Crossroads at the time I think was what it (called, what it was called.)
But
there's *no record of anyone being KILLED* there—
but it's a *possibility*
((OK.))
["**Rational**"] Uh—the records are unclear about what DID happen there, it was fairly
    swampy in that area, it was the trail leading into town—or the village there.
(Uh—)
None of the local historians, uh—Joyce Miller (or uh—
(what the hell's her name, Helen—uh—Davis—)
have been able to HELP me on that.
["**Amazed**"] But I'm *kind of trying to check it out for* **my** *curiosity, I* **DON'T BELIEVE**
    that there's **such a thing** *as a* **GHOST**—
but I damn well want to find out WHAT there was.
Tracy: Mm-hmm.
Bruce: Just to—
    (you know)
    So I can rest at nights.
    (And go in there and not think about it.)
    (Uh—)
    He's *never bothered* anybody in the sense that he's *hurt* anybody but he's (scared a
        lot of people).
    [**Conversational**] Any other questions?
Tracy: [*Nervous laugh*]
    That's pretty good.
    I didn't, I didn't know that—
    I don't talk to Fred or any of those other ones.
Bruce: *I don't know if Wilson ever worked there*—well Fred worked there for a
    WHILE—
    I don't know if he'd have been there when any of this happened.
    Uh—the *crew originally*—
    the *crew originally*—
    none of them—
    I haven't seen the original crew when I first sighted the guy in years—
    in TWO years at least.
Tracy: What, were you the—

were you the first one to—

Bruce: [**"Rational"**] *No*—

Tracy: —experience him?

Bruce: I *think Mary had seen him* before I had because when I came into the store the
next day and said,

I, you know, I saw this—

the stories started coming out about the strange things that had happened, it was
like   [*quickly*]   nobody-wanted-to-admit-it-because-everybody-else-would-have-
thought-they-were-NUTS.

Tracy: Mm-hmm.

Bruce: (Uh—)

(it was uh—)

[*Loud clang; Bruce has picked up a round pizza serving tray*].

(You know that's funny.)

Uh—

Tracy: [*Nervous laughter*].

Bruce: [*quickly*] Nobody-else-would-ADMIT-it.

Tracy: Oh.

Bruce: (It was kind of a strange—)

[**"Rational"**] But *I* saw him twice, uh—

I don't know if anybody else will admit they've seen him or HAVE seen him (either for
that matter.)

THAT'S WHY I want to find out IF there IS something there.

Am I just seeing things or is there something there.

I *THINK there's something there* because of (everybody having these spooky things
happening—)

(the noises and everything.)

Tracy: Yeah but you don't think it's a ghost?

Bruce: [**"Amazed"**] *I DON'T KNOW WHAT IT IS I **REFUSE** to believe in a ghost.*

Tracy: *Yeah*?

Bruce: [**"Rational"**] *It's just a* matter of PRINCIPLE.

Tracy: Mm-hmm?

Bruce: WHAT it is, is what I want to find out.

As far as ghosts—

uh, you know, uh—the sheets and the Hollywood version of a ghost or a spirit of the
dead, *I don't know*

I don't know *WHAT it would be*, there COULD *conceivably be something* on that *line*.

A force that we're not a*ware* of

Tracy: Like more of a spirit than a—

Bruce: Well, *say just a, a*—

Tracy: —quote, ghost?

Bruce: (—a—)

physical—force).

(OK, a—) magnetic energy (for want of a better term).

Tracy: Mm-hmm?

Bruce: But as far as a ghost that will make CONTACT with you that—would have been—
necessarily a human form because he was damned to be here for all time or something
like that, (I'm not sure of).

["**Amazed**"] (Maybe—it—was—because—of—something—but)

(I, I don't know I *want to find* out).

(I'm *curious*.)

◇

((Uh—it's—mostly I'm *scared*.))

((Being frightened, I'll be honest.))

◇

◇

((I didn't like it any, either time.))

((It's a *terrible* feeling—))

((*not* knowing what it is.))

Tracy: And not being able to explain it?

Bruce: (And not being able to explain it, right.)

Tracy: Yeah.

Bruce: ["**Rational**"] If I drop something on my foot I hurt it and I don't like it but I
know why it hurts and I know why I don't like it.

Tracy: Mm-hmm.

Bruce: ["**Amazed**"] (Uh—but when I see something like that I—*can't* explain it and—)

◇

◇

((uh—))

((my traditional frame of reference is just totally useless.))

((I can't touch it, I can't see it—))

◇

◇

Tracy: (Mmm.)

OK.

[*Recording terminated*]

Unlike the other tape, which includes much incidental chatter and scene
setting, the tape Tracy recorded is brief; Bruce evidently gave no prelude and
artificially cut off the taping at the end. It is therefore difficult to say what

discussion prefaced the recording. Almost certainly Tracy paraphrased what she had learned from Louise, since Bruce alludes to her. Further, Bruce appears to be responding consciously to the "official" legend-motif interpretation of the events when he incongruously uses Louise's term "Pizza Hut Ghost" despite his insistence that what he saw was no ghost. And his abrupt mention of checking into "it" in local history presupposes awareness of the common legend trip motif. Still, while Bruce's performance is carefully, almost symmetrically structured around the two appearances of the "ghost," Tracy's surprised, incoherent response rules out any preliminary rehearsing. Likewise, Bruce's defensive response to her challenge makes little sense if the two had previously agreed about what he would say. In sum, the tape records spontaneous dispute on two levels: between collector and performer and, simultaneously, between two sides of Bruce's personality. And like the active legend, the debate reaches no resolution.

The issue here, though, is not whether Bruce's performance is structured, but why it is structured the way it is. Gillian Bennett has proposed typical differences between legends told "for laughs" and those told "as true," which at first seem to fit the contrasting features of Louise's and Bruce's performance.[8] But laughs and "truth" are not the concepts at loggerheads here; rather, it is tradition and experience that collide. The major distinction, then, is not the subjective *purpose* of the structuring—which may be psychologically unrecoverable—but rather *what* the performers are consciously, visibly structuring. Louise is passing on a story, restructuring in words the words she has received from others. Having received the legend in a form that has already placed social interpretation on the events, she understandably distances herself from the empirical status of the events and emphasizes the entertainment value of the story. Bruce, by contrast, is structuring primary experiences—sensory impressions that came to him without the reassuring mantle of cultural explanations. His performance embodies a structure, but it is one that he has imposed, and not successfully, on the uncanny events that have challenged his rational understanding of the world. As another storyteller explained to me (in words), "This is not a story, this is some *thing* that happened to me."[9] This distinction between referents cuts deeply and—to previous scholars—invisibly through the entire corpus of legend performances.

Since Bruce's own "rational' interpretation of his experience ultimately fails, within his performance we can see two subdivisions, corresponding to the contradictory attitudes Bruce expresses about the experience. One is spoken in a normal, "rational" intonation, and one performed in what I term an "amazed" intonation.[10] The "rational" tone is more like the classic narrative intonation described in Louise's version of the Pizza Hut ghost; flattened, almost singsong, it serves to relate events without comment. It is difficult to locate adequate terms in the English language, for the "amazed" intonation, which, by contrast, is initially hushed, with quieter, lower-pitched dynamics, but it frequently includes abrupt leaps to higher pitch and louder dynamics that contrast dramatically with this background.

Bruce uses the "rational" intonation to begin each of his accounts with fact-heavy orientations and descriptions of occasions:

Bruce: OK.

["**Rational**"] The Arbordale Pizza Hut Ghost.

Uh—

I saw the Pizza Hut Ghost—

(now this was back in uh—)

◊

either late seventy-four or early seventy-five is the first time *I* saw him. (I don't remember the exact date.)

(I was working late one night.)

I was in the back of the Pizza Hut. I was washing dishes at the time in these large, industrial-size sinks.

Now there's a *wall*—

leading to a—yeah a *doorway* [*Clarifies positions with his hands*]

another portion of the wall (and then another doorway).

(And a—refrigerator there.)

The sheer amount of detail contrasts sharply with Louise's abrupt orientation: "OK, Bruce was closing once and we had this like little room in the back for his office." But the detail, though apparently inconsequential to the story that follows, is important to establish the persona telling the story as a critical, factual observer.[11] The use of the same persona in the second memorate is more telling:

["**Rational**"] Now I *once again saw* the ghost

in—nineteen—seventy—SEVEN—

(that would have been).

Late SUMMER of seventy-seven.

(Late summer—is that right)—yeah 'cause the ground was clean).

Uh—

I was walking to the BANK (which is) right next door to the building.

And it was MY store so I always checked it out to check to see if any lights were missing
outside and how it looked, looking through the windows.

Here the rational stance is necessary to the effect of the narrative. The
scrupulousness with which Bruce settles on the specific details of time and
place now applies to the details of the apparition, fitting its manifestation into
an empirical surrounding and suggesting its concreteness. Thus while Louise
indicates that the ghost was insubstantial, and all Bruce had to do was "kind
of" shake his head to make the apparition vanish, here Bruce describes the
ghost as doggedly substantial, defying all his logical hypotheses.

["**Amazed**"] And I *saw someone* moving. And I thought—
IMPOSSIBLE.
CAN'T be.
CAN'T be, it's got to be *my reflection*.
["**Rational**"] Well I moved my arm [*waves his arm*] to see
if it was my reflection and—it—didn't.
OK,
I thought, well somebody's walking out in front of the building, looked—*THROUGH the
windows* to see if anybody was moving and it WASN'T.
The *figure was moving*
◇
in a direction
OUT toward the FRONT of the store—
OK?
NINETY-degree angle to me.
[*Clarifies position with his hands*].
Moving out toward the front of the store—
just on the other side of the salad bar (which is in the center of the dining area.)

Where Louise ironically suppresses skepticism in her version but allows it
the upper hand through her playful editing of the episodes, Bruce quite deliberately incorporates the skeptic into his performance, allowing him to make
the obvious rational statement: "IMPOSSIBLE./CAN'T be./CAN'T be." The
result is a different kind of irony, as the statement is made in Bruce's
"amazed" intonation, and the careful description that follows in "rational"
intonation leads only to more exact observation of the impossible and therefore to greater certainty that something supernatural is empirically there.
Thus in both memorates the controlled "rational" intonation leads into the
contrast-ridden "amazed" intonation, as raises in pitch become more consis-

tent and extreme and frequently contrasted with much softer expressions. Both rise to two emotional peaks. The first comes when Bruce becomes convinced that he is witnessing something supernormal, as in the first episode:

Bruce: It *kept up and I finally looked up* and looked
   over.
and I ***THOUGHT*** *I* ***SAW*** someone.
(OK, a, a) man.
Standing in that second doorway by the freezer area.
And I thought—*didn't think anything of it* and went *back to washing dishes* and it *clicked—*
that
*there's somebody **STANDING** there.*

The second follows when the apparition finally docs vanish, and Bruce is forced to try to reconstruct the event and determine exactly what he did see. This, in both episodes, leads to a section in which Bruce lowers his voice to an undertone, describing his "alienation," or psychological disorientation following contact with the supernormal.[12]

["**Amazed**"] Uh—I reacted and *RAN over* to see
who in the hell was in the *store—*
   OK?
NOBODY WAS THERE.

NOT A SOUL.
*And I **SAW** him move across—*
out of the *picture*—out of my *view*—and nobody was THERE.
I *IMMEDIATELY checked all the* doors—
checked the restroom—
◇
RAN around the store—
PANICKING almost, thinking
There's GOT TO be somebody here—
It CAN'T be happening.
Uh—
◇
I didn't know what to do.
I was scareder as the devil, OK?
["**Rational**":] I *finally got myself back to the point* where I was (you know, I was just
   imagining this,

it couldn't be anything).

And

went back, finished up the dishes and left and (didn't sleep worth a *damn* that night).
(OK, it) scared me—now—

In general, then, the tension of Bruce's account of the events contrasts the "rational" perspective with the "amazed." The "rational" perspective attempts to gain or maintain equilibrium through careful, skeptical observation, while the "amazed" reacts to contradictory empirical evidence with an equally unstable, contrast-filled intonation. This linguistic phenomenon is not merely a "clue" to the narrator's emotions.[13] It appears in a consistent, dramatic way in Bruce's memorates, and in somewhat foreshortened form in the validating legend of Jim Landers's experience framed by the memorates. Louise uses extreme pitch abruptly and without warning to characterize what her characters "say," and in so doing makes them seem light-headed and foolish. By contrast, Bruce builds to climaxes of pitch and volume against flatter, more "rational" intonation, making his "amazed" reactions to genuinely supernormal events the more credible.

The Ghost Beyond the Salad Bar   Why, then, the puzzling refusal in the metacommentary to grant the cultural interpretation so blithely posited by Louise—that the apparition is the ghost of someone killed or buried there? Bruce's voice rises twice more to emotional peaks, both times in response to this theory. After acknowledging that he has looked into local history, he admits that "there's *no record of anyone being KILLED* there—/but it's a *possibility/((OK.))*." Still, even as he leaves the door open for this "possibility," he quickly claims that "I'm *kind of trying to check it out for* **my** *curiosity, I* **DON'T BELIEVE** *that there's* **such a thing** *as a* GHOST—/but I damn well want to find out WHAT there was." Later he repeats. "I *THINK there's something there* because of (everybody having these spooky things happening—/(the noises and everything.)" But as soon as Tracy presses him to call it a "ghost," he reacts emotionally, his intonations audibly contrasting with each other: ["**Amazed**"] "*I DON'T KNOW WHAT IT IS, I REFUSE to believe in a ghost./* ["**Rational**"] *It's just a* matter of PRINCIPLE./WHAT it is, is what I want to find out." Bruce's translation of his experience, therefore, is pulled in two distinct directions—toward validating the reality of the apparition ("I *THINK there's something there*") and against giving it an easily applied cultural tag ("*I* **DON'T BELIEVE** *that there's* **such a thing** *as a* GHOST").

But choice is denied to those in an environment associated with modernity. Bruce alludes to the ways in which people who told about the experiences in the Pizza Hut were ridiculed, or at least feared ridicule, the second time using a peculiar, nervous, rushed intonation to do so:

Strange things would happen, noises, voices—
You'd be *SURE somebody was talking* to you—
calling *your name*—
and, and you wouldn't—
nobody would be there or—
the people were there would say you're NUTso.

["**Rational**"] I *think Mary had seen him* before I had because when I came into the store the next day and said, I, you know, I saw this—
the stories started coming out about the strange things that had happened, it was like [*quickly*] nobody wanted-to-admit-it-because-everybody-else-would-have-thought-they-were-NUTS . . .
[*quickly*] Nobody-else-would-ADMIT-it. . . .
["**Rational**"] But *I* saw him twice, uh—
I don't know if anybody else will admit they've seen him or HAVE seen him (either for that matter.)

The Pizza Hut is not holy ground; that is, unless the performer blesses, or remythologizes it.[14] It is important that Louise prefaces her performance with the flat statement that "supposedly a man was killed on the site where the Pizza Hut was built," and Bruce spends significant time trying to locate and verify this statement in local history. Nevertheless, Bruce is faced with two sets of dilemmas. The first he states directly: "Am I just seeing things or is there something there?" The first, as we have seen with Louise's version, leaves him open to ridicule as credulous, easily fooled, or hysterical. Bruce is at pains to deny this characterization: he presents his own supernormal experiences against a background "rational" intonation, he collates them with other employees' uncanny testimony, and he investigates, instead of uncritically accepting, the culturally provided explanation of a ghost tied to a grave or death site. His metacommentary concludes, "I *THINK* there's something there." But then, if something is there, what is it?

This explains why Bruce, in spite of his refusal to believe in ghosts, is reluctant to reject this cultural model absolutely. First he admits, "it's a *possibility*"; then he says more dubiously, "a spirit of the dead, *I don't know*." The collector is anxious to end the uncertainty and prompts him to call it a ghost; when he refuses she again tries to get him to accept a slightly revised view:

"more of a spirit than a—quote, ghost?" Bruce will have none of this, although his strongest emotional reaction, leading directly to the termination of the recording, comes immediately after he has made his fullest statement of the ghost hypothesis:

["**Amazed**"] (Maybe—it—was—because—of—something—but)
(I, I don't know I want to find out).
(I'm *curious*.)
◇
((Uh-it's—mostly I'm *scared*.))
((Being frightened, I'll be honest.))
◇
◇
((I didn't like it any, either time.))
((It's a *terrible* feeling—))
((*not* knowing what it is.))

The *principle* behind Bruce's refusal, therefore, is not simply skepticism or agnosticism, though he implicitly ridicules the pop culture model, "the sheets and the Hollywood version of a ghost." He would like to believe, if he could satisfy his rationalist scruples and locate evidence that the Pizza Hut was built on an old grave or death site. Nevertheless, Bruce indicates that he would be more comfortable if he could define the manifestation in quasi-mechanical terms, as "a force that we're not *aware* of . . . (—a—/(physical—force./(OK, a—) magnetic energy (for want of a better term)." Such a "physical" force obviously, would not be out of place inside a technologically advanced fast-food restaurant and would thus baptize (and so lay) the ghost by naming it in secular, demythologized terms. But Bruce can do so only by positing that the force is one "that we're not *aware* of," so putting him, with the parapsychologists, outside the cultural definitions of reality on yet another front.

And again the belief-language is more a hindrance than a help. If Bruce buys the first of these suggestions, then he has to admit that ghosts, spirits, or whatever can appear at any place at any time. Despite culture's efforts to limit paranormal power to socially acceptable spots, who can tell when he or she is standing on a centuries' old grave? If, however, he chooses the second option, then he is left speculating about unknown forces and energies that lead to empirical results—visions, flying pizza pans—but cannot be described empirically. As Bruce says:

["**Amazed**"] (Uh—but when I see something like that)
(I—*can't* explain it and—)

◇
◇
((uh—))
((my traditional frame of reference is just totally useless.))
((I can't touch it, I can't see it—))
◇
◇

Faced with this irreconcilable dilemma, Bruce retreats into official silence. What lies behind these gaps is perhaps best expressed by Dégh and Vázsonyi:

A positive legend . . . is surrounded by innumerable concentric circles spiraling into cosmic distances. The first and closest circle will indicate that ghosts exist if there was one somewhere at a given time. Yet, if ghosts exist they must act according to the unknown rules of their existence. What is even worse, they might undermine man's faith in the normal order of things, his reason and his principle of causality, upon which the average man's feeling of the relative security of the human condition is based.

In the domain of the concentric circles at that distance, it is a mysterious twilight that rules. If ghosts do exist or can exist (in other words, if their existence cannot be disproved beyond doubt, and how could it be?), what kinds of other unfathomable things might also exist? Bodiless entities, inscrutable rules, unconceivable relationships, immeasurable forces—anything, within the confines of everyday life. . . .

Is there anything one can hang onto?[15]

Chapter 8

THE VARIETIES OF ALIEN EXPERIENCE

Whitley Strieber's fictional works such as *The Wolfen* and *The Hunger* established him as a solid, productive author in the contemporary tradition of horror fiction. In 1987, he published *Communion,* a firsthand account of his encounters with alien creatures, an event that provoked open hostility, with many reviewers assuming that Strieber was simply extending his fictional successes into a new realm. Nevertheless, *Communion* is what Strieber called it—"A True Story"—as journalist Ed Conroy demonstrated in his investigation. There is no compelling evidence that Strieber fabricated the events described in the book, nor did mental tests administered afterwards show signs of clinical psychosis. So far as can be determined, the book is a truthful account of a bizarre series of experiences, during which Strieber encountered supernatural entities whom he calls "the visitors."

However, it is difficult to see Strieber's account for exactly what it is, because many readers see the details he represents in the light of their own belief-languages. Without thinking about it, we transform the story he tells into a story of our own making. One such act of transformation occurs in a hostile review by Thomas M. Disch. Like many other reviewers, Disch begins by describing the book he thought he read: "what Strieber recounts in *Communion* is nothing less than the first contact of the human race, in the person of Whitley Strieber, with an ancient alien civilization that abducted him from his cabin in the Catskills . . . and took him aboard a flying saucer, where he communicated with a variety of alien beings and was subjected to surgical and sexual indignities. . . . Only later, in March 1986, did hypnosis reveal the true character of what had happened to him."[1] The description is inaccurate on several points. First, Strieber does not claim to have been the *first* human contacted by the visitors; in fact, he suggests that similar encounters have occurred at least since medieval times. Second, while hypnosis clarified details

142

of the experience, Strieber directly remembered the essential details before he sought help from ufologists.

Similarly, Ernest H. Taves, in a *Skeptical Inquirer* review, begins by rearranging Strieber's memories and reconstructions as if they constituted an official biography: "At the age of 12, Strieber goes out in the evening to a tent in a lot next to his backyard. He is accosted by a huge insect, similar to a praying mantis, which he had at first mistaken for a skeleton on a motorcycle. The bug pins the lad to the ground and hits the boy's head with a silver nail."[2] After three pages of unsympathetic and bald summary, Taves dismisses the story with a brusque "Enough." Like Disch, he proposes that Strieber is either mentally ill or he is consciously perpetrating a hoax, "having fun, playing a joke on his readers—and perhaps upon his publisher as well—serving up an engrossing and fanciful tale, offering as fact what is fiction."[3]

A more subtle distortion is that both reviews claim that *Communion* describes Strieber's contact with aliens. It does not. The book in fact is a more complex version of Bruce's dilemma—an attempt to "tell" an ungrammatical experience, an experience for which there is a limited cultural belief language. In fact, Strieber's story begins *after* the alleged contact, with his attempts to reduce his confused recollections of a strange night into a coherent memory. The narrative, as told through journal entries written during this interim period, describes his working through a period of mental stress and his initial reactions to other persons' abduction accounts. In January we find him in psychological disarray, alienated from his wife, unable to read or write, and suffering from a variety of physical symptoms. At this point, Strieber tells us, images began to float into his mind. Strieber began reading and talking to friends about UFOs, a process climaxing with his discovery of an account of an abduction experience that contained some minor correspondences with the images he was "recalling." This point of contact evidently led to a psychological crisis a few days later: "I was sitting at my desk when things just seemed to cave in on me. Wave after wave of sorrow passed over me. I looked at the window with hunger. I wanted to jump. I wanted to die. I just could not bear this memory, and I could not get rid of it."[4]

At this precise moment, Strieber contacted abduction investigator Budd Hopkins, who gave him assurances that his memories were indeed similar to those of others. Strieber wept in relief and "went from wanting to hide it all to wanting to understand it." Then Hopkins introduced the idea of looking for a previous encounter, and Strieber—for the first time—began to look at the October 4 events as possibly paranormal. Given this task, Strieber left this interview "a happy man."[5] After his contact with Hopkins, the book presents transcripts of hypnosis sessions, during which Strieber reconstructed the December 26 event in terms of the new belief-language that he had learned. In additional sessions, he revisits several previous moments in his life, which also can be recounted in terms of the new language. Between these transcripts, Strieber presents his comments and interpretations of the information revealed, along with his tentative conclusions, doubts, disclaimers, speculations, and follow-up experiences that confirmed his new comprehension of his experience.

Even at the end, Strieber is unwilling to do more than present a series of possible interpretations, only one being the "standard" line of ufologists— that he had been abducted by extraterrestrials doing biological experiments on humans. He admits, "I cannot say, in all truth, that I am certain the visitors are present as entities entirely independent of their observers."[6] By presenting one of Strieber's proposed interpretations as the only one authorized by the author, Disch and Taves create a straw man. And by characterizing *Communion* as fiction, Taves engages in nihilation, stating that there is no need to understand Strieber's experience because there never was any experience to understand.

The irony here is that both reviewers are imitating the creative act of fiction by rearranging and selecting details from Strieber's reported experiences to create something akin to a coherent plot. In fact, the book makes little sense as conventional fiction. Moving backward and forward in points of reference, Strieber changes his mind about events, contradicts himself, and includes damaging self-admissions about periods of mental instability and (apparent) lies that he has told about his past. The bizarre encounter at age twelve is in fact described in Strieber's *last* hypnotic regression. After this, the sessions were terminated because both the author and his analyst were becoming increasingly skeptical about the accuracy of the details recalled.[7] Such self-doubts are, of course, picked up by his critics, but in doing so they fail to acknowledge that they are only completing one response that Strieber has already sketched out for them.

The discussion begun by *Communion* in 1987 opened the way to a large number of publications on the topic. Some of these, such as John Mack's *Abduction: Human Encounters with Aliens* (1994) and *Alien Discussions* (Pritchard et al., 1994), the proceedings of a scholarly conference held at MIT, made a serious attempt to engage the phenomenon in a serious, intellectual way. Folklorists Thomas Bullard and Peter Rojcewicz engaged in this discussion. However, for the most part formal study of abductions remains part of the marginal realm of parapsychological research. Folklorists can shed more light on this kind of experience by providing insights on how individuals react to contacts with puzzling forces. The contact itself, in most cases, remains unexplainable—but as soon as individuals react to such contacts, fit available belief-language to the experience, and try to communicate it to others, folklore intrudes. Seen this way, the peculiar features of *Communion* do not reflect abnormalities in Strieber's experience but the normal process of legend formation. Critical reactions to the book are part of the same folk process. This process, perhaps inevitably, alters the experience it records at the same time as it makes it sharable with others. The final irony is that the direction of Strieber's work since *Communion* likewise reflects the same inevitable process of change.

Abductions and the Folklore Record   Collections of legends and folktales, both European and otherwise, contain a variety of "real life" accounts that contain close parallels to elements of modern abduction stories. Many of these are anonymous, migratory tales that have little weight as evidence, because, as folklorists have noted, they may circulate simply because they are entertaining stories. Some, however, contain alleged firsthand experiences. Strieber himself notes these parallels and cites them as support for the "reality" of his abduction. The more carefully recorded cases, however, make it clear that these earlier abductions were similar in many ways to Strieber's. Anne Jeffries (ca. 1624–98), an illiterate country girl from Cornwall, was one such celebrated abductee. In 1645 she apparently suffered a convulsion and was found, semiconscious, lying on the floor. As she recovered, she began to recall in detail how she had been accosted by a group of six little men. Paralyzed, she felt them swarm over her, kissing her, until she felt a sharp pricking sensation. Blinded, she found herself flying through the air to a palace filled with people. There, one of the men (now her size) seduced her, and suddenly an angry crowd burst in on them and she was again blinded and levitated. She then found herself lying on the floor surrounded by her friends. The accounts note that the experience left her ill for some time, and only after she regained her health did she recall the experience fully. Still, like Strieber, Jeffries claimed that this encounter was followed by further contacts with the "fairies," and the local authorities took her seriously enough that in 1646 she was actually arrested and imprisoned for witchcraft.[8]

Still, what should the folklorist's role be toward such stories? It is naive to assume that medieval accounts of contact with the otherworldly describe the *same* phenomena as modern abduction experiences.[9] Such studies are as reductive as skeptics' analyses, picking a significant detail out and ignoring vast differences in context and form. Another approach is to study such accounts as illustrations of "folk beliefs." The Finnish folklorist Lauri Honko has advocated such an attitude. Paranormal events comprise "numens," experiences recognized as supernormal but not yet interpreted. But, Honko continues, "during the experience itself a person does not yet know what the creature he sees is. He might already be convinced of the supernormal nature of the vision, but the interpretation does not yet occur."[10] Culture provides immediate, if controversial, models for many such events—"I saw a ghost!"; "That's a UFO!" Others take more time to interpret, and when the witness or others try to translate such unexpected visions into narratives, they use the convenient language culture gives them, and so the experiences normally are harmonized with existing cultural values. An encounter with a fairy, for instance, might be "told" as a warning or punishment for those who violate social norms. Hence, Strieber's fatigue and sensory deprivation admit the possibility of hallucination, the content of which may have been based on cultural models. Retrospection heightens their traditionality, so, as Honko noted elsewhere, "the tradition is already present in the experience."[11]

Thus in Newfoundland, residents might have called Strieber's experiences variations on the "Old Hag." In that tradition, such visitations are assumed to be caused by a witch who casts a spell on persons who have offended her. "Hagging," under a variety of names, is found in many parts of the world where witchcraft is feared. In the south of Germany, it is known as "*Hexendrüken*," "being crushed by the witch." Many remedies for this phenomenon exist in collections of folk beliefs. One advises throwing one's pillow on the floor to make the witch sit on it instead; another suggests trying to grab hold of the entity sitting on the chest to learn the witch's identity.[12]

And allusions to the phenomenon are common in the writings of contemporary anti-cult crusaders. During a revival in Canada, a Saskatoon Christian "saw in the night a figure coming towards her. She was crippled and could not move. The black figure reached out towards her. Then from the other side came another hand and pushed the black figure away with the words: 'She is my child.' This brought the attack by the powers of darkness to an end, and [she] could again pray and move her body."[13] In another case, a woman "sometimes heard footsteps coming up to her bed and had the feeling that a figure was approaching her trying to squeeze her throat or put its hands on her chest." In both these instances, the supernatural being was interpreted as a demon, perhaps even Satan, and in the second case the woman underwent a Christian exorcism ceremony to drive the unwelcome visitor away.[14] As frightening as the concepts of witchcraft or demon possession might be, they brought a common but unpredictable and terrifying experience within the ken of social experience. Members of such communities could both talk about the event and take decisive action to ward it off in the future. The

Newfoundland tradition of the Old Hag, for instance, includes counter-charms—sleeping with a sharp knife, for instance—known to be effective against repeat attacks.[15] Such practices materially reduce the anxieties of the victim (though perhaps not those of his bedmate). Failing that, such traditions provide ways of interpreting the next occurrence in a way that assured the victim that the "hagging" could be brought to an end and the entity responsible identified and supernaturally punished.

When David Hufford first studied memorates of "hagging" experiences, he assumed that the similarities he found could be explained by previous exposure to oral tradition. But when he moved his base of research to the United States, Hufford found the experience just as common there as in Newfoundland.[16] He therefore disparaged Honko's model, countering that some paranormal experiences are so widespread and consistent across cultures that they must derive from a common experience, not simply from unconscious expectations set up by contact with cultural models.[17] But Honko does not in fact say that culture is the only source of supernatural experience. Indeed, he admits that "for one reason or another, an explanatory model from tradition cannot be found for many supernatural experiences and they remain at the numen stage." He continues: "In just this way came about the ever fresh tradition which tells of indeterminate specters and ghosts. With admirable ease it has passed through those cultural changes which cause weakening and death to belief in spirits."[18]

Cultural models often do *not* help witnesses explain their encounters, which suggests that numinous apparitions are not, after all, culturally derived. In her study of ESP experiences among Finnish informants, Leea Virtanan also argues that memorates do not simply reflect "folk beliefs." This "fundamental narrowness of approach" she says, "limits the scope of investigation from its outset."[19] Like Hufford's Old Hag, numens appear to defy, indeed they threaten to destroy, artificial models set up to explain them. Convenient language does not limit the supernormal to graveyards or old country inns, but it does limit people's capacity to talk about their supernormal experiences, unless they (the witnesses, not the numina) limit themselves to hallowed turf. In this regard, the main value of Strieber's book to folklorists is that much of it was committed to writing soon after the experiences themselves. For we see more clearly than usual how the numinous experience is independent of the cultural belief-language, an indeterminate psychic threat to the author until he finds cultural explanations adequate to "name" the encounter and put its details into a narratable framework.

Abductions and Traditions of Belief   When individuals encounter forces so far outside normal experience, and cultural language provides no adequate model for relating such contacts, the legend process cannot easily deal with them. Worse, institutional experts may impose interpretations on such ambiguous experience to maintain what Gillian Bennett has called a "tradition of *dis*belief."[20] And in the responses to *Communion* we see a power-ful compulsion—on all sides—either to deny Strieber's encounters or reduce them to a "grammatical" concept within the traditions of disbelief or belief. One skeptical approach has been to "name" Strieber's apparent mental defi-ciency in the existing psychological lexicon. Two examples of this approach are the psychological analyses of abductees by Robert A. Baker and Martin Kottmeyer.[21] Both assume that alluding to and defining existing psychological processes can "name" and so contain the most threatening elements of Strieb-er's encounters within mundane explanations. Baker suggests that the experi-ence reflects a combination of "confabulation," or the tendency to add fantasy details to memory, and "inadvertent cueing" by analysts like Budd Hopkins. Strieber, in Baker's view, is a "fantasy-prone" individual who, when ufologists showed interest, was motivated "to come up with a cracking 'good story.' "

Kottmeyer suggests that Strieber has a "boundary-deficit personality" and has difficulty distinguishing states that for most people are clearly separate: sleep and waking, fantasy and reality, self and nonself. Examining the details of his life, Kottmeyer finds evidence for an impressive number of psychologi-cal problems: "Strieber . . . manifests a constellation of traits that object-relations theory explains as resulting from traumas early in childhood when the child is first developing the character armour during the phase of separa-tion and individuation. Prominent among these traits are threats of inner fragmentation . . . ; primitive emotional defences including paranoia and, most primitive of all, splitting; archaic narcissistic formation involving gran-diosity; inability to integrate the hostile and loving aspects of parental intro-jects; and a tendency to project hostility."[22]

Much of this jargon is of debatable relevance to Strieber's encounter and seems introduced more for the talismanic effect of the "names" of complexes. Leea Virtanan, likewise, found many of the skeptics' explanations of ESP events "simplistic" and often "bolstered by the addition of scientific, observa-tional, and sociopsychological jargon" that in fact may "obscure the fact that such explanations are sometimes inadequate."[23] Baker, nevertheless, endorses Kottmeyer's analysis as "brilliant" and suggests that all books based on alien encounters should be labeled "science fiction," a move that has the effect of calling all contactees' stories conscious lies.

Such explanations consistently sacrifice discordant details to the theories. Skeptical psychologists, for instance, assume that untrained hypnotists unwit-tingly lead their followers to remember a "standard" plot. Philip J. Klass warned that abductee-hunters like Hopkins were like "Typhoid Mary" in that they induced anxieties and condemned their "patients" to recurrent night-mares of continuing abductions.[24] Analysis of abduction accounts shows that this is the opposite of the case. When abductions were directly recalled by witnesses, the stories they tell are closest to those recovered by trained profes-sionals with no preconceived plot in mind. The narratives that contained the most unusual details, paradoxically, were recovered by the untrained ufolo-gists whom one would most expect to "lead" their patients. Overall, though, narratives constructed with the help of hypnosis were not significantly differ-ent from those "recovered" by hypnosis. "Maybe abductees just know their aliens," one folklorist commented.[25]

On the other hand, Strieber's reception within the UFO camp has fre-quently been stormy. Strieber and Hopkins broke off relations soon after *Communion* was drafted, and other ufologists who began in close company with him later warned others to stay away from him because he was "mentally and emotionally unstable and therefore not to be trusted."[26] The reasons for these disputes partly reflect suspicion over the profit Strieber verifiably made on the book. But there probably is a more profound reason for the cool re-sponse from the group that would ordinarily have been his natural allies. Again, the twin responses of denial and containment seem to have been as common among "believers" as among "skeptics." The rift between Strieber and Hopkins evidently began when an early draft of *Communion* was passed to the researcher. Hopkins recalled: "When I finally saw the manuscript, I was quite horrified and I thought it was totally unpublishable. . . . He said he was led off his airplane [the aliens' craft] by his penis, by these little—naked—things; it was the kind of thing where I said 'Whitley!' He had no sense as to what would go down with the reader and what wouldn't. I mean, writing fiction is one thing, but there are other rules." Strieber's status as a fiction writer made him something of a liability within the UFO camp, though Hop-kins claims that Strieber's fault was not that he embellished his experiences but that he didn't know what to leave out.

I was very upset, and it had a lot to do with making suggestions on how to handle things, what to leave out, and general sort of strategic decisions. See, one has to realize one very basic thing. He [Strieber] has little experience as a nonfiction writer. I have a great deal of experience as a nonfiction writer. . . . I certainly made a lot of suggestions, and there were many, many hundreds of changes that the editors made to the book. So it was finally whipped into shape, thanks to a lot of other minds, but at the time it was bizarre beyond belief. A lot of it was very, very good, but a lot of it was extremely bizarre.[27]

Hopkins seems to have wanted to make Strieber's accounts conform with the expectations of readers formed by John Fuller's *The Interrupted Journey* (1974) and his own *Missing Time* (1981). Bizarre details like being led around by one's penis did nothing to give credence to Strieber's experience and, through their shock value, increased the chance that the book would simply be rejected out of hand. The result was to deny the events and perceptions that Strieber felt were central to his encounter. The irony is that, after insisting that the detail be deleted from the manuscript, Hopkins later *did* encounter a case in which an abductee independently recalled being led around by his penis, a circumstance that "profoundly affected" Hopkins.[28]

Ufologists seeking physical proof of aliens' existence were also underwhelmed by what Strieber had to offer. Another researcher who read a rough draft of the book recalled reading and reading, "waiting for him to tell us something I didn't know. Well he never did, because in reality, his abduction was a very mild case."[29] Strieber replied that "the stress and extreme strangeness of the experience disrupts the ability of even the most well-intentioned witness to provide an accurate report of his or her encounter." He added that when investigators criticized accounts such as his as "confused," it showed only that they, like the skeptics, "are overly eager to dismiss that which does not fulfill their wishes."[30] It is, indeed, *Communion*'s strongest point that it is still, even after all the editorial changes, very, very bizarre. And Strieber's wife Anne reports a rather different response to the book's appeal. "We get hundreds of letters," she said, "from men and women who tell us that they have kept their experiences a secret."[31] Trying to express the bizarre, that is, allowed others to do the same thing, in a process that is essentially therapeutic.

Strieber's experiences were no more or less bizarre than many others in literature, religion, or folklore. Conventional theories proposed by skeptics or psychologists dismiss the phenomenon at the cost of denying it or trying to demote its validity. Ironically, many ufologists, including some that worked closely with Strieber initially, likewise distort the contact by trying to reduce it to "good form" in the interest of taming its essentially unpredictable, irrational nature. Strieber himself has reconstructed the event in such a way as to produce his own "tamed" version. But this is the task and duty of the legend process—to reduce private experiences to "tellable" form.

Abduction as Religious Experience   A disorienting experience like Strieber's requires some kind of reorienting process to "complete" the narrative and return the witness to a state of equilibrium. We see this dilemma in the case of theologian Henry James Sr., who also had a supernatural attack encounter with some connections to Strieber's alleged experience. One after-noon in May 1844, relaxing in his chair, James suddenly felt the presence of some invisible, ineffably evil being squatting in the room with him. Rationally, he recognized that his emotion "was a perfect insane and abject terror, with-out ostensible cause"; still he found himself completely paralyzed while (as in Strieber's experience) his mind was flooded with images of "doubt, anxiety, and despair."[32] His first step toward regaining his mental health came when he learned from a certain Mrs. Chichester that the encounter he had had was well known among Swedenborgians as "vastation."[33] Finding that such experiences were in fact shared by others and literally had a "name" was enough to relieve his anxiety, and he eventually found release in Swedenbor-gianism, while his sons dealt with the impact of this experience in their own ways. William James provided one of the first rational anatomies of paranor-mal encounters in *The Varieties of Religious Experience.* Henry James Jr. dealt with the lingering threat of such events in his fiction, ranging from *The Turn of the Screw* to "The Jolly Corner," both of which contain suggestive parallels to *Communion.* The senior James's reaction to finding the experience's name is not uncommon: Hufford reports that one surgeon unnerved by an Old Hag experience was literally reduced to tears when he found it described in psychological literature as "idiopathic SP."[34]

Strieber may, then, have sought help from alien abduction investigators like Hopkins exactly for the reasons he describes: to find convenient belief-language for a psychological event that otherwise would have to be labeled "fraud" or "madness." If Strieber was not fabricating his experience, and if he was not mentally ill, then the hard-line rationalist position, as stated by Taves, gave him no alternative but to proceed on the assumption that the aliens were real. Rather than engaging in a one-sided battle with established traditions of disbelief, most individuals prefer to stay silent, though at a con-siderable psychological cost. This corresponds with the results of psychologi-cal tests performed on Strieber in March 1986, which found that "at a price to his psychological well-being, he tries to repress strong emotional responses, rather than verbalize them so that he can deal more effectively."[35]

To reestablish a set of values by which one can regain control over one's psychological environment, *conversion* becomes almost a necessity. In the process of conversion, the human nervous system is stimulated beyond its normal capacity ("transmarginally") for long periods of time, eventually be-ginning to operate in paradoxical ways. This process may occur when people undergo a lengthy period of psychological stress. Their thought and behavior patterns begin to change and they become highly susceptible to new concepts and philosophies. It is unrealistic to expect a person to resist the process of conversion once it has begun: even recognition that one is being converted may not delay its progress.[36] Conversion has been institutionalized in the religious rites of many cultures, and the pattern frequently occurs in the narratives of "born-again" Christians.[37]

Strieber's account of events, based on the journal he kept before and during his hypnotic sessions, is structurally identical to such narratives. When he contacted Hopkins, Strieber was transmarginally excited: loss of sleep combined with obsessive, uncontrollable thought patterns "overloaded" his brain and left him susceptible to the slightest idea that would give his anxieties a licit avenue. Further, the extreme significance placed on small details—the slim correspondences that suddenly seem concrete proof of the visitations' reality—exhibits a common "paradoxical" phase of this process. In Strieber's words, "There did seem to be a lot of confusion . . . and perhaps even an emotional response on my part greatly out of proportion to what seemed a minor disturbance."[38] Strieber's first hypnosis session led to an intense moment in which he suddenly "remembered" the little man by his bed and responded with twenty seconds of prolonged screams.

This reaction, common to many other hypnotized "abductees," represents the moment of "abreaction," in which pent-up emotions are released in a controlled way through emotionally reliving the event that caused the anxieties. This process has been used therapeutically since World War II to treat stubborn cases of battle shock and trauma. Significantly, Sargant reports, it was found that it was not necessary to make the patient recall real-life incidents. Rather, "it would often be enough to create in him a state of excitement analogous to that which had caused his neurotic condition and keep it up until he collapsed; he would then start to improve. Thus *imagination would have to be used in inventing artificial situations. or distorting actual events.*"[39]

Recognizing this pattern in *Communion* explains why Strieber acts less like a playful hoaxer than a religious convert. Indeed, judging from psychological tests, the conversion experience largely restored his mental health, dispelling his self-destructive tendencies and restoring his writing abilities. Further, Strieber was left with the status of a "chosen one" and a mission whose quasireligious nature is explicit in the book's title. Where *Communion* describes clearly the process by which Strieber constructed a psychologically satisfying version of his abduction, the sequel, *Transformation,* expands on the scenario that the abduction projects. Hence, like many contactees, Strieber's visions contain apocalyptic warnings of the end of the world, along with mystical revelations and moments of profound emotional transfiguration.[40]

According to a rationalist point of view, the *source* of such narrative elements determines whether they are "true" or "false." That is, if alien abductions do not happen, then the visions Strieber had are fictional. But hard-line skeptics often assume that we can always distinguish between fiction and truth. No sympathetic observer of the legend process would agree. Legends, whatever else they are, are accounts of ambiguous experience, events that normal "factual" concepts cannot contain. Faith that all apparently paranormal events have a simple, rationalistic explanation, is itself a quasi-religious belief that some skeptics maintain with missionary zeal equal to Strieber's. A more realistic point of view concedes that such experiences, by their nature, challenge culturally derived rationality. It is therefore the job of belief-language to help those who have such experiences share them, and so integrate the paranormal into their overall sense of reality. William James, in *The Varieties of Religious Experience*, aptly describes this relationship:

I do believe that feeling is the deeper source of religion, and that philosophic and theological formulas are secondary products, like translations of a text into another tongue. . . . Feeling is private and dumb, and unable to give an account of itself. It allows that its results are mysteries and enigmas, declines to justify them rationally, and on occasion is willing that they should even pass for paradoxical and absurd. . . . To redeem religion from unwholesome privacy, and to give public status and universal right of way to its deliverances, has been reason's task.[41]

"A question can tear you apart," Strieber comments.[42] The lack of shared language for an otherworldly contact is debilitating; conversely, finding or creating language provides tremendous relief. The experience of being able to integrate such a contact with a new worldview is in itself frequently a emotional moment corresponding with religious conversion. But "conversion" is only the first stage in a total redefinition of one's life and worldview. Once Strieber accepted his initial abduction experience as real, he began constructing and reconstructing his past life, partly in subsequent hypnosis sessions, partly through testing the experiences directly remembered. And some of the reconstructions have come from subsequent encounters with the aliens, which have included visions of "a golden city," the temporary abduction of his son and his entire bank account, and magical apparitions of lights before himself and witnesses, as recorded in *Transformation*.

As Strieber has become increasingly skeptical about the ability to "prove" the visitors' physical reality, oddly he has become more convinced that the contacts *are* real. We could say that, having so drastically reformulated his memories of the past and his perspective of reality, Strieber has essentially entered a mythic world. Strieber's visions, in this regard, are no more bizarre than the encounters experienced by such minds as Joseph Smith, William Blake, or—most interestingly—Saul of Tarsus on the road to Damascus.

Thinking of a Green Monkey   There's a way you can make gold, said Manly Wade Wellman, a North Carolina fantasy writer who based his plots on American folklore. You put certain objects in a pot and say certain secret sayin's while it cooks over the fire. If you do everything right, nuggets pour out of the pot. But if anyone thinks about a blue monkey, nothing happens. In other words, human minds are programmed to "chunk" data, to make sense out of noise. Once we make a link between two ideas, we find it virtually impossible to think about one without bringing in the other. Telling us to cook the pot *without* associating the action with a blue monkey in effect forces us to do just that. So we will never, can never make gold. This explains why we are prone to see patterns quicker than fortuity: even when reality contradicts these patterns, we *still* see them. Simple debunking does little to "end" debate over paranormal claims. People won't stop, can't stop thinking about the blue monkey.

Sargant has noted that a sense of humor is one of the surest blocks to conversion, and mirth is a skeptic's first line of defense against works like *Communion* that convey a missionary message.[43] But humor, like an oversharpened razor carelessly used, may turn on its user. We need to admit that sane, intelligent people may sincerely perceive, or come to believe, that they have been attacked or abducted by paranormal agents. But such experiences are "irrational," just as many other paranormal claims have been assumed, on first hearing, to occur to people who are prone to thinking illogically. Such a presumption oftentimes leads into stereotyped thinking that has an illogical and subjective quality of its own. Gender biases, for instance, cut deeply through the contemporary discussion of the supernatural. In her study of ESP experiences, Leea Virtanen found that 81 percent of those who chose to report cases of telepathy were female. Several other surveys showed a similar trend in both the British Isles and the United States.[44] Does this prove that women are more prone than men to psychic experiences because they lack the firm intellectual powers of logic needed to explain such events rationally? Virtanan notes that as recently as the 1930s other collectors had collected such experiences predominantly from *men*.[45] And other surveys, based on random polls rather than volunteered testimony revealed no such sex-related predispositions toward ESP experiences. When the National Opinion Research Center conducted an extensive survey in 1973 on psychic experiences among Americans, it found only a 4 percent difference between males and females reporting cases of telepathy, déjà vu, and other common events.[46]

What we see here is the result of gender expectations: when cultural world-views allowed for frequent psychic experiences, males were more apt than women to take credit for them. As technological responsibilities fell more and more on males, Virtanan suggests, overt statements of psychic perceptions became more prone to ridicule and hence were repressed. Yet the debate between skeptics and believers remains colored by gender issues. The powerful political tensions pulling sexes in different directions can be seen in the predominantly male character of professional "skeptics" organizations like the Committee for Scientific Investigation of Claims of the Paranormal (CSICOP) (>95 percent male) and the heavily female (indeed feminist) membership of contemporary Wiccan or witchcraft movements. Such a sharp distinction is a factor of each sex's *freedom* to be psychic without social penalty, not some sex-linked personality or perceptual trait. And, ironically, many women have associated the power to accept psychic experiences as normal with strong positive social traits. Gillian Bennett found the firmest faith in psychic experiences in the personality that she termed the "family woman," that is, the female most motivated by reliance on and love for close relatives. Bennett conducted extensive interviews, not only concerning paranormal events but also the feelings and beliefs they provoked. She concluded that "women are far more likely to accept a supernatural belief if it is other-person centred, if it is geared to intuition, and if it helps to make the world seem safe and orderly."[47] Both Virtanan and Greeley found that individuals reporting contact with the paranormal also had "greater than normal sensitivity. . . . The joys and sorrows of life are deeply felt, and the experiences themselves indicate an exceptional interest in life." Is such a heightened sensitivity evidence for mental weakness? Greeley challenged this assumption. While psychic experiences seemed linked (weakly) to female gender, there was a much stronger correlation to youth and paradoxically to *higher* levels of education. He concluded: "It is not as simple as it used to be to write off a sex-related variable as a manifestation of feminine instability and frivolity. Even if there were no women's movement, it would still be hard to say that somehow or other the young and the better educated are emotionally inferior to the older and the less well educated. It may be that the heightened emotional and psi sensitivity to be found, apparently, in women, the young, and the better educated represents a superior mode of adjusting to the cosmos."[48]

Faced with such ambiguous social issues, it is no wonder that many folklorists have avoided the role played by the paranormal in contemporary life, preferring to deal with trivial matters or with social groups so marginal that debunking their beliefs has (up to now) had no political significance. As early as 1894, Andrew Lang, himself a psychic investigator, deplored this tendency. While he acknowledged that much alleged psychic phenomena might be the result of hallucination or trickery, he insisted that folklorists could not logically study "vague savage or popular beliefs" but refuse to deal with similar beliefs when they are held and affirmed by "educated living persons."[49] The discipline has ignored "dirty" topics like these, perhaps because any attempt to study them acknowledges the presence of threatening political and existential issues that, like the little man who wasn't there, we wish would simply go away. The result, ironically, is that folklorists have largely escaped controversy, but often at the cost of trivializing their discipline.

But Wellman's folk hero finally made gold. He warned himself and his fellow alchemists—no matter what—they should never, ever, *ever* think about a *green* monkey. Perhaps we should change the normal academic paradigm and see claims of the paranormal not as deviant but as *normal* parts of social life.[50] Supernatural sleep attacks occur commonly even in the absence of a cultural tradition, and studies summarized by Larry Danielson show that comparison of reports by "reliable" and "unreliable" percipients do not show as many differences in content as one might expect.[51] This does not mean that we accept every theory proposed to explain abductions. Work in this field, as we have seen, is as prone to slant as extreme skeptical approaches. At a conference on abduction research, Hufford took investigators to task for being unaware of relevant folklore research. Even research by professional scholars and therapists failed to recognize that paralysis attacks like the Old Hag were related to many abduction experiences. Since hagging has been reported around the world since ancient times, he notes, the phenomenon underlying abductions must also have deep historical roots and is related to other types of anomalous experience. These relationships, in fact, are often explicitly made by abductees like Strieber but often are strongly resisted by investigators who have committed to a rigid theory explaining abductions. Hufford concludes: "Adequate theory development regarding abduction experiences will require rigorous phenomenological inquiry in which the distinctions among observation, interpretation and language choice are made and empirically supported. Since all we have are reports, the reports must be as detailed and comparable as possible. Full, unedited accounts, not just summaries or frequency counts, will have to be published and analyzed.[52]

The Empirical Numen   Much more needs to be done in field study of experiences with the paranormal, a task that requires unusual sensitivity to informants' beliefs and unusual cooperation with collectors' academic needs. Folklorists are the academics best suited to this important work. We have the theoretical tools to distinguish between the experience observed, the interpretations provided by a culture, and the language choices used by an individual to mediate the two. Detailed textual studies, like that done on Bruce's Pizza Hut Ghost experience, would shed needed light on the complex social process of "naming" abduction experiences.

This puts two responsibilities on folklorists who study contemporary encounters with the paranormal. On the one hand, the actual phenomena described ought to be considered without cultural prejudice from the folklorist; too often those we collect from have already suffered enough psychic stress without our official disdain. On the other, the dispute and the precise linguistic forms needed to express such phenomena in public need to be examined and described as exactly as possible. For just as the numen is not the legend tradition, the legend tradition is not the memorate, and the three elements as often collide dissonantly as they coexist harmoniously. It is true that such analysis needs to be careful to show how these oppositions appear in other materials collected and analyzed, both by scholars and amateurs. But the issues are important, and the legend process is most active where the cultural belief-language least adequately explains empirical experiences.

But the problem of "objectivity" intrudes. "The folklore scholar is fortunate," Donald Ward says, "inasmuch as he need not concern himself with the question of the existence or nonexistence of paranormal phenomena. For the subject who is a believer, the experience is real, and it is the reality of experience and its relation to tradition which interests the folklore scholar . . . The folklorist is thus interested in the reality of the supernormal experience and not in the reality of paranormal phenomena."[53] This statement is perceptive, so far as it goes; the folklorist need not and should not believe in ghosts or in cultural anthropologists from Zeta Reticuli in order to examine how a culture sets up a belief-language to respond to the threat of the numinous.

But there is a danger in taking this approach too far. Ward prefers to see man "as a being who is governed by social restraints, fears, and who is capable of attributing mystical significance to his creative perceptions."[54] This assumes, however, that experiences or visions not sanctioned by "rational" modes of description are, ipso facto, the result of creative imagination. The supernatural experience thus becomes little more than an aesthetic puzzle to be solved, and we are free to take an abductee's terror in the face of the unknowable and dissect it for a pleasant afternoon pastime. Yet the person who has witnessed the supernormal *knows* he has had a real experience; what he is interested in is precisely the question of the existence of paranormal phenomena. In the case of persons objectively disturbed by memories of abduction, the proper response is not amusement but concern—not over the risk of UFO invaders but over the welfare of those who have encountered *it*, whatever it is. In this respect, Honko again seems closer to the mark in stressing that "Belief in the existence of spirits is founded not upon loose speculation, but upon concrete, personal experiences, the reality of which is reinforced by sensory perceptions. In this respect spirits are empirical beings. Although the investigator himself is unable to see the spirits, he must admit that his informant really saw them."[55]

Unless we grant the validity of this position, our analysis of any reported experience must necessarily reduce it to the status of untruth. We may continue to believe, in our own minds, that aliens are products of hypnogogic hallucination, or byproducts of sleep paralysis, or products of a special "part of the brain which is not normally used,"[56] or the result of "group psychosis."[57] But it is central to many informants that what they saw was real, not merely the reflection of what they wanted to see or had been culturally trained to see. Given statistics that suggest that such supernatural experiences are far more frequent than investigators have suspected, the folklorist ought to be the first not only to accept, but to defend their *empirical* status.

This is not to say that we must admit that "aliens" exist in the sense that Hopkins or Mack or Strieber or the even more extreme amateur investigators claim. For folklorists' power and utility reside in their marginal status. They have the right to *refuse*, in the best sense of the word, that is, to decline to accept as privileged *any* cultural explanation of numinous phenomena—not swamp gas, not extraterrestrials, not even vastation or idiopathic sleep paralysis. So empowered, we have the capacity, (provided that we choose to exercise it) of looking more closely at what witnesses are experiencing. We can give full value to the sociolinguistic difficulties they confront when they attempt to be true, not to the words of tradition, but to the world, to the empirical evidence they critically perceive.

And genuinely scientific studies need to focus carefully on the phenomenology of such events, which may reveal genuine correspondences among "abduction" events. Surveying the psychological and psychiatric literature relating to the experience, Hufford found no evidence that the Old Hag was linked to neurological or psychotic illnesses. The peculiar stability of the hallucinations' content across cultural boundaries and in the absence of traditions concerning it remains unexplained. If the support groups formed in the wake of the abduction publicity encourage others to produce a corpus of similar experiences, good may come from the work of abduction investigators. Professionals may be able to examine the phenomenology of the events described and determine more exactly what mechanisms lie behind them.

When we deny this power, we *refuse* in the meanest sense of the word; that is, we deny importance to our informants' critical nature and we affirm only our uncritical adherence to "rationality." For behind this kind of mean refusal, and behind the social sanctions, behind the ridicule, behind the threat of being called insane, we may hide our uneasy suspicion that the fault, after all, lies not with the "irrational" beholder but with "rationality" itself. For all our hardheadedness, we are still all amazed in this world.

So the numen, and the dispute it provokes, persist even into a contemporary age. Just as legends "conceived in technology can be the vehicles of new ideas," so too old phenomena and old ideas will continue to coexist with technology.[58] Further work in this area will have two practical values: first, we will understand how our cultural vocabulary and grammar restrict our capacity to describe experience, and second, we will hear, perhaps for the first time, what our informants so desperately are trying to say in the face of legendry.

PART THREE LEGEND AS LIFE

In 1991, a Dallas, Texas, woman wrote a letter to the popular magazine *Ebony*, claiming to be "C. J." a real-life "AIDS Mary" who was deliberately spreading the disease because she hated men. While the magazine could not verify the letter's accuracy, it printed it anyway, "as a warning to readers." Soon after, a woman contacted a local radio talk-show, identifying herself as "C. J." and agreeing to appear on a broadcast. In this, she described haunting nightclubs in the Dallas-Fort Worth area, picking up as many men as possible and having unprotected sex in order to give them AIDS. "I blame it on men, period" she told the radio audience. "I'm doing it to all the men because it was a man that gave it to me." In the end, both the author of the letter and the talk-show guest (two different women) proved to be hoaxers, but the event led to an extraordinary rise in males seeking AIDS screening and attending education seminars. "I look at what happened with C. J. as a fire drill, something that has made people aware of danger and risk," a local health official said.[1]

When "C. J." sent her letter and her counterpart appeared on the talk show, what had begun as a legend became real-life action. Similarly, when dozens of men came into health centers, legend was affecting life. Ostension is present whenever someone creates such "found narrative" out of real life or whenever someone creates a stir by manufacturing evidence for legendary events. Such cases test the boundaries of "life" and "legend" by staging actions that the players represent as real and that the audience overtly accepts as such. Yet such performances may not always be fiction: they may inspire real-life actions with lasting results.

Semiotician Umberto Eco first used this term to refer to moments in oral communication when, instead of using words, people substitute actions. "Would you like a cigarette?" might be signaled by waving a pack; "Stop talking" by a finger drawn across one's throat.[2] Entire legend plots can, in a similar way, be reduced to an allusive action. Freshmen living in dormitories often pass around a common legend in which a girl is attacked by a mysteri-

161

ous "hatchet man" and dies scratching at her roommate's door. For weeks after the story is circulated, girls frighten each other by scratching, rather than knocking, at each others' doors.[3]

A more unsettling complex of ostensive allusions came attached to a series of panics caused by rumors that sadists were trying to harm children by placing razor blades or other dangerous substances in Halloween candy.[4] Although no actual instances of anonymous sadists were ever documented,[5] parents and authority figures began altering their behavior according to the legend, cutting fruit or taking candy bags to x-ray rooms to look for razor blades. More disturbingly, children took to planting objects in their own treats to cause a stir in their community.[6] And on Halloween 1974 Ronald Clark O'Bryan of Houston killed his own son for insurance money by planting cyanide-laced candy in his trick or treat bag. Although O'Bryan tried to use the legend as a smoke screen, evidence linked him both to the candy and the poison, and he was convicted of the murder and executed in 1984.

Such complexes of legend and actions led Dégh and Vázsonyi to suggest that, even when no actual conspiracy of sadists exists, the ubiquity of information about such sadists itself tends to influence irrational individuals to commit criminal acts. Such a legend tradition, they conclude, constitutes an unorganized, nameless conspiracy unified by "a similar ideology and moral excuse for child murder and the commission of what is called 'expressive crime.' "[7] Not every legend is based on some real event, nor does it have the ghoulish ability to compel one to enact the legend in real life.[8] But the concept of ostension still helps explain a diversity of common events. Dégh and Vázsonyi propose several degrees of ostension, describing ways in which circulating narratives can influence reality, or at least the way reality is interpreted.

Ostension proper involves the literal acting out of a legend. While uncommon, some "satanic" murders have involved ostension of traditional plots. The 1989 abduction-murder of Mark Kilroy by a Matamoros drug gang influenced by the American cult movie *The Believers* seems one clear example.[9] Such instances, happily, are rare; more often what we see is some form of action that suggests the legend but does not fully enact it. Still, as we will see in the case of the Logan, Ohio, murders, ostension often cannot be totally ruled out.

Pseudo-ostension involves a hoax in which the participant produces evidence that the legend has been enacted: teens often fabricate evidence of cult sacrifices, even to the extent of killing animals and leaving occult symbols behind at the site. Often this involves a kind of initiation rite called a "legend-trip" in which experienced teens will take friends out to a remote site specially "decorated" with spooky paraphernalia to test their bravery. Many "trips" will involve mock rituals or hoaxes in which confederates imitate witches or supernatural figures.

Quasi-ostension involves a misinterpretation of naturally occurring events in terms of an existing legend: in the notorious "Toledo Dig" of 1986, law enforcement agents claimed random items of trash found in a drifter's cabin as evidence that human sacrifices had been conducted nearby.[10] And in northeastern Pennsylvania, teens have admitted being amused when they held open beer parties in an area alleged to be a "devil-worship" site and found police reluctant to approach them. In such cases, adolescents may encourage the legend to allow them to drink illegally without being molested.

Proto-ostension occurs when, to gain attention, persons take a story alleged to have happened to someone else and claim it as a personal experience of their own. Jeffrey Victor found during a cult panic in Jamestown, New York, that people swore to having seen mutilated dogs hanging from light poles; police found none.[11] Lauren Stratford gained the sympathy of several different California Pentecostal groups with a string of abuse stories, climaxing in a complex set of "baby-breeding" personal experience stories: these now seem to have been ostensive legends of this type.[12]

Obviously, when a panic strikes a community, many different forms of ostension may arise simultaneously, all tending to reinforce each other and maintain the sensation. The well-documented community panics in Missoula, Montana, in Jamestown, New York, and, as we will see, in Lansford, Pennsylvania, involved a wide range of allegedly "satanic" activities, from graveyard mischief to threatening letters.[13] In retrospect, these proved to be ostensive behavior, consisting of misinterpreting evidence, planting false evidence, and passing on legend as alleged experience. Those involved, pro and con, in the present satanic ritual abuse controversy might be well advised to keep ostension in mind when interpreting evidence. It is certainly true, as Kenneth Lanning of the FBI, has warned, that a group of child abusers might well incorporate elements from much-discussed ritual abuse cases into their acts to confuse children and make prosecution difficult.[14] Even if satanism is not a long-lived underground way of life, that is, the present publicity might well bring it into being.

On the other hand, folklore and sociological research suggests that literal ostension is far rarer in reality than the other forms. Pseudo-ostension may encourage parents who themselves abuse or even murder their own children to fabricate "legendary" evidence to direct police attention elsewhere. Quasi-ostension may lead overly anxious authorities to overinterpret evidence to make it fit police crime models when in fact the situation is less clear-cut. In a 1992 San Diego scandal, social workers used a boy's scar from a documented operation, talk about "devils and angels, people going to heaven, and fear about his grandmother dying," and a range of poorly documented "cult signals" to remove three children from their grandparents, their legal guardians. One medical expert claimed to have seen evidence of sexual abuse when he examined the youngest girl's genitals; later a respected child-abuse expert examined photographs and said, "I would use this picture to teach what normals look like." The children were released with official apologies.[15]

Finally, proto-ostension may well encourage persons sincerely trying to reconstruct a troubled youth to remember details from other stories as having happened to them as well. Clinical psychologist Sherrill Mulhern warns that the personality type most often claiming ritual abuse is also notable for being fantasy-prone and easily hypnotized, two conditions that may well lead to sincere but false memories.[16] Christian psychiatrist Basil Jackson also warned against naïveté in dealing with cases of demonic possession, a phenomenon closely related to multiple personality disorder (MPD), a mental disease characterized by apparent alternation of personalities. The fact that clients are "cured" of mental problems after sincerely undergoing exorcism, he argued, "does not prove that demons were involved or that the devil had anything whatsoever to do with the particular client or his condition." Indeed, he concludes, "the more ignorant we are of precise etiologic factors, the more esoteric are our interpretations and explanations likely to be."[17]

Events provoke stories; but it is far more likely that stories provoke events. Some forms of ostension are relatively benign; others can be deadly. As far back as 1978, evangelist Kurt E. Koch averred that devil-worshipping babysitters in the United States had actually roasted a baby in an oven.[18] A similar claim recently circulated during the Rochdale, England, panic over alleged satanic ritual abuse (SRA). Such an event has not been documented as having been committed by satanists; however, on at least two occasions young children have been killed by being placed in ovens as part of an improvised religious ceremony. In both cases, the rites were Christian exorcisms intended to banish the devil.[19]

We have to accept, as Dégh and Vázsonyi stress, "that fact can become narrative and narrative can become fact."[20]

Chapter 9

OSTENSION AS FOLK DRAMA

Camping in the United States involves playacting, by its very nature. Adults and adolescents, mainly from the city or suburbs, voluntarily give up modern comforts to live for a while in an imaginative re-creation of the "frontier" world. In the case of the institutionalized summer camp, in which campers and counselors from many different communities play at being pioneers or Indians, part of this make-believe necessarily involves initiations, by means of which the sense of a single community is formed, united against the real discomforts and reputed dangers of "the woods." Jay Mechling has recently described how the Boy Scout campfire event creates out of multiplicity a unified sense of "male solidarity and male world view."[1] Even though this event contains elements of "carefully rehearsed drama," Mechling says that comic skits performed at campfires are the only camp activities that can properly be called dramatic. In fact, there is one additional genuinely dramatic camp activity: ostensive ordeals.[2]

As Thomas A. Green has stressed, not all patterned events that use theatrical techniques can be considered dramas, and ostensive ordeals must thus be distinguished from nonmimetic events frequently collected in adolescent and camp circles.[3] Ostensive ordeals may be defined as contrived events in which a group of campers and counselors venture out to challenge supernatural beings, confront them in consciously dramatized form, then return to safety. An obligatory element is what Mechling has described as "liminal monsters," uncanny, extrahuman beings that are invoked to embody the group's psychic needs. Fully dramatized confrontations of this sort typically form part of initiation activities. Often elaborately staged with sound effects, lights, props, costumes, and other aids, they enact an encounter with the supernatural by means of several rehearsed players in front of a passive audience. Such events resemble and derive elements from both legend-trips and pseudo-ostensive

165

hoaxes popular among the same groups. Neither of these related activities, however, can be considered genuinely dramatic.

The adolescent legend-trip, as Kenneth A. Thigpen Jr. and others have noted, approaches drama in structure and is often conducted in a spirit of pretense rather than literal belief. As with the ostensive ordeal, it involves venturing out to a reputedly haunted site, invoking the supernatural, then returning to "safety" to share perceptions of what actually occurred. We might consider these three stages in the legend-trip as "scenes," but such a discussion would commit the fallacy of considering "life" as "theater." Actually, legend-trips differ from genuine drama in two ways. First, there is no clearly marked distinction between players and spectators, since all are really spectators. There may be differences in the ways adolescents perceive the events witnessed, some seeing them as genuinely supernatural, others taking the trip as mere entertainment and pretending to be scared. But no one (except perhaps the ghost) is enacting drama.

Second, the stated purpose of such activities is not entertainment but a sincere effort to test and define boundaries of the "real" world, and even the most jaded participant in a legend-trip may be genuinely terrified by a sudden, unexplained happening. Thus the legend-trip would fall under the heading of ritual, "the working, worshiping and acting on [one's] environment."[4] The overall structure may be patterned, but it is not drama.

Similarly, practical jokes, swindles, and hoaxes of all kinds, especially those played on uninitiated campers, may also involve elaborate staging and play-acting. The traditional snipe hunt (to be distinguished from the ostensive ordeal "real" snipe hunt later) is a common camp hoax that may involve elaborate role-playing and theatrical scenes and props. Groups of campers are encouraged to believe that by performing carefully prescribed actions they can lure snipe to their bags. Only after being taken to the "snipe ground" and enduring an eternity of bag holding, flashlight waving, and clucking do the uninitiated campers realize that what they had initially taken as a serious event was in fact a joke at their expense.[5] But here again there is no clearly marked separation of roles between players and spectators. Indeed, the success of the performance depends on making the spectator play a part in the hoax. Although the players recognize the contrived nature of the event, they deliberately hide this fact from the uninitiated. Following Erving Goffman, we might call such activity fabrication, or actions contrived not to entertain but to induce an audience "to have a false belief about what it is that is going on."[6]

Fabrication thus requires a difference in perspective between the hoaxer and the dupe, while true drama depends on all participants seeing the events in the same way. In order to characterize an event as genuinely dramatic, therefore, we need to establish two features over and beyond the mere use of dramatic techniques. First, there must be a clear separation between the roles of players and spectators from the outset, and, second, the spectators must be aware that the action is contrived, however engrossed they may become in the incidents.

Carefully balanced between ritual and fabrication are the events I have termed ostensive ordeals. Like the legend-trip, they begin with accounts of past happenings, journey into uncanny territory, contact the supernatural, and conclude with intense discussion. Like the fabrication, such events stage the journey and contact in such a way that contrived events are represented as real from start to finish.

Thus, from the campers' point of view, the ostensive ordeal comes close to ritual, since they are asked to believe that they are actually confronting supernatural forces. Likewise, from the counselors' point of view this type of event comes close to fabrication, since the sign of a good ostensive ordeal is that the campers apparently accept the events as literally real. Admittedly, to the extent that the counselors actually deceive and the campers actually believe, such events are not folk drama. But a close look at actual performances reveals that such a situation is unusual. If the campers did accept the incidents as real, they would fear for their personal safety and reject the camp as unsafe. Likewise, if they were to discover the event's falsity, they would feel tricked and humiliated, thus alienating them from the counselors and fragmenting the community spirit of the make-believe frontier.[7] When properly performed, however, such ostensive ordeals reinforce this sense of community by involving both campers and counselors on the same level of participation in the creation and maintenance of fantasy. A performance that does not fit the definition of folk drama, in other words, is for that very reason a failed performance.

"High Drama": Ostension as Performance   Hiram House Camp, in the East Cleveland suburbs, is especially rich in make-believe of all sorts, partly because of its social function, partly because of its flexible activities format. Originally part of a settlement project serving ethnic communities in the inner city of Cleveland, the camp now attracts mainly disadvantaged black children from the Hough district. Its staff, however, is mostly middle-to-upper-class white; therefore, cultural shock is unavoidable. As one means of minimizing conflict, therefore, the counselors resort to fantasy. Already a setting foreign to most of the urban campers, the woods are presented as hostile to counselors as well, peopled by a host of monsters, mutants, vicious animals, and ghosts. Significantly, few of them attack children; they go for the men at the top.

Since Hiram House's activities are not ruled by any particular scouting or religious institution, the counselors are relatively free to organize activities as they and their campers see fit. Thus not only stories about liminal monsters but a multitude of activities involving such beings are invented. The effect is to make the camp a self-contained liminal realm, distinct from both black and white cultures, in which representatives of the two function nearly as equals in the (fictional) battle to survive. Over the past decade Hiram House counselors have felt free to organize more and more elaborate activities as initiations into this liminal realm, which function to establish the temporary sense of community without which the camp experience at Hiram House would fail.

Not all such activities are dramatic, strictly speaking. Most, in fact, are similar to the legend-trip in that they are no more than legends deliberately left open-ended. Ross Johnson, an experienced storyteller at the camp, noted that if a narrative were given a conventional closed ending, "then everybody's dead or everybody's safe. That's no fun."[8] On the other hand, if the story were left without a conclusion, then it could be extended ostensively into present activities, with any unexpected noise or event becoming integrated into the fiction.

Two Hiram House activities, simultaneously current in tradition, do constitute genuine folk drama: a "Majaska hunt," in which the group seeks out the local camp monster, and a " 'real' snipe hunt," which features not mythical birds but horribly real vampirelike mammals. "High drama" is the term one counselor used to describe the first of these, and from the players' point of view both activities are complex scripted dramas involving multiple rehearsed incidents and roles. Of the two, the Majaska hunt is closest to the legend-trip and the open-ended legend; it is, in fact, a reenactment of one scene in the narrative describing the monster's origin. This story (which can run over an hour in the telling) relates how Majaska, an orphan of unknown origin, was raised by wild dogs when his foster parents were murdered by the tyrannical ogre Hermit Dan. When mature, Majaska confronted and killed the ogre, but by a trick of fate was himself transformed into an ogre and doomed to wander forever in the camp's thickest wilderness, an area called the Lost Trail. The story concludes:

The Lost Trail is a rather unique thing, as some of you may discover, hopefully not too soon.

You see what you think is a trail, and you start to follow it. And it becomes—harder and harder to see the trail in front of you. All of a sudden you say, "Why. there's no trail here, I think I'll go back," and you turn around—and there's no trail.

And so you stumble through the brush a little bit until you come onto another—supposed trail. And you start to follow this one. And the same thing happens: . . .

It'll be getting darker, getting to the point that it is now, you're hoping desperately for some way out, and all of a sudden you'll sense—that there's—something else—near you.

You'll walk on, and every once—in a while you'll think that you hear a step. And you stop—it stops.

And so you walk on—and you're too afraid to turn around—to see—what *fiend* may be lurking behind you.[9]

The Majaska hunt grows organically out of this open-ended conclusion, the threat of getting lost and being dogged by a fiend actually functioning as a challenge. In both cases when I heard this ending performed in context, the group immediately demanded to be shown to Lost Trail. On another occasion the narrator dropped it from the story, only to be taken to task by another counselor afterwards: "Look! We could have had a Majaska hunt tomorrow. Think about it!" Whereupon the teller defensively replied, "OK, OK, next time I will."

Channeling this spontaneous response into an activity, the counselors typically make plans to take several units (forty to fifty boys) together into Lost Trail, either that evening or the next. The first part of the narrative, of course, comes true; the counselors almost immediately "get lost." Ross Johnson, who participated in these hunts, recalled, "We knew the trails well enough that we could get the kids completely lost as far as they were concerned; simply by going up and down a ravine or two you could completely make them lose their sense of orientation." At this point the counselors would begin to adopt their roles, some playing it safe, others beginning to act foolhardy. This in turn would invite the monster's appearance. Jeff Jeske, one of the hunt's originators, described the dramatic climax:

And so they'd [the campers] be up on the other side [of a ravine] and one of the counselors would go back, or me—I got killed a couple of times in the story—would go up, and this counselor would be standing up on the other end of the ravine in plain, full view of the kids, and he'd be looking around and all of a sudden Majaska would come out wearing this really terrible mask, and robed in black and everything, sometimes in a hood, and he would have a knife.

And the kids would all be screaming because the counselor would have his back to Majaska and then Majaska would just come up behind him, and get him. And he'd [the counselor] roll down into the ravine and then another counselor would go across and he'd fight with Majaska and he'd get—And so the kids would be in a state of absolute terror . . . and the counselors would be acting really scared.

At this point the wiser counselors would give the word to withdraw, and the campers and wiser counselors would dash back over the trails to the main campgrounds. Some versions heightened the sense of panic by including further appearances by Majaska, but the drama proper was limited to the one scene in which the counselors, not the campers, were endangered by their own stupidity. The next day's discussions among the boys support this focus: Ross Johnson said, "The couple counselors that had supposedly been injured would go and get drunk that evening somewhere and come back the next day and look suitably beat up (laughs), and the next day of course, you know, the main topic of conversation was, 'Wow, we saw Majaska last night and look at these two guys, they run into him,' and of course they were saying, 'Boy, I was knocked unconscious, I could have been killed if he had had his ax,' and all this stuff. And that was sort of a highlight or a high point for the kids for the session."

The "real" snipe hunt, by contrast, does not grow out of the telling of a camp story, although its structure is recognizably similar. Indeed, since the campers do not know the plot before it is turned into action, it must be anticipated by detailed "bracketing" episodes and speeches that make clear what direction events will take next.[10] Nevertheless, the impact of this ostensive ordeal depends on having it turn out to be more complicated than the hoax of the same name (which most of the campers already know). In the performance that I taped, the action began without warning after a long period of chaotic milling around the Indian Boys' (ages 12–14) tent complex. As T. J. Miller and "Chief" Roseman, the counselors directing the activity, began to group the campers, three' other counselors—Matt Raidy, Chris Rowe, and Jon Hutchins ("Hutch")—suddenly took off up a trail toward the deep woods.

T. J. shouted up after them, "Hey, Matt, Chris, did you guys—you guys touch it? Hutch? You touch it?" When the three scouts yelled back scornfully, "Naah! No way!" the two organizers replied ominously, "You'll be sorry! Be careful!" This exchange immediately captured the campers' attention: up to this point no one had so much as mentioned that touching anything was crucial to the hunt. With the event already begun, then, the hunt's leaders explained what had happened and established a predictable structure for what was to follow.

T. J.: OK, now you guys might think this is kinda hokey but it's very true, and I'm not lying. This stick, right here that Chief is holding over there–last time, all the kids, in my group, touched that stick. I didn't touch that stick. I got bit.

Chief: He was the only one in his whole unit that went on the snipe hunt that got hurt.

T. J.: Now that's why I'm worried about Matt and Chris.

Chief: They don't believe it.

T. J.: They don't believe it.

Chief: So they didn't touch it, just—to get tough.[11]

The campers, as might be expected, then began to bombard the leaders with questions, and explanations followed: "snipe," far from being a harmless little bird to be captured alive, was a small weasel-like mammal with razor-sharp teeth and vampirelike supernatural powers. It could only be killed, or even avoided, with the aid of the unit's magic ironwood stick, given them by the area's original Indian inhabitants.[12] All these details, while they serve to make it clear that this will not be the usual hoax, are incidental to this scene's dramatic function. By establishing a narrative interdiction that the scouts have violated, and by referring to earlier hunts in which such violation brought serious consequences, the hunt leaders effectively bracketed what was to follow as yet another enactment of a predictable plot. In the past, whoever refused to touch the stick was bitten; the same can be expected to happen now.

And in fact, while the campers were attending to this episode, the three scouts were busy setting up the next one. Previously in the day a trip had been made to a local blood bank to obtain some outdated blood, so, after arranging Matt and Chris in suitably grotesque positions, Hutch poured over them a liberal amount of genuine human blood. The campers, following the scouts' trail into the deep woods, thus came upon what the first episode had led them to expect: a realistically snipe-bitten counselor. The focus of the hunt then shifted from challenging the supernatural to returning safely and, more important, saving the counselors' lives. Stretchers were brought up, and, with a rearguard set to keep more snipe from attacking, the whole unit returned with the injured to the tent complex. There followed a tense pause, while the counselors were examined at the infirmary, then the campers were gathered again to hear that Matt had only "a fifty-fifty chance" of living. At this point Crazy Ed, the unit's local sorcerer, came forward dressed in a conjurer's robe. After asking the whole group—campers and counselors—to join hands and focus its "power" on him, he invoked the "lord of the nether world" to help him revive the counselor's life. After a silence, Crazy Ed announced that the prayer was successful and Matt would live, but added, "Let no evil be spoken tonight or he will die." This ceremony marked the end of the event; campers and counselors dispersed in silence and, after a short period of whispering, they retired to their bedrolls. The next day the camp was back to normal: the wounded counselors returned, each with a token bandage on his left shoulder, and the campers enthusiastically shared their accounts of what it was that had gone on.

Both activities, seen from the perspective of the counselors who put them on, are dramatic scriptings—"high drama" in their terms. They involve assigned, rehearsed roles (including ordeal leader, victim, or monster) and their performance includes specified costuming, props, effects, and, at times, set speeches and dialogue. Much changes from year to year, since many campers return annually and would be too familiar with the previous year's production. Still, the structure of these ordeals has remained stable, the Majaska hunt since 1971, and the "real" snipe hunt since 1978. Both follow a predetermined, predictable plot in which the violation of a prohibition is followed by attack by the supernatural and the group's retreat. There is no question, therefore, that these events are dramatic in form and transmission, but it remains to be seen whether they are genuine dramas in performance: to what extent are the campers spectators who collaborate with the counselors in sustaining the illusion of "life"?

"This Is No Game": The Audience's Role   In commenting on such events, the counselors often boasted about how "realistic" the action was and how "terrified" their campers were by it. If we take such remarks literally, we would have to see these ostensive ordeals as complex fabrications exactly analogous to those perpetuated on "childlike" blacks by the Ku Klux Klan during reconstruction days.[13] There would seem, at first, little difference between the hooded, masked Klansmen who played at being revenants of Confederate dead at Shiloh and the hooded, masked Majaska player who jumps out to terrify a group of "credulous" black adolescents. Even if we concede that Hiram House counselors are not acting out of malice and that their intent is to entertain, not oppress, the issue of whether such events are genuine folk drama cannot be settled by one point of view alone. It is the perception of the event that defines its nature, and such a perception is no simple thing to characterize. Nearly all campers said the events they witnessed were "real," and suppressed any skeptic bold enough to say that they were "fake." Yet they observed the violence depicted with little anxiety about personal safety. There were some, to be sure, who did respond with genuine terror, but neither counselors nor fellow campers encouraged this reaction. The ostensive ordeal thus plays with an ambiguous response, neither skepticism nor terror, but engrossment. Central to creating this response is the way the ostensive ordeal distances the audience from the action, thus emphasizing the campers' security, while its predictable structure encourages them to join with the players as willing collaborators in unreality.

Students of related traditional performances have reported similar spectator responses. Fans of professional wrestling often assert that the matches are absolutely authentic, as Mark Workman has noted, even though all wrestlers and most spectators recognize that bouts follow stereotyped plots. The peculiar attraction of the sport, Workman concludes, is that it allows this liminal response to last an unusually long time, for "it is in the articulation between 'real life' and professional wrestling that wrestling manages to sustain its relevance in the eyes of its audience."[14] Similarly, Gary Hall has described how participants in legend-trips will "willingly suspend disbelief in supernatural haunts and other horrors" in order to become caught up in the event's excitement. At the same time, active disbelief is discouraged, since it would prevent participants from getting into the right mood. Thus adolescents need not believe that the horrors they confront are real, Hall argues, "they simply do not disbelieve. Questions of actual belief or nonbelief are largely irrelevant during the drama and excitement of the trip."[15]

Sociologist Ikuya Sato has made a similar finding studying the activities of adolescent gangs in terms of play theory. Previous analyses of youth crime, he noted, attributed delinquency to the participants' stressful environment and to peer pressure forcing individuals to conform to a group norm. But Sato's interviews with members of a Japanese motorcycle gang showed that they, like many American gang members, participated in "forbidden" activities simply because the action and risk involved were "fun."[16] Sato argues that "playlike deviance" provides groups of teenagers with a loosely constructed set of rules for generating "fun." Such rules create a liminal middle ground between conformity to norms and random actions by defining the situation in terms of an alternate reality. He concludes that such play "includes a great latitude for improvisation and often constitutes a loose dramaturgical system on the basis of which youngsters can generate their own 'street corner myth' or other narratives with more or less distinctive plots and themes. The dramaturgical system is flexible enough to allow each of the youngsters a considerable degree of improvisational performances."[17]

Such "street drama" includes exaggerated and distorted images of adult roles, and Sato suggests a parallel with Third World initiation rituals, in which "some of the values, norms, and styles in ordinary life are presented dramatically, comically, and grotesquely."[18] Sato's sociological findings fit well with summer camp situations in which excitement is generated by superimposing a fictional framework onto everyday life. This excitement mimics genuine fear and involvement in dangerous events. But it is pleasurable because participants recognize that the events are part of a structured, fictive plot, that they are insulated from the real-life implications of their actions, and that the event will eventually come to full closure and they can leave it behind. In the same way, visitors to a "haunted house" can express exaggerated responses to images of monsters and mad killers because they recognize the origins of the images in movie and fiction plots, the people enacting the bogeymen cannot cross certain boundaries and attack spectators, and the experience is limited to a certain time and place.[19] As Sato notes, "An activity can be playful only when there is an implicit or explicit assumption that a free choice exists between thrilling play and everyday life. Even a thrilling excursion into an extremely dangerous situation presupposes a secure starting point and a safe destination."[20]

Such traditional activities, as well as mass-culture performances like horror movies, become ways of playing with the boundaries of reality and fiction when participants choose to behave as if the events dramatized were real. It is therefore more likely that these campers' response—even if the counselors often do feel that their ostensive ordeals deceive their audiences—is not literal belief but dramatic engrossment that includes active cooperation with the artifice.

The premises from which the ostensive ordeals begin are strongly bracketed in time and space. That is, these dramas include, at the very outset, signals that allow the audience to predict what will happen next and where it will happen. The Majaska campfire story that precedes and informs the hunt is framed as conscious fantasy by its long-ago setting and its hero and ogre protagonists, more typical of fairy-tale plots than of legends. While campers treat it with respect and may even seriously discuss "belief" in Majaska, few of them see it as historical truth, least of all the older adolescents who engage in the hunt, and the main interest of the event is what the adults will do. The narrative simultaneously frames the ostensive ordeal that follows as part of a contrived, predictable fiction. Spatial brackets then are provided by appropriate props along the way. Ross Johnson recalled, "And then we'd be going along and—'Oh my God! Look, there's an ax in the log over there!' And we'd go over and usually there was a little ketchup or some similar item squirted on it, and of course nobody needed to say it was—Majaska's ax."

Other performances added a "bloody" shirt to the ax, but in any case the prop made it clear that the scene of the drama had been reached. Majaska's attack therefore comes as a dramatic climax to this preparation, not as an unexpected shock.

For all the supposed terror that met Majaska's appearance, counselors' accounts of the hunts make it clear that the typical bunch of campers is a belligerent, skeptical group. The part of the monster had to be cast carefully, Ross Johnson noted: "usually not one of the counselors, 'cause the kids were pretty sharp and they'd notice that he was missing." Another counselor, who often watched the campers return "panic-stricken" from these hunts, recalled that "they get down there and—'Who was that?' And pretty soon somebody comes up with who it was. Who's missing from the counselors or who isn't on duty." An immediate problem was keeping the more aggressive campers from interfering with the players. The physical boundaries of the scene, therefore, were planned not only to distance spectators emotionally from the action, but also to keep campers physically on the other side of the ravine, where other counselors could thwart any attempts to get into the act. This effort to keep the audience detached from the action is one feature that distinguishes the ostensive ordeal from most hoaxes: not only do players avoid involving spectators in the action, they actively prevent it.

Likewise in the "real" snipe hunt, few campers actually behaved as if threatened by supernatural forces. The folktale frame of the opening action, in which the hunt leaders explained how previous violators of the taboo were punished, produced dramatic expectations that were heightened by the leaders' protest that the event was not a fiction. When one counselor warned the campers, "OK, listen up, listen up fellows, this is no game. This is no game, I'm serious. This is for real. And it ain't no game," in fact he was underscoring the drama's narrative bracketing: this is not for real; what follows is a dramatic scripting with a foregone conclusion. As with the Majaska hunt, however, the campers responded warily, though skeptics were shouted down. At the scene of the first wounded counselor, one boy complained, "They keep saying that's fake blood—that's not!" And on the retreat to camp another camper went down the line, insisting, "Hey, hey, that's real blood, I took a—I tasted it—it is real blood." When a more skeptical boy challenged him with, "It taste like salt?" he shot back, "No, it tastes like blood!" The blood was indeed real, but it is unlikely that the campers would have gone to such ends to test and affirm its authenticity unless they saw it not as part of a horrifying accident but as an important stage effect that they were supposed to taste and appreciate.

As might be expected, individual responses initially ranged from extreme (though silenced) skepticism to literal belief, and a few campers did admit to being fearful at the scene of the "accident." It is thus significant that neither the counselors nor the other campers made any effort to exploit this fear. Rather, when a camper expressed anxiety, counselors immediately reaffirmed the drama's spatial brackets: touching the stick automatically provided permanent protection from snipe. If vampirelike supernatural animals exist, so does the stick's magic power that ensures that any violence be kept distant from the audience. Further magic rituals by Crazy Ed and others made it clear that the danger invoked would not touch the campers. The campers too were concerned with who was actually scared, but, rather than taunting the more credulous, the involved spectators' response was to display their own lack of fear, encouraging the fearful to play along. Even before the group returned to safe ground this display began. When the counselor supervising the rearguard asked a departing group, "Where you guys all going?" one remaining camper commented disdainfully, "They going home, boy, they scared!" Another chimed in, "I ain't scared, everybody here ain't scared—you scared?" When a third admitted, not without pride, "I'm scared, but I'm staying," the rest let it pass, boasting and brandishing their snipe-killing sticks. It was important to the campers to find out who was cooperating with the drama and who was literally taken in, but they allowed even the scared ones to share in their aggressive display of manhood.[21] The "real" snipe hunt, instead of allowing "superior" counselors and initiated campers to harass social inferiors, stressed a community response to the threat, and, instead of being singled out, the fearful were encouraged by the terms of the drama to trust in the strength of the whole unit. "Hey I tell you," one counselor reassured his group, "you guys, safe in numbers, safety in numbers, you ever heard that? We got enough here that no snipe gonna be able to do anything to us."

"I Feel Power—Being Drawn from You": Ostension and *Communitas*
Looking at both events in the larger context of the camp's social function, we see that this "safety in numbers" is central to the ostensive ordeal's success. The initial gathering of campers and counselors, as we have seen, represents distinct and often hostile ethnic communities. Forming a sense of *communitas*, in Victor Turner's term, is essential to the camp's operation, and, as several counselors told me, the worst way to accomplish this would be to assert social superiority through a process of hazing and ridiculing newcomers.[22] Such a procedure, even though it would be in line with most initiations that include a rite of passage, would resemble too closely the racist fabrications described before, and would tend to increase rather than lessen the distance between ethnic factions. In this sense, then, the ostensive ordeal at Hiram House creatively reverses the typical rite of passage. The campers here are being initiated into a temporary fictive community, but they are not subjected to abuse; rather, the counselors create a contrived liminal situation to which they subject themselves. The ostensive ordeal thus acts as an analogue

to the ritual "lowering of the high" that Turner has documented, except that the counselors, who actually are the ones who hold social power here, act as if it were the campers who were most in control of the situation. Within the terms of this pretense, the counselors are not only proven foolish but "killed" in a ceremonial fashion.

It is therefore important that the ordeal draw a strict line between players and spectators, since the forces of horror attack only the superiors, who are brought low. It is also important that the plot be seen as predictable, since if the campers can foretell what a counselor's careless act will lead to, then they are, imaginatively, in control, while the player is "helpless." In both ways the rank of the counselor, and of counselors in general, is temporarily reduced, and the campers' responsibilities within the community correspondingly become more important.

This leveling function of the ostensive ordeal makes it clear why Majaska, and not another of the camp's pantheon of supernatural beings, is the agent of a ostensive ordeal. As noted earlier, Majaska is not the usual camp bogie: although disfigured and uncanny, he is a sympathetic figure to campers. From the start the names of the antagonists suggest the campfire narrative's political significance. The name "Majaska" suggests both "majestic" and ethnic origins. (In fact, according to the narrative, he was raised by Chinese parents, but his ultimate origins remain unknown.) His counterpart, given the distinctively Anglo "Dan" for his name, is further characterized in the narrative as a vicious bigot, obsessed with murdering all ethnic trespassers found within the territory that he sees as his alone. Majaska, having grown up in the street-gang environment of a wild dog pack, finally dethrones the bigot in a climactic battle. Thus for most ethnic campers, Majaska is a heroic figure who embodies their desires to confront and defeat social repression. The Majaska hunt thus dramatizes not only the narrative's open-ended conclusion but also the monster's continuing ability to entrap and disgrace smug authority figures.

Even though an effort is made to keep campers physically separated from the action, nevertheless each counselor interviewed told of at least one instance when campers managed to get into the act. One "Majaska," in fact, was thrown over a cliff by an overzealous band of rescuers. While such instances were uncommon, they still represented a constant threat to performance, since campers who crossed the spatial boundaries of the drama and became active participants would have to be made partners with the players or else the illusion would be destroyed. The constant tendency of campers to out-Majaska Majaska, moreover, indicates not credulity but recognition that the ostensive ordeal is a moment during which traditional power structures are no longer in effect, thereby giving campers license to manhandle the Majaska player without fear of retribution. Certainly this is the case in one incident recounted by Ross Johnson:

> we had one time when the kids—we had a couple kids that were sort of old to be there, they were like fourteen or fifteen, I don't understand what they were doing at camp. Yeah, they took off after [the Majaska player] and nobody was going to stop them.
>
> And we took off right after the kids, and the kids caught up with—I forget who the person was playing the part at that time—tackled him and the two of these kids were pretty big and so two of them could pretty well handle this guy. And they weren't really hurting him, I'm sure they knew he was really the counselor and not Majaska, you know.
>
> But we stopped them and here's where the old "Well, let's play a trick on the other kids" routine came into play. And so we just got them into the act. And then we—fortunately we were out of sight and nobody really saw what was happening—we suitably dirtied them up and they came back and gave a similar story as what the counselors would do. . . .
>
> I'm sure that they were just out to spoil everybody else's fun. But we were able fortunately to turn that situation around and it turned out to be a good experience actually.

In this case the campers who disrupted the ordeal not only avoided punishment but were even rewarded by being assigned parts in the drama, thereby making them equal in social rank to the counselors. It is thus easy to see in the Majaska hunt a dramatized, and thereby controlled, rebellion against authority.

The "real" snipe hunt is structured around a similar lowering of rank but focuses less on revolt than on campers' responsibility to restore order after it has been lost through a counselor's stupidity. Once counselors have been proven fallible, though, campers take a free role in reinterpreting the significance of events, refusing to accept pat morals without emendation. One small-group discussion during a pause in the action showed Straff, one of the participating counselors, continually defending his moralistic view of the drama, while his campers picked holes in it:

Straff: Y'all touch the stick?
Chorus of voices: Uh-huh, yeah.
Straff: Matt and Chris touch the stick?
Chorus: No.
One camper: That's why they got it!
Straff: That was stupid.

Another camper: Hutch didn't touch it!

Another: Hutch didn't either!

Straff: Hutch is fast. [Laughs nervously.] Hutch is lucky. That was stupid—some guys don't—

Another: Hutch a neat ol' man!

Straff: If I didn't like them so much I'd say they deserved it! They deserved it—they should know better than to go out there without touching the stick. That's ridiculous.

Another: [sarcastically] You get bit?

Straff: Yeah, I got bit last year, we didn't have a stick, we didn't have a stick last year, that was it.

Hutch, the unit's senior counselor, was also its only black staffer, and the campers found it significant that he too flouted the stick's magic power (though less conspicuously) and yet escaped without harm. Similarly, the moralizing white counselor, in spite of his lame excuse, stood exposed as ridiculous by his own interpretation. While there was no opportunity, or reason, for mock-revolt, the terms of the ordeal still allowed campers to describe white counselors as "stupid," while recognizing the one black counselor as a heroic "neat ol' man."

The closing scene of the event, nevertheless, stressed unity of purpose, not ridicule of authority. It was the heroic Hutch who initiated the final ceremony, warning his campers, "If we want to pull Matt through, we need complete silence. You guys understand that? If you guys don't never be serious another day in your life you better be serious now." The pseudo-magical trappings of Crazy Ed's invocation are irrelevant to his speech's function as a closing frame, beginning and ending with gestures of solidarity. First, Crazy Ed insisted that everyone join hands and concentrate on Matt's condition, an act that had to be carried out with total seriousness before he would proceed. "I feel power—being drawn from you. Concern—for your counselor and friend . . . Concentrate!—you four!—concentrate! Without your help he will die." Similarly, as he dismissed the assembly (thus concluding the drama), Crazy Ed warned that the whole unit must depart without speaking out loud and keep the peace for the rest of the night, "or he will die." This closing scene restored the community's well-being through group action that was, as before, based on an inversion of roles. Instead of the counselors acting as if they had the power of life and death over the campers, here the campers' "power" was the mysterious force that healed the dying counselor. When Matt returned the next day, miraculously recovered, the ritual lowering of the high was complete, and the campers' role in maintaining the community's integrity had been duly celebrated.

Needling Whitey In this sense, the dynamics of ostensive ordeals can be compared with events that involve a more complex form of "street drama." The "snipe hunt," with its artistic use of real blood, took place in a relatively innocent time before the AIDS pandemic. A grimmer form of ostensive drama emerged shortly before Halloween 1989 in the Upper West Side of Manhattan in New York City. Beginning on October 21, black teenagers (mostly girls) jabbed needles or pins into the back or necks of randomly chosen female white pedestrians. In all, forty-one women reported being pricked by the gangs, who sometimes giggled or laughed loudly—"Joker style"—when their victims turned around.

Additional anxiety was created by television coverage that repeatedly suggested that the gang was using a syringe containing AIDS-tainted blood. Local experts discounted the fears, noting that it would be impossible for AIDS to be communicated in this way, even if the mysterious needle had been recently used by an infected drug addict. Nevertheless, residents in the area reported that they were afraid to leave home: one noted, "I'm not a coward, but I'm scared. I don't know what's in the needle."[23] Others went out wearing thick leather jackets and cautioned others to do so as well.

A *New York Times* reporter commented, "In a city where finding reasons and explanations for even horrible incidents can help people deal with their worries, residents of the Upper West Side seem most upset by the meaninglessness of the attacks. They are afraid, but in a new way, and they feel perhaps even more helpless than they would over a spate of shootings or robberies. Those are, at least, comprehensible." The article continued by quoting a social worker from the area, with part of the quote featured prominently in a boldface "call-out" on the *Times* page: "I really don't know what the purpose of using needles is. . . . Do they just want to scare you or do they want to transfer a disease or something?"[24]

New York City Mayor Edward I. Koch offered a $10,000 reward to anyone offering information to help arrest the gang responsible. On Halloween night more than seventy officers, both undercover and uniformed, patrolled the area, hoping to catch the gangs in the act. Later, *Newsweek* commented that in many sites it looked "as if martial law had been imposed." Within a week, however, ten black teenagers were arrested and charged with the incidents. The explanation offered by police was that the youths simply "felt it was fun to run down the street and stick females and see their reaction."[25]

The official explanation may well be true, as the "Mystery Assailant Syndrome" is nothing new to big cities. Michael Goss has done an intensive study of a panic that occurred in Halifax, England, in November 1938, when an unidentified "slasher" inflicted superficial cuts on a series of women with a razor blade. In his analysis, Goss traces a series of similar panics, dating back to a London "monster" who in 1788–90 pricked ladies' thighs and buttocks with a sharp knife. As in New York City, police patrols were increased and ladies wore protective clothing; one cartoonist showed women being fitted with copper petticoats. In some such panics, the attacks appear to have been the result of mass hysteria, and many "victims" later admitted that they had inflicted the evidence of an attack on themselves. But in other cases there clearly were real assailants, and, in any case, Goss concludes, "sooner or later the Slasher or someone like him will be back in our streets and in our imaginations.[26]

But one also suspects that the teens knew the old legend about unattended women walking down the street who are attacked by a man with a "poisoned needle." My mother recalled a variant from Baltimore, Maryland, ca. 1920, where the man is seeking pretty girls to sell into "white slavery" (involuntary prostitution), and the needle contains a powerful sedative or anesthetic. This rumor is at least as old as 1914, when the state of Massachusetts ordered an official investigation into "the white slave traffic, so called" and recorded a number of contemporary legends about near-abductions. One, the final report observed, "alleges the administration of a narcotic drug by the use of a hypodermic needle by a procurer, who plies the needle on his victim as he passes her on the street, or as he sits beside her in the street car or in the theatre." Such stories were thoroughly investigated, the report continues, but each one was "either found to be a vague rumor, where one person has told another that some friend of the former (who invariably in turn referred the story farther back) heard that the thing happened, or, in a few instances, imaginary occurrences explained by hysteria or actual malingering. Several of the stories were easily recognized versions of incidents in certain books or plays."[27] (As "The Attempted Abduction," Brunvand notes, this legend type remains in active circulation. Sometimes the young girls are injected with heroin, cocaine, or LSD, and the drug may be administered in the buttocks through a seat in a darkened movie theatre, a detail remembered also by my mother.)[28]

In general, though, this legend tends to reflect the Anglo majority's fears of intrusive minorities, especially blacks. Even the most commonly feared outcomes of the abductions—sale into "white" slavery or a pornography "black" market—make an explicit comparison of the privileges of the white upper class and the subjugation of the black working class. The horror behind the legend, in other words, is not that decent white girls will become prostitutes but that abducting and selling them in this way will turn them into slaves, essentially making them Negroes.

It's impossible to tell how many African Americans are aware of this level of the legend's significance for Anglos. In any case, the legend circulates among blacks as well and has its own levels of significance for their culture. In Washington D.C., Gladys-Marie Fry collected "night doctor" legends, in which white medical students abducted poor blacks to experiment on them or dissect their bodies. They were thought to sneak up behind blacks on the street and stick anesthetic needles in their backs. One informant said: "They say they'd throw some kind of a needle, or something, and it would stick you and that's the way they would catch you. . . . They say you'd stop right there and you wouldn't move another peg."[29] It's likely, therefore, that the pinprick attacks were legend performances through acts of ostension, literally "needling" the previously dominant white class and symbolically turning the tables on them. Previously, blacks were free from black slavery, but they were still subject to unauthorized sterilization and other dehumanizing acts of medical manipulation (such as the notorious Tuskegee syphilis experiments). As Patricia A. Turner has shown, African Americans widely believe that AIDS is yet another white medical "experiment" in which the CIA has used Africans as guinea pigs to test biological warfare."[30] So, to New York City blacks, it must have been fortuitous that frightened whites assumed that the gang's mysterious needle contained not a narcotic or sedative but the same virus with which Anglos supposedly infected Africans.

Now the needle was in the other hand. For the incidents took place in the middle of a bitter political campaign filled with racial innuendoes. After defeating incumbent Mayor Koch in the Democratic primary, Afro-American David Dinkins was virtually assured victory in the November general election. But in a city where Democrats outnumber Republicans five to one, the actual outcome was much closer. Blacks overwhelmingly supported Dinkins, while 70 percent of whites voted for his Italian-American opponent, and traditionally Anglo neighborhoods turned out in extraordinarily large numbers to vote against Dinkins. "Racism is too gentle a word," the mayor-elect's advisor said. "This was a pure antiblack vote."[31] Nevertheless, Dinkins won, as did black candidates in Connecticut, Virginia, North Carolina, and Washington State, claiming positions once reserved for whites only.

Probably, then, the New York City pinprick attacks, like the Hiram House ostensive ordeals, celebrated this shift of ethnic power. The wounds inflicted were superficial and harmless, but the black teenagers fully appreciated the way such events reversed traditional power structures and became—like the comic-book Joker—a legendary expression of the power of absurdity. Although these events cannot be considered true rituals in Victor Turner's sense, as they do not involve the characteristic stripping of rank from the initiates, these dramas do serve a ritual-like function by stressing that safety lies in numbers, that is, in the unit's functioning as a whole. The Hiram House campers were tested, but in such a way as to deflect the ridicule normally aimed at initiates onto their social superiors, who were proven to be fallible and in need of help from quick-witted campers.

Involvement in such ostensive ordeals is intense, but not because campers believe that the action presented "is life." Rather, involvement in the ordeal "as life" requires a creative suspension of disbelief, in which the camper is encouraged to help create the fantasy world of the camp. Moreover, by submitting to this liminal emotion and agreeing to believe in the terms of the drama—Majaska's power to entrap counselors, the stick's power to ward off snipe—the camper simultaneously agrees to believe in the *communitas,* the liminal state in which diverse individuals can live, however temporarily, in an egalitarian society that owes little to white suburbia or black inner-city. It is the desire to believe in this ideal that prompts the campers themselves to take the lead in suppressing skepticism.

At the very end of the "real" snipe hunt, as Crazy Ed was giving a last warning not to speak out loud, one camper threatened to start yelling out of his tent. The others angrily hushed him, and when he defiantly said, "I'm gonna let him die!" the others quashed him with the rules of the drama: "Get back in bed!" "You get back in bed and you cut out the light!" "Think about Matt!" "Now I'm telling you—that was real blood!"

When Drama Fails   After the "real" snipe hunt, I witnessed yet another dramalike event at Hiram House. It too involved a scripted performance with assigned roles, costumes, props, and sound effects—yet as drama it was a total failure. To begin with, it was organized solely by a group of counselors, partly as a punitive measure against a cabin of campers who had scoffed at camp fictions like Crazy Ed's "sorcery." But when they heard, out of the blue, that Ed was planning to make a night visit to the cabin, they were unnerved. Even before his arrival they actually began to sob, even though their counselors tried to shame them into courage by calling them "a bunch of girls." A shocked silence followed when Crazy Ed stormed in, threatening supernatural penalties to nonbelievers. After Ed had warmed up by "forcing" the other counselors to writhe on the ground as if demented, suddenly one of the campers began to heckle him. One of the counselors quietly rose, as if programmed like a robot, walked over to the boy's bunk, picked him up, and threw him heavily to the ground.

The camper, of course, was in on the plot, and a cot had been placed there

to break his fall. But the effect was so unexpected and realistic that it electri-
fied the whole cabin—including Crazy Ed—none of whom had any idea this
would happen. Ed tried to resume the ceremony, which involved putting a
curse on the location, but after some additional hocus-pocus he recognized
that the mood was becoming genuinely horrifying, so he abruptly broke off
his act, switched on the cabin's overheard lights, and declared the event at an
end. Still, the campers were so frightened that it took the counselors over an
hour to quiet them down for sleep. During the postmortem at a nearby bar,
one of the cabin's counselors confided, "Those campers are going to be angels
from now on." They may well have been well behaved, but the group I
lunched with the next day seemed bitter too. Normal meal preparation took
far longer than usual, while the campers complained, whined, wrangled
among themselves, and threatened to write home to their parents. Community was not achieved; indeed, once morning had come and the campers had
realized the event's true nature, their disillusionment prevented any further
attempt to unify the group.

The counselors had not intended to intimidate, they admitted later, but
only to initiate this cabin into the uncanny side of the camp's fictive realm.
But in this case what was intended as theater became fabrication: the campers,
unable to predict or control the events they witnessed, perceived them as real-
life threats to their safety and responded with terror. When the fabrication
was exposed, moreover, the counselors stood discredited in the campers' eyes,
thus making further ostensive ordeals impossible.[32] Had the sole intent been
social control, the performance might have been judged successful—by the
counselors—but as a drama that was supposed to create a sense of *communitas,* it failed.

The ostensive ordeal must thus maintain a fine distinction between apparent reality and perceived fiction. As drama that plays at being as lifelike as
possible, it is filled with inherent social risks. Those who put on an inept
performance—that is, one that does not provide enough clues that it is a
dramatic scripting after all—risk provoking resentment both from campers
and from camp administrators who must deal with campers' and parents'
complaints. As the result of one overly realistic Majaska hunt, for example,
the whole complex of Majaska lore-narrative, ostensive ordeal, and all—was
suppressed for a year by the camp's executive director. The "real" snipe hunt
I witnessed was a success among the older boys for whom it was staged, but
by accident a group of younger campers was swept up unawares in the action,
and the fright they received led to headaches for camp administrators. James
P. Leary, commenting on ostensive ordeals once performed at an Indiana
camp, reported that similar incidents have caused Boy Scout leaders to dis-

courage the use of horror in all camp activities.³³ The tradition behind such dramas is therefore tenuous, maintained so long as counselors are sensitive enough to perform them correctly, defunct as soon as accounts of botched performances come to the front desk's notice.

Yet the art, and the magic, of the camp community lies in this ambiguous response. When ostensive ordeals work successfully, they can be one of the most potent means of initiating campers into this liminal realm. Even the executive director of Hiram House was careful to distinguish what he tried to prevent—"scaring the hell out of the kids"—from the "feeling of excitement and anticipation and suspense" that he felt responsible use of horror could evoke. The trick to performing in such a context, then, is to say, "This is for real," and yet imply exactly the opposite, a complex art to which dualistic approaches to such material cannot hope to do justice. When the trick works, the highest praise would be a comment like one made to me by a camper during the "real" snipe hunt: "Isn't this fun? Isn't this kind of fun? Yeah—it's not too scary."

Chapter 10

WHAT REALLY HAPPENED AT GORE ORPHANAGE

There is this place . . . it's kind of close to my town and it's called "Gore Orphanage" and it was back in the 1800s I believe. It was an old building, all that's left is the foundation now, but, uh, it was an old guy who ran it, Old Man Gore, they called him. He was a mean guy and all the kids in there they were really deprived I know that . . . the place caught on fire. The old man Gore he got away and he left all the kids in there to burn to death. OK. I guess they screamed and all they did was make a hell of a lot of noise and, uh, they all burned, that's all. And all that's left now is the foundation and supposedly if you go back there at night now, you can still hear the screams of the kids burning in the building.[1]

This legend, in one form or another, is familiar to most teenagers in the Greater Cleveland area. Some versions blame the fire on villainous adults like Old Man Gore, malicious custodians, or greedy owners who collect the burnt orphans' insurance; others simply link the mysterious screams to an accidental fire. Other elements drop freely in and out. Some more creative informants elaborate on the supernatural phenomena said to be witnessed on the site: the smell of smoke, the roar of flames, the flickering of the orphans' ghosts as, covered with flames, they race desperately through the woods.

The site identified as Gore Orphanage is one of the focal points in north central Ohio for a popular adolescent rite of rebellion—the legend-trip. Everywhere across Ohio, teenagers gather together, tell spooky stories about a local site, and then travel by car to see the place for themselves.[2] The destinations of these legend-trips are invariably rural, however, and most are located along sparsely populated roads. Those in or near major cities appeared in undeveloped parks or along rural-seeming streets.[3] The stories attached to these sites vary widely but fall into three general categories. By far the most popular one involves persons who died violent or accidental deaths and who haunt the place of their deaths.[4] Babies proved an especially popular subject, often associated with a "Cry-Baby Bridge" where their mothers murdered them or where they were flung out the window of a crashing car, onto the path of an oncoming locomotive.[5] Decapitated revenants, usually looking for their lost heads, also showed up frequently.[6] The headless horseman still rides near Cincinnati, but near Sandusky he has become a headless motorcycle man, his head cut off by piano wire stretched across the road,[7] and near Cleveland the ghost is a headless little old lady in a yellow Volkswagen. Indeed, headless women are more popular than headless men, and again are attached to bridges where they were murdered or died in car wrecks, the most popular being "Screaming Mimi's" outside Tiffin.

A second popular subject is the haunted graveyard, where the dead return to punish those who disturb graves.[8] Several such stories warned of mysterious deaths resulting from the desecration of an alleged witch's or warlock's burial site. Another, near Wheeling on the Ohio side of the river, simply promises death to whoever sits in a chairlike grave marker. Other tombstones are not cursed but develop strange markings, sprout eyes at night, glow, or move around. One popular location near Carey is the grave of a murdered woman, whose portrait mysteriously appears on her tombstone, with the murderer's hands clutched around her neck.

Finally, many sites feature uncanny persons or creatures, some supernatural, some merely bizarre or eccentric. Witches, werewolves, zombies, and ghouls lurk around some places; but the more popular threats are maniacs and escaped mental patients who prowl around "parking" roads, looking for unwary carloads of teenagers to liquidate. "The Hook" in his various manifestations is perhaps the farthest traveled, having killed boyfriends in twenty Ohio locations and left his prosthetic murder weapon in car door latches in seven more. Less murderous is the "Green Man" near Youngstown; disfigured in an electrical accident, he simply seeks company. And some subjects of legend-trips are merely eccentric old ladies, like the "Stick Lady" of Waterville, who can be depended on to come out and scream at carloads of teenagers who disturb her.

The multiplicity of legends attached to such sites has been the downfall of most text-oriented collecting. Not only do many migratory legends circulate within a single community, but a single site will provoke as many versions of what happened there as there are informants to interview.[9] All graduates of Columbus high schools will agree that someone died near the Mooney Mansion on Walhalla Drive. But who? Did a father kill his promiscuous daughter, or did a jealous husband kill his cheating wife, or did a butler kill the maid, or did a maniac kill a young girl? Some say it was the husband, not the wife, who was killed, and others say no murder happened at all—a truck accidentally ran a girl down. The point is *something* must have happened there; otherwise no legend-trip would be necessary. Or in other words, *some* legend, it doesn't matter which, is necessary to justify the traditional ritual. When we turn from the multiplicity of legends to the accounts of the trips themselves, we find remarkable unanimity.

Some of this agreement is at first puzzling. However hard a legend-trip site was to find, once it was reached it proved easy to recognize. The area was deeply rutted with tire tracks, which often led away from the haunted site into deep woods, while the place itself was littered with beer cans and remains of campfires or was marked by vivid graffiti. On rare occasions the inscriptions alluded to the legend, but more often they named "who loved whom," celebrated alcohol and drug use, or simply shouted obscenities. These markings may record the participants' successful passage of an initiation into adult status, which would explain why initials and class symbols are often found too, but why the stress on drugs and male-female bonds?[10] Similarly, although legends often warned against disturbing gravesites, I found all such cemeteries named were heavily vandalized. To say that desecrating a witch's tombstone fulfills the terms of an initiation ritual evades the issue: Why should the ritual require vandalism? The answer seems to be that the legend-trip is more than an initiation into the supernatural; it functions in the same way as other adolescent automotive activities—that is, as a "ritual of rebellion."[11] The trip is the significant thing to the adolescent, and the legend serves mainly as an excuse to escape adult supervision, commit antisocial acts, and experiment illicitly with drugs and sex. Both legend and trip are ways of saying "screw you" to adult law and order; hence the obscene graffiti.

The locations of especially popular legend-trips are often described by participants not as threatening, mysterious places but as "party spots," where large numbers of teenagers gather to drink, smoke pot, and raise hell. An Athens informant described a local cemetery this way: "It doesn't look that scary right now, but at night it's pretty decent. On Halloween there's always parties here. Hank came down last Friday. He said there must have been about a thousand people there. They had a big fire going and beer cans were thrown all over the place."[12]

Another informant from Union City described how a certain bridge was haunted by a werewolf that only appeared to groups of six or seven guys in a car and only if they had been drinking or smoking; to others it was invisible.[13] In fact, many haunted locations seem to exist only in the minds of the participants: instructions on how to find them are unusually, perhaps deliberately, vague. At night, after a few beers and joints, doubtless any old house, bridge, or graveyard can be the "right" one.

Witches, werewolves, and the like at first seem incongruous with the desire to get high, but in fact both are means of escaping from the symbolically sterile world governed by school, parents, and police. "Cruising" itself breeds on the excitement of breaking the law, and my students have confirmed that the last day one can cruise in good form is the last day before one's eighteenth birthday: the day one could (until recently) legally buy beer in Ohio. Drinking and pot smoking, equally illegal for teens, are thus like visiting haunted sites in that both are "trips"—deliberate escapes into altered states of being where conventional laws do not operate. To this extent, actually participating in the supernatural is not a terror but a sought-after thrill. A Shelby informant, after recounting an experience of being chased by one graveyard haunt, commented, "All those stories added flavor to what would have been a dull high school year. Besides, being one of the few people to see Peter Ghoul, and one of the first, I felt rather privileged."[14] Just as the adolescent who gets drunkest and commits the most outrageous prank gains status among his peers, so too the participant who trips the farthest and sees the most tangible evidence of the supernatural is "privileged." The use of drugs or alcohol as a prerequisite to the visit makes it more likely that something out of the ordinary will be experienced; it also allows participants a rationalization for experiences that in retrospect seem *too* real.

Still more incongruously, many legend-trip sites are used for both scares and sex. Some frequently visited locations, in fact, appear first to have been lovers' lanes; yet when frightening legends became current, visits for sexual experimentation did not diminish. Why should a story describing a gruesome murder on a parking road serve as a sexual turn-on? Apparently, the couples continue to make out in spite of the threats. The illicit nature of the sexual adventure is the key: authority figures such as parents, teachers, and other chaperones are united in trying to keep the sexes apart, thus essentially castrating them until the age of socially recognized maturity. It is thus significant that the maniac or other threat is often identified with older, parental figures.[15] Sally Ann, one of the Mansfield-area witch-revenants, is characterized in life as a "dried-up [i.e., sterile] bitch" and in death as a puritanical ghost who "gets" couples who make out near her grave.[16] Likewise, one of the Columbus Walhalla Drive legends presents a ghost who behaves remarkably like a middle-class mother. She is said to "climb down the embankment and peer or pass the couple. Then she throws an emotional fit, stares at them again, and returns to the base of the grave. The results of the haunting are that the male becomes impotent or the girl just can't get it on anymore."[17] It is not hard to see that these legends project social warnings against sex onto marginal figures like ghosts and lunatics whom the participants can defy in good conscience.

The trip, not the legend, is the thing. To quote one former participant from Dover, "I am convinced that there is a basic need in people to be placed in terrifying positions where your life is in jeopardy. Very little in Dover serves as a threat, yet up on Ridge Road you can always find a full moon and a warlock. You get your adrenaline flowing on a boring evening, rush back home after a close brush with death, and somehow Dover doesn't seem so stagnant."[18] The legend provides the incentive to rebel against this "stagnant," adult-governed establishment and to confront a fictive death threat, but it is not the reflection of passive acceptance of belief in warlocks, ghosts, maniacs, and the like. Rather, such legends are what adolescents *desire* to believe in, in spite of community norms. The trip, complete with illegal drinking and drug use, illicit sexual experimentation, and explicitly antisocial behavior such as vandalism, is from start to finish a way of "giving the finger" to adult rationality. If it is true that ritual acts of rebellion provide and inform many legend texts, much of what we have accepted as "supernatural legends" needs to be reconsidered, not as expression of belief in the paranormal but as an excuse for what we adults would prefer to call juvenile delinquency.

Finally, a little-examined but essential feature of a legend-trip is the automobile. The sites visited are not just spooky; they are also remote, sometimes twenty miles or more from the informants' neighborhoods. In part, then, the legend-trip is an extension of the car's normal function for adolescents—the creation of a personal, mobile territory where they are free to make their own rules.[19] But this territory is also a sanctuary from which conventional authorities can be safely challenged. Surely the least studied kind of legend-trip is that in which an eccentric person, usually an old lady, is harassed. A Toledo source describes a typical visit to the Stick Lady of nearby Waterville: "you'd honk your horn once or twice and yell 'Hey. Stick Lady' at 'er and every now and again, if you had a good night, the Stick Lady would come out and chase you down the street and hopefully you would get away, as we always did."[20] The usual method of challenging the supernatural, interestingly, is the same: honking horns, blinking lights, shouting a name, or, in one case, conducting a Chinese fire drill. In the same way the auto itself is a refuge from outside threats, since one could drive away from Stick Lady and haunts do not open car doors and get in. Even "The Hook" gets no closer than the door latch and kills only those stupid enough to open the door and get out. More often, this legend ends when the teens return home with a trophy of their willingness to transgress cultural rules.

Nevertheless, the legends often express anxieties about the safety of this mobile territory. Many sites possess magical powers over cars, causing them to stall, refuse to start, develop mysterious electrical failures, or even roll toward cliffs. At Rogues' Hollow near Akron, ghosts are said to appear and run alongside cars as they approach a dangerous curve, hoping to startle drivers into speeding up and plunging over the ravine.[21] "The Vanishing Hitchhiker" often is found in a sinister mood: if you don't stop to pick her up, you will wreck your car, or she will race into the road in front of you, hoping to make you swerve into a tree or abutment.[22] If you see a little girl on the Randolph Hill Bridge outside of Steubenville, one informant advises, run over her.[23] Such a spirit of defiance motivates trips to "Screaming Bridge" outside of Cincinnati as well. This site is supposed to be the scene of a car wreck that wiped out an entire family, yet the highlight of the trip is the successful negotiation of "Lose-It Curve" and "Lights-Out Straightaway." The last is a strip that participants covered at speeds of up to fifty-five miles per hour without the benefit of headlights.[24] In such cases, the legends not only express anxieties about the fragility of this moving sanctuary but also challenge adolescents to play chicken with these very anxieties. What better place than the scene of a horrible wreck to display one's fearless driving skills?

Teenagers come to Gore Orphanage to brave the supernatural and also "to be alone so no one knew all the naughty things we did that good high school kids didn't do"[25]—drink beer, smoke pot, make out, and talk about what's "real." One is tempted then to dismiss the legend as a typical excuse for parking in a "spooky" place. Elements of the story could have been borrowed from any number of Ohio legends featuring the screaming ghosts of small children. The ragtag crew of adolescents' bogeys also congregates there: the Hook, the Headless Motorcycle Man, the shotgun-toting farmer trying to kill kids, even Big Foot. But the core legend of Gore Orphanage is surprisingly stable and consistent. While most adolescent legends are so variable that two informants can rarely agree on what happened and where, all versions of Gore Orphanage stubbornly agree on essentially what occurred and exactly where.

The "Truth" of the Matter   "What occurred" is more complicated than most participants realize. Local historians over and over have debunked the legend, explaining that no such fire ever occurred at the site the teenagers visit. Nevertheless, several factors made the Lorain County countryside an appropriate place to relocate the fire. First the atmospheric name suggests not only a gathering of children already touched by death (orphans) but also the blood and gore of the disaster itself. Although historians point out that there never was such a place as Gore Orphanage, Gore Orphanage *Road* does exist. It extends nearly the length of Lorain County, from its southern boundary almost to Lake Erie, losing itself in the outskirts of the small town of Vermilion. For most of its length, it is a typical midwestern country road: flat, straight, sparsely inhabited, uneventful. The romantic name, however, records no local memories of gruesome events, or even of any Old Man Gore. Rather, the road was originally laid out along the boundary line dividing Lorain County from its western neighbor, Huron County. When a surveying error was discovered, a thin strip of land resembling the gore of a dress had to be annexed to Lorain. The route then became known as Gore Road.

There was also a public school of sorts on Gore Road. In 1902, the Reverend John Sprunger, a Lutheran minister from Bern, Indiana, moved to the area, purchased several abandoned farms along Gore Road, and started the Light of Hope Orphanage. Supported by free-will, nonsectarian contributions, the institution trained orphaned and destitute children to do agricultural work and housekeeping. It operated uneventfully for twelve years; after Sprunger's death it collapsed into bankruptcy and the children were resettled into other homes.[26] One of the old dormitories may have burned—no records from the place survive—but historical sources agree that no catastrophe occurred there.

To find local traditions of tragedy—and the site of the legendary Gore Orphanage—one must pass the real orphanage's location on the heights above the Vermilion River. Traveling north, the road suddenly curves sharply right, then left, and plunges 150 feet down a ravine into what is locally known as Swift's (or Swiss) Hollow. There at the side of the road the daylight visitor finds a well-trampled footpath, liberally marked with empty beer cans, discarded plastic six-pack rings and condoms, and paper beer cases. Following these, one finds first a single sandstone column at the edge of the woods, still upright but carved all over with initials and graffiti. A few yards further is the ruin of a Greek Revival house, the Swift Mansion. Zigzagged among the underbrush lie sandstone blocks of surprising size, including several fallen columns, the remains of a stone well, and extensive brickwork and stonework foundations. This is the spot, according to legend, where the children burned and their screams still fill the air. Today, the Ohio Turnpike (Interstate 80) crosses the Vermilion River a mile and a quarter away. When the wind is right, the sound of trucks crossing the bridge is blown down the ravine, echoing and reechoing from the sides until it becomes a ghostly wail, scarcely recognizable as mechanical in origin.

This ruin, impressive by moonlight, has an equally impressive history. Built in 1840–42 by Joseph Swift, a wealthy Massachusetts farmer, the house was one of the most fashionable on Ohio's upper tier. It had fourteen rooms, including "two large front rooms with parquet ceilings and floors in varied colors." The front boasted French-style window frames and four marble columns, made in Troy, New York, and shipped to the site by flatboat and oxcart.

Surrounding the house were two acres of lawns and an extensive ornamental garden, which gave the mansion its family name, "Rosedale," though neighboring farmers preferred to call it "Swift's Folly."[27]

Indeed, Swift proved unwise. The bottomland gave him rich harvests, but he invested his savings in worthless railroad stock and, penniless, was forced to sell his house and leave the area in 1865. Nicholas Wilber and his family, natives of New York, then occupied the house until the early years of this century. Contemporary records portray him as a "progressive citizen," a farmer and active politician.[28] But oral history is unanimous in describing him as the leader of a group of Spiritualists and asserts that one of the great front rooms was specifically given over to seances. One local historian notes that "many wild and weird stories were told about the place during and after their occupancy."[29]

According to this local tradition, tracing back perhaps before the turn of the century, the Wilbers were in the habit of calling the spirits of small children back to earth during their seances. Nicholas Wilber's son, Miller, had four children, aged two to eleven, who died during the course of seven days (January 13–19, 1893) at the height of a diphtheria epidemic. Residents insist that they died at the Swift Mansion and were buried there.[30] The tragic deaths of these four children, tightly packed into a week of horror for their relatives, were vividly remembered by this tight-knit farming community.

Nicholas Wilber died in 1901, and the house thereafter sat vacant. The deaths of the younger Wilber's children grew increasingly confused with rumors about the elder Wilber's experiments with the hereafter, providing the impetus for the supernatural legends surrounding the abandoned house. One local historian mentions "neglected children's graves" along the Vermilion River's edge and comments that "their spirits were said to appear frequently at the seances held in the house. This may have led to the belief that the house, after it was finally abandoned as a home, was haunted."[31]

In any case, as early as 1905 teenagers seeking a taste of the supernatural began to visit the house. In time, youngsters began to take their first automobiles to "Gore Road" (as it was then called) to see if they could get them up the steep ravine without stalling or negotiate the sharp curves at the top and bottom without crashing. This done, the next test of bravery was "to go into the Swift Mansion at night and prove that you weren't scared of the haunted house."[32] One older resident, who recalled being taken to the "haunted house" in horse and buggy around 1908, gave this account:

You heard about the Wilburs [sic]?
They were the ones who had the seances?

No, no, they were the ones that had the four children that died in four days.
Did they die in the house?
In their mother's arms. But not in the Orphanage. Mr. Wilbur helped them build that orphanage on the count of losing those children. And Mrs. Wilbur went insane over it, naturally. . . . you know what she'd do. It's terrible, make you sick. She set the table three times a day and passed food to those kids just as if they were sitting there. Give you the creeps. And at night, she'd take the lamp, she'd light the lamp and she'd go up and say, "Time for bed, children come on." And go up the stairs with the lamp and put those kids to bed. And some people would go and watch it you know.[33]

The orphanage, having acquired the Wilber fields, allowed the mansion to deteriorate, and when it in turn disbanded, the land was sold to Cleveland real estate speculators. Architectural historians visited the house but recorded that it had become sadly dilapidated. One noted, "it became the 'Haunted House' and was regarded as fair game for all manner of vandalism. Roofs sagged, a column lay across the lawn, doors were torn from their hinges, walls were disfigured with names."[34] In December 1923, just as efforts to purchase and restore the old house were beginning, it burned down, apparently through the work of a vandal or a careless drifter using the house for shelter.[35] So at least two parts of the rural legend made direct contact with the urban history: the Swift Mansion was regarded as a place where children died and their spirits lurked, and it was destroyed by fire.

Still, some forty years passed before the site was renamed Gore Orphanage and became the object of the present legend. The ruins of the mansion were stripped by residents, but, according to at least one account, even the bricks carried with them memories of the place's uncanny past. One informant, familiar with the modern version, also recorded that his mother, who had visited the site earlier, associated the legends with the Wilbers: "they had five boys that died from diphtheria. And they buried them behind the fireplace in the house. The stones or the bricks that they used in the fireplace are now in the Tipton's house. . . . It's a new house and Mrs. Tipton's mother, she said that at first you could hear screams, sort of like they were right there. And all these kids in the whole family [the Wilbers] were supposed to be psychic, you know, and be able to have all these weird occurrences and everything. They could bring the kids back after they died."[36]

And on another level, the legend preserves a historically true story. In essence it accurately recounts one of the worst school disasters in the history of the United States, the Lake View Public School fire of 1908, in which 176 elementary school children and teachers were killed. The contemporary legend, as it turns out, combines elements from urban residents' oral accounts of the real fire with rural traditions circulating at least since the turn of the century about a spooky house where small children also died a tragic death. Gore Orphanage, then, transports urban fears to a rural setting and, by doing so, exorcises them from the urban and suburban worlds of the teenagers.

On March 4, 1908, in the Cleveland suburb of Collinwood (now incorporated into the East Cleveland inner city), 335 pupils between the ages of six and fourteen were in classes when the janitor noticed smoke coming from the basement, curling out from beneath the front stairwell. He sounded an alarm, and the children, well-trained in fire drills, began marching down the stairs toward the front exit. But by the time they had assembled, the front stairwell was blocked by flames. According to witnesses, the children at the front broke from the lines and tried "to fight their way back to the floor above, while those who were coming down shoved them mercilessly back into the flames below." Those who made it to the rear exit found it locked. Outside rescuers unlocked it but found it opened inward, so it was impossible to move against the press of dozens of desperate bodies. When the door was finally broken down, one bystander said, "we thought that the work of getting the children out would be easy, but when we attempted to release the first one we found it was almost impossible to move them at all. We succeeded in saving a few who were near the top but that was all we could do. The fire swept through the hall, springing from one child to another, catching their hair and the dresses of the girls. Their cries were dreadful to hear."[37]

The contemporary legend undoubtedly preserves details from the historical event. The status of the building as a public institution, the rapid spread of the fire, the trapping of many children inside are all details common to the real disaster but not typical of local legends like "Crybaby Lane." Further, the presence of malicious arsonists—supervisors, landowners, janitors, or Old Man Gore—arguably stems from the rumors that spread soon after the Collinwood fire that it had been set deliberately. In fact, the school's janitor, a German-American named Herter, was accused of setting the blaze (though he lost four children in the fire and was badly burned trying to rescue one), and for a time he was detained in protective custody to keep residents from lynching him.[38] The death toll, estimated at 176, devastated the community and left deep scars in the memories of those living in the Cleveland area.

In particular, the uncertainty over the fire's cause left the survivors with mixed feelings of anger and anxiety over whether children were truly safe in public institutions. One editorialist summed up the emotions by saying that the disaster represented a base betrayal of childhood by its natural protectors. The children in the Collinwood school had been told that if they followed the rules of their fire drill, they would be safe in any emergency.[39] Strangely, though, mention of the disaster in local histories is nearly impossible to find. None of the informants who knew the Gore Orphanage legend (the oldest of whom was born two generations after the disaster) consciously connected it with the Collinwood disaster, and none of the debunking historians of Lorain County explained the legend by alluding to the real-life fire. It is as if the event were so horrible that it was deliberately blotted out of the area's history, only to emerge later—and somewhere else—in the form of legend.

At first, it seems strange that the story would be retold at the place called Gore Orphanage, which is some forty miles west of the Lake View School and in a rural setting. To be sure, the disaster's original site is now not only totally obliterated, the neighborhood itself has been absorbed by Cleveland's black community. Since the legend-trip is almost exclusively a white middle-class activity, these factors alone might have forced the disaster to "move" in adolescents' minds.

The final stage in the legend's development must have occurred in the late 1960s, as the growth of Cleveland drove white families, with their submerged memories of the school fire, away from the center city and into a growing complex of suburbs on every side. The Swift Hollow legend, already analogous to the Collinwood disaster, merged with the other story to form a stable entity: a public orphanage on the site where the Wilber children died; arson; a massive loss of life; screams; the return of the children's spirits. This site became popular and subsumed any other traditions in the West Cleveland area that would express anxieties of the original disaster.

Tellingly, though, a nearly identical legend circulates in the East Cleveland suburbs, connected with the United Methodist Children's Home in Berea, an institution still in operation:

Umm I—I think it's in '65, I'm not sure. It sounds, '65 sounds right. But it was, the night was really weird about the story. It was an orange, fiery sky, the whole sky was just orange. And umm—this orphanage caught on fire, arson and in this—they say the top room, there was—babies, just tons of babies in there, and it was really weird because, like the way the house caught on fire, and the babies screaming, you could hear it for miles. . . . And you could hear these babies screaming. . at the top of their lungs, this piercing screaming at the fire and it says every year whenever that umm, day of the fire, every year you can hear these babies screaming in the wind. And supposedly the sky is that color.[40]

Like the historian in Lorain County, the current employees of the Methodist Home are mystified by the story, since no fire or similar disaster ever occurred there. The lack of any similar legends in Ohio outside the Cleveland area demonstrates that these stories are independent transformations of the real disaster.

Conclusion   Although literal-minded historians might conclude that the Gore Orphanage legend is a collection of alcohol- or drug-induced visions and borrowings from other adolescent legends, in fact the Swift Mansion was the ideal place for urban history to resurface in oral tradition. Already associated with the tragic deaths of children and with the return of their screaming, restless ghosts, its secluded nature and the ominous sound of the road's name suited it well for the purpose. But by transforming a real fire into a legendary one, teenagers simultaneously changed history into archetype.

While some (correctly) insist on the story's essential truth, many others find it irrelevant whether Gore Orphanage really existed or whether anyone really died there—and many of them actually admit that the screams they hear are really caused by trucks crossing a bridge. Rather, adolescents are celebrating their fears of a death like those of the fictional orphans and the real Collinwood children. By locating the disaster in a remote place and recasting the victims as orphans, the legend-trippers can confront the threat of their own death and prove that they are not paralyzed by it. And, since authorities can prove that neither Gore Orphanage nor the Children's Home were sites of real disaster, participants can doubly protect themselves by admitting that the catastrophe celebrated is "not for real." At worst, adolescents leave fears behind in the night, returning by daylight to the city with its public schools and fire drills not so far different from those at Lake View.

Extending this point, we could say that the legend-trip in general is a way of playing chicken with adolescent anxieties. At the same time that it dares participants to rebel against adult authority, it provides a psychologically safe way to defy the taboo against confronting fears of death itself. Violent death is at the heart of nearly all legend-trips, and if we strip away the melodrama, they are similar to today's news items. Bodies do turn up in isolated fields and roads. High schoolers are tragically killed in car wrecks. Husbands do go berserk and kill wives and family. Lunatics do haunt "parking" roads, killing whomever they find. In short, the same violence that confronts teenagers in raw form during the day is given structure during the night in these rituals. Mary Jane's Grave, for example. seems not to have been a popular spot to visit until two popular Mansfield teenagers were killed in a car wreck. The story that they had visited her grave and died on the way back seems to have been a post hoc imposition of logic on an otherwise senseless accident.

Likewise, the cursed cement chair near Wheeling seems invented to embody the threat of mortality. If you sit in it, you die within the year, or, some say, within eight years, or, others say, either you or a close friend will die within eight years. Given such latitude the odds are good that the curse will take effect; thus, any tragic event, either within the high school or within an individual's family, can be given some sense of order through this legend. One informant recalled a tombstone in the same cemetery: "It's a big long story and you read it and come to the last line, it says if you read this story you will die." Actually, the stone reads, "Reader, remember all must die, as you are now, so once was I, as I am now thou soon must be, prepare for death and follow me."[41]

In a sense, then, the informant's paraphrase of the inscription is accurate: anyone who reads the stone *will* die, just as anyone who reads this essay will die. Mortality fears, first becoming intense during adolescence, need to be relieved, and adult white middle-class society is notorious for making such fears taboo in "polite" discussion, thus evading the psychological burdens of such feelings.[42] One function, then, of the legend-trip is to create a means by which such fears can be localized, circumscribed, and defied without risk. Without actually putting oneself in physical danger (as in the literal car game of "chicken") such activities allow adolescents to experience the emotions of being in death's presence and the exhilaration of having conquered their fears without adult assistance.

Local legends and legend-trips help teenagers come to grips with this basic reality, turning elements of real-life horror into part of a ritual of orderly disorder. By carousing, flirting with danger, and testing their limits, to the tune of synthetic screams produced by I-80, West Cleveland adolescents reaffirm their ability to enjoy life even though it passes. The horror they name is fictitious, a ghostly howl in the midnight hours, but the horror they learn to face is the banal violence of daylight, the AP statistics of automobile accidents, disease, tragic fires, and explosions, and lives casually snuffed in the cause of national security. The fire drill bell needs to be tested every so often—just in case. So, too, does one's capacity to be human—to enjoy life in the face of death.

That's what really happens at Gore Orphanage.

Chapter 11

THE DEVIL WORSHIPERS AT THE PROM

Toward the end of May 1987, students at Panther Valley High School in Lansford, Pennsylvania, began to spread the news that a satanic cult in the area was planning mischief for the school's prom night. The story quickly multiplied into a legion of variants: One type held that "there was to be three suicides and three murders that night. . . . the first six people in the door would be the six to die." Another common version held that the first four couples to arrive would die; or perhaps it would be the first five persons to leave. Others specified that girls wearing a given color dress (usually pink) would be the first to die. How? Some sources thought that the satanists would open fire during the "King and Queen Dance," the dance following the election and coronation of the lucky couple; others speculated that the refreshments would be laced with drugs or poison; still others thought that people would simply be stabbed at the tables or shot on the parking lot as they left.[1]

The panic spread rapidly among the student body and so came to parents' attention. Within a few days, residents of McAdoo, Lansdale, Lehighton, and Jim Thorpe began calling police and school officials. Phillip Rader, principal at Panther Valley, began holding public conferences to assure press and public that fears were unfounded. But since the prom was to be held at Stefanisko's, a popular roadhouse just south of the Hazleton city limits, teens in nearby Hazleton soon became aware of the panic. So on the day of Hazleton High School's prom, the principal, Rocco Mussoline, began receiving dozens of phone calls from concerned parents asking about the danger. The rumor did not say which prom would be disrupted, so Mussoline contacted officials at Bishop Hafey, Hazleton's Catholic high school, which was also holding a prom that night. When Robert Hines, coordinator of the prom, asked students about the story, they confirmed that they "had heard stories of animal sacrifice and things like that" conducted in the Conyngham Valley where Hafey's prom was scheduled. At that point, Hines said, "we figured that there might be something going on," and both schools asked for help from state police.

Panther Valley had metal detectors installed at the door of the banquet room, and all three schools hired extra security guards. Undercover agents mingled with students, and state police cruised the roads outside. No fatalities were recorded.

Ostension and "Collective Delusion"

As sociologist Joel Best once asked, "Why would anyone . . . do any of the . . . terrible things Satanists are said to do?" Tradition gives us no satisfactory answer, he concluded. "They are, apparently, just the sorts of terrible things Halloween sadists and the other new bogeymen do. . . . irrationality gives these threats their emotional power."[2] True, such beliefs assume that satanists are not controlled by the same rational codes of conduct as "normal" people. But are they themselves expressions of "irrationality"? When sociologists call events such as the prom-panic "collective delusions," they often unconsciously imply a condescending attitude toward those who pass them on, as if "rational" people were immune to such ideas. But when these events are examined, they often prove not to be "irrational" at all.

Previous studies of "collective delusions" have often proved naive. Donald Johnson studied the 1944 "phantom anesthetist" panic of Mattoon, in which a mysterious assailant sprayed victims with poisonous gas, then vanished. First he commented that he was concerned lest such phenomena were "disappearing," since he could find only one sociological study of an analogous event in the literature.[3] Then he limited himself to determining that residents of "low educational and economic level," especially women, were the most "suggestible."[4] More recent studies have likewise focused on demographic concerns, assuming that factors like sex, education, and social position inflexibly determine one's ability to resist irrational ideas for life.[5] Victor, in stressing the economic pressures on the small towns prone to cult panics, suggests a similar approach, though he finds it puzzling that some towns in his study area were affected by the outbreak and others were not.[6]

Being skeptical about the reality of the devil and shadowy cults does not, however, make communities immune to such panics. Residents of Great Britain are much less apt to believe in Satan (only 21 percent compared with 60 percent of Americans), but throughout the 1960s communities there were shocked by rumors that satanists were holding occult ceremonies and exhuming graves for the purposes of black magic.[7] And neighborhoods and schools there are still subject to similar panics focused on vicious gangs like "The

Chelsea Smilers" or mysterious beings like a "vampire with iron teeth" in a neighborhood cemetery.[8] Authorities assumed that one Glasgow "vampire" panic in 1954 was simple hysteria, brought on by too many American comic books and science-fiction movies. But Hobbs and Cornwall concluded, after interviewing witnesses and locating a number of earlier "hunts" in the Glasgow area, that the participants enjoyed the panic, seeing it as an adventure, not a nightmare. They suggest that calling the hunt "mass hysteria" was inaccurate.[9] That there was no vampire is obvious; that the vampire hunt was therefore irrational and socially dysfunctional seems not so obvious.

A few studies have suggested a more complex interpretation of such events. In the 1957 Seattle "windshield pitting epidemic," many well-educated and presumably rational adults were willing to believe that recent H-bomb tests had left holes in their car's glass.[10] Yet doing so, Medalia and Larsen argue, revealed deep-seated anxieties—hardly irrational—about the effects of open-air nuclear testing. There was legitimate concern about the health effects of fallout drifting over the Pacific Northwest from Pacific tests, not to mention anxiety over the tests' political effect on the Cold War. Such broader concerns, we might say, constituted a broad warrant for claiming that minor pitting of windshields was connected to The Bomb. And by focusing these fears "on a narrower area of experience," Medalia and Larsen found, believers "succeeded in bringing to a focus and in reducing diffuse anxieties" about the threat of atomic fallout. Their normal reactions, such as "calling the police, appealing to the Governor and President for help, covering windshields and cleaning them," were "magical practices," since they had in themselves no power to suck radioactivity out of the air. Nevertheless, by engaging in them, people were able to convince themselves that they were constructively solving the problem; they "named" and hence controlled their anxieties.[11] So despite its scientifically irrational conclusions, this debate succeeded in calming rational fears.

We might expand this specialized definition of "magic" to include other kinds of apparently sensible reactions to perceived threats that do not in fact directly protect one against danger. Most superstitions, of course, are implicitly or explicitly magical—for instance, protecting oneself from auto accidents by having a priest bless the family car or by hanging a lucky rabbit's foot from the rearview mirror. But many other ambiguous threats provoke "magical" responses: in the wake of two brutal murders in Huntsville, Texas, women insisted on being escorted to their cars on dark parking lots, even though both murders had taken place in broad daylight and in places other than parking lots.[12] If one function of legend is to "name" previously undefined threats and so gain psychological control over them, then when people change their behavior based on such legends, they are engaging in magical practices. This is so even if the participants perceive them as "good common sense," since their actions do not act directly on the threat but simply reassure individuals that they are somehow controlling their fates.

The Structure of Ostensive Panics   Drawing global conclusions from the fact of panic itself is misleading, because we fail to see why a variety of people found such actions appropriate at the time. In fact, opinions varied during the event from extreme belief to cynical skepticism, a spectrum of response found even today in witnesses' memories. Yet whether skeptical or convinced of the legend's credibility, a large number of people found their actions influenced, even dictated, by the story's terms. For events like these are not static but dynamic events, traditional performances of legends through *ostension*. Véronique Campion-Vincent has recently argued that legends enter into ostension because of a combination of factors:

1. *Underlying stress:* "social situations of unrest or of crisis" must be present as underlying or "faraway causes."
2. A *"triggering event"* dramatizes this unrest in an "exceptional and traumatic" way.
3. A period of *collective action* then embodies the community's reaction to the threat, and
4. This leads to a *showdown,* or climactic moment in which the legend is "fulfilled."[13]

When such legend-derived panics occur, *all* the activities of the participants constitute a collective performance of the legend. That is, few participants put their fears into oral narrative form, but their responses constituted a resolution of the warning's implicit narrative content: "if you don't do something, innocent people may die."[14] We can see this process clearly in the periodic "mass murder" panics that regularly occur at college campuses. One such, the so-called "Nostradamus panic," occurred in 1991.

1. *Underlying stress.* The papers had been filled that summer and fall with gruesome accounts of mass murders. On July 22, a Milwaukee man, wearing handcuffs, hailed a police car and said he had been attacked by a man with a knife. Police went with him to the upstairs apartment of Jeffrey L. Dahmer and found three heads kept in a refrigerator, along with seven skulls, decomposed torsos, and photos of mutilated bodies. Dahmer eventually confessed to seventeen cases of murder and cannibalism dating back to 1978. Neighbors in Dahmer's apartment complex recalled hearing screams and a buzz saw and complaining of a foul odor but evidently failed to contact police.[15]

On October 10, Joseph M. Harris of Paterson, New Jersey, who had recently been fired from the Post Office, stabbed his former supervisor to death and fatally shot her boyfriend; then he drove to his office where he shot and killed the first two postal workers who arrived. Armed with hand grenades, a samurai sword, and two machine guns, he threatened to murder more persons before surrendering to police after a four-hour standoff. A letter found in his room said that his actions were inspired by a 1986 incident in which an Oklahoma postal worker killed fourteen people.[16] And on October 16, George Hennard drove a pickup truck through the plate-glass window of Luby's Cafeteria in Killeen, Texas, and began firing randomly on diners with two semiautomatic pistols. When police arrived, Hennard shot himself, but not before he had killed twenty-three patrons in the worst mass shooting in U.S. history.[17]

2. *Triggering event.* During the week of October 6, a rumor began to emerge among American college students predicting a mass murder in a specified building at their campus. Appearing first at Boston College, it quickly spread to nearby institutions, appearing by Friday, October 11, at Boston University, the College of the Holy Cross in Worcester, and the University of Massachusetts in Amherst. This rumor stated that an unspecified psychic had appeared on a TV talk show (most sources named *The Oprah Winfrey Show*) and predicted that by Halloween another mass murder would occur at a collegiate site with specific characteristics. The Holy Cross version, for instance, stated that the murder would occur in an L-, F-, or T-shaped building with a tower situated on a hill overlooking a cemetery and near a body of water. The University of Massachusetts version likewise specified a letter-shaped building (L-shaped in this case) near a pond and a cemetery and added that it would be named after an assassinated president (Kennedy Hall was the most likely candidate). Most versions named Halloween as the date of the murders, though the Boston University version held that the massacre would take place on the party weekend preceding the holiday. The rumor soon cropped up at more colleges.[18]

At some point, the name of the psychic was given as Nostradamus, the sixteenth-century cryptic poet whose writings had been recently cited as predicting the Persian Gulf War.[19] The detail that the murder was to occur in a "reversible year" (i.e., 1991) perhaps added warrant to this otherwise unlikely connection. Nevertheless, Alan Bash, an editor for Georgetown University's daily student newspaper, consulted Charles A. Ward's widely available *Oracles of Nostradamus* and located a likely entry in the section containing quatrains "which may well be applied to the present and to the days immediately to follow":

> Entre deux fleuues se verra enserré,
> Tonneaux & caques vnis à passer outre:
> Huict ponts pompus chef à tant enferré,
> Enfans parfaicts sont iugulez en coultre.

Or, as Ward rendered the verse (Century VIII, quatrain 55): "Between two rivers shall he see himself enclosed, tuns and casks shall be joined together in order to pass across: after eight bridges have been broken up, the chief shall at that moment be run through, and perfect children shall have their throats cut with a knife."[20]

The verse seemed to refer to a mass murder of young people in the vicinity of a body of water, but it was unclear who the man enclosed between two rivers was, and the relevance of the nine pontoon bridges and the assassination of "the chief" was also foggy. (In the original context, "he" alludes to a new "Henry the Great" who, the preceding quatrain predicts, would wage a successful war on Spain. The passage quoted presumably predicts the climactic battle of this campaign.[21]) As Halloween neared, the rumor came to national attention. On October 28, the *Boston Globe* summarized its spread and gave reactions from various college administrators. And on October 30 both the Associated Press and *USA Today* reported on the legend, publishing disclaimers from Oprah Winfrey and assurances from several sources that the rumor was untrue. Reports also appeared on CNN, on NBC's morning news program, and on many local radio call-in talk shows.[22]

3. *Collective action.* Reaction at campuses was mixed. Many students immediately discounted the story as an obvious hoax, some speculating that it had been concocted as a psychology experiment. Others commented facetiously that the term "perfect children" could not possibly apply to them. "I mean, hey, according to the baby boomers, there ain't a perfect child in our entire generation, so . . ." commented the *Bucknellian*, while another Bucknell student commented, "all the perfect children go to Ivy League schools."[23] But in other cases the rumor provoked fear. At the University of Massachusetts at Amherst, seventy to a hundred female dorm residents met on October 24 with John Luippold, the campus police chief, who commented, "there was definitely some concern because the rumor was so widespread." A spin-off rumor, found at Wheaton, held that other campuses had already shut down for fear of murders.

At Syracuse, after several parents called the university, the Public Relations office issued a statement debunking the story, but the university promised to increase security at Halloween. Sergeant Grant Williams said, "Naturally we're concerned, and if putting extra (security) people around certain buildings is going to make the kids feel better, we'll do something about it." At Day Hall, a letter-shaped building over-looking a cemetery and a body of water, extra security officers were posted, and off-duty police were hired to patrol the outside, while RAs (resident advisors) were told to patrol the building every hour. Some students were not reassured. "Ninety percent of my floor is going to leave," one freshman said: "There are so many ways around security. The murderer could have an SU ID [Syracuse University identification card]. . . . My mother would rather be safe than sorry."[24]

At Bucknell, Barbara A. Shailor, vice president for student services, issued a letter to all students on October 22, which summarized the rumor and noted its appearance at several other colleges. The letter ended: "Although some of you may be frightened by the interpretations of a philosopher's written verse over 400 years ago, others will think it somewhat absurd. Whatever your interpretation, we want to assure you our Public Safety Office will have extra patrols on duty that night because of Halloween. Because it is Halloween, we urge you to take extra precautions."

The letter did not quiet students' fears. One commented, "At first I just thought the whole thing was kind of ridiculous. But after getting the letter from the school, it's kind of scary. I don't believe that it is taken so seriously. Now that everybody has heard of it, I'm afraid that some psycho might go crazy and act it out."

By October 25, many freshmen at one U-shaped dormitory had made arrangements to stay overnight at another hall or in a local motel. Local chains advertised special "Medieval Prophecy One-Night Rates" for jittery students. Shortly after, the student paper published an RA's concern that freshmen's fears could be justified: "People are afraid that some weirdo will hear about this and fulfill the prophecy." Bucknell's director of public relations conceded that security was being increased because of this specific fear. "There was a discussion with our director of public safety about someone acting out, but we didn't want to talk about it (in the letter to the students) because we didn't want to give anybody any ideas. It was deliberately left out of our note to students because we didn't want to frighten them."

On the other hand, some students saw the rumor as an occasion for humor. One girl told press, "If I knew where (the massacre) was definitely supposed to take place, I'd be there. I need more excitement." A call-in campus radio talk show aired the rumor on October 24, and soon afterwards a merrymaking mob of 250 students gathered outside the freshman dorms, requiring the efforts of several security officials and RAs to break it up. One officer noted that the students were not threatening, "just being celebratory."[25]

4. *Showdown.* No deaths occurred at the campuses affected. However, on November 1, Gang Lu, a recently graduated Ph.D. student in physics at the University of Iowa, attended a faculty meeting at Van Allen Hall. Apparently upset over being passed over for an academic award, he stood up and fatally shot two faculty members involved in the decision and Linhua Shan, who received the award. Leaving the room, he went to two other offices to kill the chair of the Department of Physics and the associate vice president of academic affairs before committing suicide.[26] The Associated Press story connected the shooting to the Killeen mass murder and alluded to the college rumors as possibly related. The nightly tabloid TV news show *A Current Affair* aired a study of the Iowa shooting, which included the claim that Lu's actions had "proved" Nostradamus correct. The broadcast repeatedly showed an engraving of the astrologer and also interviewed students who agreed that the prophecy had come true. Barry Stark, an editorialist for Syracuse's *Daily Orange*, commented, "When the rumors of the Day Hall massacre were circulating, the furthest thing from my mind was that the rumor was actually going to become reality. . . . While SU left Halloween without a scare, the University of Iowa had tragedy that surpassed our wildest rumors."[27]

The excitement caused by "The Devil Worshipers at the Prom" must therefore be seen against the background of the area's narrative and customary traditions. Most immediately, two *underlying tensions* gave the legend warrant in the Hazleton area: 1) the community's religious conservatism and mythological worldview, and 2) teenagers' adoption of "satanic" symbolism as a rebellion against the older generation's dogma. The *triggering event* was the unexplained suicide of a popular Panther Valley student. Out of the ensuing tangle of rumors came the claim that shadowy devil worshipers were involved. This claim, amply supported by institutional warrants, created a satisfactory magical scapegoat for the tensions provoked and led to *collective action.* Localizing the satanic threat to prom night, an event already charged with marginal dangers in American culture, delimited the crisis to a single night and created a logical moment for *showdown.* Ironically, the panic, as painful as it was for many participants, was socially therapeutic. It exorcised the threat created by the suicide and put a rational mask on events otherwise seen as chaotic.

Underlying Stress: Satan Is Alive and Well   The area's worldview is strongly *mythological*; that is, as Thomas L. Berger and Thomas Luckmann say, it "posits the ongoing penetration of the world of everyday experience by sacred forces."[28] A survey conducted in September 1989 at Penn State's Hazleton Campus showed that a majority of students believed in Satan as "a real supernatural being who causes evil in the world." (See table.) The figure—56 percent—is in line with figures compiled by various researchers between 1973 and 1982, which consistently have found that between 48 and 70 percent of Americans believe in the devil as an empirical force for evil.[29] Likewise, when asked if "God works miracles if you pray to him," 48 percent agreed and only 18 percent disagreed (34 percent uncertain); a similar plurality agreed that devil worshipers go to hell (45 percent vs. 20 percent; again 34 percent uncertain). Students from the Hazleton area were, in fact, considerably more willing to credit the reality of Satan (70 percent) and Hell (55 percent).[30] True, the sample may not represent a random sampling of area teens, but if it is biased, it probably represents a group that is better educated and economically better off than average.

Outside canonical liturgies, the magical power of prayer is also supported by informal groups within many congregations. In the Lutheran church to which I belonged, a "prayer network" has been in operation for many years: if one calls in a problem needing the Lord's intervention, one member will call another, the next will pass on the word to the next, until all are notified. Then all will pray simultaneously at a set moment for the troubled member. Benefits mentioned have ranged from healing the cancer-ridden to finding athletic scholarships for college-age children. The local paper regularly prints "novenas" in its "Personal" section that provide formulas for working miracles. Typically, the novena will provide a skeleton prayer to the Holy Spirit, St. Jude, or another of the Catholic pantheon, with a blank for the specific petition desired. Generally, it must be repeated nine times a day for nine days, then republished in the paper without mentioning the favor granted. Most assure the reader that even though the request may seem difficult or might require a miracle, the novena "has never been known to fail."

Accounts of black magic are also common among the older generation, including accounts of people tempted to make pacts with the devil or afflicted by witchcraft. One source described in detail her grandmother's death by witchcraft and the means that a wise woman used to identify the culprit, who was compelled to come and sit at the foot of the dead woman's coffin. The informant concluded about the witch, "Her day will come. Because if she did that, there is a God, the Devil will take her; believe me. And that's it."[31] Another elderly resident of an ethnic mining town recalled that a boarder in his house claimed to have met the devil. "You go with me, I'll give you all this money," the devil said. But when the boarder took the money and ran home, he found that it had turned to oak leaves.

Such lore has previously been found in rural areas, most notably in the

College Students' Opinions on Satanism and Suicide (Percentages only)

	Strongly Agree	Agree	Don't Know	Disagree	Strongly Disagree
Satan is a real supernatural being who causes evil in the world.	17	39	10	20	13
God works miracles if you pray to him.	9	39	34	9	9
People can gain supernatural power by worshipping Satan.	1	7	24	27	40
People who worship Satan will go to Hell when they die.	15	30	34	7	13
Satanic cults are operating in my hometown.	16	15	42	21	6
Satanic cults have killed animals in my hometown.	12	15	48	18	7
Satan could harm me or my family personally.	3	10	22	28	37
I have met people who said they were Satanists.	13	25	4	21	37
Teenage suicides are associated with Satanism.	7	18	36	24	15
There are always warnings before a person commits suicide.	28	46	10	12	3
Many teen suicides are pact-related.	4	24	48	19	4
I personally knew someone who committed suicide.	30	6	3	13	48

Ozarks and in the Schoharie Hills of New York State.[32] Such practices, being difficult to collect and often dramatic in form, have sometimes been regarded as idiosyncratic survivals of more primitive lore. But the depth of belief in religious magic, both good and evil, obviously reflects strong belief in religion, and local informants made it clear that the beliefs they passed on were fully relevant to the present. When a house in nearby West Pittston was the site of "demonic" manifestations, the case was given front-page publicity in Hazleton.[33] The local diocese declined to say whether the phenomena—which included opening doors, ghostly glows, hoofbeats and pig grunts, and foul stenches—was caused by a demon. But an official source said that the Catholic Church took the occupants' claims quite seriously: "The church believes that people and buildings can be possessed by demons."[34] The event remains fresh in Hazleton residents' minds as empirical evidence for the existence of devils. The source of the "oak leaf" story concluded: "Now the devil's at work. He's the one that's causing all this stuff that's going on around the world. You take—where did you hear of stuff like this years ago? You never heard of it. People killing themselves, shooting themselves, committing suicide, on drugs and everything."[35]

Moreover, local religious groups perceive themselves as beset by less dramatic threats that are nevertheless satanically inspired. Even before Martin Scorsese's *The Last Temptation of Christ* was released, violent protests in the Hazleton area led town and city councils to pass injunctions forbidding local theaters from showing the film. On the basis of an advance script, the local diocese's bishop called the movie "an outrageous insult to all Christians" and urged "the faithful" to "protest as vigorously as you can within the law and pray." Viewing the movie, he warned, would cause "untold confusion and harm." The local dean of priests agreed that "people who don't have a firm grip on the nature of Christ are going to come out of this film with a thoroughly negative view."[36] Indeed, when Cinemax broadcast the movie in 1989, the area's cable company, without warning or precedent, interrupted its broadcast and transmitted only a blank screen. The cable company later reversed the decision, under pressure from the local newspaper and the American Civil Liberties Union, but noted that viewers who called at the time seemed either pleased with the decision or "didn't much care" one way or the other.[37]

Movies presenting unconventional views of the Christian mythos are only one of many threats that make local church leaders uneasy. In a public meeting on satanic cults, Father Raymond of St. Anthony's Catholic Church in Freeland stressed that secularism itself was equivalent to Satanism:

[Most people are] denying that Satan exists. And guess what? That's what he loves. He doesn't want to be acknowledged. Believe that he doesn't exist, and he can do all his damage. . . . If he can get us to believe that he doesn't exist, boy! he can work tremendous things in this world. He can overturn our spiritual lives and really hurt us spiritually. . . . And he never comes as he really is, because if he did, we see him as ugly, and easy to reject. He comes as a college professor, he comes as a doctor, he comes as a teacher, and he's always bringing something good like he did to the Lord. . . . Believe it. Don't deny him because that's what he likes.[38]

One may argue that such views are intrinsically irrational, in that they reject the objectivity of the college professor for the perpetual warfare of the saint. But even if this is true in the academy, the Hazleton community still rests firmly with the American majority that accepts the world as a battleplace between God and Satan. For most living in this area, it seems more rational to side with priests and politicians who uphold the myth than to opt for the dubious good of the college professor.

The Cult   The younger generation has at least partially accepted this mythological worldview, but this group showed little fear of black magic or demonic threats. Only 8 percent agreed that people can gain supernatural power by worshipping Satan, and no more than 13 percent felt that Satan could cause them or their family personal harm. Yet satanic cults were quite real to many students, especially from the immediate area. Local students were twice as likely to agree that cults were operating in their hometown (48 percent to outsiders' 22 percent), and they were nearly four times more likely to add that cults had sacrificed animals there (46 percent to 12 percent). Part of this tendency may be owing to aggressive anticult programs in local Catholic schools—but 50 percent of locals also agreed that they had met people who said that they were satanists (vs. only 31 percent of outsiders).

Anecdotal accounts from students and parents, and the testimony of local police confirm that local adolescent gangs have widely adopted satanic symbolism as part of their antisocial activities. Graffiti incorporating traditional satanic symbols like inverted stars and "666" are commonplace throughout the community, and many students have been willing to appear in allegedly satanic folk dress. Students often wear black T-shirts with "heavy metal" bands, sometimes featuring overtly satanic symbols. And two girls at Bishop Hafey graduated wearing black nail polish and white face makeup to show that they were "brides of Satan." During long, dull summers, groups of teens sometimes while away the weeks by playing at satanism. In August 1986, shortly after the West Pittston manifestations were made public, gangs of more than two hundred bikers wearing devil insignias entered the neighborhood, standing on the lawn of the "possessed" house to chant, "We love Satan."[39] In nearby Monroe County a gang of teens was arrested in August 1989 after they forced a younger teen to go with them to an abandoned barn, where he was made the centerpiece in what purported to be a "Black Mass." Tied down in the middle of a pentangle marked by lighted candles, the younger teen's blood was let and tasted by the leader. Police confiscated satanic paraphernalia from the leader's house, including a black hooded robe and a fake skull.[40]

Such signs are, of course, no more than evidence of normal "tough" gang images and hazing with a contemporary touch. The traditional "jock" (athletic-oriented) versus "head" (alcohol/drug-oriented) rivalry often incorporates such imagery, the "jocks" sporting all-American crew cuts and patriotic symbols, while the "heads" complement their disheveled look with demonic tokens. Legend-trips may include rituals to "raise" evil spirits and so verge on satanism, and some psychiatrists have treated cases of teens whose obsession with devil-worship has led them to improvise "black masses" and kill small animals. Some adults sincerely accept such evidence as proof that a shadowy underground cult is ready to abuse their children and involve their teens in human sacrifices.[41]

After a fatal child abuse case in 1982, the Luzerne County District Attorney's office set up a specially trained squad to combat this threat.[42] Former Duryea police chief Gary Sworin was hired as a specialist in child-abuse cases and sent to attend a training seminar on detecting signs of trouble. The seminar was conducted by Kenneth Wooden, a former TV journalist who, after making a sensational documentary for ABC's *20/20* news series, became a self-styled expert on cult abduction and murder of children and satanic infiltration of child-care centers.[43] In addition to investigating child-abuse cults, Sworin also conducted a series of public meetings, passing on to parents a version of the satanic "Gang Initiation" legend.

But in 1983 he became involved in a particularly difficult case. Larry and Leona Cottam, a fundamentalist couple, claimed that their children had been forced to participate in satanic animal sacrifices and blood drinking at their church-affiliated school. Sworin could not press charges because the couple suddenly dropped out of sight, but he gave credence to their story and alluded to their allegations in his public meetings. The Cottams reappeared early in 1989; fearful for their children's safety, they had withdrawn from society and, out of funds, they had decided to go without food, trusting that God would save them. They contacted authorities only after their twelve-year-old son starved to death. Although Sworin testified in the Cottams' defense, the new district attorney pressed for and won a third-degree murder conviction.[44]

Encountering evidence of animal sacrifices is a regular part of teens' stories about satanism, and while some of these are obviously hearsay, a few teens claim firsthand knowledge. One student recalled coming across a ritual site marked by goats' heads with horns and crosses: "But in the middle of this was a huge stone with a flat top. And on top of it—which was sad—were several animals, all dismembered and stuff like that, with flies all over it; it was really disgustingly ugly." This informant added that other adults had confirmed that sacrifices did occur there, and "they say that children who get curious out there, usually get abducted out there. . . . So I could have been a statistic, I almost was a statistic if it wasn't for maybe God looking over me, watching me, you know."[45]

State police officers admit that they are aware of occasional animal killings but again blame such acts on local gang activity. In the same spring as the prom night panic, a local meatpacking house reported that a lamb had been stolen from a pen and found slaughtered nearby inside a stone ring. The investigating trooper assured me that he had located the gang responsible and confirmed that it was only a drunken adolescent prank. Nevertheless, the incident was widely assumed to be part of a cult sacrifice, especially since it had occurred during the Easter season. The lamb is a common image for Christ, and figures of lambs made of butter are commonly placed in blessed Easter baskets during Holy Week. Hence the killing of a lamb during this season would naturally have been seen as an insult to Christ and perhaps even a blasphemous parody of the Eucharist. It seems likely, too, that the gang would have recognized these implications and enjoyed the sensation the killing caused. Still, as the investigating trooper pointed out, *real* satanists wouldn't be "advertising" their activities, and in any case the local incidents did not fit police-circulated descriptions of genuine cult sacrifices: "You can distinguish between somebody who's playing games, or trying to imitate it [and] where the actual thing is occurring . . . and kids don't know how it works. They're playing their games, they're going with what they think is right. But there's actually set ways of doing everything."

Thus whether or not specific evidence could be found for cult activities, the consensus received from officials in the area was that cults were, in fact, a real threat. Beliefs were also reinforced through media presentations (such as Geraldo Rivera's various presentations on cult activities), and also through the deep involvement of the Catholic Church in trying to combat satanism. In Louisiana, workshops and counseling given by Father Joseph Brennan have been formally sanctioned and blessed by the local archbishop. Brennan estimates that there are 8,000 organized covens nationwide, amounting to more than 100,000 practicing satanists, not counting "self-induced" loners.[46] Such statistics may be dismissed as themselves irrational and incredible. Still, when the church and the police combine to give warrant for this belief in some form, it is both rational and normal for large numbers of people to accept cults as a credible threat for areas like Hazleton.

Triggering Event: The Panther Valley Suicide   Two weeks before the prom, a popular Panther Valley student spent a perfectly normal night out drinking with a group of friends. When he arrived home, his mother challenged him about his drinking. The boy went upstairs, returned a few minutes later with a gun, and shot himself in front of his mother. Friends claimed that he had shown no signs of depression and had expressed no suicidal ideas, so they were badly shaken by the event. About a week later (a week before the prom) rumors began to circulate connecting the senior's death with cult activities. Chief suspects were a small group of "weirdos" who were observed doing suspicious things like writing the alphabet backwards and singing "in a strange voice." According to hearsay, they said of the suicide, "Some sacrifices are made in the name of the devil," and they seemed to enjoy the unrest that their new "satanic" status caused.[47] At any rate, they did nothing to refute the rumors, and their alleged involvement turned into a legend in itself. A Hazleton-area student heard this from teachers: "There were five students who attended Panther Valley that were members of an organized cult. A pact was made within the group that these five students were to commit suicide before their school prom that year. One boy did and the other four members backed out. Because of this, the cult threatened to kill someone in area schools before each prom that year."[48]

The situation then turned ugly. Soon a group of athletes, close friends of the dead student, received written threats signed with satanic symbols, warning "you will be the next one." Someone spray-painted a skull on the suicide's gravestone, and rumor held that four persons had been observed in black capes performing some kind of chant over the grave. At the same time, crank phone calls began to threaten the lives of Principal Rader, other school officials, and their families. The actual persons who made these threats were never positively identified, but both adults and students suspected the "weirdos." They thus became the subject of an intense investigation: examination of their school and public library records showed that some of them had checked out "suspicious" books, and Principal Rader claimed to have received good information that some of the group had attended a "meeting" of satanists in the vicinity of Allentown, the nearest major metropolitan area.

Though confronted with this evidence, the "weirdos" continued to deny that they had been responsible for the threats. A fellow student remarked that the leader refused to answer questions "and basically got weirder than he already was," though she admitted that "when you're trying to find something wrong with someone, it usually doesn't take very long to come up with something. . . . There was not much confession to anything and still no denial either."[49] In the end, the principal told me (not without satisfaction) that a group of the dead student's friends simply accosted some of the weirdos on the street and "busted ass."

The violence of this initial phase of rumors was a reaction to the threat posed by the student's suicide. Since there was no rational reason for the act, and no apparent warnings, the death at first seemed irrational, absurd. In fact, a study done in Luzerne County during the same period showed that only eight of twenty recorded suicide victims signaled their intentions in any way, even by writing a suicide note.[50] Nevertheless, 73 percent of students surveyed agreed that "There are always warnings before a person commits suicide." The student's abrupt act therefore seemed to contradict most people's expectations and required a more "rational" explanation. The idea that satanists had caused his death fit at least a germ of logic to the event. Satan is the spirit that negates, as many authorities in the area preach, and satanists enjoy power over other people. One of the ways, according to cult "experts," is to induce recruits to kill themselves, as a pledge to the devil or as the only way to leave the cult once they have been initiated. Although only 25 percent of students polled agreed that there was a connection between satanism and suicide, local authorities insist that it explains some recent cases they have seen. During his talks, detective Sworin showed parents a binder belonging to a local teenaged suicide victim; it contained "satanic" symbols, lyrics of an Ozzy Osbourne song, and a suicide note that ended "I have nothing to live for but Satan."

"Heavy metal" music and satanism are synonymous for many adults, particularly since some musicians have in fact been influenced by occult writers like Aleister Crowley, and many others have incorporated satanic trappings into their music and stage acts.[51] Some critics of this music have gone so far as to say that the songs are satanically inspired and, if played backwards, reveal subliminal messages magically inducing the listener to commit suicide or worship Satan.[52] Even doodling the logos of such bands or jotting down their lyrics may be dangerous: Father Keck, counselor at Bishop Hoban High School in nearby Wilkes-Barre, warned a Sugarloaf PTA meeting in October 1989 that devil worship first manifested itself in such doodles, which were an early warning of suicide. Sworin too commented that "drawings of evil beings ... [and those] concerning the rock groups that are around" were an "indicator" of potential suicide. "A contributing factor?" he added: "Very *definitely* a contributing factor."

Dying for Satan, however horrifying, at least affirms the community's mythology; issuing death threats, however ugly, at least presents the student's suicide as part of an ordered plan, not as a random, absurd act. Both sides, as unlikely as it seems at first, appear to have tried to contain the threat that the suicide occurred by connecting it to existing rational belief structures. But since the "weirdo" group could not have been involved in any pact with the dead student, there was no real point in blaming them for the suicide. Official sanctions, even unofficial violence, could not therefore provide closure for the tensions produced by the suicide. These required a showdown more in line with community norms and myths, a magical event that would focus and limit fears more effectively.

The Prom-Panic as Showdown Nothing unusual occurred at the three area proms, and interest in the suicide and in dangerous cult activity declined rapidly afterward. One student's reaction, recorded on a survey form, was typical: "It was bullshit nothing happened a hoax." Why prom night? Most obviously, it was the next significant social event for the community. But popular culture also provided useful models for presenting a prom as an occasion for violent death. Stephen King's novel *Carrie*, memorably filmed in 1976 by Brian de Palma, describes one such event that ends in a bloodbath. A shy girl with supernatural powers is crowned Queen of the Prom but is immediately soaked in pig's blood as part of a cruel prank. In a fit of rage, she destroys most of the attending senior class in a pyrotechnic display of PK. (One of the Panther Valley legends, we recall, said that the satanists would open fire at this very moment.) Another popular movie, *Prom Night*, appeared in 1980. Starring Jamie Lee Curtis, the lead of a series of teen-oriented "slasher" movies, this film is about a mysterious murderer who stalks a group of girls during their senior prom.

It therefore makes sense to see the senior prom as more than simply an occasion for adolescents to celebrate: it becomes a potentially dangerous rite of passage. During the prom, an adolescent "comes out" into young adult status, and so failure to attend, or failure to be invited, is sometimes a crushing psychological blow. Likewise, those who attend risk making some memorable blunder, or not measuring up to others' display of fancy clothing or other means of conspicuous consumption. So extending this already marginal experience by adding satanic threats was, for many, a logical and realistic move.

The Panther Valley principal perhaps summed up the response of many administrators when he determined to go ahead with the prom in spite of the death threats, "to show these guys that we were not going to let them scare us out of our prom." A persistent element in students' memories was that some other high schools canceled their proms out of fear of the satanists. (In fact, other proms were held as scheduled, and in most cases the sponsoring high schools were not affected by the rumor.) Could the prom have been a drama, a sort of mock-ordeal, intended to create a sense of *communitas* by fabricating some kind of fictitious threat, then repelling it through group action? Perhaps some students saw the event as a positive event for "our" school; by contrast, "other" schools let satanists make cowards of them and canceled their rites of passage out of fear.

I think not. One telling sign is that few students remember the night of the prom with any sense of pride. One recalled that "the prom was horrible, there was all kinds of security cops there, everyone had to be searched when entering, and there was such an atmosphere of gloom, that it was impossible to have a good time." If those who spread the rumor intended to use it to create *communitas*, they clearly failed. In any case, it is hard to see how such a drama could have been staged. The intensity of the rumor set up a model for ostension, the projection of legend into real-life actions. Everyone knew what might happen on prom night, so if some teen had been so unwise as to show up in the parking lot in a black robe, the police and security might have shot first and done performance-analysis later. In fact, police have noted that armed vigilante groups aiming to eliminate satanists pose more of a threat to teenagers than shadowy cult recruiters.[53]

So the event was primarily an expression of *adult* fears about adolescents' rites of passage. During this night's rite of passage, many teens want to exercise their new adult status through extravagant drinking and sexual encounters; parents recognize this as part of the event and obviously want to limit their kids' activities. Principal Mussoline recalled that during the weeks leading up to the prom, students at Hazleton High School were bombarded with a series of movies and special programs warning them not to drink and drive. On TV and radio, the prom season is marked by a public-service blitz, during which students are warned that if they don't confide in parents and watch what they do, their prom night might be their last night on earth. Hence prom night is already an uneasy mix between adolescent license and adult authority. Drinking for teens is illegal in Pennsylvania, so the threat of sudden death is rational, but less immediate than that of being confronted with a grim adult with a gun and a summons. Waiting for devil worshipers at the prom was a more visible and extreme form of local administrators' efforts to contain adolescents' normal acts of rebellion. Holding the prom at all, even with the discomfort that the tight security caused, allowed school administrators to put on a test of local safety procedures, even a display of force for the benefit of parents. "Whenever something happens like that," the Bishop Hafey prom coordinator admitted, "we might tend to overreact. But in the long run that's usually the safer way of going." Hazleton Principal Mussoline likewise was skeptical about the story but felt that it was best to get the police involved "and at least BE there in the event (God forbid) something happened." Indeed, he recalled that he and his superintendents "spent the biggest part of the prom that night outside in the parking lots."

Certainly adolescents participated in the welter of rumors and threats that came out of Panther Valley, but when the legend spread to Hazleton High and Bishop Hafey, only parents and school officials took it seriously. And, as one Hazleton student commented, Principal Mussoline spent a lot of time out on the parking lot looking for troublemakers anyway, so the legend only justified his normal response. The extremes to which they went may have, in fact, negated the ritual's normal significance for teens, reinforcing their perception that, in the eyes of parents and principals, they were still children to be monitored.

Another student response, more sympathetic to administrators' reactions, claimed that "the police successfully prevented anyone from killing themselves." The show of force, that is, left the impression that aggressive adult intervention could prevent future suicides. Since most area suicides occur without warning, this idea is illogical but comforting. But the Lansford area did institute a crisis intervention center in the wake of the panic, and Panther Valley High School invited a string of experts on teenage suicide and supposed "suicide pacts" to the area. These "magical practices" both heightened faculty members' sensitivity to suicide danger signals and gave them the impression that they were somehow warding off irrational acts in the future. Whether coincidental or somehow related, so-called "clusters" of teen suicides are a common fear, and high school administrators feel that unless some kind of constructive-seeming action is taken, the act will somehow become contagious. "Satanism," whatever else it may be in a rural community, is at least one handy "name" used to contain and limit the threat of an unexplained suicide.

Morals and Magic   The two major responses—that it was a hoax and that it successfully prevented suicide—grow organically out of the definition of the prom as a physical confrontation between satanists and community members. When no satanists appeared, either there were no satanists in the area, or the existing satanists were too cowardly to stand up to the community's show of force. In either case, the fears embodied in the legend were exposed as unfounded, and the community could return to its normal routine.

We should, however, resist assuming that the message was the same for everyone at the same time. For some adolescents, making such a prom deadly may have heightened its status as a rite of passage, making their attendance doubly a proof of their adult status. The participants may not have been simply adolescents dabbling in the occult; the Lansford death threats, police later discovered, were written by a parent who had grudges against administrators and used the cult stories as an opportunity for revenge.[54] For some school administrators, turning the prom into a show of force may have been a way of assuring edgy parents that they were, after all, in control of their children. For a few members of the community, the currency of the story might in itself have been proof that satanic cults are prevalent. As Medalia and Larsen point out, when people lost interest in the phenomenon, they did not automatically drop the belief that it embodied.[55] Finally, for a few participants, the event may have been seen as a hoax proving that adolescent "quasi-satanic" rebellion was justified, since grown-ups are prone to hysterical delusions and really do not understand what Ozzy Osbourne is all about. Hence the event carries the seeds of future panics, and indeed, as we will see, the same material was recycled in the area in 1996, with similar results.

True, the devil worshipers never came to the prom, nor could local and state police produce evidence of dangerous cults in the area. From this point of view, the panic was a delusion. Phillips Stevens correctly argues that folklorists ought to be outraged when satanic rumors like these turn into crusades directed against ethnic or social groups, or when they unintentionally threaten innocent parties.[56] And there were ugly aspects to the event: the investigation of the "weirdos" was possibly unjustified and certainly violated their civil rights. The presence of armed security guards meant at least the potential for fatal mistakes if any disruption was perceived as "satanic."

Yet we too should not overreact, if it means that we ignore the background of such legends in community anxieties. Approaching satanic cult panics purely as delusions denies that communities like the Hazleton area need such stories to give them a handle on diffuse anxieties. In other words, daring the satanists to come to the prom puts a human face and rational motives onto situations otherwise perceived as chaotic. The Panther Valley student's suicide remains a puzzle whose threat to the community could not directly be focused or contained except through "magical" means. The Hazleton-area prom night panic was successful magic in that it focused participants' unresolved tensions onto a single community event. Overall, it helped deflect attention away from specific students and provided a logical point of closure, after which it was simply unnecessary to discuss satanic cults further. If the Hazleton area's prom night was a delusion, it was on some level a therapeutic one.

Chapter 12

DEATH BY FOLKLORE

By the middle of October, Ohio seemed ripe for the frost. The last of the harvest festivals wound to a close in a whirl of orange crepe and pumpkin queens, while homeowners doggedly raked dead leaves and bagged them for the trash collectors. The morning air was crisp, even if the first hard freeze had not yet killed the tomatoes, not yet. Still, in 1982, with the aftermath of the Chicago Tylenol murders crowding the papers, the atmosphere seemed icier than usual.

Especially unwelcome was the arrival of the Halloween season, and the fragile boundary between legend and fact was easily broached. Police vainly scoured farmland near Columbus after residents reported hearing a baby crying, night after night, out in the surrounding fields.[1] On October 14 local "haunted houses" opened amid complaints that simulated horrors were psychologically damaging to children. One authority complained, "You have given the message that destruction of human beings is laughable, that it is fun to pretend to kill people and chop them up."[2] Meanwhile, some forty miles southeast of Columbus, the county sheriff was fishing out of the Hocking River the chopped-up pieces of two human torsos.

The story of Annette Cooper and Todd Schultz, the teenagers who owned these torsos, has, like all legends, neither resolution nor end. They may have been murdered by the man who was first convicted and sentenced to death for the crime, then freed on appeal. Or they may have been ritually killed by a satanic cult, as some argue. Or they may have died, like the Tylenol victims, in some unexplained and hence grimmer way. In any case, their fates were intimately tied to the region's traditional narratives, to the spirit of the macabre Halloween 1982, and to the dynamics of the legendary process itself: in more than one way, their murder was legend.

Legends are normative definitions of reality, maps by which one can determine what has happened, what is happening, and what will happen. We can never determine the truth behind the Cooper/Schultz murder and similar cases in which folklore and murder combine. But the concept of ostension allows us to look at such crimes from a new perspective. Legends can help the folk relieve themselves of contemporary fears, but they may also serve as patterns for psychotics, cunning criminals, or desperate communities for provoking the same fears.

Animal Mutilation as Ostension
To comprehend the impact of the Cooper/Schultz murders, one must first examine the legends and rumors against which the crime was seen. Largely rural, southeastern Ohio depends on strip mining, backyard oil wells, farming, forestry, and, in small towns like Athens and Logan, small industry. Residents are quiet, suspicious of strangers. A student from the region observed, "The vast majority of people in this area found life hard and living sparse. It was these rural people that had a much stronger belief in the legends and stories."[3] One of the most persistent of these concerns an underground cult of witches or satanists who periodically sacrifice and mutilate animals during weird rites. This belief is not limited to the Logan area but forms part of a much larger corpus of legends and beliefs found throughout rural America. Jeffrey Victor, surveying outbreaks of panics concerning dangerous satanists, found that nearly all of them occurred in "small towns and rural areas . . . rather than in large, urban areas" where one would expect "urban legends" to circulate. He argued that increased economic stress in rural America, combined with anxieties over disintegrating family relations, fueled such stories: "The metaphorical language of the rumors tells the story of families, whose world is falling apart and whose ideals are being threatened by evil forces."[4]

As one expression of this panic, beginning in the summer of 1974, farmers across rural America began to report "cattle mutilations": cows were found drained of their blood, stripped of their sex organs "with surgical precision," and marked with enigmatic geometrical patterns. Many amateur investigators, puzzled by the lack of footprints around such carcasses, hypothesized that the cows had been taken aboard UFOs, mutilated, then dropped back to earth. Others postulated complex theories featuring weird cults. In Oklahoma, a special committee was appointed by the governor in 1974 to investigate such incidents. By March 1975 this team concluded that there was no evidence that "ritualistic practices or Satanic cults" were involved in any way. But the report noted that such rumors were commonplace in Nebraska and Minnesota and that Texas authorities seriously believed that satanists were involved. A near panic had occurred in Kansas when one official stated publicly that "the type of person who would mutilate cattle might do the same thing to children."[5]

This theory was elaborated by the Aerial Phenomenon Research Organization (APRO), working in cooperation with sympathetic Texas law enforcement agents. They found evidence that many of the mutilations had indeed been committed by a "bizarre Satanical group":

It is believed that members of the Satanic group would stalk the intended sacrificial victims under cover of darkness. They probably used large pieces of cardboard to distribute their weight so as not to leave any tracks. To avoid a struggle the animals were immobilized by being shot with a tranquilizer dart. This was substantiated when autopsies disclosed traces of nicotine sulfate in the livers of some of the mutilated animals.[6] The next step was to administer a heart stimulant, designed to make the animal's heart pump very fast. The throat artery was then punctured and the gushing blood, literally down to the last drop, was caught in large plastic bags. Upon completion of the mission everything, including the blood, organs and cardboard, is carried away from the scene, leaving no clues.[7]

This theory was "proved" to the satisfaction of one FBI agent when two convicted Texas convicts confessed their involvement in the cult. They added that the sex organs were used in sex orgies and that at least four teenagers had also been murdered in much the same way. The other details were left, according to this confession, to make people believe that UFOs were involved. The real culprits, the cult, consisted of about fifty devoted cult members and four to seven hundred part-time members, including many otherwise respectable lawyers, doctors, and citizens. Their goal: "to graduate to people so they can usher in a 1000 year Reign of Darkness while Satan rules supreme."[8]

Similar mutilation incidents had occurred in southeastern Ohio since November 1966, when a registered nurse complained to the FBI that mysterious cattle rustlers had "expertly butchered" some of her cows, draining them of their blood.[9] In 1976, a whole series of animal mutilations briefly panicked the area. In separate incidents, rabbits, and chickens were slashed open, a dog was tortured to death with cigarette burns, and a pet llama was impaled through the vagina with a wooden stake. During the same summer, rumors of "black robed men . . . performing strange rituals" spread through the region, climaxing when investigators came across a stone ring near Logan, enclosing a cow's skull propped up like a religious icon. Hocking County residents stocked up on firearms and combed the woods for satanists, but none were found, the mutilations eventually stopped, and the incidents were left to become legend.[10]

In several other areas of Ohio, local police conducted extensive investigations into apparently real satanists. In 1977, the year after the Hocking County mutilations, police in Sidney (Shelby County) found a cow's head in a phone booth; its eyes had been gouged out and bizarre patterns had been sliced into its hide. Shortly after, residents reported seeing groups of white-robed figures walking in procession along country roads, holding lighted candles. Investigators allegedly learned that "the activity was indeed linked to Satanic worship, which in turn was linked to prostitution and sales of illegal drugs." Regrettably, they concluded, before they could collect enough information to make arrests, "the Satanists went even deeper underground" and the incidents remained a mystery. Rumors circulated widely among police officials that babies had been murdered in satanic rites. An anonymous Fairfield County woman claimed to have been taken, at the age of thirteen, to a satanic ceremony "at a huge open field in a remote area of Northern Ohio," where a baby was ritually murdered. Police took her story seriously but admitted that it was difficult to sort out the fiction from fact.[11] An altar marked with animal blood was found in Belmont County in 1982, and, just before Halloween 1983, a mutilated dog was found in the middle of a pentagram drawn on the floor of an abandoned house in a county adjacent to Hocking.

Adolescents and college students kept these rumors alive as part of their legend-trips. In the Cleveland area, for example, teens said that "Witchy People" gather along the Cuyahoga River: "they're like in these monk outfits and they have a fire burning and they sacrifice things like animals and if anybody bothers them they just stand there and look at you." Likewise, near Toledo, "The Candlemen" hold occult services once a year, during which a human is sacrificed; those who spy on their rites likewise are stripped naked, stabbed, and strangled.[12] Near Logan, one popular legend-trip focuses on a broad ridge running north and west of Athens, alternatively known as Peach Ridge or Mount Nebo. One of the small cemeteries on the ridge, according to these adolescent stories, contains the graves of witches and therefore serves as a meeting place for those practicing black magic.[13] Adding to the cemetery's power is its position in the exact center of a natural pentagram formed by the peaks of five surrounding hills.[14]

No informant provided any firsthand accounts of the rites, but nearly everyone knew a cautionary story telling how "someone" had spied on the cult and had come to a bad end. One recalled, "I heard that one time a girl came down here [Peach Ridge] by herself and nobody ever saw her again. A few days later one of her girlfriends went down—she made [it] back but she was all sliced up, like with a razor or something."[15] The degree to which informants take such stories seriously, as usual, varies. One was quite willing to go to the graveyard at night, commenting, "Guys take their chicks down there to scare the shit out of them. They probably think they'll get a fuck out of it." Still, he recalled that his source for the legend was "scared shitless" and refused to get out of the car when they went there.[16] Another source was eagerly planning to test the site's supernatural nature: "We've been reading up on the occult and things and we are gonna go on out there go camping and we are gonna raise some spirits. I want to see a spirit—I really do." Yet, even as he planned to emulate the Peach Ridge witches, he too described contrary reactions:

Now, I went there a second time and we talked to people around there asking where this place is and people are strange. They'd say, "What are you looking there for, you don't go near there." They are just really weird. I don't know what it is about it. People really act strange about this place. They are scared shitless. I don't know why. . . .

They told us, this one farmer we stopped at, he said "Wow, you just don't go near there—stay away," and he just refused to talk about it, closed the doors. He didn't want to talk to us, and we went there, it was day time this other time, and . . . down there we found a dead horse that had been tied down and left to die, sitting there the thing couldn't have been dead much more than a week, and it's the strangest situation.[17]

Probably all these rumors and legends reflect a complex assortment of deliberate acts, misinterpreted evidence, and exaggeration. Each animal mutilation must remain at heart a mystery, since investigators looking for evidence of natural causes will find it and seek no further and those who "confess" to the acts may be lying. But the concept of ostension, as Dégh and Vázsonyi adapt it, allows us to identify the common variations. *Quasi-ostension* is the observer's interpretation of puzzling evidence in terms of narrative tradition. Accordingly, those who believe in satanism will interpret the phenomena they witness as evidence for cult activity.[18] In fact, most experts feel that "mutilated" animals have died of natural causes and then have been partially dismembered by predators like crows and feral dogs. And "satanic" altars may have been erected as fireplaces by partying youths or by local residents for picnics. Still, observers prepared to find evidence of satanism will "map" such evidence in terms of known rituals. The evidence thus is a sign to the observer, communicating, "The satanists have been here too!" In such cases, the act of interpretation is the legend performance, not the actions that actually produced the evidence.

Alternatively, some evidence could be produced by *pseudo-ostension*, or imitating the outlines of a known narrative to perpetuate a hoax. Adolescents may feel that they can get a rise out of adults by mimicking an animal sacri-

fice, using a handy carcass or even killing a farm animal to provide the necessary evidence. Teens who spray-paint inverted pentangles and "666" in public
places also act from the same impulse. Such actions do not reflect genuine
cult sacrifices; still, real animals may be killed and mutilated to communicate
the possibility of such cultic rites. Such pranksters are leaving signs that tell
the observer, "See? The legend is true after all!"

Finally, there is the option of *ostension* proper. Intrigued by such stories,
an individual or individuals may decide to don robes, light candles, mumble
chants, and really kill animals—or humans—in some ceremonial fashion, in
the hopes of raising a spirit. The interest expressed by the informant quoted
earlier is, in fact, a nascent form of this impulse: "we are gonna raise some
spirits. I want to see a spirit—I really do. I really would like to. If I were to
see one it would change my attitude of thinking so much."[19] As one adolescent told me, "If the devil exists, then God must, too." While the number of
teens dabbling with satanism may be exaggerated in the popular press, apparently some individuals have admitted to improvising "black masses" and even
to killing small animals to see what would happen.[20] It seems likely that all
three forms of ostension function synergistically. That is, the more naturally
occurring incidents are explained in terms of "satanism," the more certain
people, especially adolescents, will be tempted to experiment with ostension,
either by acting out narratives as hoaxes, or, more dangerously, by taking
satanism seriously and becoming, however temporarily, part of the legend
itself. And when a dimension of the tradition suggests human mutilation and
murder, one option unavoidably includes sliced-up torsos in the river.

The Logan "Satanic" Murders   The hysteria that followed the discovery
of the dismembered corpses near Logan in 1982 thus becomes readily comprehensible. At first the discovery of the decomposed torsos, followed by the
location of Cooper and Schultz's heads, arms, and legs in a series of small
graves, seemed explicable in no other terms than cult sacrifice. Although the
bodies were "badly decomposed," still investigators reported that dismember-
ing had been done by a "skilled professional" like a surgeon. Almost at once
the 1975–76 animal mutilations were recalled, and Logan residents blamed
devil worshipers. "This has to be a cult thing," one commented. "That's the
only thing that explains why the bodies were so mutilated." Another speculated that the two had "discovered something that someone didn't want them
to see."[21] For their part, police refused to discount the possibility of real satanists but attributed the murders to "a screwball of some type." A spokesman
noted, "People are upset. We've heard a lot of rumors since the word has

gotten out. . . . People are wondering about their kids. And Halloween is coming up."[22] Trick-or-treat was first rescheduled to the afternoon of Halloween, then canceled altogether in favor of a city-sponsored daylight party. The holiday passed, uneasily, without incident, but still without an explanation of the couple's deaths.

Nearly a year later, as Halloween again loomed on the calendar, police finally made an arrest, and an alternative story became public knowledge.[23] From the first, Annette Cooper's avuncular stepfather, Dale Johnston, had seemed unusually anxious to help the investigators. He told of "visions" in which he had seen "a place with water and tall trees" even before the bodies were found in a matching site. To assist with identification of the bodies, Johnston produced a photo of Annette in the nude. He had taken it as a joke, he explained, but police became suspicious and learned that Annette had complained that her stepfather had raped her more than once. A former boyfriend told police that when he had dated Annette, he received threatening phone calls, promising that if he did not leave Annette alone he would be killed and castrated. The voice sounded a lot like Johnston's, he recalled, and Todd Schultz's body had indeed been castrated. On the basis of such evidence, Logan authorities obtained an indictment and, in January 1984, brought Johnston to trial.

The case was followed closely by the community, even broadcast live over a local radio station from a hookup in the courtroom. The prosecution portrayed Johnston as an unbalanced child molester who was jealous over his stepdaughter's attachment to Schultz and feared public exposure of his abuse. He lured the couple to his farm and shot them; then, to make disposal of the bodies easier, he cut them up and transported the pieces to nearby fields and the river. The defense, however, stressed crucial gaps in the evidence: no murder weapon was found; no blood, fibers, or ballistic traces linked Johnston conclusively to the bodies. No witnesses saw Johnston near where the bodies were found. Only one person saw the three together on the day of the murder—even he had to be hypnotized to recall important details. Johnston admitted that he sometimes masturbated in his family's presence "to relieve a prostate problem," but he, his wife, and his other stepdaughter all testified that their family life was normal and happy. Bizarrely, Annette herself corroborated this point, via a videotape she had made for a local beauty contest.

Despite these gaps, though, a three-judge panel deliberated less than two hours before finding Johnston guilty. Warned against demonstrations, the crowd inside the courtroom remained quiet, but as the verdict was broadcast over the radio, pandemonium erupted in the court's outside hallways and spread into the streets. Finally liberated from the specter of hidden satanists, residents screamed, cheered, pounded on trash cans, honked car horns, and shouted the good news to each other. "Justice has been done," stated Todd Schultz's mother, with tears glistening on her cheeks, as she went home to open a bottle of champagne.[24] Not so, claimed Johnston's attorneys, who began the process of appeal. The community's jubilation marked, in their eyes, only the catharsis of certifying their client as a scapegoat. Fearing community panic, they argued, police had evaded the evidence that suggested satanic involvement. The real killers were still at loose among the seemingly normal residents.

Support for this defense came from Jeff F. Hilson III, a Columbus high school teacher and forensic specialist in cult murders. Hilson was subpoenaed by the defense but never called, and after the conviction his testimony became part of the defense's motion for a new trial.[25] Examining the autopsy report, Hilson found strange markings on Schultz's torso that suggested satanic symbolism: a cross over the solar plexus with "rays" emanating from it, corresponding to "stations of the Satanic cross dedicated to the Satanic trinity of Lucifer, Beelzebub and Baal." He concluded that the Cooper/Schultz murder "beyond question was an operation carried out by five or more dedicated, totally perverse Satanists."

What probably happened was this, he said: the couple, naked, were "lying closely together on the ground" near where their bodies were later found, when a satanic cult member surprised and shot them. The killer than left to gather the other devil worshipers for a "midnight ceremony." The couple's blood was drunk "as part of a ritual," while their sex organs and fingernails were removed. They are, according to Hilson, "probably in use by the killers as amulets." Todd's body was then mutilated and dismembered according to satanic symbolism "with the consummate skill of the group leader, who was no stranger to the task," while Annette's body, more brutally hacked, "was subject to the novices." Hilson warned that "each time Satan is summoned forth, the offering up of a sacrifice must be greater than before. . . . At a future date, the Satanists of the Hocking Hills must better this rite when they next call up their deity."

Dale Johnston, interviewed after the conviction, denied involvement and endorsed the satanic hypothesis. He recalled that friends warned him when he moved to Hocking County that animal mutilations were "frequent" and stated that he had "always" believed devil worshipers responsible for his stepdaughter's death. Yet another vision, he mentioned, had informed him that "a well-known local man" was linked to the crime, but he did not elaborate.[26] Appeals continued over the next five years, and eventually, in October 1988, the Ohio Court of Appeals ruled that the judges had erred in admitting the testimony of the hypnotized witness and quashed the verdict. When the judge in the new trial refused to allow this and other evidence, prosecutors dropped the case, and Johnston was freed on May 11, 1990.[27] While Johnston announced plans to hire a private detective to find the real killers, no definitive account emerged of how or why Annette Cooper and Todd Schultz died. These remain mysteries; what is clear is that the murder was some sort of traditional performance.

Murder as Legend Performance Looking at the evidence from the perspective of ostension, we can suggest several possible interpretations. Some are less likely than others. Perhaps Cooper and Schultz died as a murder-suicide, then were mutilated by predators? In this case, the mutilation and dismemberment of the bodies might have had no intrinsic significance, but, like the cattle mutilations, were given meaning by a hysterical populace looking for hints of satanic activity. The difficulty here is that the pieces of the body were found buried in five or six small graves, and parts of Todd Schultz's penis were found tucked inside a sock that had been left by railroad tracks near the field, as if to lead searchers to the body.[28] These facts suggest that a human murderer chose to dismember and scatter the bodies in a way that they would be found and inspire horror. Given the currency of legends involving animal mutilations in the area, it is also likely that the culprit intended the evidence to be read in terms of existing folk tradition: "It's happened; they *have* graduated to humans after all." The question, though, is at which point folklore entered the performance.

One possibility is that the crime was a form of pseudo-ostension; that is, satanism had nothing to do with the murder itself but everything to do with how the murderer intended his crime to be seen by the community. Thus the crime came first, folklore second. If Johnston were guilty, for instance, then he might have disposed of the body in such a way as to throw police off his track and direct them toward legendary characters who have a habit of going "even deeper underground" when sought. Such a tactic resembles the way in which legends and popular images of "missing children" have been used by individuals to cover their tracks. In the most benign form, youngsters have tried to cover up all-night partying sprees by claiming the next morning that they had been "abducted."

But more sinister variations exist. Brunvand notes that "The Attempted Abduction," a contemporary legend involving a child snatched from its mother at a shopping mall, began one of its periodic cycles of popularity after a TV docudrama about the abduction-murder of Adam Walsh was aired in

October 1983. The legend passed for genuine in many parts of the country throughout spring and summer of 1984 and gained additional credibility when columnist Ann Landers published it on November 21.[29] Shortly afterwards, on January 3, 1985, Sharon Comitz told police that she had left her month-old baby Garret alone in her car for a few minutes at Ames Plaza in Philipsburg, Pennsylvania. When she returned, the baby was gone; its body was found the next day in a nearby stream. The family lawyer commented: "This just doesn't fit the pattern of crime we have here. None of it makes any sense. This is a small area and if someone were crazy enough to do this, people would know who it was. The person would start with minor crime and work his way up to a crime like this. We're near Route [Interstate] 80 so I think a transient probably did it."[30]

A police investigation showed, however, that Sharon Comitz had a history of abusing children and that the parents had taken out a $3,000 insurance policy on the baby's life the day before it was "abducted." Eventually, the mother admitted that she had killed the child herself and fabricated the story; she was sentenced to eight years in a prison psychiatric program.[31]

A similar case occurred in Philadelphia four years later. On January 10, 1989, Tanya Dacri claimed that while visiting the Northeast Shopping Center, two young men ran up, snatched her two-month-old son, Zachary, and sped away in a waiting four-door brown Ford with no license plate. Again, though, Dacri proved to have a history of child abuse, and she soon confessed that she had drowned the baby in his tub and cut him into six pieces. Then she and her husband disposed of the parts by throwing them off bridges in rural areas northwest of the city.[32] In both cases, the abduction story was initially reported in the media as genuine and so served as a smoke screen to deflect attention away from clues that would lead back to the family circle itself.

More ambiguous is the case of Timothy O'Bryan, an eight-year-old from Houston, Texas, who died on Halloween night 1974 from eating trick-or-treat candy laced with cyanide. His father, Ronald Clark O'Bryan, claimed that his son had received the fatal treat from a "hairy-handed" weirdo at one of the houses they had visited together, but police found circumstantial evidence that suggested that O'Bryan himself had purchased the cyanide and given it to Timothy to collect on an insurance policy he had taken out on the child's life. The case was widely publicized in Texas and was partially responsible for temporary bans on trick-or-treating there. In a bizarre twist, O'Bryan's execution was originally set for midnight on Halloween 1982, a time that the judge chose as especially appropriate for the crime. In fact, O'Bryan won several stays, but when he was finally killed, shortly after midnight on March

31, 1984, Texans all over the state showed up in bars wearing Halloween costumes.[33]

This festive reaction suggests that his execution, like Johnston's conviction,
was seen as a ritual to rid the community of the threat posed by the legend.
For unlike Sharon Comitz and Tanya Dacri, O'Bryan may have killed his own
son with the help of a legendary plot; he may have been guilty (as Grider says)
"of acting out an 'urban legend' and carrying it to the ultimate conclusion—
murder."[34] But O'Bryan maintained his innocence to the end, and if he was
not the murderer, then both he and his son died as victims of folklore performed as ostension.

Did Cooper and Schultz likewise die as the result of literal ostension? It is
possible, but not likely, that a group of five or more "totally perverse" satanists live in or near Logan, and that they could drop everything to rush off to
a midnight ceremony of blood drinking and mutilation without making other
people suspicious. Given the hysteria that followed the bodies' discovery, how
could such clues escape police attention? It is possible, however, that folklore
came first, the crime second: unbalanced persons could have used existing
legends as models for real-life actions. Certainly the case of Richard Kasso, a
Long Island teenager and heavy metal admirer, illustrates this model. In July
1984, angered over the theft of drugs, Kasso stabbed and mutilated a fellow
teen during a mock satanic ritual. After forcing the victim to say "I love
Satan," Kasso gouged out his eyes and, announcing that "the devil had ordered him to kill," struck the fatal blow. Apprehended by police, he committed suicide soon after. Local law enforcement agents blamed Kasso's gang, the
"Knights of the Black Circle," for a series of "charred or tortured animals,
apparent victims of ritual sacrifice," found over the previous three years. Although residents of Kasso's hometown, Northport, denied police statements
that the area was "infested" by satanic cults, it is clear that Kasso's actions
were guided by legendary accounts of devil worship.[35]

Likewise, Texas confessed serial murder Henry Lee Lucas claimed to have
received guidance from a cult. Convicted of killing his mother in 1960, Lucas
had spent ten years in prisons and mental institutions. After he was arrested
in 1982 for killing his fifteen-year-old common-law wife and cutting her body
into "little teeny pieces," he began to confess to a long series of random
murders. After being sentenced to death for killing a female hitchhiker alongside Interstate 35 on Halloween, he admitted to being a member of "a devil's
organization" called "The Hands of Death." This cult killed both animals and
humans in ritual crucifixions "supposed to bring the devil back to life," and
some of the members, Lucas recalled, ate human flesh and blood. "For initiation," he added (following the Gang Initiation Legend scenario), "you would

have to go out and kill a person." His companion in crime, Otis Edward Toole (who once confessed to the abduction killing of Adam Walsh) also mentioned belonging to a cult and admitted eating human flesh, and a Catholic lay worker in Texas prisons said that she had heard of The Hands of Death from other inmates who claimed membership.[36]

Law enforcement agents took Lucas's allegations seriously, though they admitted that he could not have committed all the crimes he confessed to. Still, after a three-day conference in October 1983, attended by officers from twenty states, he and Toole were linked firmly to ninety-seven murders. The Texas Rangers maintained a "task force" for police seeking to link their unsolved murders and disappearances with Lucas's stories. In the end, investigators from twenty-six states used his confessions to close their books on more than two hundred murders. But such stories, like those told by Texas convicts to "explain" cattle mutilations, may well have been hoaxes to gain attention, special treatment, and status among other prisoners. After running his toll to six hundred murders, Lucas finally recanted in April 1985 and claimed that he had really killed only one person—his mother. He had followed detectives' lead in fabricating his confessions, he told a Dallas reporter, proving that police were "really stupid." He added, significantly, "Now we'll see who the real criminals are." Undoubtedly many of Lucas's tales were his own elaborations of police- and convict-transmitted legends about cults and serial murderers. But if we take a middle ground and assume that he did kill more than one and fewer than six hundred people, then Lucas may well have patterned some random murders after legendary accounts of ritual murder.

During early stages of the Cooper/Schultz investigation, ostension was considered a real possibility. A railroad trestle near the field where the bodies were found was known as a "hangout" for drifters and drug-using adolescents, who often gathered there to drink and do drugs. If some of the animal mutilations committed in Hocking County in 1976 were committed by psychotics or disturbed teens eager to "copycat" the sensation or "see a spirit," it is plausible that a serial murderer like Lucas or a drug-crazed group like Kasso's might have been responsible for the crime. Such groups, as Gary Alan Fine's study of the Manson Family shows, have distinctive folk cultures, which might well include literal ostension to express antisocial, "helter-skelter" messages.[37] Whether or not the group or individual was involved in organized satanic "worship," the trappings of devil worship could give pattern to essentially nihilistic acts, saying, "Satan made me do this, and his power to destroy extends to any human life."

But it is equally possible that Johnston, or someone else, could use these same trappings to make another statement: not "Satan made me do it," but

"Satan made them do it—*them*—not us God-fearing, Bible-reading, family-rearing members of the community." Neighborhoods like Logan, seeking release from the anxiety of having undetected satanists in their midst, might have demanded another human sacrifice, in this case Dale Johnston. Certainly the celebration that erupted after his conviction dramatizes the sacrificial nature of his sentence. Likewise, police across the country proved surprisingly willing to close unsolved cases on the word of Henry Lee Lucas, suggesting that they too could not abide the possibility of unknown killers living among them. The irony is that Johnston's new trial and Lucas's further revelations get us no closer to ridding our society of the demons they were used to exorcise. We cannot be sure when communities, basing their actions on contemporary legends like those about satanism, will demand another human life.

The Peanut Butter/Ritual Child Abuse Link

Six-year-old Angie McMahon bit down on a tremendous potato chip, as if to prop open her mouth. . . . [She] concentrated harder on the snacks than on the prosecutor's questions, and Judge [William L.] Harth cautioned the attorneys: "We may have to be more patient with this child than we have with others." Angie's responses were shot all over the place.

[Prosecutor] Glenn [Goldberg] asked, "What did you see Kelly [Michaels] do with peanut butter?"

"She, uh, put it on herself," said Angie, in long wide words. Then, swirling her finger in her mouth, playing with potato chip mulch, she provided the next bit of information: Kelly had used both peanut butter and jelly.

Glenn asked: "Where did the jelly come from?"

Angie was breathless, little gasps between her words, "Mm, um, from her vagina."

Out in the courtroom, her grandfather groaned.

"Did you have to lick that off her?"

"Yes," she slurred.

Feet braced on the conference table, Angie reached forward for the bag of chips.[38]

Based on this and similar evidence, on April 15, 1988, a jury found Kelly Michaels guilty of 115 counts of sexual abuse of small children. Michaels had worked as a teacher and teacher's aide at Wee Care Day Nursery in Maplewood, New Jersey, for seven months in 1984–85, without raising any suspicions or complaints from children or staff. But shortly after she left the center for another job, she became the focus of an intense investigation by county prosecutors and the New Jersey Division of Youth and Family Services. Suspicions were raised when one child, whose pediatrician was taking his temperature rectally, remarked, "That's what my teacher does to me at nap time at school. . . . Her takes my temperature." (Michaels told investigators that she and other aides used a forehead strip to take temperatures, and, ironically, the jury acquitted her of the charge of anal penetration that this remark produced.)

Intensive questioning of this child and the others at the day care center produced a complex story, in which she had assaulted children with kitchen implements and Lego blocks, played "Jingle Bells" on the piano in the nude, and forced them to consume human waste and menstrual blood. In August 1988, Michaels was sentenced to forty-seven years in prison. Her case became a cause célèbre among critics of ritual child abuse investigators, and eventually Morton Stavis, founder of the Center for Constitutional Rights, took on her case at no charge. After his death in December 1992, the noted trial lawyer William M. Kunstler directed her appeal.

On March 26, 1993, a New Jersey appeals court overturned the verdict, finding that Michaels had been denied a fair trial. The decision was particularly critical of expert witnesses, who used the theory of child sexual abuse accommodation syndrome "as an alleged scientific process of determining whether the children were actually sexually abused . . . [leading] the jury to believe that the process was rooted in science and thus was a reliable means of determining sexual abuse." It also criticized Judge Harth for playing with the children and holding them on his lap, whispering encouragement in their ears, as they gave testimony against Michaels. "The required atmosphere of the bench's impartiality was lost in this trial," the decision concluded. Prosecutors promised a retrial, but Michaels was freed on bail four days later.[39]

The two most sensational charges were that Kelly Michaels had, variously, smeared peanut butter on herself and made children lick it off, or that she herself had licked it off the children's genitals. Investigators at first found such details almost too bizarre to investigate, but were struck by how the children seemed to attest them independently. The charge remained one of the strongest against Michaels, although coworkers testified that they had never seen peanut butter go missing from the day care's kitchen. However, in June 1994 folklorists found a version of "The Surpriser Surprised" circulating on computer discussion groups and in print and broadcast media. Earlier versions featured the discovery of a nude man or couple.[40] The newer version involved an unclothed woman with peanut butter smeared on her genitals, which her pet dog is licking off. One of the earliest media accounts of the legend appears in *Frank*, the Canadian satirical magazine:

A story that sounds suspiciously like an urban legend is making the rounds at the Dept. of [National] Defence and Canada Post.

The apocryphal tale goes like this: A popular DND (or Post Office) employee is celebrating a birthday, so her co-workers decide to organize a surprise party. During coffee break, one of them rifles through her purse, takes her keys, and makes a copy of her house key. Then a group leaves the office early, enters her house, and waits in the basement to surprise her.

Shortly after, the woman comes home and goes upstairs to the bedroom. Ten minutes later, the woman's dog comes bounding down into the basement, followed by the woman calling, "Lucky? Lucky?"

When she turns on the lights, her friends jump out and yell "surprise!"

And what a surprise it is—the woman is standing stark naked, with peanut butter slathered all over her nether regions. The woman is so mortified that she calls DND/Post Office the next day and resigns. . . or so the story goes.[41]

Now, the coexistence of a contemporary legend scenario with a real-life trial involving perverse peanut butter licking raises disturbing questions. True, folklorists documented the legend *after* the trial, so it might have incorporated submerged details from the intense media publicity given the Kelly Michaels case, with the child transformed to a family pet to transpose the story from horror to bawdy humor. But there are many other contemporary legends about women "caught in the act" performing kinky acts with animals and objects that far predate the Wee Care case. It seems more likely that children or investigators projected details from the legend into the case, producing a form of what Dégh and Vázsonyi term *proto-ostension,* or claiming a legend as a personal experience.

This seems more likely, since a second major charge that appeared from children's disclosures is plainly linked to a contemporary legend found before the date of the trial. The children, coached by adult investigators, said Michaels had played the piano in the nude and taught the children "Buffalo Bill," a game in which they took their clothes off and rolled around together. This scenario is identical with the "Sex Education Horrible Example" contemporary legend actively circulating at least as far back as 1969. A Florida reader, distressed by columnist Abigail Van Buren's support of public school sex education, wrote:

Why, I heard that one teacher got so carried away while conducting a sex education lecture that she completely DISROBED in front of the class!

In another school, the teacher herded the whole class into a dark closet and told them to "feel" each other!

I could tell you much more, but you wouldn't believe it.

Abby responded: "I have heard all these wild tales (and more) but have been unable to locate the teachers who supposedly did the above, the schools in which these incidents were supposed to have occurred, or any of the children who were actually present."

At the same time, Ernest Dunbar found such stories widespread in literature being circulated by the John Birch Society and Billy Hargis's Christian Crusade, two militant right-wing organizations. In one especially popular story, "In some other city (usually quite distant), a teacher . . . put some very young children in a dark room and encouraged them to experiment sexually with each other." Such acts, Dunbar finds, are said to be part of "an international Communist conspiracy to subvert America by corrupting the minds of our young." The media, Parent-Teacher Associations, and the American Medical Association were also said to be part of this communist plot.[42]

Proponents of the trial maintain that Michaels was let off by a coalition of liberal influences and that the children's testimony is true. If so, she might have used details from a bizarre legend in the hopes that the children would not be believed if they tried to tell what had happened. But it remains far more likely that the charges against Kelly Michaels reflect not independent witnesses of criminal acts but knowledge of common legend types.

Folklorists must acknowledge that traditional narratives exist not simply as verbal texts to be collected, transcribed, and archived. They are also maps for action, often drastic action. Our conception of folklore, therefore, must be expanded to consider the ways in which legends reflect both what has "really" happened but also what a person or persons can make happen. In contemporary times too, legends about satanic murder and ritual abuse are not just expressions of fictive horror, they are paradigms for making the world more horrifying. The haunted house and the outside world are always in danger of merging, and some adults find that it is fun to kill people and chop them up. Many more adults find that it is incredibly fulfilling to find scapegoats for their fears of what might happen and punish them—by locking them up or, ultimately, by sacrificing them to the gods of civilization.

Folklorists cannot suppress such legend performances, and they dare not refuse to study them. For legend is not limited in scope to verbal art alone but also includes serious threats in real life.

Conclusions: What Next?

In a brief but pointed critique titled " 'Contemporary Legend'—To Be or Not To Be?" one traditional folklorist chided her more adventurous fellows for having proposed "contemporary legend" as a banner for research without having clearly defined what it is. Legend scholars would be better advised to begin by examining, classifying, and ordering existing archival materials. Once "we know what we are dealing with," she argued, folklorists can follow the traditional path of folkloristics to planned fieldwork, documentation of typical performances, social context, channels of transmission, and other descriptive projects. "Interpretations will have to wait until the data are assembled," she admonished.[1]

It is appropriate the title of this critique quotes the opening of Hamlet's great soliloquy. Hamlet is the archetypal self-indulgent intellectual who fusses with fine distinctions when the situation demands action. Ironically, he finds that even the act of avoiding his duties through suicide is loaded with too many fine points and moral ambiguities, and Hamlet concludes with regret:

> . . . thus the native hue of resolution
> Is sicklied o'er with the pale cast of thought,
> And enterprises of great pitch and moment
> With this regard their currents turn awry
> And lose the name of action.[2]

Certainly Hamlet's words identify a problem that has affected legend scholarship (and folkloristics in general) for decades. We do avoid much of the "muddle" in contemporary legend research if we retreat to the archives and handle our material by its motif numbers and genre descriptions.

But this involves a retreat from the nature of the subject itself. Whatever else we may say about the defining characteristics of contemporary legend, it is *urgent*. It presses on us as something that has "just happened" or is "just about to happen," and it often requires a decision to take quick, decisive action to avoid danger. Such action, as I have suggested, can hardly be judged as "illogical" or a "delusion," as it frequently confronts a symbolic danger with a symbolic response.

The 1990 Persian Gulf conflict shows that this dynamic is hardly limited to small towns and credulous individuals. After Iraq's attempt to annex Kuwait, allies led by Great Britain and the United States succeeded in imposing several economic sanctions on the aggressor. These sanctions, overall, proved effective, and there was little reason to doubt that they would eventually lead to Iraq's capitulation. Why then did pressure build at the end of the year to begin a full-scale military war?

A White House aide noted that George Bush normally looked at issues objectively, fully aware of their complexities. But with Iraq, the aide noted, he "is unlike he is on any other issue. . . this touches some deep inner core. He was deeply offended by the aggression against Kuwait. Later, the atrocities also upset him deeply." Bush himself echoed this sentiment in a statement to college students, saying that while much in this world is "washed in shades of gray," the "brutal" acts of Saddam Hussein are "black and white."[3]

The act most cited by Bush to justify his rush to war was the story, reported in a December 19 Amnesty International report, that when Iraqi soldiers took over a Kuwaiti hospital, they tore more than three hundred premature babies out of incubators and left them to die on the floors while the medical equipment was shipped to Baghdad.[4] Shortly after the report was issued, Bush met with his spiritual advisor, Episcopalian bishop Edmond Browning, who advised Bush to handle the affair patiently. Bush responded, "You should read the Amnesty International report. Then you tell me what I should do."[5] In his address announcing the start of the air war, Bush referred to the fates of "innocent children," seen as another allusion to the atrocity.

Objective commentators commented that it was unlikely that any Kuwaiti hospital would have as many as three hundred incubators, when most children's hospitals in the United States have fewer than fifty. Doctors and nurses who held senior positions at the hospital in question consistently told interviewers that no such incident occurred.[6] Doubtless violent acts were committed during the invasion and later, as tensions grew in the area. But the rationale for a shooting war in the Persian Gulf seems based less on objective military or moral need than on Americans' need to use force as a symbolic way of exorcising a ruler already equated with baby-killing satanic forces.

Not that Saddam Hussein could claim many attributes of a legendary martyr-leader: having written a political tract published in Switzerland as *Unser Kampf*, he repeatedly turned hostages and captured pilots into media shows that allowed the allies to portray him as an unfeeling, sadistic kidnapper. But the problem with atrocity stories is that they tend to turn those who act on them into the agents they think they are fighting. And, of course, the need to take arms against a satanic foe in the Middle East meant that *we* would kill hundreds of real children—however "surgical" our bombings might be.

Another example: several years after the events described in "The Devil Worshippers at the Prom," many of the same themes emerged again in the area in the fall of 1996.[7] The new panic began again with speculation over a teenage suicide, this time the pact-like mutual deaths of two adolescents. It escalated rapidly through rumor and public warnings about teenage satanism into the dubious therapy of "expert" advice. The *Scranton/Wilkes Barre Times Leader*'s September 24 issue boldly announced "2 teens' deaths linked to satanic worship." Much of the article quoted and paraphrased the speculations of Luzerne County district attorney Peter Paul Olszewski, who felt that "there are numbers of other children who are in similar states of the occult as these two were. . . . In Luzerne County, there are more children than we had thought involved in the preliminary stages of black magic."

In fact, the links were not much in evidence; even Olszewski conceded that signs of the teens' involvement with satanism were "not real obvious. . . . By all accounts they were disguising it very well." In fact, the only overt sign of behavior change was that both had dyed their hair black, "one possible sign of satanic worship." Their high school's superintendent, Andrew Marko, told press that the two were both good students and neither had shown signs of problems: "We had no signs of what the lieutenant and the district attorney are talking about." Nevertheless, the crisis brought Detective Gary Sworin back into media attention. Sworin indicated that interest in occultism had been on the wane until recently: "It just seemed like it died down." But with the new affair in the news, he revived old theories about teens entering satanism through fantasy games such as Dungeons and Dragons and through interest in heavy metal music. One new wrinkle, he noted, was teenage swapping of regionally produced "death metal" cassettes with lyrics centering on suicide and self-mutilation. Officials added that dressing in all-black clothing was another danger sign.

On Friday, September 27, the mother of a disturbed fifteen-year-old girl from Wyoming Valley West told press that she had learned that her daughter and others had made a suicide pact to die with the two teens. "Without that part of my child's covenant fulfilled, my daughter's life is in danger," she said, adding that there were ten other serious devil worshippers at the high school. She had the girl committed to a local mental hospital, the fifth time she had been there for drug use and threatened suicide. "It is not drugs alone," the mother said. "It is satanic. . . . She told me her spirits would visit her during the night." This time, she told press, she would not allow her to return home for fear that she would carry out the suicide pact.

On the evening of Sunday, September 29, the Luzerne County District Attorney's Committee on Youth and Violence sponsored a vigil on the county courthouse steps. Olszewski gave brief remarks, followed by a series of local psychologists and counselors who offered advice (often contradictory) to students, parents, and police on how to detect signs of satanism. Bishop James C. Timlin, head of the local Catholic synod, closed the meeting with prayer. Several parents remained behind to ask experts questions, and more lists of trouble signs—including collections of animal bones and occult jewelry such as pentagrams—were distributed. Several teens told a reporter that they often wore black clothes, dyed their hair black, and used black lipstick with white pancake makeup. "We're just different," one fifteen-year-old girl said, complaining that she had been expelled from Wyoming Valley West for showing up for school in "satanic" dress. "It's just a phase," her mother said, agreeing that the school had overreacted. "And black is a slimming color," she added. The outfit, her daughter explained, was just a protest against her classmates' fad of wearing expensive clothes "from the Gap," a clothing chain specializing in pricey youth attire. It did not signal suicidal or satanic tendencies, the girl continued, and denied that she had ever practiced any form of occultism. "I can vouch for that," her mother said. "I searched her room."

A more frightening problem, one of the girl's friends said, was the way in which other students were targeting those who wore such protest clothing. One student who dressed in black had received an anonymous hate letter saying, "Die, freaks!" Other teens, using the paper's thirty-second anonymous phone-in editorial service, addressed other problems. One noted that when his parents forced him to attend church, he noticed that the priest and most of the congregation were wearing black. "Are these people disguised, are they really devil worshipers? . . . You people should learn what you're talking about before you report things. You're really making yourselves look like fools." Another suggested, "If you expect us kids not to do drugs, smoke or drink, then have some classes for our parents on how to listen and understand us. All they do is fight and watch TV and lie to us about everything. . . . We need love and understanding and someone to talk to and listen to our problems."

Initially, these exchanges of opinion seemed to conclude the panic. But on Sunday, October 20, Penn State University's Wilkes-Barre campus announced a daylong workshop on "Dealing with Satanism and the Occult" for police officers and public safety officials, to be held on October 29. The person assigned to offer the course was "a Harrisburg area educator" with no publications on the topic, no academic training in the area, no affiliation with Penn State, and only limited part-time community college teaching experience. "We link the resources of the university to public needs," said a campus continuing education specialist in announcing the course, for which academic credit was promised.

On Tuesday, October 22, I sent a fax to the campus, expressing concern over this workshop and asking for the educator's credentials. "The occult," I cautioned, "particularly as it relates to law enforcement, is a controversial topic that is plagued with a high level of amateurish and pseudo-scientific misinformation. To study it objectively requires a background in anthropology, adolescent sociology, folklore, and/or comparative religion." I also warned that such a workshop might contain slurs on legitimate religious groups like the Wiccan/Women's Spirituality movement and even encourage law enforcement abuses. Knowing nothing about the content of the workshop, I urged that it be refereed by experts with training in the field and offered to provide contacts.

Philip Jenkins, Penn State's director of religious studies, was less charitable, calling the proposed workshop "nonsense" and "idiocy." He had already heard of the workshop from colleagues in England, where, he observed, "courses of this kind are regularly reported in the UK as a humorous comment on American gullibility and 'witch-hunt' mentality." Cautioning that the course might discredit Penn State internationally, he concluded, "There is NO excuse for undertaking the proposed course." This and a number of other protests mobilized the administrators at Penn State, and by Thursday the dean responsible for the decision to hold the workshop gave this report on the course's credentials: "The training he conducts has been approved for police officers and deputy sheriffs in the commonwealth through the Commission on Crime and Delinquency, and this particular workshop, which is not academic and not for academic credit, has been approved through the proper state and university channels."

Meantime, as word of the approaching workshop circulated by e-mail, a number of American experts were starting to check in with protests. On the same day, Phillips Stevens Jr. asked Penn State to reconsider the advisability of the workshop. For some time now, he advised, "anthropologists and folklorists have known that satanic cults do not exist. They are a variant of a standard legend type that crops up from time to time throughout history and all over the world." By allowing the workshop to go on, he concluded, Penn State might waste money, misinform police, and perform a public disservice.

This letter, entering the Penn State administrative conduit, brought a response from the dean on Saturday, October 26:

Dr. Stevens, I agree totally with your conclusions that such cults do not exist. I am from the west where such legends abound. However, I also know, as do you, that often individuals—usually juveniles, commit acts ranging from vandalism to genuine atrocities, imitating what they think a "Satanist" might do.

I believe that a police officer at a crime scene, or trying to anticipate what s/he may encounter on the beat on a given night, should be aware of such faux Satanist attempts. That is the purpose of the seminar—not to hunt down and burn witches wherever they may be imagined.

In short, I do not believe in the Occult nor in Satan nor in Satanists. But I also know that if we let our black cat out around Halloween, it will be killed—probably stoned or soaked in gasoline and burned. This is a widespread and well-known phenomenon.

There are others that are less well known, and I believe that police officers can benefit from being aware of them.

Notwithstanding the dean's assurances, however, the workshop began with the following theme: "When confronted with satanic information, individuals usually react by either denying it exists entirely, or there is an attempt to hide it. Unfortunately, this does not change the reality of the existence of Satanism, or of its potential devastating effects on society or individuals." Numerous satanic cults are involved in illegal activities such as child abuse, kidnapping of both adults and children, animal mutilation, rape or sexual mutilation, and murder, the officers were told. "Main satanic cult groups," the presentation continued, include adult groups who use children for sex and sale of drugs, adult/adolescent groups who also use children to sell drugs, and adolescent groups with an adult leader. Such "devious cults" are the most dangerous; they believe that the supernatural is real and that "illegal activities must occur to achieve that level." Teenagers are tempted into Satanism with sex, drugs, and alcohol. "Beyond this stage," the educator warned, "it is difficult to turn individuals away from Satanism." The next stage is "serious involvement," which includes acquisition of "satanic books" and "serious attempts at learning satanic activities," followed by "criminal involvement," in which, the educator reiterated, the participant "believes that criminal action *must* occur in order to reach the reality of the supernatural."

The workshop went on to list classic "signs of involvement," including involvement in fantasy/role-playing games, collecting of "occult books," owning objects used for spells and rituals (including mainly neo-pagan paraphernalia such as candles, bells, and ritual knives), and wearing symbolic jewelry such as pentagrams. A list of "Signs of Satan" to help decode graffiti featured the 6-pointed Star of David and the Islamic Star and Crescent as dangerous satanic symbols. Robert Hicks, author of a study critical of such cult exposés, identified this document as having been photocopied from materials circulated by Dale Griffis.[8] His "Signs of Satan," Hicks notes, is a common photocopylore item that was first authored by an anti-Semitic fundamentalist Christian group and was, in fact, simply made up.

Once the contents of the workshop became known, a series of protests descended on the dean. I conceded that a workshop on teenage ostensive pranks based on Satanism would have been valuable. "But this was *not* the workshop's purpose," I said. "Penn State's name has been used to preach an extreme faction's philosophy of religious and civil intolerance. The community deserved better." Robert Hicks agreed that police should investigate crimes with a ritualistic component, but, he characterized much of the educator's information as "bogus" and "outdated" and said that the conspiracy of satanic adults recruiting kids for sex and drug trafficking "has no basis in fact." Hicks also recognized a listing of "Common Signs of Preschool Abuse" as one that was repeatedly used in investigations of ritual child abuse cases in preschools during the 1980s. This point was underscored by Professor Jean S. LaFontaine, who wrote the British Department of Health's critical report in the wake of the United Kingdom's Rochdale and Orkney Islands scandals.[9] She suggested that "Penn State dissociate itself from the disinformation presented by the conference. This case shows that universities must be careful lest they allow their concern for freedom of speech to be exploited in order to disseminate material of this dishonest and misleading kind. I am sure that Penn State would not wish to be seen as endorsing it, even unawares."

Finally, Phillips Stevens Jr. admitted disappointment: "Many of us have given a lot of time and effort, for no remuneration, to countering the dangerous sensationalism propagated by people like [the educator] over the past 15 years. To learn that he has been given carte blanche to profess this nonsense, all over again . . . is discouraging. . . . For a respected state university to sponsor such an event, with—apparently—no exposure to the several other sides of this demonology, its history, anthropology, and social implications, is shameful." The dean, after a decent interval, acceded, informing all participants that he had now "requested that those in the path of approval for the course not approve another without first verifying the nature of the content and the approach to it. I have also asked that if we approve such workshops in the future we invite one of the vocal opponents to present their side." Neither the public nor the police officers, however, were informed of this decision.

The lesson: contemporary legends have their meaning and power as events unfold, not in the otherworldly calm of the archived and annotated text. We should see "modern" legends as part of an age-old folk process, and many historical surveys of legend complexes wait to be done. Still, our work cannot "lose the name of action." Legends should be spotted as they emerge and interpreted while they—and we—are at the cutting edge. If, as I said at the beginning of this volume, legend telling is often a fundamentally *political* action, then the act of observing a legend is also a political act. Collecting, documenting, and interpreting make up one political *re*action to a legendary performance; but refusing to do so is equally and inescapably political as well. No academic can escape the implications of inaction: we risk condoning by our silence actions that perpetuate intolerance and even age-old bigotry. It's a start to bringing the discussion of legends out of the archives and into the real world.

Notes

Introduction

1. In the United States, research into "urban" legends began with the students and colleagues of Richard Dorson, most notably Linda Dégh and Jan Harold Brunvand. As editor of *Indiana Folklore* from 1968, Dégh repeatedly published articles by herself and her students on contemporary legends, while Brunvand's books (1981, 1984, 1986, 1989, and 1993) served to introduce the genre to both an academic and a broad popular audience. In the British Isles, Paul Smith (1983) took the lead in collecting and annotating these legends. Subsequently, collections of contemporary legends have appeared in a number of European countries and languages, including Belgium (Top 1990), the Netherlands (Burger 1992), France (Campion-Vincent and Renard 1992), Italy (Carbone 1990), Poland (Czubala 1985 and Simonides 1988), South Africa (Goldstuck 1990), Sweden (Klintberg 1990a), and Finland (Virtanen 1987). Bennett and Smith (1993) provide a comprehensive bibliography.

2. Dégh and Vázsonyi 1973.

3. Bauman 1977.

4. See chapter 3, "When Is a Legend Contemporary?"

5. Best 1987 and Fine 1988, 1989.

6. See, for example, Toelken 1979, 266.

Part I

1. Sociologists such as Jeffrey Victor, Gary Alan Fine, and Joel Best have attended contemporary legend conferences and shared their methods and concepts. French scholars such as Jean-Noel Kapferer and Veronique Campion-Vincent have also brought their expertise in the social sciences to our field.

2. Dégh 1979b, 1.

3. Max Lüthi, for instance, stressed that the so-called "biology of narrative" was a way of looking at "the personality of the narrator [and] the significance of the story and story telling for the individual and for the community." Will-Erich Peuckert made a similar application to the telling of traditional legends as early as 1959, saying, "Today, we like to speak of a 'biology' of the legend, by which the folklorist means ascertaining the 'where' and 'how' of legend-telling, as well as the age, sex, occupation, background, homeland, and spirit of the teller" (1979b, 2; translation Dégh's).

4. 1979b, 4.

5. Qtd. by Dégh 1979b, 4.

6. 1979b, 4.

7. 1972, 9–10; emphases mine.

Chapter 1

1. Thompson 1946, 8.
2. Dégh and Vázsonyi 1976, 94.
3. 1965, 441.
4. Honko 1964, 13.
5. Blehr 1967, 261.
6. Dégh and Vázsonyi 1976, 119.
7. 1980, 218.
8. Ibid., 219; emphasis mine.
9. Ibid., 232.
10. 1998, 356–57.
11. 1969, 316.
12. Ibid., 316, 324. Under pressure from more traditional folklorists, Georges later reaffirmed his faith that "continuities and consistencies in human behavior" exist after all and are worth studying, but he still redenied the belief that stories exist as entities outside of unique performances (1980, 40, 1981, 250–52).
13. Dégh 1972, 73.
14. 1965, 82. Elsewhere in the same work she characterized one narrator by saying that she "is not guided by artistic inspirations, she claims only to tell the truth." She characterized another narrator by saying that she "is not guided by artistic principles and will not clothe her stories in the form of polished legends; her aim is to tell her audience about as many hair-raising events as possible" (1969a, 255). Another narrator "paid no attention to presentation; on the contrary, she talked in choppy sentences, jumped from one point to the other, and said what was passing through her head—whatever she thought it was necessary to tell the uninitiated stranger" (127).
15. Dégh and Vázsonyi in particular have described the printing of "emasculated fabulates" (1974, 234) and Dégh insists that the "remodeled, rewritten, and improperly recorded legend . . . is of no use at all" (1965, 78).
16. 1972, 74. Emphasis mine.
17. 1965, 86. Georges has questioned this kind of description as "conventional," saying that such elements are merely linguistic "clues," not formulas, that a legend is being told (1971, 10). But such elements are reported by several scholars dealing with the same kind of narrative, including those known by the teller to be fictional. The "contextual elements" identified by Blehr as the essence of the folk belief story involve placing incidents in a specific time and place and associating it with a given person (1967, 259). In the case of accounts of individual experience, William Labov and Joshua Waltezky have observed that an "orientation" section typically is present in natural contexts (1967, 32). All three sources admit that this frame is variable in content from telling to telling, but all agree that such an opening structure is characteristic, establishing the incident's exact place in time and space.
18. Patrick B. Mullen, considering "modern" legends, notes that often they derive from rumors that "arise from actual situations of crisis or unusual events"; hence they "point to modern concerns about anxiety-producing situations" (1972, 105). The same is true for personal narratives, observes Livia Polanyi, since they assume that "members of a group share a model of what the world is like" and that "the violation of a norm is a narratable topic" (1979, 212).
19. See Goffman 1974, 504.
20. Dégh and Vázsonyi maintain that "Every legend states something. . . . It takes a stand and calls for the expression of opinion on the question of truth and belief" (1976, 119). Indeed, this

statement, or "point" of the narrative is seen as essential by all critics, whether it is defined in terms of "folk belief" (Dégh 1965, 80–81, Blehr 1967, 259), "rumor" (Mullen 1972, 105), "traditional attitude" (Stahl 1977b, 20–21), "evaluation" (Labov and Waletzky 1967, 37–39), or "cultural presupposition" (Polanyi 1979, 212–13).

21. Thigpen has shown, for instance, that adolescents' fascination with the supernatural is linked not with credulity but with their psychological need to "experiment with the alternatives to conventional reality" (1971, 107).

22. Dégh and Vázsonyi 1976, 101.

23. Such a difficulty is familiar to ethnographers of Native American material. Dennis Tedlock (1972), John McDowell (1974b), and Barre Toelken (1976) have severally demonstrated the inadequacy of dictated or artificially taped narratives compared with recordings of actual performances by the same informants. Richard Bauman, commenting on their work, has warned that even the most verbatim of texts may represent "recordings of informants' abstracts, resumes, or reports of performance and performance forms rather than true performances" (1977, 8).

24. Fine 1984, 87.

25. Labov and Waletzky suggest that narratives normally begin with an "orientation section," but they admit that such a section is sometimes missing and that later sections of these narratives take over this role (1967, 32).

26. Emil J. Marginean, Ohio State University Folklore Archives (OSUFA), Mar. 1979.

Chapter 2

1. Publications on camp horror legends are uncommon. "The Walking Coffin" is studied comparatively by William H. Clements (1980, 279–86). Longer and more serious legends are discussed by James P. Leary (1973), and by Lee Haring and Mark Breslerman (1977). Paul J. Bartos (1979) and Jay Mechling (1980) also touch on such legends.

2. Among others, Sandra K. D. Stahl (1977b) has challenged the definition of tradition in terms of whole-item repetition by more than one storyteller. The implications of this new definition to the area of legends proper have not yet been explored.

3. Leary 1973, 178ff., and Bartos 1979, 135. Both use concepts originally formulated by Gladys Marie Fry (1975), to discuss Ku Klux Klan harassment of blacks.

4. The dichotomy is William Bascom's (1965, 4).

5. This characterization is Max Luthi's, quoted by Linda Dégh (1972, 73).

6. 1971, 121.

7. Dorson 1959, 131.

8. 1971, 103–4.

9. 1971, 17–18.

10. Text in the OSUFA, 1978. Collected by Elizabeth Blair from Ross Johnson, former counselor at Hiram House Camp, Moreland Hills, Ohio.

11. Goffman 1974, 6, 136–37.

12. OSUFA, 1975. Collected by Jane Core from Dave Linkhart, former counselor at Camp Clifton, Clifton, Ohio.

13. "Headless Hattie [Haddie, Haddy]" is an especially wide-traveled revenant of this type. Legends about her have been collected for OSUFA at camps near Medina, Marion, and Montgomery, as well as by the author at Hiram House.

14. Information about Henry and his version of the legend are drawn from the author's per-

sonal interview with him on 13 July 1979. Unless otherwise noted, all quotes in the text are from this interview. Personal names in his quotes have been replaced by pseudonyms at his request.

15. Ross Johnson, author's personal interview of 22 June 1979. His version of "Ralph and Rudy" was collected for OSUFA by Elizabeth Blair.

16. Johnson's version expands on this point slightly: "Rudy was just sort of really introverted and just always kept to himself a whole lot. And Ralph and Rudy worked together real well and they worked with the horses all the time and they got along just fine, except when Ralph would come back drunk sometimes Rudy would get on his back about it and then the two of them would sorta fight it out but they always forgot about it and forgave each other in the morning." (Text in OSUFA.)

17. Henry had told the legend the night before at a campfire and so had it fresh in memory, but this variant was collected artificially—in a cabin during daylight, with a few counselors present. Thus Henry continually broke off his performance of the legend to comment on the fine points of how it should be told. The moments of metanarration I have included inside parentheses.

18. This song is printed as "The Hearse Song" by Carl Sandburg in *The American Songbag* (1927, 444). Iona and Peter Opie include a British children's version in *The Lore and Language of Schoolchildren* (1959, 33).

19. In recent years several "cut and slash" movies have adopted this narrative structure, some, like *Friday the Thirteenth* and *Friday the Thirteenth, Part Two,* adopting the camp setting as well. Despite consistently hostile reviews from critics, such films have enjoyed considerable box-office success with teenagers.

20. "Short Arm" is from OSUFA, 1977, collected by Susan Muskat from Jim Fracker, former high school student at New Concord. The "witch" rituals are from OSUFA, 1975, collected by Toni Kidwell from a high school student (name withheld) in Montgomery, and from OSUFA, 1978, collected by Molly Birnbaum from Jeff Curtis, former college student at Hocking Tech, Athens.

21. OSUFA, 1975, collected by Toni Kidwell from a former counselor (name withheld) at Camp Meecher.

22. This mournful howling is paralleled in the legend of "Moana" at Lutheran Memorial Camp, Fulton, Ohio. After losing her eyeballs in an accident, Moana prowls the camp, trying to gouge out campers' own eyes and announcing her arrival with drawn-out wails of "MOOOOAAAANNNNAAAA!"

23. Certainly this was Johnson's sense of the narrative; this is his paraphrase of the incident: "at night, far off in the distance you could hear Ralph, *he'd be so lonely and he missed his brother so much* you could hear him way off in the distance, going, 'Ru-dy, Ru-dy,' and it scared everybody at the camp" (OSUFA text; emphasis mine).

24. I provided a more detailed discussion of the camp, its philosophy, and camper population in "Majaska: Mythmaking in Greater Cleveland" (1982).

25. Haring and Breslerman 1977, 15–16.

26. Collected by the author from Don Page, former counselor at Hiram House, in a personal interview on 12 June 1979. Page, who worked at the camp from 1970 to 1977, was famous for this story.

27. The counselor herself confirmed this account during the author's visit to the camp, 28 June 1979.

28. The concept of ostension is discussed in greater detail in Part IV of this book.

29. Green 1978, 847–48. This passage deals only with examples in which a single person mimics

drama by adopting two conflicting personalities. In personal communication, he agreed that the concept of protodrama could be extended to cover cases in which several persons adopt roles, but in which no antagonist appears and no resolution occurs.

30. Luthi 1970, 85–86.

31. See Danielson 1979, 214–19.

Chapter 3

1. 1981, 188–89.

2. Baker 1976, 372; Carey 1970–71, 10.

3. Mullen 1972, 95.

4. 1993, xi.

5. Klintberg 1990a.

6. Pettitt 1995, 1996.

7. Mayor 1995.

8. Mayor 1992; Brunvand 1984, 31–34.

9. Lassen 1995, 1996, 1998.

10. Dorson 1981, 228. Dorson's informant dated the story "about 1965," but Dorson found it many times among his students and lecture audiences in 1975 and afterwards. Additional incidences in oral tradition and mass media, all localized in urban or suburban areas nationwide, were noted by Ridley (1967, 155–56), Hippensteel (1969, 75), Mullen (1972, 103), and Toelken (1979, 177–78). Studies of this legend complex include Brunvand (1978, 117) and Campion-Vincent (1990).

11. Langlois 1983.

12. *FOAFTale News* 24 (Dec. 1991): 11; Brunvand 1993, 134–38.

13. *FOAFTale News* 29 (Mar. 1993): 11.

14. Wachs 1990.

15. *FOAFTale News* 25 (Mar. 1992): 11.

16. 1988.

17. Sparks 1979, 111–12.

18. *FOAFTale News* 25 (Mar. 1992): 10.

19. *FOAFTale News* 31 (Nov. 1993): 5.

20. Clarke 1974, 9–10.

21. Minucius Felix 1931, 337, 339. Further references to this text are cited in the text of the essay by chapter and line.

22. Tertullian 1931, 37. Further references to this text are cited in the text of the essay by chapter and line.

23. Grant 1958, 361–62.

24. Sallust 1921, 39.

25. Cassius Dio 1914, 149.

26. Cohn 1975, 6, 10–11.

27. Ibid., 20–21; Zacharias 1980, 47–48.

28. Zacharias 1980, 49.

29. Motif V361: *Christian child killed to provide blood for Jewish rite.* A comprehensive survey of this belief-complex is provided by Alan Dundes (1991). Although Ridley traced the legend to a fifth-century incident set in Syria (1967, 153), the Jewish scholar Joseph Jacobs previously had shown that this case could not have spawned the legend because it involved no intentional

murder or ritual use of blood (1902, 3:261). Jacobs (3:260); and Hippensteel (1969, 77–82) agree that its origin lay in ancient Greece but that it was not definitively attached to the Jews until late medieval times, beginning with the case of William of Norwich in 1144. Both Jacobs (3:266–67) and Hippensteel (134–36) have comprehensive bibliographies on the history of this motif from 1144 A.D. to recent time. *The Jewish Encyclopedia*'s entries on "Anti-semitism" (1902, 1:642) and on "Apion" (1902, 1:668) also provide valuable information on the early history of the rumor.

30. Josephus 1926, 329–33.

31. Grant 1958, 362.

32. Mullen 1972, 106.

33. Toelken 1979, 178.

Chapter 4

1. Georges 1971, 18.

2. Bennett (1988, 200) has called this tendency a "riffle and pool" effect.

3. Blehr 1967, 259–60.

4. Nicolaisen 1984, 177.

5. Translated and quoted by Ward 1981, 369.

6. See, in particular, Richard Dorson's version of "The McDonald Boys" (1952, 5, 169–76).

7. Todorov 1973, 163–64. Emphasis added.

8. Dégh and Vázsonyi 1973, 27.

9. Ibid., 5.

10. I draw this insight from an unpublished paper by the late Carol Edwards (1984).

11. Todorov 1973, 31–33.

12. Ibid., 89–90.

13. Barnes 1984a.

14. Samuelson 1980.

15. Hufford 1982, 51–52.

16. Dégh and Vázsonyi (1974) define the "proto-memorate" in similar terms, as the inferential experience that lies behind the widely circulated fabulate.

17. Janet Langlois (1985) has uncovered a striking example of how legends express unspoken community values through a cycle of stories about an Indiana mass murderess.

18. On the audience's role in forcing revisions of personal experience narratives, see Polanyi 1979.

19. Bennett 1988, 250.

20. In a parallel fashion, a resident of Hazleton told me of a woman who made it her business to learn and repeat every conceivable belief for avoiding bad luck and demonic possession. She evidently was not prone to phobias but found that capacity to remember a superstition for each conceivable situation made her an essential part of every community undertaking.

21. Hufford 1982, 64. Bennett notes the same about stories told by narrators "with a positive or open-minded attitude to traditional beliefs." She argues that such stories are best described as "cyclical . . . clusters of events organized round some central idea in a loose associative pattern" (1984, 83).

22. Dégh 1979, 99.

23. Susan Kalcik (1975) has observed this phenomenon among women storytellers.

24. Kalcik called these expressions "kernel narratives," but I adopt the more flexible term suggested at the same time by Robert J. Smith (1975, 98–100).

25. See the various metonymic forms of the contemporary legend "The Hatchet Man" among adolescent girls, described by Sylvia Grider (1980). Grider, as dormitory resident advisor to the girls, found that the legend in fact had not deteriorated in tradition, and she collected finished versions as part of her own "initiation." Rather, she concluded, the group's use of the legend had become more and more metonymic as the girls gained confidence in themselves and their environment.

26. Grider 1984.

27. Narrated and collected by Theresa Luthman, a transfer student from Miami University (name of second participant altered at her request), Apr. 28, 1978. Text in OSUFA. Transcription by Luthman.

28. Fine 1984, 99.

29. Toelken 1979, 51. A more detailed consideration of this problem is Haring 1972.

30. The transcriptions of legend texts in this book use the following orthographic conventions:

a) Square brackets enclose italicized descriptions or characterizations of sounds by the transcriber ([*Nervous laugh*]), as well as editorial clarifications (someone there [*near Fisher Hall*]).

b) Momentary pauses are indicated by commas, more definite pauses by line breaks, and pauses of longer than a second by a diamond. Lines that run too long to fit on the printed page are indented at the left margin on continuation.

c) Momentary use of louder dynamics is indicated by printing the passage in capital letters ("people, you know, RETARDED people").

d) Slight elevation of pitch for emphasis is noted by *italics*.

e) More extreme elevation of pitch is noted by ***bold italics.***

f) Softening of dynamics (usually accompanied by lowering of pitch) is noted by (parentheses); more extreme softening is noted by ((double parentheses)).

g) Lowering of pitch without softening of dynamics, for ironic purposes, is noted by underlining; heavy irony is noted by **underlining**.

h) A dash (—) is used within the line to indicate the drawing out of words for effect or for thought ("she called out to—see who it *was*"). At the end of a line a dash indicates a pause on a leveled pitch tone, indicating incomplete expression ("Um—there's the Alumni—").

31. Collected by Carol Bennison (informant was at the time a student at Miami University; her name has been altered at her request), May 18, 1979. Text in OSUFA. Text retranscribed by the author from the original tape.

32. 1963.

33. Balliett 1986, 93.

Chapter 5

1. 1993.

2. 1989, 2.

3. Ibid., 96–97.

4. Ibid., 192.

5. Ibid., 198.

6. Ibid., 192.

7. 1993, 20.

8. Ibid., 19.

9. Ibid., 26.

10. 1994, 23.

11. Szapir 1995.

12. See Toelken 1979.

13. Besides Preston 1976 and Welsch 1988, sample chain letters with analysis have been printed by Halpert 1956 and by Dundes and Pagter 1978, 3–10. Sann 1968, 97–104, gives a detailed account of the 1930s manias caused by early versions. The Himmelsbrief tradition is best discussed by Fogel 1908 and "Himmelsbrief" 1908; Hand 1959 and Stoudt 1977 give briefer discussions with examples.

14. 1994, 23.

15. Sann 1968, 97–101.

16. Anna Guigne (1993) has produced a detailed history of the affair, which includes a copy of the actual appeal. This is precisely the study of "mutation rates" Goodenough and Dawkins call for.

17. *FOAFTale News* 19 (Oct. 1990): 9; 21 (Mar. 1991): 10–11; 22 (June 1991): 11.

18. Fine 1991.

19. 1989, 322.

20. Ibid., 325.

21. Dennett 1993, 232.

22. 1991, 156.

23. See Gould 1983, 121–45, and 1991, 416–31. Particularly disturbing is the way Dawkins comes close to dismissing as "massively infected" anyone who defends religious activities such as Judaic dietary rules. He might keep in mind that Adolf Hitler, influenced by the version of natural selection that was current in his day, used the "infected mind" image for his own political ends: "What had to be reckoned heavily against the Jews in my eyes was when I became acquainted with their activity in the press, art, literature, and the theater. . . . This was *pestilence, spiritual pestilence*, worse than the Black Death of olden days, and the people was being *infected* with it. . . . And bear in mind that there is no limit to their number; bear in mind that for one Goethe Nature easily can foist on the world ten thousand of these scribblers who poison men's souls like *germ-carriers* of the worse sort, on their fellow men" (1943, 57–58; emphasis added). Dawkins attacks religion for training people to kill in the name of God and praises science for being a haven for "good ideas"—but never mentions Nazi scientists' active collaboration in the Holocaust.

24. 1995.

25. In *Western Folklore*'s special issue on "Contemporary Legends in Emergence" (1990) Véronique Campion-Vincent, Jeffrey Victor, and I used a model adapted from sociology to describe the structure of intense legend outbreaks in Latin America and the rural United States. French researchers Jean-Noel Kapferer (1993) and Jean-Bruno Renard (1991) have studied the panic caused when the LSD tattoo rumor passed through France late in 1991. Their research identifies many of the conduits through which the rumor passed, and together their articles give a detailed picture of who was most affected by it and how.

26. Qtd. in Dawkins 1989, 3.

27. Ibid., 231; emphasis his.

28. Nossal 1993, 55; emphasis mine.

29. Dégh and Vázsonyi 1973, 12–14; see also Vlach 1971.

30. *FOAFTale News* 36 (Jan. 1995): 4–5.

31. 1961, 233–35.

32. 1980, 390–92.

33. Mulhern 1991, 166.

34. 1980.

35. E.g., Passantino and Passantino 1992; Hertenstein and Trott 1993.

36. 1980.

37. Barnes 1984a, 77; emphasis added. Or as Dégh and Vázsonyi have argued, the legend telling event somehow compels participants to respond to the narrative: "The teller of the legend, and often the listener, the active or passive participant of the legend telling event, has to speak his [sic] mind" (1973, 5).

38. This is precisely what Dégh and Vázsonyi hypothesized in their "conduit theory" of transmission (1975) and what Gary Alan Fine confirmed in his analysis of legend transmission among a group of preadolescents (1992, 86–119).

39. See Fine 1985 and Turner 1993, esp. 165–79. Turner's discussion has an interesting parallel in Dawkins's biological analysis of warning signals. When an individual bird in a flock perceives a predator, it may give a warning call to alert the others. This may seem a disinterested act, but Dawkins notes that the alternatives are actually much more dangerous to the individual. Flying off by oneself makes the individual "an odd bird out," a potentially suicidal move since predators often select those that stray from the flock. Staying put as if nothing had happened does nothing to remove one from the danger observed. The most selfish, and therefore best policy, Dawkins says, "is indeed to fly up into a tree, but to make sure everyone else does too" (1989, 169–70).

40. Bennett 1991, 190; 1994.

Part II

1. Adams 1984, 54.

2. Quoted in Dégh and Vázsonyi 1973, 33.

3. Adams 1984, 59–60. Ellipsis points are the author's and do not indicate omission. Other similar examples from Ohio are the Old Mansion Restaurant, Columbus, and the Columbian House, Waterville, both described in "Beyond Incredible" 1980, 40, 42, 45. The author recalls similar stories cheerily circulated about the Old Worthington Inn, Worthington, and the Buxton Inn, Granville.

4. See chapter 10, "What Really Happened at Gore Orphanage."

5. Adams 1984, 69. Ellipsis points are the author's and do not indicate omission.

6. The dialectics of legendry, as Dégh and Vázsonyi point out, "enable the recipient to make his choice between belief . . . and disbelief . . . without experiencing qualms of conscience or dangerous social consequences" (1973, 5). Indeed, Kenneth A. Thigpen observed that adolescents' actual contact "with what is thought of as the supernatural does not necessarily have a profound or stable influence on one's belief system" (1971, 207).

7. Hufford 1982, 52–53.

8. Grimm and Grimm 1981, 1:3.

9. This reading of supernatural experience follows Berger and Luckmann 1967, 112–16.

10. Fuller 1978, 13–35.

Chapter 6

1. For a history of paranormal investigation as a movement, particularly in the area of spiritualistic phenomena, see Evans 1982 and Bennett 1999, 139–72.

2. Korson 1968, 61–70.

3. See Rose 1981.

4. "Fact or Fiction Is Undetermined," *Shippensburg [Pa.] News-Chronicle*, 28 Apr. 1980, 16; Yvonne J. Milspaw, "Folklore Is Part of the Modern Era," *Harrisburg [Pa.] Evening News*, 28 Oct. 1980, 25.

5. Motif E322.3.3.1 in Baughman's version of the Motif Index. It could indeed be more closely identified as Version B in Richard K. Beardsley and Rosalie Hankey's exhaustive catalog of Vanishing Hitchhiker variants: *vanishing hitchhiker predicts some impending disaster*. Baughman found this motif so prevalent that he gave it a distinct pigeonhole in his catalog: E332.3.3.1 (d). For versions of this type collected in New York State in the 1970s, see Fish 1976.

6. Rosanne M. Hall, "Bizarre Tales of a Mysterious Hitchhiker," *Shenandoah [Pa.] Evening Herald*, 4 Feb. 1994, 1, 19; Leon Bogdan, "Angel or Fable? Hitchhiker Warns 'The End Is Near,' " *Bloomsburg [Pa.] Press-Enterprise*, 16–17 Apr. 1994.

7. Bram Boroson, alt.folklore.urban, 6 Feb. 1994.

8. Cindy Stauffer, "The Vanishing Hitchhiker: Lancaster's Latest Legend," *Lancaster [Pa.] New Era*, 14 Mar. 1994, A-1, A-4; " 'Urban Legends': Infamous 'Hitchhiker' Tale Surfaces Again," *Shenandoah [Pa.] Evening Herald*, 16 Mar. 1994, 13.

9. Bakker and Bakker 1980. The booklet is unpaginated; the story appears in the devotion for March 29. Brian Finn, "Hitchhiking Angels? *Challenge Weekly*, 31 Oct. 1990. B. O. Jans, "Hitchhiking Angels in Holland," *FOAFTale News* 22 (June 1991): 5–6.

10. Carl Gundlach, folklore@tamvm1.tamu.edu.

11. Discussed in more detail in part 3 of this book.

12. Self-collected by Neil R. Mortine, OSUFA, 1975; reprinted in *FOAFTale News* 20 (Dec. 90): 4.

13. Fine 1979.

14. Bogdan, "Angel or Fable?"

15. Simonides 1988, 274.

16. From a modern broadside distributed by J.M.J. Book Co., Necedah, Wisconsin. The rest of the broadside conforms to the "Himmelsbrief" tradition that produced the modern "chain letter."

17. *FOAFTale News* 19 (Oct. 1990): 2–3.

18. Doris Cohoon, "If You Believe in Ghosts, Read On," *Shenandoah [Pa.] Evening Herald*, 4 Mar. 1994, 4.

19. Petzoldt 1989, 1. Compare accounts from African American girls in the Indianapolis area: "And if you, if you stop and say you not going that way, you'll get killed or something," and "if you don't give her a ride you will crash at the next stop light" (Langlois 1980, 209–10).

20. Simonides 1988, 274.

21. Hind 1979; Goss 1984, 121–28; *FOAFTale News* 19 (Oct. 1990): 3.

22. Glazer 1984, 110.

23. Reprinted in Betty Harlor, "Women, Some Infamous, Make History," *Hazleton Standard-Speaker*, 11 Mar. 1987.

24. Sanderson 1981; Brunvand 1986, 52–55; Bronner 1988, 149–50, 312–13.

25. PSUHFA, Nemchick, 1987. Retranscribed from audiotape by the author.

26. Grimm and Grimm 1981, 146–49 (nos. 153–56).

27. Briggs 1976, 352.

28. Briggs 1971, B.1 11 (Motif B.15.4.3).

29. *FOAFTale News* 13 (Mar. 1989): 2.

30. 1991, 89–90.

31. Czubala 1992b, 2.

32. Alford 1992, 129. This episode was dramatized in a scene from the movie *Superman*.

33. Di Salvatore 1988, 39; cited in *FOAFTale News* 11 (Oct. 1988): 5.

34. Bord and Bord 1985, 42ff.

35. Rojcewicz 1987, 152–53.

36. *FOAFTale News* 18 (June 1990): 10.

37. Clements 1991, 87.

38. Badone 1987, 104.

39. Hufford 1982.

Chapter 7

1. Brunvand 1978, 183, 223–25.

2. Greeley 1975, 7, Bennett 1999, 9–14.

3. Tracy C. McCullough, "The [Arbordale] Pizza Hut Ghost," Mar. 1979, OSUFA. All texts have been retranscribed by the author from the original interview tapes. At the collector's request, all personal names have been replaced by pseudonyms. My thanks to McCullough for providing me with these tapes and allowing me to use them.

4. E 411.10: *Site of tragic death haunted by ghosts*. Out of 175 "haunted" sites, at least 80 had this motif attached to the locale.

5. E 334.2: *Ghost haunts burial site*.

6. Dégh and Vázsonyi 1973, 5.

7. Ibid., 8–9. They actually contrast "extinct" legends, which are "not heated by internal flames nor strained by internal forces" to "active" legends, which are "dominated by thrill, anguish, the mysterious, the dismal, the extraordinary." They leave room, however, for legends that might seem extinct but prove "to be only dormant" and "By some unexpected cause . . . might warm up again."

8. 1988, 25–26.

9. He was, of course, pretending, but his orientation-heavy narrative was rhetorically convincing. A few scholars have touched on this distinction: William Labov and Joshua Waletzky note, for instance, that "orientation sections are typically lacking" in narratives that "fail in other ways to carry out referential functions," for instance, a child's "narrative of vicarious experience" from a TV show (1967, 32). But, as they warn, and Edgar Slotkin (1988) dramatically shows, not all narratives that emphasize experience (or serve referential functions) are memorates; nor are all memorates orientation-heavy. Labov and Waletzky emphasize that "it is essential to preserve the context of the narrative. Because such originating context is often missing and cannot be reconstructed in traditional folktales, it is more difficult to relate analysis to the originating functions." See also Dégh and Vázsonyi 1974, 225–39, and Stahl 1977a, esp. 22–31.

10. English is notoriously weak on terminology relating to the supernormal. The germ of this choice of descriptive terms is Will-Erich Peuckert's assertion that the legend "documents the wrestling of a *magic* or *mythic Weltanschauung* with that of the *rational*, the sensible." Certainly one side of Bruce is self-consciously rational: but I doubt that one can call the other magical or mythical. Another of Peuckert's terms, "alienated," is more accurate in the sense he uses it, describing the witness's state of mind after he has encountered the supernormal (Dégh and Vázsonyi 1973, 28). But this term carries a special meaning in American English that I find confusing here. "Amazed" seems the best of a poor set of options, particularly if we combine the usual psychological sense with a folklorist's knowledge of the supernormal experience known as being

"pixy-led": being bewitched by a supernormal power into seeing the natural world as a maze or puzzle that cannot rationally be solved. See Briggs 1976, 33–34.

11. Otto Blehr, among others, has observed how important details as to time, place, and person are to narratives involving folk belief. He argues that such elements in "folk belief stories" should not be considered for their own content but "rather for how convincing they make the folk belief elements in the same story" (1967, 260). This is fair, but in this case it seems that the rationality of the narrator is the matter being "proved," rather than any particular folk belief. The role of what William Labov has called "orientation" in personal narratives remains to be analyzed in its complexity.

12. Dégh and Vázsonyi 1973, 28.

13. As Robert A. Georges would have it (1971, 10).

14. Compare Hufford's account of an interview with a Pennsylvania family who lived in a house plagued by poltergeists: "They thought it unusual that a new house should have such phenomena associated with it, but this was tentatively explained by the possibility that the house had been built over 'an Indian grave,' as had been suggested by a neighbor" (1982, 101).

15. Dégh and Vázsonyi 1973, 27–28.

Chapter 8

1. Disch 1987, 328.

2. Taves 1987, 90.

3. Ibid., 95.

4. Strieber 1987, 40.

5. Ibid., 41.

6. Ibid., 294.

7. Strieber 1988, 93.

8. Briggs 1971, 17, 177; Briggs 1976, 239–42.

9. See Bullard 1989c and Clark 1990.

10. Honko 1964, 16.

11. Quoted by Dégh and Vázsonyi 1974, 237.

12. Sebald 1978, 66. A Hazleton area variation holds that if you could ever snatch the entity's hat (an impossibility, as the paralysis fades as soon as you move any part of your body) you could make it "shit gold" and make you wealthy.

13. Koch 1973, 81.

14. Koch and Lechler 1970, 180.

15. Hufford 1982, 34; Hyatt 1965, 270, 273

16. Hufford 1982, 245.

17. Ibid., 14 n.1.

18. Honko 1964, 17.

19. Virtanen 1990, 3.

20. 1999, 32–36.

21. Baker 1987–88; Kottmeyer 1988.

22. Kottmeyer 1988, 6.

23. Virtanen 1990, 5.

24. Klass 1987.

25. Bullard 1987, 1989b, 1989c.

26. Conroy 1989, 161.

27. Ibid., 159.

28. Ibid., 163.

29. Ibid, 165.

30. Ibid., 174.

31. Ibid., 149. Many of these letters were published as Strieber and Strieber 1997.

32. Edel 1953, 30.

33. Ibid., 32.

34. Hufford 1982, 161.

35. Conroy 1989, 52.

36. Sargent 1961.

37. Turner 1977; Clements 1982.

38. Strieber 1987, 51.

39. Sargant 1961, 51; emphasis added.

40. It is worth noting that Strieber, who was raised Catholic during the doctrinally more conservative pre-Vatican II years, understood that the Eucharist prepared during Holy Communion underwent a transformation into the Body and Blood of Christ. Hence the titles of his first two books on abduction clearly underline the religious nature of the abduction experience, as he finally understood it.

41. James 1958, 329–30.

42. 1988, 35.

43. 1961, 233

44. Larry Danielson's survey of paranormal memorates in American folklore publications and archives also found a preponderance of female informants and noted that the same sex bias was found in the British Society for Psychical Research's 1890 Census of Hallucinations and D. J. West's 1962 Mass Observation survey of psychic events (1983, 201). Even the amateur Central Premonitions Registry, after issuing an appeal for premonitions in 1968–71, found that 70 percent of their respondents were female and that the majority of male psychics were over 65 in age (Greenhouse 1971).

45. Interestingly, Robert Kirk reported in 1692 that the gift of "second sight" in Scotland was almost exclusively handed down from father to son, and that female seers were the exception, not the rule.

46. Discussed in Greeley 1975.

47. Bennett 1987, 138.

48. Greeley 1975, 32.

49. Qtd. in Bennett 1987, 102, and 1999, 158.

50. Bennett (1999, 21) found that 77 percent of her informants believed in "premonitions" or "omens," mainly because of first- or secondhand experiences; the NORC survey found that 58 percent of Americans have experienced ESP, 24 percent "several times," and 8 percent "often"— figures that extrapolate to hundreds of millions of individuals.

51. Danielson 1983.

52. Pritchard et al. 1994, 352.

53. Ward 1977, 216.

54. Ibid., 218.

55. Honko 1964, 10.

56. Ward 1977, 222, 225.

57. Dégh 1971, 66.

58. Ibid., 60.

Part III

1. *FOAFTale News* 25 (Mar. 1992): 11.

2. Eco 1976, 224–26; Dégh and Vázsonyi appropriated the term to refer to ways in which "the reality itself, the thing, the situation or event itself functions in the role of message" (1983, 6).

3. Grider 1980.

4. Grider 1984, 1985.

5. Best and Horiuchi 1985.

6. Ellis 1994.

7. Dégh and Vázsonyi 1983, 15.

8. Sociologist Joel Best (1991) criticized Dégh and Vázsonyi for overstressing the prevalence of "copy-cat crimes"; in fact, he notes, genuine cases of criminal ostension are extremely rare, although the media tends to give them exaggerated attention. He cautions that ostension, sloppily used, may simply "explain events which have not occurred" (118).

9. Raschke 1990, 4–25; cf. Green 1991.

10. Ellis 1991, 290.

11. Victor 1989, 30; 1990, 52.

12. Passantino, Passantino, and Trott 1989.

13. Balch and Gilliam 1991.

14. Qtd. in Victor 1989, 22.

15. *FOAFTale News* 25 (Mar. 1992): 7.

16. Mulhern 1991.

17. Jackson 1976, 260.

18. Koch 178, 198.

19. Watkins 1983, 134–35; *Portland [Maine] Press Herald*, 20 Nov. 1985.

20. 1983, 29.

Chapter 9

1. Mechling 1980, 37.

2. I initially applied the term "mock-ordeal" to this material because of the way these events mimicked more serious ordeals normally connected with rites of passage. The more flexible term "ostension" became available a few years later, and I happily adopt it in this version. In the Ohio State Folklore Archives, John F. Wolary's collection project, "Boy Scouts and Their Legends," Dec. 1975, describes a variety of ordeals once active at Camp Lazarus, near Delaware, Ohio. Some of these, involving glowing heads, levitating Indians, headless horsemen, and the like, seem more complicated than Hiram House's ordeals. I also recall being initiated by ostension while a Cub Scout in Portsmouth, Ohio, ca. 1960. A ritual ordeal performed for prank value but involving similar theatrical effects and staging is described in Leary 1973.

3. Green 1978.

4. Ibid., 846.

5. Brunvand gives a normative description (1978, 291); it has also been collected many times in the OSU Folklore Archives.

6. Goffman 1974, ch. 4. Goffman's distinction between fabrication and "keying" (play or drama) is developed with reference to "folk crime" by Barnes (1979).

7. See Goffman's remarks on the exposure of fabrication, ch. 4.

8. Ross Johnson, author's personal interview of 22 June 1979. All quotes from Johnson in this chapter are from this interview.

9. Quoted from Jeff Jeske's performance of the Majaska narrative during Hiram House's counselor orientation, 28 June 1979. Jeske performed the narrative regularly at this camp from 1968 to 1978. For more on this legend, see Ellis 1981.

10. The concept of "bracketing" is drawn from Goffman 1974, 45, who uses it to refer to the cues that warn an audience when a keying begins and ends, and where it applies and where not.

11. All quotes in my discussion of the "real" snipe hunt are taken from the performance of 7 August 1979, which I recorded on a portable tape recorder while running up and down ravines, etc. This ostensive ordeal is normally performed weekly by the counselors, as campers usually come for a seven-day session. This performance was the last of eight successfully performed that summer by this group of counselors.

12. More traditional snipe hunts are regularly conducted among the younger campers (ages six to eleven). This particular variant of the hunt, according to the counselors, was adapted from a California version, which I have been unable to trace. A similar weasel-like snipe was hunted at Quaker Hills camp in southwestern Ohio, though without the ostensive ordeal trappings.

13. Described by Gladys Marie Fry (1975, 122–47).

14. Workman 1977.

15. Hall 1973, 170–71. Compare Iona and Peter Opie's observation of children's "belief" in Father Christmas: "for five or six years the children believe the make-believe; for one year they are gloriously uncertain; and from then on (in our experience) they find it even more fun than before knowing that it is a pretense, and pretending that they do not know, and indeed pretending that they do not know that their parents know that they know that it is a pretense. And, curiously, in this quadruple make-believe the original feeling of magic continues to permeate the ritual" (1959, 251 n.).

16. Sato 1988, 197.

17. Ibid., 201–2.

18. Ibid., 200.

19. Magliocco 1985.

20. Sato 1988, 205.

21. The Quaker Hills Snipe Hunt, even though it did not become an ordeal, also exhibited this same feature: more experienced campers, even though they knew the activity to be a hoax, nevertheless participated and collaborated with counselors to keep the younger campers from recognizing the fabrication—even after the hunt was over (personal interview with Nancy Beattie, former camper and counselor, 26 Feb. 1981).

22. This discussion is based on Turner 1977, "Liminality and Communitas," 94–130.

23. James C. McKinley, "Needle Attacks Spreading Fear on West Side," *New York Times*, 1 Nov. 1989, B3.

24. Sarah Lyall, "Pinprick Attacks on Upper Broadway Magnify Crime Fear," *New York Times*, 4 Nov. 1989, 27, 29.

25. "Stabs" 1989, 49.

26. 1987, 42–43.

27. Qtd. in *Prostitution* 1976, 22.

28. 1984, 79–80.

29. 1975, 196.

30. Turner 1993, 151–63.

31. Fineman 1989, 52–53.

32. See Goffman 1974, 106, 122–23.

33. Leary 1973, 181, 186–87.

Chapter 10

1. Legend text in the OSUFA, collected by Deborah Kay Bryan, 21 May 1975, 16. (Collections in this archive are catalogued by the collector's last name and by the page number in his/her collection project.) A series of legend texts concerning Gore orphanage was published by Rudinger 1976, 44–52.

2. This ritual activity was christened the "legend-trip" by Hall 1973. Dégh made influential accounts of legend-trips and their function: 1969a, 77–81, and 1971, 62–66. As editor of *Indiana Folklore*, Dégh printed several of her students' studies of legend-trips, of which the following are the most comprehensive: Thigpen 1971, Hall 1973 (also in Dégh 1980, 225–57), and Clements and Lightfoot 1971. Sue Samuelson (1979) gives a rare view of a legend-trip near San Francisco. Their analyses, however, have focused on single locations or on single legend motifs, and, aside from Dégh's work, little effort has been made to characterize legend-trips in general.

3. This paper does not attempt an in-depth study of any single Ohio tradition; rather, it draws some preliminary conclusions from a broad range of legend-trips reported in the OSUFA, especially about the behavioral patterns that remain constant over a variety of locations. This survey is based on 117 collections, supplemented by some original interviews, which relate 218 narratives attached to 175 locations, attested to by 303 informants. A few generalizations about the tradition-bearers: all but one were white, and all came from middle-to upper-middle-class neighborhoods. No bias, other than European origin, was found in ethnic background, and none was seen in religious preference. Informants were about equally balanced male and female; some came from rural areas or towns of fewer than 5,000 residents, but the majority lived in towns of more than 10,000, with significant clusters around the major industrial areas of Cleveland, Youngstown, and Cincinnati. Most informants were interviewed while attending college, but they agreed that the peak age for participation was "cruising age"—sixteen to eighteen. The legend-trip thus is linked to the coming-of-age crisis among white small-town or suburban adolescents.

4. Motif E411.1O

5. Cognate material from Indiana is given in Dégh 1969a, esp. 73–75, 83–84.

6. Motif E422.1.1.

7. A full set of texts is given by Rudinger 1976, 52–62.

8. Motif E235.

9. This conclusion is also reached by Clements and Lightfoot 1971, 127–28, and by Dégh 1980, 194.

10. See Dégh 1971, 65.

11. Licht 1974, 51–52 and passim.

12. OSUFA: 1976, Morosco.

13. OSUFA: 1974, Chew.

14. OSUFA: 1974, Daniel.

15. Also observed by Samuelson 1979, 20–21, 24–25.

16. OSUFA: 1976, Williams.

17. OSUFA: 1974, Stuts. Compare the consequences of the "White Witch's" appearance to parking couples, Samuelson 1979, 27.

18. OSUFA: 1975, Rulon.

19. Licht discusses this aspect of adolescent behavior in more detail (1974, 45–46, 51).

20. OSUFA: 1975, Carroll.

21. OSUFA: 1975, Stripe.

22. Also reported from Indiana by Langlois 1980, 199, and from Louisiana by Alphonso 1981, 31–32.

23. OSUFA: 1975, DeSeyn.

24. OSUFA: 1977, Halvorson.

25. OSUFA, Van Wormer (collector's comment on his own participation in the legend-trip), Mar. 1978, 4. One of his informants confirmed, "The only thing that is haunting about that place is the 'mystic air' of alcohol that lingers over the place on weekends. I don't know whether or not anyone was killed, but if that place is haunted why isn't anyone scared to go necking at the old place?" (19).

26. Untitled and undated clipping, "The Sprunger Orphanage and Swift House," in Lorain Public Library, Lorain, Ohio. Quoted in OSUFA, Mary Ann Ross, Dec. 1976, 8.

27. For descriptions of the Swift Mansion in its prime, see O'Donnell 1924, 109–13; Frary 1936, 160–63; Metcalf 1968, IA; and "Sprunger Orphanage," quoted in OSUFA, Ross, 10.

28. *Biographical Record* 1894, 1174. My thanks to Tom Stetak of the Lorain County Historical Society for this information.

29. Metcalf 1968, 4; "Sprunger Orphanage," quoted in OSUFA, Ross, 10.

30. In fact, they are buried in the Maple Grove Cemetery south and west of Vermilion, in Huron County, and the younger Wilbers were probably then residing nearby in Berlin Heights.

31. Metcalf 1968, 4.

32. OSUFA, Ross, collected 12 Nov. 1976, 22.

33. Ibid., 27–28.

34. Frary 1936, 163.

35. Ibid., O'Donnell 1924, 111.

36. Rudinger 1976, 44; three other versions collected by him attach this motif to a variant of the contemporary Gore Orphanage legend and also specify that sometimes the orphanage administrators' voices can be heard from the bricks, planning to burn the building to collect insurance money (46–47).

37. *New York Times*, 5 Mar. 1908.

38. *Cleveland Plain Dealer*, 6 Mar. 1908, quoted in OSUFA, James S. Kahn, Mar. 1981, 19–20. My thanks to Mr. Kahn for first identifying the relevance of this historical event.

39. "National Crime" 1908, 2.

40. OSUFA. Kahn, collected 1 Feb. 1981, 7.

41. OSUFA, 1976, Macri. Interestingly, Simpson (1973) records a "not very serious" belief of the same kind. According to legend, if you run around the tomb of a local eccentric seven times, he "will jump out and chase you; it is even asserted that the verses on the tomb (now very worn) say that this will happen. In fact, of course, they say nothing of the sort, but are simply the ordinary type of pious verse popular at that period [1793]" (45). The history of the legend-trip before modern times, especially in England and Scotland, remains to be traced.

42. A treatment of this taboo in Western cultures is Aries 1974, 87 ff.

Chapter 11

1. Basic information on the event comes from Elena Boyle, "The Cult," collection project in Folklore Archive, Penn State—Hazleton Campus, and from interviews with Phillip Rader, principal, Panther Valley High School, Lansford, Pa.; Rocco Mussoline, principal, Hazleton High School, Hazleton, Pa.; Robert Hines, sociology teacher and prom coordinator, Bishop Hafey High School, Hazleton, Pa.; Robert Ritz, Principal, West Hazleton High School; and Trooper Henry of the Hazleton office of the Pennsylvania State Police.

The folklore that has recently emerged around rumors of dangerous satanic cults has provoked a small but growing literature among folklorists. Persistent rumors about "devil cults" responsible for mysterious cattle deaths provoked extensive fieldwork by University of Arkansas anthropologist Nancy H. Owen (1980) and a brief publication of texts by Arkansas State folklorist Martha Long (1985). The more recent connection between mysterious serial murders and underground "satanists" was touched on by Dégh and Vázsonyi (1983). The growing network of police officials who specialize in detecting "satanic" involvement in rural communities was noted by Guinee (1987), who observed that such "expert" information encouraged law enforcement agents and other community officials to interpret innocent events in terms of dangerous cults. The growth of this network, based essentially on officially circulated folklore, since then has been noted—and deplored—by Stevens (1989). Victor (1989) and Balch (1989) analyze specific cases of panics caused by rumors of cults, compounded by official misinformation. They also discuss social factors that make rural communities susceptible to such rumors.

2. Best 1991. In another of his essays, Best suggests a stronger methodology when he applies Stephen Toulmin's principles of rhetorical analysis to controversy over the extent of missing children in the United States. Best surveys the organizations and individuals responsible for exaggerating the numbers of abducted children. He argues that the perception of the problem was created not so much by the statistics themselves—the facts or literal grounds for the claim that a problem exists—but rather the implicit reasons, or warrants, that people find for justifying drawing certain conclusions from the facts. These warrants, even though they may be oblique or glossed over by advocates of a conclusion, Best finds most critical to understanding what values are exhibited by a social problem (1987, 108–9). Rumor-panics are more localized, intense versions of the social problems studied by Best, and so we should not study the claims made by participants as things in and by themselves but rather as manifestations of quieter, normally unobservable dynamics that give the claims warrant.

3. Johnson 1945, 175.

4. Ibid., 183–85.

5. Such as James Stewart's study of the South Dakota cattle mutilation panic (1977).

6. Victor 1989.

7. Barham 1973, 58–61.

8. Roud 1989; Hobbs and Cornwall 1988.

9. 1988, 127–28.

10. Studied by Medalia and Larsen 1958.

11. Ibid., 186.

12. Davis 1990.

13. 1989.

14. Similarly, Grider (1980) showed that when rumors about impending mass murder in college dormitories spread, college coeds expressed their fears in terms of traditional oral narratives such as "The Roommate's Death." But this was only one part of a complex of reactions that includes both verbal art and ostension, including hoaxing and changes in normal behavior.

15. Associated Press, 24 and 26 July 1991.

16. Ibid., 10 and 11 Oct. 1991.

17. Ibid., 18 and 21 Oct. 1991.

18. The spread of the rumor followed two apparent conduits. One linked Catholic-affiliated institutions: Holy Cross, Salve Regina (Newport, R.I.), Siena College (Loudonville, N.Y.), Catholic University, and Georgetown University (both in Washington, D.C.). The other touched a variety of liberal-arts-oriented colleges, many in the vicinity of the Catholic-related campuses: Syracuse University (Syracuse, N.Y.), Russell Sage College (Troy, N.Y.), Franklin Pierce College

(Rindge, N.H.), Wheaton College (Norton, Mass.), Bucknell University (Lewisburg, Pa.), and University of Pittsburgh at Johnstown.

19. *FOAFTale News* 21 (Mar. 1991): 8–9.

20. Ward 1940, 345.

21. See Roberts 1947, 260.

22. Jean Caldwell, "Spooky murder rumor is no treat for colleges," *Boston Globe*, 30 Oct. 1991; Tony Rogers, AP release, 30 Oct. 1991; Anita Manning, "Massacre rumor has students running scared," *USA Today*, 30 Oct. 1991, D1.

23. Peter Lalos, "The Collegiate Perspective (and other fairy tales)," *Bucknellian*, 1 Nov. 1991, 5; Chris Courogen, "Rumor brings both fear, laughs at BU," *Lewisburg [Pa.] Daily Journal*, 25 Oct. 1991, 1, 11.

24. Rob Owen, "Murder prophecy plagues SU," *Daily Orange*, 24 Oct. 1991, A1, A6; Robert Shields, "Security tightened on Mount Olympus," *Daily Orange*, 31 Oct. 1991, A1, A3.

25. Travis Elliott, "Nostradamus prediction gives campus goosebumps," *Bucknellian*, 25 Oct. 91, 1; Bob Ritter, "November 1st and we're all still alive," *Bucknellian*, 1 Nov. 1991, 1,2; Courogen 1991.

26. Associated Press, 2 and 4 Nov. 1991.

27. "Iowa episode instills fright," 5 Nov. 1991, 5. As a final irony, on 14 November, Thomas McIlvane, another disgruntled postal employee, entered a post office in Royal Oak, Michigan (a suburb of Detroit) and shot ten fellow workers, killing four supervisors before shooting himself. Police took McIlvane to a local hospital, where he was pronounced dead and his organs harvested for transplant. A coworker commented, "Everybody said if he didn't get his job back, he was going to come in and shoot. . . . Everybody was talking about it." Another called him a "waiting time bomb," recalling that when he was enrolled in the U.S. Marines, "there was a guy he was mad at and he drove a tank over his car." The U.S. Postal Service, noting that this was the fifth post office massacre since 1985, planned to review the background of all its employees and revise grievance policies to give workers more control over personnel disputes. Associated Press 14, 15, and 16 Nov. 1991.

28. 1967, 110.

29. Truzzi 1989, xiii–xiv.

30. Similarly, Balch 1989 found positive correlations between belief in satanic cult rumors and belief in Satan, in the literal reality of miracles, and in speaking in tongues as part of religious experience.

31. PSUHFA, Nemchick 1987.

32. Randolph 1947, 264 ff; Gardner 1937, 66 ff.

33. "House terrifies demonologist," *Hazleton Standard-Speaker*, 22 Aug. 1986, 1; see also Curren 1988.

34. Ed Conrad, "Roadblocks keep curious away from 'haunted' W. Pittston home," *Hazleton Standard-Speaker*, 22 Aug. 1986, 16.

35. PSUHFA, Valeant, 1988. Emphasis is the source's.

36. Pat Collier, "Council Planning Resolution about 'Last Temptation,' " *Hazleton Standard-Speaker*, 8 Aug. 1988, 21.

37. Bill Berry and Carl Christopher, "Service Electric Pulls Plug on 'The Last Temptation,' " *Hazleton Standard-Speaker*, 3 Oct. 1989, 1–2.

38. Sworin 1988.

39. Conrad 1986.

40. Robert H. Orenstein and Sean Connolly, "5 Arrested in Satanist kidnapping," *Allentown Morning Call*, 27 July 1989.

41. E.g., Johnston 1989.

42. Jill Graham, "Officials urge unity in handling child abuse," *Wilkes-Barre Times-Leader*, 4 Feb. 1990, 1A+.

43. Wooden is mentioned in Best 1987, 108; the satanic child-care controversy, started over the notorious McMartin case in the Los Angeles area, is surveyed in Carlson 1989, 81–87. An authoritative survey of the evidence behind such cases, compiled by the FBI, is found in Lanning 1989a.

44. This summary is based on Sworin 1988 and coverage in the *Hazleton Standard-Speaker*, 7 Jan. 1989, and 6–14 Sept. 1989.

45. PSUHFA: Gryn 1989.

46. Brennan 1989, 29, 41.

47. PSUHFA: Boyle 1987.

48. PSUHFA: Kilmer 1988.

49. PSUHFA: Boyle 1987.

50. Bob Salitza, "Luzerne County suicides typical, study indicates," *Hazleton Standard-Speaker*, 13 Jan. 1990, 14.

51. Seay and Neely 1986, 248–52; Lyons 1988, 161 ff., Hicks 1991, 302–7.

52. McIver 1988.

53. Owen 1980, 20–21.

54. *Hazleton Standard-Speaker*, 25 Nov. 1991.

55. Medalia and Larson 1958, 186.

56. 1989.

Chapter 12

1. *Columbus Dispatch* [henceforth *CD*], 7 Oct. 1982, B1.

2. *CD*, 14 Oct. 1982, E1.

3. OSUFA, 1978, Birnbaum.

4. Victor 1989.

5. Rommel 1980, 241–44.

6. A similar scenario was proposed by a veterinarian in an official inquest on a "mutilated cow" (Rommel 1980). Rommel comments that nicotine sulfate is found in many insecticides found on farms and ranches and so would naturally be accessible to cattle (296).

7. Spencer 1976, 112.

8. Smith 1976, 38–39.

9. Spencer 1976, 103.

10. OSUFA, 1980, Cannata. Details on the case, as collected by the Ohio Department of Agriculture, are summarized in Baird 1984, 10. The same incidents are narrated with variants by two informants (collected by Birnbaum) who associated them with satanism and the Peach Ridge tradition.

11. Don Baird, "Sympathy for the Devil," *Capitol: Sunday Supplement to the Columbus Dispatch*, 15 July 1984, 14.

12. Indian Hill, near Cincinnati. is also mentioned as a site of cult sacrifices (OSUFA, 1975, Kidwell). One core motif, that of a passing stranger whom cult members seize and sacrifice, is an ancient one, traced to Greek myth by Frazer (1922, 429). Baird adds that another story "told of the death of two policemen who were attacked by devil worshippers after the officers crossed the boundaries of a five-pointed star used for a ritual. The story [Baird notes] was investigated but never documented" (1984, 14).

13. But which? Birnbaum found that five cemeteries on Peach Ridge fit the description of the legends, with the Haning private cemetery being the most frequently visited. Local historian W. E. Peters recalled legends from the period 1939–42, alleging that Mary T. Roberts, buried in the nearby Simms private cemetery, was a witch (OSUFA).

14. Some informants reduce the number to three hills. Birnbaum attempted to trace the pentagram on survey maps but found that "all pentagrams are somewhat shady and due to she topography of the area I could make such perfect pentagrams anywhere" (OSUFA).

15. OSUFA, 1975, Morosco. A similar story involves "a young girl" who, warned by her mother not to go out with "a certain group of people" (presumably on a trip to Peach Ridge), "told her mother to go to hell and went out anyway. When she defied her mother the candles on the table turned from white to blood red. She didn't come home again. She was found buried at Peach Ridge. She had been raped and had been buried alive" (OSUFA, 1978, Birnbaum). Other stories develop the animal mutilation aspect. One tells of a group of kids who spied on witches, apparently undetected; yet a week later they found piles of mutilated dogs and cats on their front lawns, evidently put there by the witches in revenge (author's field notes, Hiram House Camp, Moreland Hills, Ohio [Informant from Athens, Ohio], 23 June 1981). Other adolescent stories relate the usual migratory graveyard motifs: gates opening and closing, glowing eyes, mysterious shotgun blasts, etc.

16. OSUFA, 1975, Morosco.

17. OSUFA, 1979, Dore.

18. See Guinee 1987 for an illustration of how three different witnesses saw a neo-pagan gathering around a campfire in terms of their differing belief systems.

19. OSUFA, 1979, Dore.

20. Bourget, Gagnon, and Bradford 1988, 197–201.

21. *CD*, 20 Oct. 1982, B1.

22. *CD*, 17 Oct 1982, A1.

23. Details of the trial are drawn from the coverage in *CD*, especially the issues of 17, 19, 21, 24, 25, and 29 Jan. 1984.

24. *CD*, 19 Jan. 1984, C3.

25. Hilson's testimony was summarized in *CD* on 30 Jan. and 8 June 1984.

26. *CD*, 31 Jan. 1984, C1.

27. *FOAFTale News* 19 (Oct. 1990): 8. A useful summary of the case and the rumors it provoked is found in Canaan 1989.

28. *CD*, 18 Oct. 1982, A1; *CD*, 19 Oct. 1982, A1.

29. Brunvand 1986, 148–56.

30. *Harrisburg [Pa.] Sunday Patriot-News*, 13 Jan. 1985, 1.

31. *Harrisburg [Pa.] Sunday Patriot-News*, 27 Jan. 1985, 1; *Hazleton Standard-Speaker*, 26 Oct. 1985.

32. AP releases of 10 and 11 Jan. 1989. Interestingly, many adolescent traditions about "Cry-Baby Bridges" describe how cruel mothers throw their infants off bridges into streams or onto railroad tracks.

33. The O'Bryan case is discussed in detail by Grider (1984) and by Dégh and Vázsonyi (1983).

34. Grider 1984, 128.

35. AP releases of 7, 8, and 15 July 1984. St. Clair (1987) gives a journalistic account of this case.

36. See *New York Times*, 2 Oct. 1983, 33; 16 Oct. 1983, 34; 9 Nov. 1983, 20; 12 Apr. 1984, 19; 13 Oct. 1984, 30; and 14 Jan. 1985, 8. For his recantation and its effect, see 14 Apr. 1985, 40; 18 Apr. 1985, 17; 24 Apr. 1985, 16; and 30 Nov. 1985, 8. Jenkins 1988 is a critique of police handling of his confessions.

37. Fine 1982, 47–60.

38. Manshel 1990, 219–20.

39. Manshel 1990 presents the prosecution's side of the affair; defenses of Michaels came from Debbie Nathan (1988) and from Dorothy Rabinowitz (1990). Manshel responded to her critics (1991), which led to thorny exchanges in *Washington Journalism Review* with Debbie Nathan ([Sept. 1991]: 9–10) and with Stephen Squire ([Oct. 1991]: 8–9). The reverse on appeal and Michaels's release were covered in the *New York Times* ([27 Mar. 1993]: A26) and ([31 Mar. 1993]: B5). Michaels later published a bitter account of her experience (1993).

40. See Brunvand 1981, 140–46, and Jansen 1979, 64–90.

41. "Crunchy or Smooth?" 1994, 13.

42. Cited by de Caro 1970, 124–27.

Conclusions

1. Jason 1990.

2. III.i.84–88.

3. Drew 1991, 82–83.

4. Cockburn 1991, 114.

5. Trexler 1991.

6. Cockburn 1991, 114.

7. The following account is based on my "Satanic Deja Vu in Northeastern Pennsylvania," *FOAFTale News* 40–41 (Dec. 1996): 4–8.

8. For his critique of Griffis, see Hicks 1991, 85–96.

9. 1994.

References Cited

Adams, Charles III. 1984. *Ghost Stories of Berks County: Book Two*. Reading, Pa.: Exeter House.

Alford, Peggy E. 1992. "Anglo-American Perceptions of Navajo Skinwalker Legends." *Contemporary Legend* 2: 119–36.

Alphonso, Patricia. 1981. " 'We Don't Wanna Hear the Scientific Reason': Teenage Lore of St. Bernard Parish." *Louisiana Folklore Miscellany* 1: 31–32.

Ankarloo, Bengt, and Gustav Henningsen, ed. 1990. *Early Modern European Witchcraft: Centres and Peripheries*. Oxford: Oxford University Press.

Aries, Philippe. 1974. *Western Attitudes toward Death*. Trans. Patricia N. Ranum. Baltimore: Johns Hopkins University Press.

Badone, Ellen. 1987. "Death Omens in a Breton Memorate." *Folklore* 98: 99–104.

Baker, Robert A. 1987–88. "The Aliens among Us: Hypnotic Regression Revisited." *Skeptical Inquirer* 12: 148–61.

———. 1989. "Q: Are UFO Abduction Experiences for Real? A: No, No, a Thousand Times No!" *Journal of UFO Studies*, n.s., 1: 104–10.

Baker, Ronald L. 1976. "The Influence of Mass Culture on Modern Legends." *Southern Folklore Quarterly* 40: 367–76.

———. 1982. *Hoosier Folk Legends*. Bloomington: Indiana University Press.

Bakker, Jim and Tammy. 1980. *The Lord Is on Your Side*. Ed. Mary McLendon. Charlotte, N.C.: PTL Television Network, 1980.

Balch, Robert W. 1989. "The Social Construction of Satanism: A Case Study of the Rumor Process." Paper presented at the annual meeting of the Society for the Scientific Study of Religion, Salt Lake City.

Balch, Robert W., and Margaret Gilliam. 1991. "Devil Worship in Western Montana: A Case Study in Rumor Construction." In *The Satanism Scare*. Ed. James T. Richardson, Joel Best, and David G. Bromley, 249–62. New York: Aldine de Gruyter.

Balliett, Whitney. 1986. "Poets Needed," *New Yorker*, 23 June, 93.

Barden, Thomas E., ed. 1991. *Virginia Folk Legends*. Charlottesville: University Press of Virginia.

Barham, Tony. 1973. *Witchcraft in the Thames Valley*. Bourne End, Bucks, Eng.: Spurbooks.

Barnes, Daniel R. 1979. " 'The Pigeon-Drop' and Other Traditional Confidence Games." Paper presented at the meeting of the American Folklore Society, Los Angeles.

———. 1984a. "Interpreting Urban Legends." *ARV* 40: 67–78.

———. 1984b. "Surprise Packages: Some Relations Between Urban Legends and Practical Jokes." Paper presented at the Annual Meeting of the American Folklore Society, San Diego.

Bartos, Paul J. 1979. "The Royal Order of Siam." *Indiana Folklore* 12: 132–35.

Bascom, William. 1965. "The Forms of Folklore: Prose Narrative." *Journal of American Folklore* 71: 4.

Baughman, Ernest W. *Type and Motif Index of the Folktales of England and North America*. The Hague: Mouton, 1966.

Bauman, Richard. 1977. *Verbal Art as Performance*. Rowley, Mass.: Newbury House.

Beardsley Richard K., and Rosalie Hankey. 1942. "The Vanishing Hitchhiker." *California Folklore Quarterly* 1: 303–35.

Ben-Amos, Dan. 1972. "Toward a Definition of Folklore in Context." In *Toward New Perspectives in Folklore*. Ed. Américo Paredes and Richard Bauman, 3–15. Austin: University of Texas Press.

Ben-Amos, Dan, ed. 1976. *Folklore Genres*. Austin: University of Texas Press.

Bennett, Gillian. 1984. "Women's Personal Experience Stories of Encounters with the Supernatural: Truth as an Aspect of Storytelling," *ARV* 40: 79–87.

———. 1987a. *Traditions of Belief: Women, Folklore, and the Supernatural Today*. New York: Viking Penguin.

———. 1987b. "Problems in Collecting and Classifying Urban Legends: A Personal Experience." In *Perspectives on Contemporary Legend*, vol. 2. Ed. Gillian Bennett, Paul Smith, and J. D. A. Widdowson, 15–30. Sheffield, Eng.: Sheffield Academic Press.

———. 1988. "Legend: Performance and Truth." In *Monsters with Iron Teeth: Perspectives on Contemporary Legend*, vol. 3. Ed. Gillian Bennett, Paul Smith, and J. D. A. Widdowson, 13–36. Sheffield, Eng.: Sheffield Academic Press.

———. 1989. "Playful Chaos: Anatomy of a Storytelling Session." In *The Questing Beast: Perspectives on Contemporary Legend*, vol. 4. Ed. Gillian Bennett and Paul Smith, 193–212. Sheffield, Eng.: Sheffield Academic Press.

———. 1991. "Contemporary Legend: An Insider's View." *Folklore* 102: 187–91.

———. 1993. "The Color of Saying: Modern Legend and Folktale." *Southern Folklore* 50: 19–32.

———. 1994. "Geologists and Folklorists: Cultural Evolution and 'The Science of Folklore.'" *Folklore* 105: 25–37.

———. 1999. *Alas, Poor Ghost! Traditions of Belief in Story and Discourse*. Logan: Utah State University Press.

Bennett, Gillian, and Paul Smith, eds. 1988. *Monsters with Iron Teeth: Perspectives on Contemporary Legend*, vol. 3. Sheffield, Eng.: Sheffield Academic Press.

———, eds. 1989. *The Questing Beast: Perspectives on Contemporary Legend*, vol. 4. Sheffield, Eng.: Sheffield Academic Press.

———, eds. 1993. *Contemporary Legend: A Folklore Bibliography*. New York: Garland.

Bennett, Gillian, Paul Smith, and J. D. A. Widdowson, eds. 1987. *Perspectives on Contemporary Legend*, vol. 2. Sheffield, Eng.: Sheffield Academic Press.

Berger, Peter L., and Thomas Luckmann. 1967. *The Social Construction of Reality: A Treatise in the Sociology of Knowledge*. New York: Doubleday Anchor.

Best, Joel. 1987. "Rhetoric in Claims-Making: Constructing the Missing Children Problem." *Social Problems* 34: 101–21.

———. 1991. "Bad Guys and Random Violence: Folklore and Media Constructions of Contemporary Deviance." *Contemporary Legend* 1: 107–21.

Best, Joel, and G. T. Horiuchi. 1985. "The Razor Blade in the Apple: The Social Construction of Urban Legends." *Social Problems* 32: 488–99.

"Beyond Incredible," 1980. *Ohio Magazine*, Nov., 40 +.

Biographical Record of Lorain County. 1894. Lorain, Ohio: n.p.

Bird, Elizabeth. 1989. "Invasion of the Mind Snatchers." *Psychology Today*, Apr., 64 +.

Blehr, Otto. 1967. "The Analysis of Folk Belief Stories and Its Implications for Research on Folk Belief and Folk Prose," *Fabula* 9: 259–63.

Bord, Janet, and Colin Bord. 1985. *Alien Animals: A Worldwide Investigation*. London: Panther Books.

Borges, Jorge Luis. 1963 [1939]. "Pierre Menard, Author of the Quixote." Trans. Anthony Bonner. In *Ficciones*. Ed. Anthony Kerrigan, 45–55. New York: Grove Press.

Bourget, Dominique, Andre Gagnon, and John M. W. Bradford. 1988. "Satanism in a Psychiatric Adolescent Population." *Canadian Journal of Psychiatry* 33: 197–201.

Brednich, Rolf Wilhelm. 1990. *Die Spinne in der Yucca-Palme: Sagenhafte Geschichten von Heute.* Munich: Verlag C. H. Beck.

Brennan, Father Joseph. 1989. *The Kingdom of Darkness.* Lafayette, La.: Acadian Press.

Briggs, Katharine. 1971. *A Dictionary of British Folk-Tales.* Bloomington and London: Indiana University Press.

———. 1976. *Encyclopedia of Fairies.* New York: Pantheon Books.

Britton, James. 1970. *Language and Learning.* Baltimore: Penguin Books.

Bromley, David. 1989. "Satanic Conspiracy: The Social Construction of a Demonic Subversion Myth." Paper presented before the Society for the Study of Social Problems, San Francisco.

Bronner, Simon. 1988. *American Children's Folklore: Annotated Edition.* Little Rock: August House.

Brunvand, Jan Harold. 1978. *The Study of American Folklore: An Introduction.* 2nd ed. New York: Norton.

———. 1981. *The Vanishing Hitchhiker: American Urban Legends and Their Meanings.* New York: Norton.

———. 1984. *The Choking Doberman And Other "New" Urban Legends.* New York: Norton.

———. 1986. *The Mexican Pet: More "New" Urban Legends and Some Old Favorites.* New York: Norton.

———. 1989. *Curses! Broiled Again! The Hottest Urban Legends Going.* New York: Norton.

———. 1993. *The Baby Train and Other Lusty Urban Legends.* New York: Norton.

Bullard, Thomas E. 1987. "Klass Takes on Abductions; Abductions Win." *International UFO Reporter* 12 (Nov./Dec.): 9 +.

———. 1989a. "UFO Abduction Reports: The Supernatural Kidnap Narrative Returns in Technological Guise." *Journal of American Folklore* 102: 147–70.

———. 1989b. "Hypnosis and UFO Abductions: A Troubled Relationship." *Journal of UFO Studies,* n.s., 1: 3–40.

———. 1989c. "How to Make an Alien." *International UFO Reporter* 14 (Nov./Dec.): 10 +.

———. 1991a. "Why Abduction Reports Are Not Urban Legends." *International UFO Reporter* 16, no. 4: 15–20, 24.

———. 1991b. "Folkloric Dimensions of the UFO Phenomenon." *Journal of UFO Studies,* n.s., 3: 1–57.

Burger, Peter. 1992. *De Wraak van de Kangoeroe: Sagen uit het Moderne Leven.* Amsterdam: Prometheus.

Campbell, Joseph. 1969. *The Masks of God: Primitive Mythology.* New York: Viking.

Campion-Vincent, Véronique. 1989. "Complots et avertissements: legendes urbaines dans la ville." *Revue francaise de sociologie* 30: 91–105.

———. 1990. "The Baby-Parts Story: A New Latin American Legend." *Western Folklore* 49: 9–26.

Campion-Vincent, Véronique, and Jean-Bruno Renard. 1992. *Légendes urbaines: Rumeurs d'aujourd'hui.* Paris: Payot.

Canaan, Don. 1989. *Horror in Hocking County.* Cincinnati: Land of Canaan Publications.

Cannon, Anthon S. 1984. *Popular Beliefs and Superstitions from Utah.* Ed. Wayland D. Hand and Jeannine E. Talley. Salt Lake City: University of Utah Press.

Carbone, Maria Teresa. 1990. *99 Leggende Urbane*. Milan: Oscar Mondadori.

Carey, George. 1970–71. "Some Thoughts on the Modern Legend." *Journal of the Folklore Society of Greater Washington [D.C.]* 2: 3–10.

———. 1971. *Maryland Folk Legends and Folk Songs*. Cambridge, Md.: Tidewater Publishers.

Carlson, Shawn, et al. 1989. *Satanism in America: How the Devil Got Much More than His Due*. El Cerrito, Calif.: Gaia Press.

Cassius Dio Cocceianus. 1914. *Dio's Roman History*, vol. 3. Translated by Earnest Cary. Loeb Classical Library. New York: Macmillan.

Child, Francis James. 1965. [1882–84.] *The English and Scottish Popular Ballads*, vol. 1. New York: Dover Publications.

Clark, Jerome. 1990. "The Thickets of Magonia." *International UFO Reporter* 15 (Jan./Feb.): 4–11

Clarke, G. W. 1974. *The Octavius of Marcus Minucius Felix*. New York: Ancient Christian Writers No. 39.

Clements, William H. 1980. "The Walking Coffin." In *Indiana Folklore: A Reader*. Ed. Linda Dégh, 279–86. Bloomington: Indiana University Press.

———. 1982. " 'I once was lost': Oral Narratives of Born-again Christians." *International Folklore Review* 2: 105–11.

———. 1986. "Mythography and the Modern Legend." *Journal of Popular Culture* 19, no. 4: 39–46.

———. 1991. "Interstitiality in Contemporary Legend." *Contemporary Legend* 1: 81–91.

Clements, William H., and William E. Lightfoot. 1971. "The Legend of Stepp Cemetery." *Indiana Folklore* 5: 92–141.

Cockburn, Alexander. 1991. "Beat the Devil." *Nation*, 4 Feb., 114–15.

Cohn, Norman. 1975. *Europe's Inner Demons: An Enquiry Inspired by the Great Witch-Hunt*. New York: New American Library.

Conroy, Ed. 1989. *Report on Communion: An Independent Investigation of and Commentary on Whitley Strieber's Communion*. New York: William Morrow.

"Crunchy or Smooth?" 1994. *Frank* 171 (7 July): 13.

Curren, Robert, et al. 1988. *The Haunted: One Family's Nightmare*. New York: St. Martin's Press.

Czubala, Dionizjusz. 1985. *Opowiesci z Zycia: Z Badan nad Folklorem Wspolcsesnym*. Katowice: Uniwersytet Slaski.

———. 1992a. "The Death Car: Polish and Russian Examples." *FOAFTale News* 25 (Mar.): 2–5.

———. 1992b. "Mongolian Contemporary Legends: Field Research Report, Part One." *FOAF-Tale News* 28 (Dec.): 1–5.

Danielson, Larry. 1979. "Folklore and Film: Some Thoughts on Baughman Z500–599." *Western Folklore* 38: 214–19.

———. 1983. "Paranormal Memorates in the American Vernacular." In *The Occult in America: New Historical Perspectives*. Ed. Howard Kerr and Charles L. Crow. Urbana: University of Illinois Press.

Davis, Amma. 1990. "Narrative Reactions to Brutal Murders: A Case Study." *Western Folklore* 49: 99–109.

Dawkins, Richard. 1989 [1976]. *The Selfish Gene*. Oxford: Oxford University Press.

———. 1993. "Viruses of the Mind." In *Dennett and His Critics: Demystifying Mind*. Ed. Bo Dahlbom, 13–27. Oxford: Blackwell.

de Caro, Rosan Jordan. 1970. "Sex Education and the Horrible Example Stories." *Folklore Forum* 3: 124–27.

Dégh, Linda. 1965. "Processes of Legend Formation." *Fourth International Congress for Folk-Narrative Research in Athens*. Ed. Georgios A. Megas. *Leographia* 22: 78–87.

———. 1968a. "The Haunted Bridges Near Avon and Danville and Their Role in Legend Formation," *Indiana Folklore* 1: 77–81.

———. 1968b. "The Hook." *Indiana Folklore* 1 (1): 92–100.

———. 1969a. *Folktales and Society*. Trans. Emily M. Schossberger. Bloomington: Indiana University Press.

———. 1969b. "The House of Blue Lights Revisited." *Indiana Folklore* 2, no. 2: 11–28. Also in Dégh 1980, 179–95.

———. 1971. "The 'Belief Legend' in Modern Society: Form, Function, and Relationship to Other Genres." In *American Folk Legend: A Symposium*. Ed. Wayland Hand, 55–68. Berkeley and Los Angeles: University of California Press.

———. 1972. "Folk Narrative," In *Folklore and Folklife: An Introduction*. Ed. Richard M. Dorson, 53–83. Chicago: University of Chicago Press.

———. 1979a. "Grimm's Household Tales and Its Place in the Household: The Social Relevance of a Controversial Classic." *Western Folklore* 38: 83–103.

———. 1979b. "Biology of Storytelling." *Folklore Preprint Series* 7, no. 3 (Mar.). Also in Dégh 1995, 47–61.

———, ed. 1980. *Indiana Folklore: A Reader*. Bloomington: Indiana University Press.

———. 1991. "What Is the Legend After All?" *Contemporary Legend* 1: 11–38.

———. 1995. *Narratives in Society: A Performer-Centered Study of Narration*. Ed. Linda Kersey Adams. FF Communications No. 255. Helsinki: Academia Scientiarum Fennica.

Dégh, Linda, and Andrew Vázsonyi. 1973. "The Dialectics of the Legend." *Folklore Preprint Series* 1, no. 6 (Dec.).

———. 1974. "The Memorate and the Proto-Memorate," *Journal of American Folklore* 87: 225–39.

———. 1975. "The Hypothesis of Multi-Conduit Transmission in Folklore." In *Folklore: Performance and Communication*. Ed. Dan Ben-Amos and Kenneth A. Goldstein, 207–52. The Hague: Mouton. Also in Dégh 1995, 173–212.

———. 1976 [1971]. "Legend and Belief," In *Folklore Genres*. Ed. Dan Ben-Amos, 93–123. Austin: University of Texas Press.

———. 1983. "Does the Word 'Dog' Bite? Ostensive Action: A Means of Legend-Telling." *Journal of Folklore Research* 20: 5–34. Also in Dégh 1995, 236–62.

Dennett, Daniel. 1993. "Back from the Drawing Board." In *Dennett and His Critics: Demystifying Mind*. Ed. Bo Dahlbom, 203–35. Cambridge, Mass.: Blackwell.

Di Salvatore, Bryan. 1988. "A Reporter at Large: Large Cars—Part I." *New Yorker*, 12 Sept., 39 + .

Disch, Thomas M. 1987. "The Village Alien." *Nation*, 14 Mar., 328 + .

Dobos, Ilona. 1978. "True Stories." Trans. Peter Vari. In *Studies in East European Folk Narrative*. Ed. Linda Dégh, 165–205. Bloomington: Indiana University Folklore Institute.

Dorson, Richard M. 1952. *Bloodstoppers and Bearwalkers*. Cambridge: Harvard University Press.

———. 1959. *American Folklore*. Chicago: University of Chicago Press.

———. 1981. *Land of the Millrats*. Cambridge: Harvard University Press.

Drew, Elizabeth. 1991. "Letter from Washington." *New Yorker*, 4 Feb., 82–90.

Dundes, Alan. 1971. "On the Psychology of Legend." In Hand 1971, 21–36.

———. 1980. "Texture, Text, and Context." In *Interpreting Folklore*, 20–33. Bloomington: Indiana University Press.

———. 1989. "The Psychoanalytic Study of the Grimms' Tales: 'The Maiden Without Hands' " (AT 706). In *Folklore Matters*, 112–50. Knoxville: University of Tennessee Press.

———. 1991. "The Ritual Murder or Blood Libel Legend: A Study of Anti-Semitic Victimization through Projective Inversion." In *The Blood Libel Legend: A Casebook in Anti-Semitic Folklore*, 336–76. Madison: University of Wisconsin Press.

————. 1993. "Introduction." *Contemporary Legend: A Folklore Bibliography*. Ed. Gillian Bennett and Paul Smith, ix–xiii. New York: Garland.

Dundes, Alan, and Carl R. Pagter. 1978. *Work Hard and You Shall Be Rewarded: Urban Folklore from the Paperwork Empire*. Bloomington: Indiana University Press.

Eco, Umberto. 1976. *A Theory of Semiotics*. Bloomington: Indiana University Press.

Edel, Leon. 1953. *Henry James: 1843–1870*. New York: Lippincott.

Edwards, Carol L. 1984. "Closure in the *Märchen* and Legend." Paper presented at the Annual Meeting of the American Folklore Society, San Diego.

Edwards, Frank. 1967. *Stranger than Science*. New York: Bantam Books.

Ellis, Bill. 1981. "Majaska: Mythmaking in Greater Cleveland," *Kentucky Folklore Record* 27: 76–96.

————. 1991. " 'Contemporary Legend'—Cracks or Breakthroughs?" *Folklore* 101: 183–85.

————. 1994. " 'Safe' Spooks: New Halloween Traditions in Response to Sadism Legends," in *Halloween and Other Festivals of Death and Life*. Ed. Jack Santino, 24–44. Knoxville: University of Tennessee Press.

————. 1995. "Kurt E. Koch and the 'Civitas Diaboli': Germanic Folk Healing as Satanic Ritual Abuse of Children." *Western Folklore* 54: 77–94.

Evans. Hilary. 1982. *Intrusions: Society and the Paranormal*. Boston: Routledge and Kegan Paul.

Fine, Elizabeth C. 1984. *The Folklore Text: From Performance to Print*. Bloomington: Indiana University Press.

Fine, Gary Alan. 1979. "Cokelore and Coke Law: Urban Belief Tales and the Problem of Multiple Origins." *Journal of American Folklore* 92: 477–82. Also in Fine 1992, 79–85.

————. 1982. "The Manson Family: The Folklore Traditions of a Small Group." *Journal of the Folklore Institute* 19: 47–60.

————. 1985. "The Goliath Effect: Corporate Dominance and Mercantile Legends." *Journal of American Folklore* 98: 63–84. Also in Fine 1992, 141–63.

————. 1987. "Welcome to the World of AIDS: Fantasies of Female Revenge." *Western Folklore* 46, no. 3 (July): 192–97. Also in Fine 1992, 69–75.

————. 1988. "The Third Force in American Folklore: Folk Narratives and Social Structures." *Fabula* 29: 342–53.

————. 1989. "Mercantile Legends and the World Economy: Dangerous Imports from the Third World." *Western Folklore* 48: 153–62. Also in Fine 1992, 164–73.

————. 1991. "Redemption Rumors and the Power of Ostension." *Journal of American Folklore* 104: 179–81. Also in Fine 1992, 205–8.

————. 1992. *Manufacturing Tales: Sex and Money in Contemporary Legends*. Knoxville: University of Tennessee Press.

Fineman, Howard. 1989. "The New Black Politics." *Newsweek*, 20 Nov., 52–53.

Finn, Brian. 1990. "Hitchhiking Angels?" *Challenge Weekly*, 31 Oct.

Fiore, Edith. 1989. *Encounters: A Psychologist Reveals Case Studies of Abductions by Extraterrestrials*. New York: Macmillan.

Fish, Lydia. 1976. "Jesus on the Thruway: The Vanishing Hitchhiker Strikes Again." *Indiana Folklore* 9: 5–13.

Fogel, Edwin M. 1908. "The Himmelsbrief." *German American Annals* 6: 286–311.

Fox, William. 1993. "Thanks for the Meme-ories: Folkloric Transmission as Self-Replication." Paper presented at the Annual Meeting of the American Folklore Society, Eugene, Ore.

Frary, T. 1936. *Early Homes of Ohio*. Richmond: Garrett and Massie.

Frazer, James George. 1922. *The Golden Bough: A Study of Magic and Religion*. Abridged ed. New York: Macmillan.

Fry, Gladys-Marie. 1975. *Night Riders in Black Folk History.* Knoxville: University of Tennessee Press.

Fuller, John G. 1978. *The Ghost of Flight 401.* New York: Berkley Medallion.

Gardner, Emelyn E. 1937. *Folklore from the Schoharie Hills, New York.* Ann Arbor: University of Michigan Press.

Georges, Robert A. 1969. "Toward an Understanding of Storytelling Events." *Journal of American Folklore* 82: 313–28.

———. 1971. "The General Concept of Legend: Some Assumptions to be Reexamined and Reassessed." In *American Folk Legend: A Symposium.* Ed. Wayland D. Hand, 1–19. Berkeley and Los Angeles: University of California Press.

———. 1980. "Toward a Resolution of the Text/Context Controversy." *Western Folklore* 39: 34–40.

———. 1981. "Do Narrators Really Digress? A Reconsideration of 'Audience Asides' in Narrating." *Western Folklore* 40: 245–52.

Glazer, Mark. 1984. "Continuity and Change in Legendry: Two Mexican-American Examples." In *Perspectives on Contemporary Legend.* Ed. Paul Smith, 108–27. Sheffield, Eng.: CECTAL.

Goffman, Erving. 1974. *Frame Analysis.* New York: Harper and Row.

Goldstuck, Arthur. 1990. *The Rabbit in the Thorn Tree: Modern Myths and Urban Legends of South Africa.* Johannesburg: Penguin.

Goode, Erich. 1992. *Collective Behavior.* New York: Harcourt Brace Jovanovich.

Goodenough, Oliver R., and Richard Dawkins. 1994. "The 'St Jude' Mind Virus." *Nature* 371 (1 Sept.): 23–24.

Goss, Michael. 1984. *The Evidence for Phantom Hitch-Hikers.* Wellingborough, Northamptonshire: Aquarian Press.

———. 1987. *The Halifax Slasher: An Urban Terror in the North of England.* London: Fortean Times.

Gould, Stephen Jay. 1983. *The Panda's Thumb: More Reflections in Natural History.* Harmondsworth: Penguin.

———. 1991. *Bully for Brontosaurus: Reflections in Natural History.* New York: Norton.

Grant, Michael. 1958. *Roman Readings.* Baltimore: Penguin Books.

Greeley, Andrew M. 1975. *The Sociology of the Paranormal: A Reconnaissance.* Beverly Hills, Calif.: Sage Publications.

Green, Thomas A. 1978. "Toward a Definition of Folk Drama." *Journal of American Folklore* 91: 843–50.

———. 1991. "Accusations of Satanism and Racial Tensions in the Matamoros Cult Murders." In *The Satanism Scare.* Ed. James T. Richardson, Joel Best, and David G. Bromley, 237–48. New York: Aldine de Gruyter.

Greenhouse, Herbert B. 1971. *Premonitions: A Leap into the Future.* New York: Warner Paperback.

Grider, Sylvia. 1980 [1973]. "The Hatchet Man," *Indiana Folklore: A Reader.* Ed. Linda Dégh, 147–78. Bloomington: Indiana University Press.

———. 1984. "The Razor Blades in the Apples Syndrome." *Perspectives on Contemporary Legend: Proceedings of the Conference on Contemporary Legend, Sheffield, July, 1982.* Ed. Paul Smith, 128–40. Sheffield, Eng.: CECTAL.

———. 1985. "Razor Blades in the Apples: The Proto-Legend That Is Changing Halloween in America." Unpublished paper presented at the annual meeting of the American Folklore Society, Cincinnati.

Grimm, Jacob, and Wilhelm Grimm. 1981. *The German Legends of the Brothers Grimm.* Trans. Donald Ward. Philadelphia; Institute for the Study of Human Issues.

Guigne, Anna Elizabeth. 1993. "The 'Dying Child's Wish' Complex: A Case Study of the Relationship Between Reality and Tradition." Master's thesis, Memorial University of Newfoundland.

Guinee, William. 1987. "Satanism in Yellowwood Forest: The Interdependence of Antagonistic Worldviews." *Indiana Folklore and Oral History* 16: 1–30.

Gutowski, John A. 1980. "Traditions of the Devil's Hollows." In Dégh 1980, 74–92.

Hall, Gary. 1973. "The Big Tunnel." *Indiana Folklore* 6: 139–73. Also in Dégh 1980, 225–57.

Halpert, Herman. 1956. "Chain Letters." *Western Folklore* 15: 287–89.

Hand, Wayland D. 1959. "A North Carolina *Himmelsbrief.*" In *Middle Ages-Reformation Volkskunde: Festschrift for John G. Kunstmann,* 201–7. Chapel Hill: University of North Carolina Press.

———. 1965. "Status of European and American Legend Study." *Current Anthropology* 6: 439–46.

———, ed. 1971. *American Folk Legend: A Symposium.* Berkeley and Los Angeles: University of California Press.

Haring, Lee. 1972. "Performing for the Interviewer," *Southern Folklore Quarterly* 36: 383–98.

Haring, Lee, and Mark Breslerman. 1977. "The Cropsey Maniac," *New York Folklore* 3: 15–27.

Henningsen, Gustav. 1980. *The Witches' Advocate: Basque Witchcraft and the Spanish Inquisition (1609–1614).* Reno: University of Utah Press.

Hertenstein, Mike, and John Trott. 1993. *Selling Satan: The Tragic History of Mike Warnke.* Chicago: Cornerstone Press.

Hicks, Robert D. 1991. *In Pursuit of Satan: The Police and the Occult.* Buffalo, N.Y.: Prometheus Books.

"Himmelsbrief." 1908. *Pennsylvania-German* 9: 217–22.

Hind, Cynthia. 1979. "Girl-Ghost Hitches Ride." *Fate* (July): 54–59.

Hippensteel, Faith. 1969. " 'Sir Hugh': The Hoosier Contribution to the Ballad." *Indiana Folklore* 2, no. 2: 75–140.

Hitler, Adolf. 1943 [1925]. *Mein Kampf.* Trans. Ralph Manheim. Boston: Houghton Mifflin.

Hobbs, Sandy, and David Cornwell. 1988. "Hunting the Monster with Iron Teeth." In Bennett and Smith 1988, 115–37.

Honko, Lauri. 1964. "Memorates and the Study of Folk Beliefs." *Journal of Folklore Research* 1: 5–19.

Hopkins, Budd. 1987. *Intruders: The Incredible Visitations at Copley Woods.* New York: Ballantine.

Hufford, David J. 1982. *The Terror that Comes in the Night: An Experience-Centered Study of Supernatural Assault Traditions.* Philadelphia: University of Pennsylvania Press.

———. 1992. "Folk Medicine in Contemporary America." In *Herbal and Magical Medicine: Traditional Healing Today.* Ed. James Kirkland et al., 14–31. Durham, N.C.: Duke University Press.

———. 1995. "The Scholarly Voice and the Personal Voice: Reflexivity in Belief Studies." *Western Folklore* 54: 57–76.

Hyatt, Harry Middleton. 1965. *Folk-lore from Adams County. Illinois.* Hannibal, Mo.: Alma Egan Hyatt Foundation.

Jackson, Basil. 1976. "Reflections on the Demonic: A Psychiatric Perspective." In *Demon Possession: A Medical, Historical, Anthropological, and Theological Symposium.* Ed. J. W. Montgomery, 256–67. Minneapolis: Bethany Fellowship.

Jacobs, Joseph. 1902. "Blood Accusation." In *The Jewish Encyclopedia.* Ed. Isidore Singer et al. 3: 261–67. New York: Funk and Wagnalls.

James, William. 1958 [1902]. *The Varieties of Religious Experience: A Study in Human Nature*. New York: Mentor.

Jans, B. O. 1991. "Hitchhiking Angels in Holland," *FOAFTale News* 22 (June): 5–6.

Jansen, William Hugh. 1979. "The Surpriser Surprised: A Modern Legend." In *Readings in American Folklore*. Ed. Jan Harold Brunvand, 64–90. New York: Norton.

Jason, Heda. 1986. Review of Paul Smith, ed., *Perspectives on Contemporary Legend*. *Asian Folklore Studies* 45: 206–8.

———. 1990. " 'Contemporary Legend'—To Be or Not To Be?" *Folklore* 101: 221–23.

Jenkins, Philip. 1988. "Myth and Murder: The Serial Killer Panic of 1983–85." *Criminal Justice Research Bulletin* 3 (Nov.): 1–7.

Johnson, Donald. 1945. "The 'Phantom Anesthetist' of Mattoon: A Field Study of Mass Hysteria." *Journal of Abnormal and Social Psychology* 40: 175–86.

Johnston, Jerry. 1989. *The Edge of Evil: The Rise of Satanism in North America*. Dallas: Word Publishing.

Jones, Suzi. *Oregon Folklore*. Eugene: University of Oregon, 1977.

Josephus. 1926. *Against Apion*. Translated by H. St. J. Thackery. In *Josephus,*, vol. 1. Loeb Classical Library. New York: Putnam.

Kagan, Daniel, and Ian Summers. 1983. *Mute Evidence*. New York: Bantam Books.

Kalcik, Susan. 1975. ". . . like Ann's Gynecologist: or the Time I was Almost Raped." *Journal of American Folklore* 88: 3–11.

Kapferer, Jean-Noël. 1993. "The Persuasiveness of an Urban Legend: The Case of 'Mickey Mouse Acid.' " *Contemporary Legend* 3: 85–101.

Keel, John A. 1975. *The Mothman Prophecies: An Investigation into the Mysterious American Visits of the Infamous Feathery Garuda*. New York: Saturday Review Press.

Klass, Philip J. 1987. "Intruders of the Mind." *Skeptical Inquirer* 12: 85–89.

Klintberg, Bengt af. 1988. " 'Black Madame, Come Out!': On Schoolchildren and Spirits." *ARV* 44: 155–67.

———. 1990a. *Die Ratte in der Pizza: Und Andere Moderne Sagen und Grosstadtmythen*. Kiel: Wolfgang Butt.

———. 1990b. "Do the Legends of Today and Yesterday Belong to the Same Genre?" In *Storytelling in Contemporary Societies*. Ed. L. Röhrich and S. Wienker-Piepho, 113–26. Tübingen: Gunter Narr Verlag.

Koch, Kurt E. 1973. *Revival Fires in Canada*. Grand Rapids, Mich.: Kregel.

———. 1978. *Occult ABC*. Grand Rapids, Mich.: Kregel.

Koch, Kurt E., and Alfred Lechler. 1970. *Occult Bondage and Deliverance: Advice for Counseling the Sick, the Troubled, and the Occultly Oppressed*. Grand Rapids, Mich.: Kregel.

Korson, George. 1938. *Minstrels of the Mine Patch: Songs and Stories of the Anthracite Industry*. Philadelphia: University of Pennsylvania Press.

———. 1968. *Black Rock: Mining Folklore of the Pennsylvania Dutch*. Baltimore: Johns Hopkins University Press.

Kottmeyer, Martin. 1988. "Abductions: The Boundary Deficit Hypothesis." *Magonia* 32: 3–7.

Labov, William, and Joshua Waletzky. 1967. "Narrative Analysis: Oral Versions of Personal Experience." In *Essays on the Visual and Verbal Arts*. Ed. June Helm, 12–44. Seattle: University of Washington Press.

LaFontaine, Jean S. 1994. *The Extent and Nature of Organized and Ritual Abuse*. London: HMSO.

Langlois, Janet. 1980. " 'Mary Whales, I Believe in You': Myth and Ritual Subdued." In Dégh 1980, 196–224.

———. 1983. "The Belle Isle Bridge Incident: Legend Dialectic and Semiotic System in the 1943 Detroit Race Riots." *Journal of American Folklore* 96: 183–99.

———. 1985. *Belle Gunness: The Lady Bluebeard*. Bloomington: Indiana University Press.

Lanning, Kenneth V. 1989a. *Child Sex Rings: A Behavioral Analysis*. Arlington, Va.: National Center for Missing and Exploited Children.

———. 1989b. "Satanic, Occult, Ritualistic Crime: A Law Enforcement Perspective." *Police Chief* 61, no. 10 (Oct.): 62+. Also in Carlson 1989, B1–12.

Larsen, Leonard E. 1990. "U.S. Seems Foolish, Careless with Truth." Syndicated column, *Columbus Dispatch*, 28 Jan.

Lassen, Henrik R. 1995. " 'The Improved Product' A Philological Investigation of a Contemporary Legend." *Contemporary Legend* 5: 1–37.

———. 1996. "Contemporary Legends and Traditions of the Past: The Regenerative Approach." In *Modern Legends and Medieval Studies*. Ed. Henrik Lassen and Tom Pettitt. Odense, Denmark: Odense Universitet.

———. 1998. *The Idea of Narrative: The Theory and Practice of Analyzing Narrative Types, and Legends of Suppressed Inventions*. Ph.d. thesis, Odense Universitet.

Leach, Maria, ed. 1950. *Standard Dictionary of Folklore Mythology and Legend*. New York: Funk and Wagnalls.

Leary, James P. 1973. "The Boondocks Monster of Camp Wapehani." *Indiana Folklore* 6: 174–90.

Legman, G. 1968. *Rationale of the Dirty Joke*. New York: Grove Press.

———. 1975. *No Laughing Matter: Rationale of the Dirty Joke, 2nd Series*. New York: Breaking Point.

Licht, M[ichael]. 1974. "Some Automotive Play Activities of Suburban Teenagers." *New York Folklore Quarterly* 30: 44–65.

Long, Martha. 1985. "Is Satan Alive and Well in Northeast Arkansas?" *Mid-American Folklore* 13, no. 2: 18–26.

Long-Wilgus, Eleanor. 1984. " 'Spit on a Wooly Worm, but Don't Iron a Shirt-Tail': Tradition as Function in Folk Belief." Paper presented at the Annual Meeting of the American Folklore Society, San Diego.

Luthi, Max, 1970. *Once Upon a Time: On the Nature of Fairy Tales*. Bloomington: Indiana University Press.

Lyons, Arthur. 1989. *Satan Wants You: The Cult of Devil Worship in America*. New York: Mysterious Press.

Mack, John E. 1994. *Abduction: Human Encounters with Aliens*. New York: Charles Scribner's Sons.

Magliocco, Sabina. 1985. "The Bloomington Jaycees' Haunted House." *Indiana Folklore and Oral History* 14: 19–28.

Manshel, Lisa. 1990. *Nap Time*. New York: Morrow.

———. 1991. "Reporters for the Defense in a Child Abuse Case." *Washington Journalism Review* (Jul./Aug.): 17–21.

Mayor, Adrienne. 1992. "Ambiguous Guardians: The 'Omen of the Wolves' (A.D. 402) and the 'Choking Doberman' (1980s)." *Journal of Folklore Research* 29: 253–68.

———. 1995. "The Nessus Shirt in the New World: Smallpox Blankets in History and Legend." *Journal of American Folklore* 108: 54–77.

McDowell, John. 1974a. "Coherency and Delight: Dual Canons of Excellence in Informal Narrative." *Folklore Forum Bibliographical and Special Series* 12: 97–106.

———. 1974b. "Some Aspects of Verbal Art in Bolivian Quechua." *Folklore Annual of the University Folklore Association* 6: 68–81.

McIver, Tom. 1988. "Backward Masking, and Other Backward Thoughts about Music." *Skeptical Inquirer* 13: 50–63.

Mechling, Jay. 1980. "The Magic of the Boy Scout Campfire." *Journal of American Folklore* 93: 35–56.

Medalia, Nahum, and Otto L. Larsen. 1958. "Diffusion and Belief in a Collective Delusion: The Seattle Windshield Pitting." *American Sociological Review* 23: 180–86.

Melton, J. Gordon. 1986. "The Evidences of Satan in Contemporary America: A Survey." Paper presented at the meeting of the Pacific Division of the American Philosophical Association, Los Angeles.

Metcalf. George P. 1968. "The Swift's Hollow Mansion." *Pathways of the Pioneers* (Lorain County Historical Society) 2, no. 4 (June): IA.

Michaels, Kelly. 1993. "Eight Years in Kafkaland." *National Review*, 6 Sept., 37.

Milligan, Linda. 1990. "The 'Truth' about Bigfoot." *Western Folklore* 49: 83–98.

Minucius Felix, Marcus. 1931. *Octavius.* Translated by Gerald H. Rendall. In *Tertullian/Minucius Felix.* Loeb Classical Library. New York: Putnam.

Montgomery, John Warwick. 1976. "Not Suffering Witches to Live." In *Demon Possession: A Medical, Historical, Anthropological, and Theological Symposium.* Minneapolis: Bethany Fellowship.

Mulhern, Sherrill. 1991. "Satanism and Psychotherapy: A Rumor in Search of an Inquisition." In *The Satanism Scare.* Ed. James T. Richardson, Joel Best, and David G. Bromley, 145–72. New York: Aldine de Gruyter.

Mullen, Patrick B. 1972. "Modern Legend and Rumor Theory." *Journal of the Folklore Institute* 9: 95–109.

Nathan, Debbie. 1988. "Victimizer or Victim? Was Kelly Michaels Unjustly Convicted?" *Village Voice*, 2 Aug.

"A National Crime." 1908. *Collier's*, 21 Mar., 2.

Nicolaisen, W. F. H. 1984. "Legends as Narrative Response." In *Perspectives on Contemporary Legend.* Ed. Paul Smith, 167–78. Sheffield, Eng.: CECTAL.

———. 1989. "Definitional Problems in Oral Narrative." In *The Questing Beast: Perspectives on Contemporary Legend,* vol. 4. Ed. Gillian Bennett and Paul Smith, 77–89. Sheffield, Eng.: Sheffield Academic Press.

Niles, John. 1989. "The Berkeley Contemporary Legend Files." In *The Questing Beast: Perspectives on Contemporary Legend,* vol. 4. Ed. Gillian Bennett and Paul Smith, 103–11. Sheffield, Eng.: Sheffield Academic Press.

Nossal, Gustav J. V. 1993. "Life, Death and the Immune System." *Scientific American*, Sept., 53–62.

O'Donnell, Thomas Edward. 1924. "The Early Architecture of the State of Ohio: 4. The Joseph Swift House; An Example of Greek Revival Architecture." *Western Architect* 33 (Oct.): 109–13.

Opie, Iona, and Peter Opie. 1959. *The Lore and Language of Schoolchildren.* London: Oxford University Press.

Owen, Nancy H. 1980. "Preliminary Analysis of the Impact of Livestock Mutilations on Rural Arkansas Communities." Report prepared for the Arkansas Endowment for the Humanities, Little Rock.

Parochetti, JoAnn Stephens. 1965. "Scary Stories from Purdue." *Keystone Folklore Quarterly* 10: 49–57.

Passantino, Gretchen, and Bob Passantino. 1992. "Satanic Ritual Abuse in Popular Christian Literature: Why Christians Fall for a Lie Searching for the Truth." *Journal of Psychology and Theology* 20: 299–305.

Passantino, Gretchen, and Bob Passantino, with Jon Trott. 1990. "Satan's Sideshow." *Cornerstone* 18 (90): 24–28.

Pettitt, Thomas. 1995. "Legends Contemporary, Current, and Modern: An Outsider's View." *Folklore* 106: 96–98.

———. 1996. "Introduction: The Contemporaneity of the Contemporary Legend." In *Modern Legends and Medieval Studies*. Ed. Henrik Lassen and Tom Pettitt, 7–14. Odense, Denmark: Odense Universitet.

Petzoldt, Leander. 1989. "Phantom Lore." In *Storytelling in Contemporary Societies*. Budapest: ISFNR Theory Commission, 9th Congress of the International Society for Folk-Narrative Research.

Polanyi, Livia. 1979. "So What's the Point?" *Semiotica* 25: 207–41.

Preston, Michael J. 1976. "Chain Letters." *Tennessee Folklore Society Bulletin* 42, no. 1 (Mar.): 1–14.

Pritchard, Andrea, et al., ed. 1994. *Alien Discussions: Proceedings of the Abduction Study Conference*. Cambridge, Mass.: North Cambridge Press.

Prostitution in America: Three Investigations. 1976. New York: Arno Press.

Rabinowitz, Dorothy. 1990. "From the Mouths of Babes to a Jail Cell." *Harper's*, May, 52–63.

Randolph, Vance. 1947. *Ozark Superstitions*. New York: Columbia University Press.

———. 1976. *Pissing in the Snow*. Urbana: University of Illinois Press.

Raschke, Carl A. 1990. *Painted Black*. New York: Harper and Row.

Renard, Jean-Bruno. 1991. "LSD Tattoo Transfers: Rumor from North America to France." *Folklore Forum* 24, no. 2: 3–26.

Ridley, Florence H. 1967. "A Tale Told Too Often." *Western Folklore* 26: 153–56.

Roberts, Henry C., ed. 1947. *The Complete Prophecies of Nostradamus*. Oyster Bay, N.Y.: Nostradamus Co.

Robinson, John A. 1981. "Personal Narratives Reconsidered." *Journal of American Folklore* 94: 58–85.

Rojcewicz, Peter M. 1987. "The 'Men in Black' Experience and Tradition: Analogues with the Traditional Devil Hypothesis." *Journal of American Folklore* 100: 148–60.

———. 1989. "The Folklore of the 'Men in Black': A Challenge to the Prevailing Paradigm." *ReVISION* 2, no. 4: 5–16.

Rommel, Kenneth M., Jr. 1980. *Operation Animal Mutilation*. Report of the District Attorney, First Judicial District, State of New Mexico.

Rose, Dan. 1981. *Energy Transition and the Local Community: A Theory of Society Applied to Hazleton, Pennsylvania*. Philadelphia: University of Pennsylvania Press.

Roud, Steve. 1989. "Chelsea Smilers: Interim Report on a Gang-Violence Rumor." *FOAFTale News* 15: 1–2.

Rudinger, Joel D. 1976. "Folk Ogres of the Firelands: Narrative Variations of a North Central Ohio Community." *Indiana Folklore* 9: 41–93.

Sallust. 1921. *The War with Catiline*. Translated by J. C. Rolfe. In *Sallust*. Loeb Classical Library. Cambridge: Harvard University Press.

Samuelson, Sue. 1979. "The White Witch: An Analysis of an Adolescent Legend." *Indiana Folklore* 12: 18–37.

———. 1980. "Infanticide in Folk Narration." Paper presented at the Annual Meeting of the American Folklore Society, Pittsburgh.

———. 1981. "European and American Adolescent Legends." *ARV* 37: 133–39.

Sandburg, Carl. 1927. *The American Songbag*. New York: Harcourt Brace.

Sanderson, Stewart. 1981. "From Social Regulator to Art Form: Case Study of a Modern Urban Legend." *ARV* 37: 134–39.

Sann, Paul. 1968. *Fads, Follies and Delusions of the American People.* New York: Bonanza Books.

Sargant, William. 1961. *Battle for the Mind: A Physiology of Conversion and Brain-Washing.* Baltimore: Penguin.

Sato, Ikuya. 1988. "Play Theory of Delinquency: Toward a General Theory of 'Action.' " *Symbolic Interaction* 11, no. 2: 191–212.

Seay, Davin, with Mary Neely. 1986. *Stairway to Heaven: The Spiritual Roots of Rock 'n' Roll.* New York: Ballantine.

Sebald, Hans. 1978. *Witchcraft: The Heritage of a Heresy.* New York: Elsevier.

Shorrocks, Graham. 1990. "Body Bag Backlog: A Contemporary Legend?" *FOAFTale News* 20 (Dec.): 5.

Simonides, Dorota. 1988. "Moderne Sagenbildung im polnischen Großstadtmilieu." *Fabula* 28: 269–78.

Simpson, Jacqueline. 1973. *The Folklore of Sussex.* London: B. T. Batsford Ltd.

Singer, Isidore, et al., eds. 1902. *The Jewish Encyclopedia,* vol. 1. New York: Funk and Wagnalls.

Slotkin, Edgar M. 1988. "Legend Genre as a Function of Audience." In *Monsters with Iron Teeth: Perspectives on Contemporary Legend,* vol. 3. Ed. Gillian Bennett and Paul Smith, 89–111. Sheffield, Eng.: Sheffield Academic Press, 1988.

Smith, Barbara Herrnstein. 1980. "Narrative Versions, Narrative Theories." *Critical Inquiry* 7: 213–36.

Smith, Fredrick W. 1976. *Cattle Mutilation: The Unthinkable Truth.* Cedaredge, Colo.: Freedland Publications.

Smith, Paul. 1983. *The Book of Nasty Legends.* Boston: Routledge and Kegan Paul.

———, ed. 1984. *Perspectives on Contemporary Legend,* Sheffield, Eng.: CECTAL.

———. 1992. "Defining the 'Canon'—Subdividing the 'Canon.' " Paper presented at the Tenth International Seminar on Perspectives on Contemporary Legend, Sheffield, Eng.

Smith, Robert J. 1975. *The Art of the Festival.* Lawrence: University of Kansas Publications in Anthropology.

Sparks, Beatrice. 1979. *Jay's Journal.* New York: New York Times Book Company.

Spencer, John Wallace. 1976. *The UFO Yearbook.* Springfield, Mass.: Phillips Publishing Company.

"Stabs in the Dark." 1989. *Newsweek,* 13 Nov., 49.

Stahl, Sandra K. D. 1977a. "Oral Personal Narrative in Its Generic Context." *Fabula* 18: 18–39.

———. 1977b. "The Personal Narrative as Folklore." *Journal of the Folklore Institute* 14: 9–30.

St. Clair, David. 1987. *Say You Love Satan.* New York: Dell Books.

Stevens, Phillips, Jr. 1989. "Satanism: Where Are the Folklorists?" *New York Folklore* 15: 1–22.

Stewart, James. 1977. "Cattle Mutilations: An Episode of Collective Delusion." *Zetetic* 1: 55–66.

Stonor, Chris. 1992. "The Haunted Car." *Fortean Times* 61: 50.

Stoudt, John Joseph. 1977. "Himmelsbrief: The Letter from Heaven." *Historical Review of Berks County* 42 (Summer): 102–3, 115.

Strieber, Whitley. 1987. *Communion: A True Story.* New York: Beech Tree Books/Morrow.

———. 1988. *Transformation: The Breakthrough.* New York: Avon Books.

Strieber, Whitley, and Anne Strieber. 1997. *The Communion Letters.* New York: HarperPrism.

Sworin, Gary. 1988. "Public Meeting on Satanic Cults." St. Anthony's Catholic Church, Freeland, Pa., 8 Oct.

Szapir, Michael. 1995. "Mind Viruses." *American Scientist* 83 (Jan./Feb.): 26–27.

Tangerlini, Timothy R. 1990. " 'It Happened Not Too Far From Here . . .': A Survey of Legend Theory and Characterization." *Western Folklore* 49: 371–90.

Taves, Ernest H. 1987. "Communion with the Imagination." *Skeptical Inquirer* 12 (Fall): 90–96.

Tedlock, Dennis. 1972. "On the Translation of Style In Oral Narrative." In *Toward New Perspectives in Folklore*. Ed. Americo Paredes and Richard Bauman, 11–33. Austin: University of Texas Press.

Tertullian. 1931. *Apology*. Trans. T. R. Glover. In *Tertullian/Minucius Felix*. Loeb Classical Library. New York: Putnam.

Thigpen, Kenneth A. 1971. "Adolescent Legends in Brown County: A Survey." *Indiana Folklore* 4: 141–215.

Thompson, Stith. 1946. *The Folktale*. New York: Holt, Rinehart, and Winston.

Todorov, Tzvetan. 1973. *The Fantastic: A Structural Approach to a Literary Genre*. Trans. Richard Howard. Ithaca, N.Y.: Cornell University Press.

Toelken, Barre. 1968. "The Folklore of Academe." In *The Study of American Folklore: An Introduction*. Ed. Jan Harold Brunvand, 317–37. New York: Norton.

———. 1976. "The 'Pretty Languages' of Yellowman." In *Folklore Genres*. Ed. Dan Ben Amos, 145–70. Austin: University of Texas Press.

———. 1979. *The Dynamics of Folklore*. Boston: Houghton Mifflin.

Top, Stefaan. 1990. "Modern Legends in the Belgian Oral Tradition." *Fabula* 31: 272–78.

Trexler, Edgar R. 1991. "The Raging 'Storm.' " *The Lutheran*, 20 Feb., 50.

Truzzi, Marcello. 1989. Foreword. In Lyons 1989, xi–xv.

Turner, Patricia A. 1993. *I Heard It Through the Grapevine: Rumor in African-American Culture*. Berkeley and Los Angeles: University of California Press.

Turner, Victor. 1977. *The Ritual Process: Structure and Anti-Structure*. Ithaca, N.Y.: Cornell University Press.

Vargo, Beth. 1993. "Satanism, Ritual Child Abuse, and Urban Legends." *Believe the Children Newsletter* 10: 3.

Victor, Jeffrey A. 1989. "A Rumor-Panic About a Dangerous Satanic Cult in Western New York." *New York Folklore* 15: 23–49.

———. 1990. "Satanic Cult Legends as Contemporary Legend." *Western Folklore* 49: 51–82.

Virtanan, Leea. 1987. *Varastettu Isoäiti: Kaupungin Kansantarinoita*. Helsinki: Tammi.

———. 1990. *"That Must Have Been ESP!": An Examination of Psychic Experiences*. Trans. John Atkinson and Thomas DuBois. Bloomington: Indiana University Press.

Vlach, John M. 1971. "One Black Eye and Other Horrors: A Case for the Humorous Anti-Legend." *Indiana Folklore* 4: 95–140.

Wachs, Eleanor. 1990. "The Mutilated Shopper at the Mall: A Legend of Urban Violence." In *A Nest of Vipers*. Ed. Gillian Bennett and Paul Smith, 143–60. Sheffield, Eng.: Sheffield Academic Press.

Ward, Charles A. 1940. *Oracles of Nostradamus*. New York: Modern Library.

Ward, Donald. 1977. " 'The Little Man Who Wasn't There': Encounters with the Supranormal." *Fabula* 18: 212–25.

———. 1981. "Epilogue." *The German Legends of the Brothers Grimm*, vol. 2. Philadelphia: Institute for the Study of Human Issues.

Watkins, Leslie. 1983. *The Real Exorcists*. London: Methuen.

Watson, Lyall. 1990. *The Nature of Things*. London: Hodder and Stoughton.

Wehse, Rainer. 1991. "Topical Narrative Research in German: Bengt af Klintberg and Rolf Wilhelm Brednich." *FOAFTale News* 22 (June): 4–5.

Welsch, Roger L. 1988. "Endless Chain." *The World and I*, Sept., 500–511.

Williams, Noel. 1984. "Problems in Defining Contemporary Legends." In *Perspectives on Contemporary Legend*. Ed. Paul Smith, 216–28. Sheffield, Eng.: CECTAL.

Winick, Charles. 1958. *Dictionary of Anthropology*. Ames, Iowa: Littlefield, Adams and Co.

Workman, Mark E. 1977. "Dramaturgical Aspects of Professional Wrestling Matches." *Folklore Forum* 10: 14–20.

Zacharias, Gerhard P. 1980. *The Satanic Cult*. Boston: Allen and Unwin.

Index